New Zealand Yearbook of International Law

New Zealand Yearbook of International Law

(this *Yearbook* covers the period 1 January 2016 to 31 December 2016)

General Editor

Róisín Burke (*University of Canterbury, New Zealand*)

Associate Editor

Christian Riffel (*University of Canterbury, New Zealand*)

Book Reviews Editor

Annick Masselot (*University of Canterbury, New Zealand*)

Editorial Assistant

Emily McGeorge (*Graduate, University of Canterbury, New Zealand*)

VOLUME 14, 2016

The titles published in this series are listed at *brill.com/nzyb*

New Zealand Yearbook of International Law

Volume 14
2016

Edited by

Róisín Burke
Christian Riffel

BRILL
NIJHOFF

LEIDEN | BOSTON

Typeface for the Latin, Greek, and Cyrillic scripts: "Brill". See and download: brill.com/brill-typeface.

ISSN 1176-6417
ISBN 978-90-04-34590-4 (hardback)
ISBN 978-90-04-34591-1 (e-book)

Contents

The Year in Review

New Zealand State Conduct

Book Reviews

Preface

The editors are pleased to publish this 14th volume of the *New Zealand Yearbook of International Law* covering the year 2016.

The articles in this volume commence with an article by Ozlem. In light of potential violations of humanitarian law and human rights law posed by developments in robot weapons, the author explores how a "world community interest" approach might develop and whether International Court of Justice ("ICJ") provisional measures could be used to prevent the use of "robot weapons". The author discusses the role the ICJ could play in providing clarification of state obligations regarding use of "robot weapons". The author uses the hypothetical case of Pakistan requesting provisional measures from the ICJ in examining this proposition. This is followed by a paper by Abbasi, who engages in an intriguing theoretical discourse on the implications of democracy in international law-making. The author elaborates on conceptual inquiries on the very notion of democracy in international law-making, with the objective of providing international scholars with new literature in the discourse on democracy and international law-making. In doing so, the author draws on theories developed by the Iranian philosophers *Jalāl ad-Dīn Muhammad Balkhī* and *Shahab al-Din Suhrawardi*. The paper discusses conceptual skepticisms in the literature regarding the very existence and effectiveness of international law and global governance models, then introducing the idea of what he describes as "fragmented democracy" as a response.

Using land-based pollution as a case study, Naporn's article provides an interesting reflection on the possible role and contribution of the International Tribunal for the Law of the Sea in handling environmental cases from Regional Sea Programmes, in addition to the challenges and legal obstacles it would face. Naporn considers why the service of this Tribunal has been so infrequently utilized in light of its potential advantages. The author argues that the potential role of the Tribunal is limited given procedural prerequisites set out by the *United Nations Convention on the Law of the Sea*. The author discusses treaty parallelism and various dispute settlement provisions of the Regional Sea Programmes' environmental agreements, assessed against the compulsory dispute settlement procedure of the *United Nations Convention on the Law of the Sea*, with a view to evaluating the possibility of a land-based pollution case reaching the International Tribunal for the Law of the Sea. Lenard's article takes us to the area of cyber operations. Introducing the reader to the novel notions of cyber blockades and zones, the author highlights the need for developments in international law to better regulate this space. The author discusses recent cyber operations against Estonia and Georgia in the late 2000s as examples, which, the author explains, appeared to constitute cyber blockades. These cyber operations or blockades, as the author suggests, were the cause of considerable disruption and harm to both states, highlighting difficulties posed by the lack of current positive law regulating cyber blockades and zones. The author engages in an interesting discussion of the legalities of state actions if wishing to instigate a cyber blockade or zone, or to defend one. She draws corollaries with the law of navel and aerial blockades and zones, explaining their history, legal content, the purpose of these tactics, and their legal regulation. Lenard does this to assess whether the law applicable to these types of operations could similarly regulate cyber blockades and zones, whether in their current forms or with adjustments to the particularities of cyber operations. She argues for adaption of these existing regulatory rules to cyber operations, given similarities of purpose across these various forms of blockades and zones, while congnizant of the need for legal adjustments.

Kafedzic's article examines the utility of common purpose (via the doctrine of joint criminal enterprise ("JCE")) and control over crime theories in the complex task of determining liability of co-perpetrators of mass atrocity crimes before international criminal tribunals and the International Criminal Court. The author critiques both approaches, arguing that JCE is the strongest legal response to mass atrocity crimes, given its focus on common intention. She notes that common intention is one of the key characteristics of mass atrocity crimes. Kafedzic argues that the doctrine of JCE enables international courts to hold to account a broader spectrum of those responsible for the perpetration of these crimes, regardless of the essential nature of their conduct's contribution to perpetration. This brings us to the next paper, by Thamir, who introduces readers to the theory of "background-vernacularism" developed by the author. The author poses this approach as a theoretical framework aimed at enabling better comprehension as to how the persistence of cultural and social norms might be navigated and boundaries pushed in promoting human rights norms in particular cultural and religious contexts. Thamir's arguments, and the tool proposed by the author, are underpinned by feminists and legal anthropology discourses. The central focus of the paper is the promotion of gender norms in Muslim-majority countries. The author engages in a re-interpretation of some Islamic feminist arguments, using the lens of a background vernacularist approach. The author's intention is to demonstrate how religious backgrounds can and have been challenged through putting forward alternative religious discourses with the aim of promoting women's human rights. The author argues that understanding the resistance cultural backgrounds give rise to is an imperative first step towards compliance with human rights conventions.

This volume includes a regular update, this year by Angelo, on the activities and developments with respect to the Pacific Island Forum. Yearly, the Yearbook encourages submissions on issues of international law affecting the South Pacific Region. The Year in Review section focuses inwardly and outwardly on New Zealand and its role in contemporary international law during the 2016 year. It covers international human rights law, indigenous peoples' rights under international law, international economic law, international environmental law, law of the sea and fisheries, the Antarctic treaty system, international criminal law and international humanitarian law, and international law and security. The commentators provide a brief overview and commentary on New Zealand's practice and developments with respect to each of these areas of international law during 2016. The Year in Review continues with a comprehensive report on New Zealand state conduct with respect to Treaty Action and Implementation in New Zealand for the 2016 period. The Yearbook ends with a number of book reviews.

The views of the authors throughout are naturally their own.

The Editors wish to extend their gratitude to the Advisory Board, the academics who continue to provide annual contributions to the Yearbook Year in Review, the authors contributing to this volume, and other academics, practitioners and government officials from New Zealand and globally who continue to support the development of this publication. A particular thank-you goes to members of the Advisory Board and those taking the time to review contributions.

Finally, we would like to thank a number of individuals, without whom the publication of this Volume would not have been feasible. We would like to thank our Book Reviews Editor, Professor Annick Masselot, and our Editorial Assistant, Emily McGeorge, for their valuable contributions and hard work in producing the Yearbook. We would also like to thank the staff at Brill for their input in developing this publication.

Dr Róisín Burke
Editor

Dr Christian Riffel
Associate Editor

Articles and Commentaries

∵

"World Community Interest" Approach to Interim Measures on "Robot Weapons": Revisiting the *Nuclear Test Cases*

*Ozlem Ulgen**

1   Introduction

Forty-four years after the ICJ provisional measures orders in the *Nuclear Test Cases* requesting France stop atmospheric nuclear weapons testing in the South Pacific, we are facing another deadly threat from the use and development of "robot weapons". Back in the 1970s nuclear weapons were seen as the new frontier in state defensive capability, just as "robot weapons" are today. The ICJ set a precedent for using provisional measures to prevent harm caused by new weapons technology. The orders under art 41 ICJ Statute requested France to avoid nuclear tests causing the deposit of radioactive fall-out on Australian and New Zealand territories. The *Nuclear Test Cases* are instructive on how the Court may deal with new weapons technology, providing clarification on an urgent basis while a case is pending. Although provisional measures were ordered only in relation to atmospheric tests, the ICJ remains the only international judicial body to have ordered cessation of nuclear tests pending a case. In contrast, individual complaints before the HRC and the ECtHR were refused provisional measures to prevent nuclear tests.

2   What are "Robot Weapons"?

Throughout history new weapons have been developed with the aim of limiting combat fatalities and costs, yet causing devastating effects. Technological advances in warfare have created greater distance between the soldier and the battlefield, so the phenomenon is nothing new. What makes "robot weapons"

---

*   Visiting Fellow, Lauterpacht Centre for International Law, University of Cambridge. Senior Lecturer in Law, School of Law, Birmingham City University, UK. An initial draft of this paper was presented at the "Urgency and Human Rights Conference", 29–30 May 2015, Radboud University Nijmegen, The Netherlands. I am most grateful to Eva Rieter and Dinah Shelton for comments on an earlier draft, and to the anonymous reviewers for their constructive critical comments.

different? "Robot weapons" are weapons with varying degrees of autonomy in critical functions (i.e. acquiring, tracking, selecting, and attacking targets) that administer lethal harm (i.e. injury, suffering or death).[1] They aim to replace human combatants from the theatre of operation and limit casualties, but will lead to gradual removal of "human central thinking activities"[2] from the lethal force decision-making process with legal and ethical implications. Examples of robot weapons include the development of lethal autonomous weapons using robotics and artificial intelligence; automated weapons systems; remotely-controlled robotic soldiers; bio-augmentation; and 3D printed weapons.[3] Below we consider in more detail different types of robot weapons based on their level of autonomy, and utilitarian perspectives on whether robot weapons represent a malevolent or benevolent potential in weapons technology.

2.1   Types of Robot Weapons and Varying Degrees of Autonomy

Robot weapons generally fall into one of two categories: (1) semi-autonomous, involving levels of automation and remotely controlled human input (e.g. UAV or "drones"); and (2) autonomous, involving higher levels of independent thinking as regards acquiring, tracking, selecting and attacking targets, without the need for human input. Varying degrees of robot weapon autonomy (i.e. a level of independent decision-making and action output without the need for human input) can be measured in terms of functionality: the ability to observe,

---

1   Sharkey makes the distinction between "automatic robots" carrying out pre-programmed sequence of operations or moving in a structured environment (e.g. painting a car); and "autonomous robots" which are controlled by a program but operate in open or unstructured environments and receive information from their sensors to adjust speed and direction: Noel Sharkey, "Automating Warfare: Lessons Learned from the Drones" (2011/2012) 21(2) *Journal of Law, Information and Science* 140, 141.

2   Ozlem Ulgen, "Autonomous UAV and Removal of Human Central Thinking Activities: Implications for Legitimate Targeting, Proportionality, and Unnecessary Suffering" (forthcoming) 1–45.

3   Automated weapons systems (e.g. unmanned maritime aircraft such as Global Hawk; tactical unmanned aircraft such as Watchkeeper; technology demonstration vehicle (TDV) such as Taranis; the Pulsed Energy Projectile; tetanizing beam weapon; laser weapons; and the Precision Airborne Standoff Directed Energy Weapon (PASDEW)). Bio-augmentation (involves using neurotechnologies, including neural implants, to improve performance of the human mind and body. Currently developed by the United States of America Defence Department's Defense Advanced Research Projects Agency (DARPA), and United States of America government commissioned Brain Research Advancing Innovative Neurotechnologies (BRAIN) initiative). See, United Kingdom Ministry of Defence Joint Doctrine Note 2/11, *The UK Approach to Unmanned Aircraft Systems* (30 March 2011) ("*JDN 2/11*"); Peter Singer, *Wired for War: The Robotics Revolution and Conflict in the Twenty-First Century* (Penguin, 2009) 84–86.

orient, decide, and act; and the ability to replicate human situational aware-ness.[4] Critical functions of acquiring, tracking, selecting and attacking targets are specific robot weapon autonomy measurements, and robot weapons may possess some or all of these functions.[5]

Unmanned armed aerial vehicles ("UAV"), often referred to as "drones", such as MQ-9 Reaper and Predator, are the most ubiquitous and controversial type of robot weapon in current use. UAV are aircraft without pilots remotely con-trolled by human pilots and intelligence analysts, carrying lethal missiles used to target and kill individuals. They have been used in Afghanistan, Pakistan, Somalia, Yemen, Libya, and now in Syria. They have caused devastating effects such as targeting and killing individuals without due process; killing civilians, including children; and terrorising local populations living in fear for their own safety, lives, mental well-being, and property.

Remotely controlled UAV may have autonomy in terms of navigational deci-sions but still require human input for key decisions (e.g. Elbit/Thales Hermes 450 and General Atomics MQ-9 Reaper). These UAV are manually controlled during take-off, can follow flight paths autonomously, and need manual con-trol for diversions, camera steering and landing. All targeting actions are per-formed manually by a human operator. Elbit/Thales Hermes 450 operates without a lethal payload, undertaking extensive and persistent intelligence, surveillance, and reconnaissance ("ISR"). It provides tactical level imagery and imagery intelligence to unit and formation commanders in the land environ-ment, as used by the British Army in Afghanistan. Autonomy exists in being airborne without a pilot, operating with an automated GPS based system for take-off and landing. But its capability is heavily circumscribed through pre-programming and human input, with an in-built inability to undertake in-dependent lethal targeting.[6] General Atomics MQ-9 Reaper operates with a lethal payload and sophisticated armed ISR capability. It provides real-time intelligence data to commanders and intelligence specialists. It has an infrared sensor, for night-time surveillance, a colour/monochrome daylight camera, an image-intensifier, a synthetic aperture radar system to see through smoke and clouds, and ground moving target indicator. Video images are streamed to re-mote human pilots who take lethal targeting decisions to release laser guided bombs and missiles.[7]

---

4 Ulgen, above n 2.
5 *Report of the ICRC Expert Meeting, Autonomous Weapon Systems: Implications of Increasing Autonomy in the Critical Functions of Weapons* (15–16 March 2016) (*"2016 ICRC Report"*).
6 *JDN 2/11*, above n 3, Annex A, A.5.
7 Ibid A.6-A.7; United States of America Department of Defense, Office of the Secretary of Defense, *Unmanned Aircraft Systems Roadmap 2005–2030* (2005) 10 (*"US Roadmap"*).

Semi-autonomous robot weapons may be developed with greater autonomy in "acquiring, tracking, and identifying potential targets; cueing potential targets to human operators; prioritizing selected targets; timing of when to fire; or providing terminal guidance to home in on selected targets".[8] Human input would still be required in terms of decisions to select individual targets and specific target groups.

At the higher end of autonomy, fully autonomous robot weapons will have a lethal targeting capability, without human input controlling what, when, and how it targets. Such weapons require the highest level of situational awareness, replicating "human central thinking activities".[9] The US Navy X-47B is an example. Developed as a surveillance, strike and reconnaissance system, public information to date reveals it has autonomous capability in relation to take-off and landing, completing the first autonomous aerial refuelling in 2015. As a combat system it may conceivably develop more autonomous features relating to critical functions.[10]

2.2 *Utilitarian Perspectives on the Use of Robot Weapons*

Development and use of robot weapons represents a huge shift in the rules, consequences and responsibilities of warfare. They take the impact of distance between the soldier and the battlefield to another level, especially if developed to be fully autonomous. Technology possessing states are keen to pursue greater autonomy for robot weapons without relying on any human input. The US and UK military have active policies developing robotics technology, which they share with friendly states.[11] The US has a declared policy of use and development of fully autonomous robot weapons.[12] The UK is not far behind in pursuing robot weapons technology development, although current policy is not to pursue fully autonomous capability. China, India and Pakistan are developing or selling such technology. But there are varying perspectives

---

8   United States of America Department of Defense Directive, *Autonomy in Weapons Systems,* No. 3000.09 (21 November 2012) 14 (*"US Directive"*).

9   See Section 3.2 below.

10   Northrop Grumman, "X-47B UCAS Makes Aviation History ... Again!", <http://www.north ropgrumman.com/Capabilities/x47bucas/Pages/default.aspx>; *US Roadmap,* above n 7, 11.

11   United Kingdom Ministry of Defence Report *Strategic Trends Programme: Global Strategic Trends – Out to 2045* (30 April 2014) 67–73; *JDN 2/11,* above n 3; United States of America Department of the Navy, *The Navy Unmanned Undersea Vehicle (UUV) Master Plan* (9 November 2004) (*"US Master Plan"*); *US Roadmap,* above n 7; *US Directive,* above n 8.

12   *US Master Plan,* above n 11; *US Roadmap,* above n 7.

on whether robot weapons represent a malevolent or benevolent potential in weapons technology.

2.2.1   The Moral Duty to Protect Soldiers

Strawser argues that the principle of unnecessary risk provides a moral duty to use UAV because they do not violate the demands of justice, do not make the world worse, or expose your own combatants to potentially lethal risk unless incurring such a risk aids in the accomplishment of good in some way that cannot be gained via less risky means.[13] Although he considers fully autonomous robot weapons "morally impermissible", it is worth engaging with Strawser's argument to see if it can be applied to justify fully autonomous robot weapons.

Warfare presents a unique set of circumstances in which combatants face inherent risks. From a national interest and utilitarian perspective, the moral duty to protect soldiers is understandable. But, apart from cases of state negligence in training, preparing, and equipping military personnel, combatant casualties are expected and unavoidable. They do not constitute an "unnecessary risk". Replacing combatants with robot weapons disregards the former's professional training and dignity derived from a military code of ethics based on discipline, courage, and restraint. There is also an inherent asymmetry between states using robot weapons and states reliant on human combatants, creating insecurity and unpredictability in the conduct of warfare which makes neither the combatant nor target safe.[14]

2.2.2   Cost-benefit Reasoning

Arguably, resourcing and financing costs of conventional warfare may be outweighed by potential savings made from replacing combatants with efficient machines. Time and money may be saved by investing in robot weapons technology to engage in combat situations with precision and efficiency.[15] Autonomy in unmanned air systems, for example, reduces the number of personnel needed to operate them.[16] It may require only one person to control multiple

---

13   Bradley Jay Strawser, "Moral Predators: The Duty to Employ Uninhabited Aerial Vehicles" (2010) 9(4) *Journal of Military Ethics* 342–368.

14   In relation to inherent asymmetry and human dignity, see Ozlem Ulgen, "Human Dignity in an Age of Autonomous Weapons: Are We in Danger of Losing an 'Elementary Consideration of Humanity'?" (2016) 8(9) ESIL *Conference Paper Series* 1–19, 7–8 <https://papers.ssrn.com/sol3/papers.cfm?abstract_id=2912002> (forthcoming in OUP edited collection – updated copy with author).

15   *JDN 2/11*, above n 3, paras 102–103.

16   United States of America Department of Defense, *Unmanned Systems Integrated Roadmap FY2011-2036* (2011) 44.

unmanned systems with automated processing and analysis of information. Robot weapons might also be used to substitute or expand existing ground forces.[17] Such practical, cost-benefit reasons sit rather uncomfortably with more pressing concerns about compliance with international humanitarian law principles of legitimate targeting, proportionality, and prevention of unnecessary suffering.[18] It also raises concerns about the extent of human input and supervision to be able to establish legal responsibility. Indeed, the cost-benefit is not entirely evident given the extensive financial resourcing that will be necessary to ensure robot weapons are predictable, reliable, and operationally compliant with international humanitarian law.[19] Cost-benefit reasoning may also be susceptible to efficiency-driven, short-term decisions which in the long-term result in combatant casualties or breaches of international humanitarian law.[20]

2.2.3   Saving Civilian and Combatant Lives?

It may be argued that the potential sophistication and superior capability of robot weapons in precision targeting will reduce civilian and combatant casualties. Such a speculative utilitarian rationale operates outside the basic common rules of international humanitarian law which apply to all parties and require interaction and interrelatedness between human combatants and human targets in order to limit harm (e.g. prohibition on use of poison and poisoned weapons under art 23(a) of the Regulations annexed to the 1899 *Hague Convention II* and the 1907 *Hague Convention IV*; fundamental guarantees under art 75 of the 1977 *Additional Protocol I to the Geneva Conventions* of 12 August 1949 ("API")). Too much faith and optimism is placed in the precision and casualty-reducing capability of robot weapons. If we look at the example of current use semi-autonomous robot weapons such as UAV, there is

---

17   United States of America Department of Defense, *Unmanned Systems Integrated Roadmap FY2013-2038* (2013) 19 and 68.

18   See, Ulgen, above n 14, 24–25.

19   Ozlem Ulgen, "Pre-deployment common law duty of care and Article 36 obligations in relation to autonomous weapons: interface between domestic law and international humanitarian law?" (forthcoming) 1–18.

20   See, eg, *Smith and Others v Ministry of Defence* [2013] UKSC 41 (negligence claims by military personnel against the United Kingdom Ministry of Defence for failures to provide target identity devices that allow automatic confirmation as to whether a vehicle is a friend or foe; and situational awareness equipment that permits tank crews to locate their position and direction of sight accurately).

a disparity between perceived UAV precision targeting capability and actual harm caused.[21]

2.2.4 The "Irrational Soldier" Argument

The "irrational soldier" argument maintains that soldiers are susceptible to fatigue, emotions (e.g. revenge), and unpredictability which can debilitate a soldier's performance and ethical judgment to the extent of enabling commission of war crimes and atrocities.[22] Such "negative" human characteristics can be eliminated by using robots weapons. But this argument makes questionable assumptions about human and robotic rational thinking capacity and conduct in warfare.[23] Humans have rational thinking capacity to prevent unethical conduct. Human emotions (e.g. fear, shame, anger) are not always to be considered as detrimental to conduct in warfare and may operate as restraints against excesses. They may also assist in navigating complex environments requiring human judgment. So it is by no means certain that an unemotional robot can better perform tasks in warfare. This argument also disregards human agency in the creation and failures of robot weapons, which may be programmed to follow set tasks using calculating logic but with limited, defective, or no ethical considerations.

Having considered the utilitarian arguments relating to development and use of robot weapons, we now turn to consider specifically why robot weapons represent a global interest issue impacting on humanity and require a "world community interest" approach to interim measures.

3 "World Community Interest" Approach to Interim Measures

Elkind's early work on interim protection considered the function performed by principles of legal systems in protecting common specific interests.[24] A comparative analysis of international and municipal legal systems revealed that both serve an interest in trying to prevent disputing parties resorting to

---

21   See, Section 4.5 below.

22   Ronald C Arkin, *Governing Lethal Behaviour in Autonomous Robots* (CRC Press, 2009); Ronald C Arkin, "Lethal Autonomous Systems and the Plight of the Non-combatant" (2014) 1 *Ethics and Armed Forces* 1 (work was supported in part by the U.S. Army Research Office under Contract #W911NF-06-1-0252).

23   Ulgen, above n 14, 15–16.

24   Jerome B Elkind, *Interim Protection: A Functional Approach* (Martinus Nijhoff Publishers, 1981) 17–19.

self-help or violence. The general principle of interim measures, found in both international and municipal systems, seeks to protect the specific interest of preventing violence. In Roman law, for example, interdicts were used to prohibit violence against a person placed in possession of property. In the Middle Ages, possessory assizes in England instituted expeditious trials to prevent men, who were in fact in possession, from being disturbed pending trial of their title. The purpose was to prevent the issue from being fought in battle. Today's use of injunctive relief, whether at municipal or international level, is rooted in the need to preserve the peace.[25] At the international level, prevention of aggravation or extension of a dispute is the primary function of provisional measures, which necessarily involves prevention of violence as mirrored in municipal law. Threats to the peace occur when a party perceives it may be "irreparably injured or that it will be forced to endure an unendurable situation", leading to desperation and desperation leading to violence.[26]

New Zealand's pleadings in the *Nuclear Test Cases* were characterised as "asserting some world community interest" concerning the threat posed by atmospheric nuclear tests to world peace and security, human health of present and future generations, and the environment.[27] "World community interest" can be defined as global interest issues that impact on humanity, transcend individual state interests and the inter-state dimension, and typically require transnational regulation.[28] Disputes that transcend parties' interests with potential impact on global security and humanity represent a "world community interest" over which the ICJ should have jurisdiction.[29] In *Costa Rica v Nicaragua*, Judge Cançado Trindade reasserts the "autonomous legal regime" of provisional measures, and how the principle of humanity has expanded their

25   Ibid Ch 2.

26   Elkind, above n 24, 222–230.

27   Ibid 222; "Application Instituting Proceedings submitted by the Government of New Zealand", *Nuclear Tests Cases* (*New Zealand v France*) [1978] II ICJ Pleadings 7–8.

28   See, eg, Antônio Augusto Cançado Trindade, *International Law for Humankind – Towards a New Jus Gentiumn* (Martinus Nijhoff Publishers, 2010); *Questions relating to the Obligation to Prosecute or Extradite* (*Belgium v Senegal*) (*Provisional Measures*) [2009] ICJ Rep 139, 174 [21]–[25] (Judge Trindade) (provisional measures transcending inter-state dimension), 190 [71] (*erga omes* obligations as superior common values in the international law for humankind), 196 [92] and 199 [104] (the legal community of the whole of humankind) (*"Obligation to Prosecute or Extradite"*).

29   See, eg, *Ahmadou Sadio Diallo* (*Republic of Guinea v Democratic Republic of Congo*) (*Judgment*) [2010] ICJ Rep 639, 806 [227]–[228] (Judge Trindade) (*"Ahmadou Sadio Diallo"*).

scope of protection beyond the inter-state dimension.[30] More recently in *Obligations Concerning Negotiations Relating to Cessation of the Nuclear Arms Race and to Nuclear Disarmament (Marshall Islands v India)*, Judge James Crawford referred to the possibility that "disputes can crystallize in multilateral fora involving a plurality of States",[31] and the *South West Africa Cases* are authority for this.[32]

There is a "world community interest" in the potential use of robot weapons because they may aggravate or extend inter-state disputes, and violate human rights and international humanitarian law. States possessing such weapons technology can use violence against individuals/groups within other states without recourse to due process. Targeted individuals/groups are killed, and local populations may suffer collateral physical and psychological harm. Obviously the loss of life constitutes "irreparable injury", which is a traditional circumstance for authorising interim measures. But there is also a less apparent form of harm in being forced to endure an "unendurable situation" (i.e. living in a constant state of fear and anxiety; not knowing when, where or who a robot weapon will strike and kill; and the potential for violation of territorial sovereignty at any time). "Irreparable injury" covers a definitive harmful result when a robot weapon is deployed to kill an individual, whereas an "unendurable situation" relates to ongoing harmful effects which the complainant cannot be expected to endure pending the outcome of a dispute. Both circumstances exist in the potential use of robot weapons and three possible grounds emerge to stop their use through interim measures: prevention of aggravation or extension of inter-state disputes; prevention of human rights violations; and prevention of violations of international humanitarian law. These grounds are developed in more detail in Section 4 in relation to a hypothetical case of Pakistan requesting ICJ provisional measures.

3.1   *Emerging* Opinio Juris *under the* UN CCW *Process*
On 16 December 2016 the Fifth Review Conference on the UN *Convention on Certain Conventional Weapons* ("CCW") agreed a Final Declaration to formalise states parties' discussions on lethal autonomous weapons systems ("LAWS")

---

30   *Certain Activities carried out by Nicaragua in the Border Area (Costa Rica v Nicaragua) (Judgment)* [2015] ICJ Rep 665, 1 (Judge Trindade) (*"Certain Activities by Nicaragua – Judgment"*).

31   *Obligations Concerning Negotiations Relating to Cessation of the Nuclear Arms Race and to Nuclear Disarmament (Marshall Islands v India) (Jurisdiction)* (International Court of Justice, General List No 158, 5 October 2016) [19]–[21] (Judge Crawford).

32   *South West Africa Cases (Ethiopia v South Africa; Liberia v South Africa) (Preliminary Objections)* [1962] ICJ Rep 319, 346.

through the establishment of a Group of Governmental Experts ("GGE").[33] After several informal and expert meetings since 2014, this is a historic step towards multilateral deliberation of the legal and ethical issues surrounding LAWS, demonstrating increasing state concern. Although the process is fraught with political and practical obstacles, it is the first global institutional initiative at norm-creation and codification of rules governing robot weapons which may even lead to a legally binding instrument. The first set of GGE meetings, due to take place in August 2017, were cancelled due to unpaid state contributions. Subject to sufficient funds being available, the next meeting is scheduled for November 2017.[34]

With 125 states parties to the CCW, the CCW process brings together diplomats, legal, and military experts to deliberate and draft rules on weapons control and disarmament. At the Fifth Review Conference the majority of states agreed that LAWS represent new and complex challenges to international humanitarian law requiring further in-depth discussions. Switzerland and Cuba prepared position papers respectively proposing consideration of scientific and technological advances in the context of compliance with international humanitarian law, and expressing concern that LAWS would not be able to comply with the principles of distinction and proportionality.[35] Many other states referred to ethical concerns about humans delegating life and death decisions to machines,[36] and considered LAWS to be contrary to human dignity,

---

33   *Final Document of the Fifth Review Conference,* Agenda Item 18, UN Doc CCW/CONF.V/10, (23 December 2016) 9 <https://documents-dds-ny.un.org/doc/UNDOC/GEN/G16/441/02/pdf/G1644102.pdf?OpenElement>.

34   *Letter from Chair of Convention on Certain Conventional Weapons,* 6 June 2017, UNOG <https://www.unog.ch/80256EDD006B8954/(httpAssets)/3D20EDEBBF0E6B68C125813A00566285/$file/Letter_CCW+MSP+Chairperson_6Jun2017.pdf>.

35   Swiss Working Paper, *Towards a "compliance-based" approach to LAWS,* Informal meeting of experts on lethal autonomous weapons systems (LAWS) Geneva, 11–15 April 2016 <https://www.unog.ch/80256EDD006B8954/(httpAssets)/D2D66A9C427958D6C1257F8700415473/$file/2016_LAWS+MX_CountryPaper+Switzerland.pdf>; Swiss Working Paper, *S&T and the CCW – Consideration of developments in science and technology that may be relevant to the work of the Convention on Certain Conventional Weapons (CCW),* 5 December 2016, CCW/CONF.V/WP.4; Cuban Working Paper, *Considerations on Lethal Autonomous Weapons System* <https://www.unog.ch/80256EDD006B8954/(httpAssets)/2EC2FA3DC75A50FFC12580820056F458/$file/Cuba+WP.pdf>.

36   UN Digital Recordings Portal, *CCW 5th Review Conference of the High Contracting Parties,* Exchange of Views: Austria, Brazil, Holy See, Mexico, Pakistan, Panama, The Netherlands, Venezuela (12 December 2016); Algeria, Colombia, Croatia, France (13 December 2016) <http://conf.unog.ch/digitalrecordings/#> ("UN Digital Recordings Portal").

humanity, and the Martens Clause.[37] Oral and written *Exchange of Views* reveal three main state positions emerging: (1) potential user or developer states; (2) preventative prohibition states; and (3) the Russian abstention. In between are "undecided" states supportive of formalised discussions but, as of yet, unclear about what LAWS are and their potential impact.

3.1.1 Potential User or Developer States

Potential user or developer states are generally open to formal discussions yet reiterate the importance of military necessity and the need to protect the civilian technology industry. Korea and Japan expressed support for the GGE but with concern that discussions should not hamper developments in civilian technology. As a leading country in the development of fibre optics, Japan noted the dual-use purpose of LAWS and that it would not be easy to distinguish between civilian-use (e.g. disaster relief and domestic law enforcement) and military-use. But it also affirmed that it would not develop LAWS for warfare.[38] State representatives often characterised the CCW's main objective as "balancing military necessity with humanitarian considerations",[39] suggesting that regulation or prohibition of robot weapons should be guided by national security interests as well as compliance with principles of international humanitarian law. But states also recognise that military necessity should be framed within a broader context of ethical, human rights, and international humanitarian law considerations. Mexico, for example, favours discussions "with the objective to prioritise an ethics-based approach since assumptions that enhance their [LAWS'] military value have been superseded and have no place in the CCW."[40]

---

37 Ibid Exchange of Views: Ecuador, Panama (12 December 2016); Costa Rica, Guatemala, (13 December 2016).

38 Ibid Exchange of Views: Japan (12 December 2016), Korea (13 December 2016).

39 Ibid Exchange of Views: Cameroon, China, Cuba, Korea, Russia, Turkey (12 December 2016); *Statement by Mr Neil Benevides, Chargé d'Affaires, Permanent Representation of Brazil to the Conference on Disarmament*, 12 December 2016 – "CCW has been paramount in striking a balance between humanitarian concerns and military needs" (copy with author); *Statement by Ambassador Amandeep Singh Gill, Permanent Representative of India*, 12 December 2016 <https://www.unog.ch/80256EDD006B8954/(httpAssets)/7C66638FB6B0C169C125808E00467D04/$file/India.pdf>. It mentions "stipulating measures to mitigate humanitarian concerns arising from the use of specific weapons and weapons systems also take into account the military necessity of such weapons, thus striving to strike a balance between the two concepts".

40 Cf *Statement by Mexican at the 2016 Meeting of Experts in LAWS*, 11 April 2016 <https://www.unog.ch/80256EDD006B8954/(httpAssets)/44FB014A6029D721C1257F920057E636/

During the 2015 UN negotiations, the UK favoured restricting discussions to "emerging technologies" rather than weapons technology, such as UAV, currently in use.[41] At the 2016 Fifth Review Conference the UK, France, and the Netherlands insisted that any further discussion of LAWS should be in relation to "emerging technologies", and this position was adopted by consensus in the final text of the Declaration, which refers to the establishment of "an open-ended Group of Governmental Experts related to emerging technologies in the area of lethal autonomous weapons systems".[42] This potentially excludes consideration of UAV and other types of robot weapon technologies currently in development or partial use. Given that states have yet to define what constitute LAWS and "emerging technologies", and they are not legally required to disclose or share information, this leaves too much scope for individual state discretion to classify robot weapons as falling outside any multilateral norm-creation and codification framework. A number of states also take the position that discussions include semi-autonomous weapons, such as UAV, or that categorisation of LAWS should be on the basis of level of autonomy.[43]

3.1.2   Preventative Prohibition States

A second group of states support formal discussions leading to a preventative prohibition of LAWS through the adoption of a legally binding instrument.[44] The prohibition would be extensive, covering acquisition, development, testing, production, deployment, and use of LAWS, and modelled on Protocol IV (Blinding Laser Weapons), which serves as a precedent for prohibition of a weapon prior to its deployment.[45] With reference to the precautionary

---

$file/2016_LAWS+MX_GeneralExchange_Statements_Mexico.pdf>; UN Digital Recordings Portal, above n 36, Exchange of Views: Mexico (12 December 2016).

41   Harriet Grant, "UN Delay Could Open Door to Robot Wars, Say Experts", *The Guardian* (online), 6 October 2015 <https://www.theguardian.com/science/2015/oct/06/autonomous-weapons-un-delay-robot-wars>.

42   *Final Document of the Fifth Review* Conference, above n 33.

43   See, eg, UN Digital Recordings Portal, above n 36, Exchange of Views: Panama and Nicaragua (12 December 2016), Venezuela (13 December 2016).

44   As of 30 July 2017, out of 124 states parties to the CCW 19 states support a ban: 16 states parties (Algeria, Argentina, Bolivia, Chile, Costa Rica, Cuba, Ecuador, Guatemala, Holy See, Mexico, Nicaragua, Pakistan, Panama, Peru, State of Palestine, Venezuela); 1 signatory state (Egypt); 2 states that are not parties (Ghana, Zimbabwe).

45   *Additional Protocol to the Convention on Prohibitions or Restrictions on the Use of Certain Conventional Weapons which may be Deemed to be Excessively Injurious or to have Indiscriminate Effects (Protocol IV, Entitled Protocol on Blinding Laser Weapons)*, opened for signature 13 October 1995, 2024 UNTS 163 (entered into force 30 July 1998) (*"Protocol IV*

principle, they call for an immediate ban and regard LAWS as ethically, morally, and legally undesirable.[46] But with greater state interest in more in-depth discussions about the nature, definition, and impact of LAWS, some states in this group have modified their position to take account of the need for further information and the possible beneficial uses of robotics and artificial intelligence. Algeria, for example, supports a preventative prohibition on the acquisition, development, testing, deployment, and use of LAWS, but with a somewhat modified position. It distinguishes LAWS from robotics and artificial intelligence used in non-lethal autonomous systems for humanitarian, medical, military, and scientific use. It recognises potential advantages "for the well-being of humanity and the legitimate rights of developing countries to technological and socio-economic progress."[47]

3.1.3   The Russian Abstention

The Russian Federation abstained from voting for formalisation of LAWS discussions under the GGE. Apart from the abstention, not really having any binding effect as decisions are made by consensus, Russia's statements leading up to the vote revealed concerns about premature formalisation of discussions without clarity on the definition of LAWS, and state defence interests:

> In principle our country is not against a discussion within the CCW of matters related to arms development. At the same time we are convinced that the substantiveness of such discussions directly depends on a clear understanding of their subject. We doubt that it is reasonable to prematurely formalize the discussion on lethal autonomous weapons systems (LAWS), which has been conducted for several years. We will

---

on *Blinding Laser Weapons"*); See, UN Digital Recordings Portal, above n 36, Exchange of Views: Egypt and Costa Rica (13 December 2016).

46   UN Digital Recordings Portal, above n 36, Exchange of Views: Nicaragua (12 December 2016), Guatemala, Peru, Egypt (called for a moratorium on development of LAWS until an eventual ban could be agreed) (13 December 2016); Pakistan (12 December 2016) <https://www.unog.ch/80256EDD006B8954/(httpAssets)/11B913BABEA32AB2C125808E003697BB/$file/PakistanStatement-CCW+++RevCon-General+Debate-12Dec.pdf>; *Statement by H.E. Archbishop Ivan Jurkovič, Permanent Observer of the Holy See*, 12 December 2016 (copy with author).

47   Cf *Statement by Algerian Delegation at the 2016 Meeting of Experts in LAWS*, 11 April 2016 <https://www.unog.ch/80256EDD006B8954/(httpAssets)/EBA56386AE5E61A1C1257F9200579F4F/$file/2016_LAWS+MX_GeneralExchange_Statements_Algeria.pdf>; UN Digital Recordings Portal, above n 36, Exchange of Views: Algeria (13 December 2016).

share our approaches in a more detailed way at the meetings of the Main committees.[48]

The abstention is in relation to supporting or not supporting the establishment of a GGE to formally discuss LAWS, and any future decisions of the GGE. It seems a tactical position to adopt in order to see to what extent, in particular, potential user or developer states genuinely engage with, or undermine, the GGE process. Judging by the financial difficulties of the CCW and the resultant cancellation of the first GGE meeting, perhaps Russia is prudent in holding back from discussions which will lead to disclosure of technological capability and potentially compromise state defence. For a dominant world power and Security Council permanent member to take such a position points to the potential for robot weapons to become the next arms race, creating further instability in the international legal order. This further bolsters the need for a "world community interest" approach to interim measures on robot weapons.

3.2   Removal of "Human Central Thinking Activities"

From an ethical standpoint there is a question as to whether humans should delegate ultimate decisions of life and death to machines. "Human central thinking activities" are essential in warfare and involve the ability to feel, think and evaluate, and the capacity to adhere to a value-based system in which violence is not the norm governing human relations.[49] Such ability and capacity uniquely identifies how humans engage in qualitative analysis through exercising judgment and reasoning in the theatre of operation. With the capacity to feel, think, and evaluate, humans can adhere to a value-system, show empathy, experience fear and shame, which all represent potential restraints or qualifiers on the use of force and any resultant harm.

Judgment is used in deciding the extent and timing of force. Soldiers engage in automatic reasoning when they obey orders, warn and take action against incoming threats, and distinguish between military targets and civilians in uncomplicated and controlled scenarios. Commanders engage in deliberative reasoning, implementing the principle of proportionality under art 51 API, by assessing whether an attack is expected to cause excessive incidental loss of civilian life in relation to the concrete and direct military advantage anticipated, taking into account location, terrain, accuracy of the weapon used, weather

---

48   *Statement by the Head of the Delegation of the Russian Federation, Deputy Director-General of the Department for Nonproliferation and Arms Control of the Ministry of Foreign Affairs of the Russian Federation, Vladimir I. Yermakov,* 12 December 2016, 3–4 (copy with author).

49   Ulgen, above n 14; Ulgen, above n 2.

conditions, the nature of the military objective, and technical skills of combatants. If the loss is deemed excessive then they must abort the attack under art 57(2)(b) API. Deliberative reasoning is also required to distinguish between military targets and civilians in mixed and uncontrolled scenarios, such as counter-insurgency operations and internal conflicts.[50] These examples illustrate how combatants use judgment and reasoning to implement principles of feasible precautions, distinction, and proportionality.

Remotely-operated UAV currently in use have varying degrees of autonomy, with some human input exhibiting these attributes. But the more autonomous the UAV becomes the less likely it is to possess "human central thinking activities"; namely, the complex cognitive capabilities to appraise a given situation, exercise judgment, and restrain from taking action or limiting harm. Unlike humans who can pull back at the last minute or choose a workable alternative, robot weapons have no instinctive or intuitive ability to do the same. In complex scenarios of asymmetric warfare perception and attribution of intentions, fears, and desires in human targets becomes important. If a robot weapon cannot attribute intentions, fears, and desires to others it has limited ability to distinguish between threatening and non-threatening behaviour, which is crucial for identifying legitimate targets.

Comparing humans to machines, there is a clear difference between the logic of a calculating machine and the wisdom of human judgment.[51] Machines perform cost effective and speedy peripheral processing activities based on quantitative analysis, repetitive actions, and sorting data (e.g. mine clearance; and detection of improvised explosive devices). They are good at automatic reasoning and can outperform humans in such activities, but lack the deliberative and sentient aspects of human reasoning necessary in warfare. The use

---

50   See Noel Sharkey, "Towards a Principle for the Human Supervisory Control of Robot Weapons" (2014) 2 (May–August) *Politica & Società* 1–16. Sharkey explores the strengths and weaknesses of automatic and deliberative reasoning, and their impact on supervisory control of robot weapons.

51   Joseph Weizenbaum, *Computer Power and Human Reason: From Judgment to Calculation* (W.H. Freeman and Company, 1976) 213. Weizenbaum discusses limitations of computer-based logical thinking after he developed the ELIZA computer programme to mimic the behaviour of a psychoanalyst; argues that computer intelligence is "alien to genuine human problems and concerns" 213, and that "there is an aspect to the human mind, the unconscious, that cannot be explained by the information-processing primitives, the elementary information processes, which we associate with formal thinking, calculation, and systematic rationality" 223.

of discretion in decisions regarding preventing unnecessary suffering, taking feasible precautions, and assessing proportionality, is absent in robots.[52]

Having established that robot weapons represent a global interest issue impacting on humanity and requiring a "world community interest" approach to interim measures, let us now consider how this would work in the case of Pakistan requesting provisional measures from the ICJ and whether the requirements would be satisfied.

4   Hypothetical Case of Pakistan Requesting Provisional Measures

Article 41 of the ICJ Statute provides that the Court has the power to "indicate, if it considers that circumstances so require, any provisional measures which ought to be taken to preserve the respective rights of either party." As this is a purely inter-state procedure, states are the relevant parties and, in theory, would have standing to make an application on the basis that continued use of robot weapons constitutes an "unendurable situation". In practice, applications are more likely to be made by states directly affected. Article 41 does not define or stipulate "circumstances" appropriate for provisional measures, highlighting the Court's discretionary power. The Court's jurisprudence has developed basic requirements of prima facie jurisdiction over a dispute, and risk of irreparable prejudice and urgency.

4.1   *Prima Facie Jurisdiction under 1959 US–Pakistan Treaty of Friendship and Commerce*
Provisional measures are part of the Court's incidental jurisdiction so it must be established that it has prima facie jurisdiction over a dispute in the main case. The Court need not be satisfied definitively of jurisdiction, yet it ought not to act under art 41 where there is a manifest absence of jurisdiction.[53] This represents a compromise between protecting the Court's power to deal with urgent cases and give effect to final judgments, and protection of state sovereignty through consent to jurisdiction.[54] A dispute exists where there is

---

52   Eliav Lieblich and Eyal Benvenisti, "The Obligation to Exercise Discretion in Warfare: Why Autonomous Weapons Systems Are Unlawful" in Nehal Bhuta, Susanne Beck, Robin Geiβ, Liu Hin-Yan, Claus Kreβ (eds), *Autonomous Weapons Systems Law, Ethics, Policy* (Cambridge University Press, 2016).

53   *Obligation to Prosecute or Extradite* [2009] ICJ Rep 139, 147 [40]; *Fisheries Jurisdiction Cases (UK v Iceland) (Provisional Measures)* [1972] ICJ Rep 12, 15 [15] (*"Fisheries Jurisdiction"*).

54   Karin Oellers-Frahm, "Expanding the Competence to Issue Provisional Measures – Strengthening the International Judicial Function" (2011) 12(5) *German Law Journal* 1279, 1284.

a "disagreement over a point of law or fact, or a conflict of legal views or of interests between two persons".[55] It could also involve a difference of opinion on interpretation of an ICJ judgment.[56] Prima facie existence of a dispute constitutes a necessary condition for establishing prima facie jurisdiction.

A key early start in the use of robot weapons has been American UAV strikes in Afghanistan, Iraq, Pakistan, Yemen, Somalia, Libya and now Syria. Among these states, Pakistan is the only one with potential to establish ICJ prima facie jurisdiction. American UAV strikes in Pakistan violate Pakistan's territorial sovereignty and cause loss of life, contrary to customary international law and treaty law, which means there is prima facie existence of a dispute over which the Court could exercise jurisdiction. Reports of Pakistan's apparent consent to strikes under former President Musharraf have not been officially confirmed, and the current government considers them a violation of Pakistan's territorial sovereignty.[57]

In *Writ Petition No. 1551-P/2012*, the Pakistani Peshawar High Court held that American UAV strikes violated Pakistan's territorial sovereignty, and the prohibition on the use of force. It called upon the Pakistani government to complain to the UN Secretary General and request that an independent war crimes tribunal be set up to consider whether American actions constituted war crimes. In recognizing such a tribunal's jurisdiction the Court also recognized its incidental jurisdiction:

> to direct the US Authorities/Government to immediately stop the UAV strikes within the airspace/territory of Pakistan and to immediately arrange for the complete & [sic] full compensation for the victims' families of the civilians of Pakistan both for life & [sic] properties at the rate & [sic] ratio laid down under international standards.[58]

---

55   *Mavrommatis Palestine Concessions* (*Greece v United Kingdom*) (*Judgment*) [1924] PCIJ (ser A) No 2, 7, 11.

56   See, eg, *Request for Interpretation of the Judgment of 15 June 1962 in the Case Concerning the Temple of Preah Vihear* (*Cambodia v Thailand*) (*Provisional Measures*) [2011] ICJ Rep 537, 544 [31] (*"Temple of Preah Vihear"*).

57   Mark Mazetti, "A Secret Deal on Drones, Sealed in Blood", *New York Times* (online), 6 April 2013 <http://www.nytimes.com/2013/04/07/world/asia/origins-of-cias-not-so-secret -drone-war-in-pakistan.html?_r=0>; Nic Robertson and Greg Botelho, "Ex-Pakistani President Musharraf Admits Secret Deal with U.S. on Drone Strikes", *CNN* (online), 12 April 2013 <http://edition.cnn.com/2013/04/11/world/asia/pakistan-musharraf-drones/>; Amnesty International Report, *Will I Be Next? US Drone Strikes in Pakistan* (2013), Section 8, <http:// www.amnestyusa.org/sites/default/files/asa330132013en.pdf>.

58   *Writ Petition No. 1551-P/2012*, 11 April 2013, [6], [22(ii)], [22(vii)], (Peshawar High Court, Pakistan).

The provisional measure request is to "immediately stop the drone strikes" before commencing proceedings on substantive matters alleging war crimes and violations of human rights, and whether state responsibility is established to require compensation.

Pakistan recognized the ICJ's compulsory jurisdiction back in 1960, but the US terminated its declaration accepting compulsory jurisdiction during the *Nicaragua Case* and this remains in place today.[59] Pakistan's declaration excludes disputes relating to multilateral treaties so that a dispute alleging violations of the *UN Charter* would not work, although it could accept jurisdiction under special agreement. Given the complete withdrawal by the US, the next best option is to establish jurisdiction on the basis of the *1959 US–Pakistan Treaty of Friendship and Commerce*. Article XXIII(2) contains a compromissory clause recognizing the Court's jurisdiction for both parties:

> Any dispute between the Parties as to the interpretation or application of the present Treaty, not satisfactorily adjusted by diplomacy, shall be submitted to the International Court of Justice, unless the Parties agree to settlement by some other pacific means.

Compromissory clauses are common in bilateral treaties of amity or establishment and the intention of the parties in accepting them is clearly to provide a right of unilateral recourse to the ICJ in the absence of agreement to employ some other pacific means of settlement.[60] They have a "sleeping beauty" quality; contained in an otherwise dormant treaty but may be revived at any point to establish the Court's jurisdiction over a dispute.[61] The Treaty provides that

---

59   *Pakistan Declaration Recognising the Jurisdiction of the Court as Compulsory*, 13 September 1960, <www.icj-cij.org/jurisdiction/?p1=5&p2=1&p3=3&code=PK>; *United States Department of State Letter and Statement concerning Termination of Acceptance of ICJ Compulsory Jurisdiction*, (1985) 24 ILM 1742. For reasons and consequences of the American withdrawal, see, Sean D Murphy, "The United States and the International Court of Justice: Coping with Antinomies" in Cesare Romano (ed), *The Sword and the Scales: The United States and International Courts and Tribunals* (Cambridge University Press, 2009).

60   *Military and Paramilitary Activities in and against Nicaragua (Nicaragua v USA) (Jurisdiction)* [1984] ICJ Rep 392, 427 [81] (*"Military and Paramilitary Activities – Jurisdiction"*); see earlier case, *United States Diplomatic and Consular Staff in Tehran (United States of America v Iran) (Judgment)* [1980] ICJ Rep 3, 27 [52]. In the case the US invoked a similar clause against Iran and the ICJ confirmed the clause was intended to enable unilateral recourse to the Court.

61   Christian J Tams, "The Continued Relevance of Compromissory Clauses as a Source of ICJ Jurisdiction" (2009) 21 <http://ssrn.com/abstract=1413722>; Matina Papadaki,

both parties are "desirous of strengthening the bonds of *peace* and friendship traditionally existing between them and encouraging closer economic and cultural relations between their peoples",[62] which necessarily means upholding customary international law principles of territorial sovereignty, prohibition on the use of force, good faith, and peaceful cooperation. UAV strikes violate the Treaty's purpose and customary international law.

Precedent exists for using compromissory clauses to establish jurisdiction even when the respondent state objects. In the *Nicaragua Case*, Nicaragua successfully relied on art XXIV of the *Treaty of Friendship, Commerce and Navigation between the United States of America and Nicaragua* of 21 January 1956 in so far as it related to a dispute concerning the interpretation or application of the Treaty.[63] Jurisdiction was still established in the *Nicaragua Case* despite the US subsequently terminating the Treaty. Thus, if Pakistan brings proceedings but the US objects and seeks to terminate the Treaty under art XXIV(3), it could only terminate after giving Pakistan one year's written notice and even then there is no guarantee that the Court will decline to exercise jurisdiction.

4.2   *Risk of Irreparable Prejudice and Urgency*

Article 41 ICJ Statute does not refer to "irreparable harm" or "irreparable injury" but the Court's jurisprudence has developed to assess whether there is a risk of "irreparable prejudice" to the rights of parties pending a decision.[64] What constitutes "irreparable prejudice" depends on case-specific facts and the rights claimed, which must be plausible and linked to the claim on the merits (otherwise known as the plausibility requirement).[65] At a general level, a *risk* or *possibility* of harm to the practical implementation or enforceability of rights

---

      "Compromissory Clauses as the Gatekeepers of the Law to be 'Used' in the ICJ and the PCIJ" (2014) 5(3) *Journal of International Dispute Settlement* 560–604.

62   *Treaty of Friendship and Commerce between the United States of America and Pakistan*, United States of America-Pakistan, 404 UNTS 259 (entered into force 12 February 1961), Preamble (emphasis added).

63   *Military and Paramilitary Activities – Jurisdiction* [1984] ICJ Rep 392, 426–429 [79]–[83].

64   *Fisheries Jurisdiction* [1972] ICJ Rep 12, 16 [21]; *Nuclear Tests Case (Australia v France) (Provisional Measures)* [1973] ICJ Rep 99, 103 [20] (*"Nuclear Tests Case – Australia"*); *Nuclear Tests Case (New Zealand v France) (Provisional Measures)* [1973] ICJ Rep 135, 139 [21] (*"Nuclear Tests Case – New Zealand"*).

65   *Obligation to Prosecute or Extradite* [2009] ICJ Rep 139, 151 [56]–[57]; *Certain Activities carried out by Nicaragua in the Border Area (Costa Rica v Nicaragua) (Provisional Measures)* [2011] ICJ Rep 6, 18 [53]–[54] (*"Certain Activities by Nicaragua – Provisional Measures"*); *Temple of Preah Vihear* [2011] ICJ Rep 537, 545 [33]; International Court of Justice, *Rules of Court* (adopted 14 April 1978) art 73(1).

constitutes "irreparable prejudice."[66] It has been deemed to exist in situations involving imminent execution of individuals, violations of territorial sovereignty, illegal military and paramilitary activities in another state, and ongoing genocidal acts.[67] Even if rights can be restored at a later stage, the Court does not need to be satisfied of absolute irreparability and can still grant an order.[68]

Provisional measures apply to urgent situations where there is a "real and imminent risk" that irreparable prejudice may be caused to the rights in dispute before the Court gives its final decision.[69] Irreversibility of prejudice is a key determining factor in cases where the Court has ordered provisional measures (e.g. individuals awaiting the death penalty; nuclear testing; gross human rights violations).[70] In the *Nuclear Test Cases* urgency was in relation to the risk of "irreparable, and harmful, somatic and genetic effects" from exposure to radiation, "the uncertain physical and genetic effects to which contamination exposes the people ... causes them acute apprehension, anxiety and concern", and "there could be no possibility that the rights eroded ... could be fully restored".[71] Other examples of urgency include the *Nicaragua Case* where Nicaragua claimed "the lives and property of Nicaraguan citizens, the sovereignty of the State and the health and progress of the economy are all

---

66 *Nuclear Tests Case – Australia* [1973] ICJ Rep 99, 105 [29] referring to "the possibility that damage to Australia might be shown to be caused by the deposit on Australian territory of radio-active fall-out resulting from such tests and to be irreparable"; *Questions of Interpretation and Application of the 1971 Montreal Convention arising from the Aerial Incident at Lockerbie (Libyan Arab Jamahiriya v United Kingdom) (Provisional Measures)* [1992] ICJ Rep 3, 84 [6] (Judge Ajibola).

67 *Military and Paramilitary Activities in and against Nicaragua (Nicaragua v USA) (Provisional Measures)* [1984] ICJ Rep 169 (*"Military and Paramilitary Activities"*); *Application of the Convention on the Prevention and Punishment of the Crime of Genocide (Bosnia and Herzegovina v Serbia and Montenegro) (Provisional Measures)* [1993] ICJ Rep 3 (*"Crime of Genocide"*); see generally Eva R Rieter, *Preventing Irreparable Harm. Provisional Measures in International Human Rights Adjudication* (Intersentia, 2010) 14–36.

68 *Arbitral Award of 31 July 1989 (Guinea-Bissau v Senegal) (Provisional Measures)* [1990] ICJ Rep 64, 81–83 (Judge Thierry).

69 *Certain Activities by Nicaragua – Provisional Measures* [2011] ICJ Rep 6, 21 [64]; *Obligation to Prosecute or Extradite* [2009] ICJ Rep 139, 152–162.

70 *LaGrand (Germany v USA) (Provisional Measures)* [1999] ICJ Rep 9; *Nuclear Tests Case – Australia* [1973] ICJ Rep 99; *Nuclear Tests Case – New Zealand* [1973] ICJ Rep 135; *Crime of Genocide* [1993] ICJ Rep 3.

71 *Nuclear Tests Case – New Zealand* [1973] ICJ Rep 135, 140–141 [28]. See also *Nuclear Tests Case (Australia v France) (Judgment)* [1974] ICJ Rep 253, 425–426 (Judge Barwick).

immediately at stake";[72] and the *Genocide Case* involving an emergency humanitarian crisis in the former Yugoslavia.

4.3   *Prevention of Aggravation or Extension of Dispute*

Using violence through advanced weapons capability to inflict serious harm on individuals, without recourse to due process or non-violent means, serves to aggravate a dispute by causing desperation of victims and/or their families to seek revenge through violent retaliation. The potential multiple harm impact from robot weapons is an aggravating feature: violation of territorial sovereignty to attack individuals; violation of fundamental human rights to life, due process, freedom from torture and freedom from crimes against humanity; and the threat to international peace and security. Robot weapons attacking humans pose an existential threat to present and future generations, adversely impacting on communities' liberty and their ability to create secure and stable environments. Unless and until international legal rules are established to regulate or ban UAV and other robot weapons, their inherent danger can only be prevented by interim measures. Possession and deployment of robot weapons is perceived by states as a strategic political and military advantage rather than a "world community interest". Early developers of robot weapons may set legal or non-legal standards according to their own rather than wider international community interests, and may abuse their position by coercing or threatening other states to comply with their demands, undermining the principle of equality of states. Use of robot weapons constitutes a significant change in how harm is created and prevented in international society, lowering the threshold for use of force making conflict more likely.[73]

4.4   *Prevention of Human Rights Violations*

States possessing robot weapons technology can use violence against individuals/groups within other states without recourse to due process. This potential capability to target and eliminate individuals clearly denies the right to life and due process, requiring urgent action. Robot weapons with autonomous capability in the critical functions of selection and attack represent a real and immediate risk of irreparable harm to the person in causing injury, suffering, and death. This breaches the rights to life and due process, and the principle of human dignity in life and death, guaranteed under international human

---

72   *Military and Paramilitary Activities* [1984] ICJ Rep 169, 182 [32].

73   See generally, Report of the ICRC Expert Meeting on *Autonomous weapon systems: technical, military, legal and humanitarian aspects* (9 May 2014) 9–10.

rights law and many constitutions.[74] In *Legality of the Threat or Use of Nuclear Weapons,* the ICJ noted that deprivation of life concerns human rights but then moves into *lex specialis* of international humanitarian law when involving lethal "use of a certain weapon in warfare". In principle, the right not to be arbitrarily deprived of life applies in the context of war, and the test of what constitutes arbitrary deprivation of life is determined by international humanitarian law. Thus, whether a particular loss of life, through use of a certain weapon in warfare, is to be considered an arbitrary deprivation of life contrary to art 6 ICCPR, can only be decided by reference to the law applicable in armed conflict and not deduced from the terms of the ICCPR itself.[75] But where robot weapons are used during peacetime (e.g. for domestic law enforcement) human rights law will still apply. The ability of UAV to target and eliminate individuals in Pakistan clearly denies the right to life and due process, requiring urgent action.

4.5   *Prevention of Violations of International Humanitarian Law*

International humanitarian law does not contain specific rules relating to robot weapons. However, they would still have to comply with existing international humanitarian law principles of distinction, proportionality, unnecessary suffering, and feasible precautions. And here lies a real concern: the technology does not exist to make fully autonomous robot weapons compliant with international humanitarian law, especially not the possibility of replicating "human central thinking activities". UAV and other robot weapons are not advanced enough to guarantee legitimate and accurate targeting, and crucially lack human cognitive abilities to exercise judgment in challenging situations to make proportionality decisions.[76] This can lead to collateral physical and psychological harm to local populations, and adversely impact on the liberty of communities living under constant fear of attack on life, property, security

---

74   See *Universal Declaration of Human Rights,* GA Res 217A (III), UN GAOR, 3rd sess, 183rd plen mtg, UN Doc A/810 (10 December 1948) art 3 *("UDHR")*; *International Covenant on Civil and Political Rights,* opened for signature 19 December 1966, 999 UNTS 171 (entered into force 23 March 1976) art 6(1) *("ICCPR")*; *UDHR* art 5 and *ICCPR* art 7; *UDHR* art 6 and *ICCPR* art 16; *UDHR* art 10 and *ICCPR* art 14(1); Paolo Carozza, "Human dignity in constitutional adjudication" in Tom Ginsberg and Rosalind Dixon (eds), *Comparative Constitutional Law* (Edward Elgar, 2011).

75   *Legality of the Threat or Use of Nuclear Weapons (Advisory Opinion)* [1996] ICJ Rep 226, 240 [25] *("Legality of the Threat or Use of Nuclear Weapons")*.

76   Ulgen, above n 2. Ulgen addresses how UAV violate principles of legitimate targeting, proportionality, and unnecessary suffering.

and livelihoods.[77] The sound and visual effect of the UAV attacking and killing could amount to serious psychological violence; an act of inhumane treatment, under crimes against humanity, against family members, friends and the local population, even though they were not subject to the attack and killing.[78]

Does this mean robot weapons are indiscriminate and capable of causing unnecessary and superfluous injury? Moreover, similar to the prohibition of blinding laser weapons under Protocol IV, should they therefore be prohibited before they are developed or deployed?[79] Robot weapons are potentially indiscriminate and capable of causing unnecessary suffering. The level of autonomy and extent of human control are determinative factors. In any case, the greater the level of autonomy, especially in relation to selecting and attacking human targets, the greater the ethical and legal dilemmas.

Significant numbers of civilian casualties from UAV strikes potentially make them indiscriminate because their effects cannot be limited in accordance with art 51(4)(c) API. Effects include civilian casualties and fatalities, destruction of civilian property, loss of livelihood due to fear of venturing outside, and severe psychological harm officially diagnosed as Post Traumatic Stress Disorder.[80] UAV strikes have caused civilian deaths without necessarily evidencing a concrete and direct military advantage. Since the first reported UAV strike in Yemen in 2002, persistent strikes have taken place in Pakistan's north western territories with reports of civilian casualties.[81] UAV strike figures in relation

---

77   Stanford International Human Rights and Conflict Resolution Clinic and Global Justice Clinic at NYU School of Law, *Living under drones: death, injury, and trauma to civilians from us drone practices in Pakistan* (September, 2012) (Stanford Report) Ch 3; Sudarsan Raghavan, "In Yemen, US airstrikes breed anger, and sympathy for al-Qaeda", *The Washington Post* (online), 29 May 2012 <https://www.washingtonpost.com/world/middle _east/in-yemen-us-airstrikes-breed-anger-and-sympathy-for-al-qaeda/2012/05/29/ gJQAUmKIoU_story.html?utm_term=.67f8c5f1c277>. Raghavan cites the case of a Yemeni soldier who initially fought against al-Qaeda but, after learning that his nephew was killed by a drone strike, left the army and sympathized with the group.

78   *Prosecutor v Aleksovski (Judgment)* (International Criminal Tribunal for the Former Yugoslavia, Trial Chamber I, Case No IT-95-14/1-T, 25 June 1999) [190]. The Court stated that broadcasting on loudspeakers the noise and screams of prison inmates subjected to physical violence by prison guards, constituted "serious psychological abuse of the detainees".

79   *Protocol IV on Blinding Laser Weapons*, above n 45; See UN Digital Recordings Portal, above n 36, Exchange of Views: Egypt and Costa Rica (13 December 2016).

80   United Kingdom, *Written evidence from the All Party Parliamentary Group on Drones (APPG)*, House of Commons 772 Defence Committee, 24 March 2014, [24] (Dr Peter Schaapveld's, forensic psychologist, evidence on drones in Yemen).

81   "168 children killed in Pakistan drone strikes", SOS Children's Villages' (online), 12 August 2011 <http://goodbye.soschildrensvillages.org.uk/news/archive/2011/08/168-children-killed -in-pakistan-drone-strikes>.

to Pakistan show disparity between perceived precision targeting capability and actual harm caused: one study shows from 2004 to 2011 an estimated 280 UAV strikes resulted in between 1,717 and 2,680 estimated total deaths of which 17%–17.5% were classified as non-militant;[82] another shows 114 UAV strikes from 2004 to 2010 resulted in between 830 and 1,210 individual deaths of which around 550 to 850 were described as militants in reliable press accounts, resulting in a civilian fatality rate of 32 per cent.[83] A 2014 analysis of UAV strikes in Pakistan and Yemen found attempts to kill 41 targeted men resulted in an estimated 1,147 deaths.[84]

States testing new robot weapons technology, exposing unsuspecting local populations to harm in the name of targeting terrorist suspects, are likely to be acting negligently. Awareness of possible risk of harm, or its mitigation through restricted strikes and location, fails to address why people should be exposed to any sort of risk of harm in the first place. Testing and development of robot weapons involves an ongoing obligation under art 36 API to appraise compliance with the principle of proportionality.[85] Article 51(5)(b) API prohibits:

> an attack which may be expected to cause incidental loss of civilian life, injury to civilians, damage to civilian objects, or a combination thereof, which would be excessive in relation to the concrete and direct military advantage anticipated.

Use of robot weapons with limited or no human control with potential to kill, injure or cause any harm or damage, needs to satisfy principles of humanity and public conscience under the Martens Clause; a fundamental principle of customary international law protecting civilians and combatants in all circumstances not regulated by international law.[86] In *Legality of the Threat or Use of*

---

82   Ian S Livingston and Michael O'Hanlon, *Pakistan Index*, 29 December 2011, Brookings, <https://www.brookings.edu/pakistan-index/>.

83   Peter Bergen and Katherine Tiedemann, *The Year of the Drone An Analysis of U.S. Drone Strikes in Pakistan, 2004–2010*, 24 February 2010, New America Foundation, <http://vcnv.org/files/NAF_YearOfTheDrone.pdf>.

84   Spencer Ackerman, "41 men targeted but 1,147 people killed: US drone strikes – the facts on the ground", *The Guardian* (online), 24 November 2014 <www.theguardian.com/us-news/2014/nov/24/-sp-us-drone-strikes-kill-1147>.

85   See Ulgen, above n 19.

86   *Additional Protocol I to the Geneva Conventions of 12 August 1949*, opened for signature 8 June 1977, 1125 UNTS 3 (entered into force 7 December 1978), art 1(2); *Hague Convention IV Respecting the Laws and Customs of War on Land*, opened for signature 18 October 1907, 187 CTS 227 (entered into force 26 January 1910), preamble; *Hague Convention II*

Nuclear Weapons, the ICJ recognised that the Martens Clause is "an effective means of addressing rapid evolution of military technology".[87]

We now turn to consider the prospects of success for provisional measures to be ordered for robot weapons in the light of ICJ jurisprudence and case law from the UN Human Rights Committee ("HRC") and the European Court of Human Rights ("ECtHR").

5   International Jurisprudence on New Weapons Technology

In the *Nuclear Test Cases,* the ICJ addressed the harmful impact of new weapons technology on an urgent basis, and was the first case to eventually order provisional measures halting atmospheric nuclear tests. It is instructive to consider whether the inter-state applications were based on a "world community interest", and how the Court dealt with these. It is also worth considering how individual complaints procedures before the HRC and the ECtHR dealt with requests by individuals and groups to halt nuclear tests and other nuclear weapons-related matters. Since the orders in the *Nuclear Test Cases* several requests have been made by individuals and groups for provisional measures to halt nuclear tests and other nuclear weapons-related matters. HRC jurisprudence reveals unease between recognition of a "world community interest", and unwillingness to engage with complaints deemed politically sensitive, even if these involve potential human rights violations.

5.1   *The Nuclear Test Cases*
Despite France's objection to the ICJ's jurisdiction, on 22 June 1973 the ICJ issued two provisional measures orders requiring the Governments of Australia, New Zealand, and France to each:

> ensure that no action of any kind is taken which might aggravate or extend the dispute submitted to the Court or prejudice the rights of the other Party in respect of the carrying out of whatever decision the Court may render in the case; and, in particular, the French Government should avoid nuclear tests causing the deposit of radio-active fall-out

---

  Respecting the Laws and Customs of War on Land opened for signature 29 July 1899, 32
  Stat 1803 (entered into force 4 September 1900), preamble.
87 *Legality of the Threat or Use of Nuclear Weapons* [1996] ICJ Rep 226, 257 [78].

on Australian territory, and on the territory of New Zealand, the Cook Islands, Niue or the Tokelau Islands.[88] In the end, the Court focused specifically on irreparable prejudice to Australia's and New Zealand's right to territorial sovereignty, which includes no radioactive fall-out entering their territories, airspace, or territorial waters.[89]

Some criticism may be levelled at the order's insufficiently prohibitory language: "avoiding" rather stopping nuclear tests, and specifically identifying nuclear tests that cause "the deposit of radio-active fall-out" leaving it open to continue tests that do not cause radioactive fall-out. Yet the orders also recognise the "world community interest" in preventing aggravation or extension of inter-state disputes; a primary function of provisional measures. The Court chose not to grant an order based on New Zealand's wider international community claims because "the circumstances of the case do not appear to require the indication of interim measures of protection in respect of other rights claimed by New Zealand".[90] This does not exclude the possibility of future "world community interest" claims and leaves open to consideration what types of "circumstances" may warrant interim measures. Would there need to be a certain level of worldwide state and public condemnation of the new weapons technology? Emerging *opinio juris* of preventative prohibition states evinces a level of condemnation of robot weapons and, at the very least, the majority of states recognise ethical, legal, and humanitarian implications.

In *Legality of the Threat or Use of Nuclear Weapons*, the Court acknowledged increasing international concern and the undesirability of nuclear weapons. International treaties prohibiting acquisition, manufacture, possession, deployment and testing of nuclear weapons, although not constituting a general prohibition on nuclear weapons, were "foreshadowing a future general prohibition."[91] The majority opined that the threat or use of nuclear weapons would "generally be contrary to the rules of international law applicable in armed conflict, and in particular the principles and rules of humanitarian law". Ultimately, however, it could not definitively conclude whether nuclear weapons would be lawful or unlawful in an extreme circumstance of self-defence involving a state's survival.[92] Strong dissents from Judges Shahabuddeen,

---

88   *Nuclear Tests Case – Australia* [1973] ICJ Rep 99, 105–106 [35]; *Nuclear Tests Case – New Zealand* [1973] ICJ Rep 135, 142–143 [36].

89   *Nuclear Tests Case – Australia* [1973] ICJ Rep 99, 105 [30]; *Nuclear Tests Case – New Zealand* [1973] ICJ Rep 135, 141 [31].

90   *Nuclear Tests Case – New Zealand* [1973] ICJ Rep 135, 141 [32].

91   *Legality of the Threat or Use of Nuclear Weapons* [1996] ICJ Rep 226, 253 [62].

92   Ibid 265–267 [105].

Weeramantry and Kormoa relied on a "world community interest" approach to deem nuclear weapons illegal under any circumstances. According to Shahabudden, uniquely destructive qualities of nuclear weapons (e.g. threatening survival of human species and annihilation of mankind; after effects remaining for future generations) override any concern not to prohibit them in order to protect states' right of self-defence.[93] Weeramantry detailed the harmful effects of nuclear weapons and their incompatibility with international law.[94] Comprehensive and universal limitations on nuclear weapons imposed by treaty make them prohibited, and they would always be contrary to international humanitarian law. Threat or use of nuclear weapons in any circumstance is prohibited under international law.[95] Koroma opined that the threat or use of nuclear weapons is illegal under any circumstances, including self-defence, and believed there was ample evidence for the Court to reach a decisive conclusion on this point.[96]

The Court's Advisory Opinion recognises a "world community interest" in terms of the harmful effects of nuclear weapons on humanity, generally favouring a prohibition. To this extent, there is a degree of international condemnation. But the Court's focus on the inter-state dimension hampers its ability to take sufficient account of overriding interests of humanity leading to indecision on prohibition and an exception for states. This is a significant shortcoming for the primary judicial organ of the UN responsible for maintaining international peace and security. The dissents support a "world community interest" approach which in recent years has been pursued more clearly by the Court.[97]

Unresolved issues at the inter-state level shifted litigation of the "world community interest" approach to the UN Human Rights Committee ("HRC") and the European Court of Human Rights ("ECtHR"), where individuals and groups claimed human rights violations.

5.2 HRC Cases with Potential "World Community Interest"

HRC General Comments of the 1980s made some headway on the status of nuclear weapons. *General Comment No.6* recognises that art 6 ICCPR (right to life) "should not be interpreted narrowly", and states have a "supreme duty"

---

93   Ibid 377, 380, 383, 387, 393–397 (Judge Shahabuddeen).
94   Ibid 450–475, 553 (Judge Weeramantry).
95   Ibid 433, 435, 553 (Judge Weeramantry).
96   Ibid 556 (Judge Koroma).
97   See, eg, *Ahmadou Sadio Diallo* [2010] ICJ Rep 639, (Judge Trindade); *Certain Activities by Nicaragua – Judgment* [2015] ICJ Rep 665, 1 (Judge Trindade).

to prevent wars, acts of genocide and other acts of mass violence causing arbitrary loss of life. Averting war, "especially thermonuclear war", and trying to strengthen international peace and security constitutes "the most important condition and guarantee for the safeguarding of the right to life."[98] *General Comment No.14* goes further in recognising a "world community interest". It identifies threats to life from use of new weapons technology, and the need to stop nuclear weapons development. It recognises that "the designing, testing, manufacture, possession and deployment of nuclear weapons are among the greatest threats to the right to life which confront mankind today", and this threat is compounded by "the danger that the actual use of such weapons may be brought about, not only in the event of war, but even through human or mechanical error or failure." It requires "the production, testing, possession, deployment and use of nuclear weapons should be prohibited and recognized as crimes against humanity", and "in the interest of mankind, calls upon all States, whether Parties to the Covenant or not, to take urgent steps, unilaterally and by agreement, to rid the world of this menace."[99]

Yet when it comes to application of art 6 and *General Comments No.6* and *No.14*, the HRC appears to retreat. In *Aalbersberg and others v The Netherlands*, 2,084 Dutch citizens alleged violation of art 6 due to the Dutch government's official position on use of nuclear weapons and its failure to provide "any active measures of protection against the actual use of nuclear weapons".[100] The complaint was deemed inadmissible because the petitioners could not demonstrate "an existing or imminent violation of their right to life". In *E.W. et al. v The Netherlands*, 6,588 Dutch citizens alleged violation of art 6 due to the Dutch government agreeing to deploy cruise missiles fitted with nuclear warheads on Dutch territory. While repeating its earlier position in *General Comment No.14* (that nuclear weapons are "among the greatest threats to the right to life"), the HRC noted the complaints procedure "was not designed for conducting public debate over matters of public policy, such as support for disarmament and issues concerning nuclear and other weapons of mass destruction."[101] The complaint was deemed inadmissible because "preparations for deployment of cruise missiles between 1 June 1984 and 8 December 1987 and the continuing

---

98   *Human Rights Committee, General Comment No 6: Article 6 (Right to life)*, 16th sess, (30 April 1982) [1]–[2].

99   *Human Rights Committee, General Comment No 14: Article 6 (Nuclear weapons and the right to life)*, 23rd sess, UN Doc HRI/GEN/1/Rev.9 (Vol. I) (9 November 1984) [4], [6]–[7].

100   Human Rights Committee, *Views: Communication No 1440/2005*, UN Doc CCPR/C/87/D/1440/2005 (12 July 2006) (*"Aalbersberg and others v The Netherlands"*).

101   Human Rights Committee, *Views: Communication No 429/1990*, UN Doc CCPR/C/47/D/429/1990 (8 April 1993) [6.2] (*"E W et al v The Netherlands"*).

deployment of other nuclear weapons in the Netherlands did not, at the relevant period of time, place the authors in the position to claim to be victims whose right to life was then violated or under imminent prospect of violation."[102]

In *Bordes and Temeharo v France*, French citizens were refused provisional measures to stop French underground nuclear tests in French Polynesia, which they alleged violated art 6, and their right not to be subjected to interference to their privacy under art 17.[103] They argued that radioactive material from underground nuclear tests escaping into the atmosphere and environment constituted an unlawful interference with the right to privacy under art 17, because it posed a real risk to family life in terms of death from cancer, leukaemia, or ciguatera.[104] The HRC did not comment on this aspect of the case and *General Comment No.16* does not refer to radioactive material release as constituting a form of unlawful interference in family life. However, the Committee's interpretation of "arbitrary interference" requires that any lawful interference "should be in accordance with the provisions, aims and objectives of the Covenant and should be, in any event, reasonable in the particular circumstances."[105] Thus, any interference caused by testing nuclear weapons must be proportionate and reasonable if it is not to breach art 17. Although the Committee deemed the overall claim inadmissible because the petitioners did not satisfy the victim requirement, it reasserted its position under *General Comment No.14*.[106]

These cases suggest a disconnect between interpretation and application of the law. On the one hand, the Committee expounds a "world community interest" on the undesirability and harmful effects of nuclear weapons. On the other, the strict evidentiary standard of direct and immediate irreparable harm excludes many claims without consideration of long-term harmful effects and "unendurable situations".

5.3 *ECtHR Cases on Nuclear Weapons*

Prior to the HRC's decision in *Bordes*, the same petitioners filed a complaint with the European Commission on Human Rights alleging breaches of ECHR arts 2 (right to life), 3 (prohibition of torture, inhuman or degrading treatment), 8 (right to privacy), and 1 of Protocol 1 (peaceful enjoyment of possessions).

---

102 Ibid [6.4].

103 Human Rights Committee, *Views: Communication No 645/1995*, UN Doc CCPR/C/57/D/645 /1995 (22 July 1996) (*"Bordes and Temeharo v France"*).

104 Ibid [4.8].

105 *Human Rights Committee, General Comment No 16: Article 17 (The right to respect of privacy, family, home and correspondence, and protection of honour and reputation)*, 32nd sess, UN Doc HRI/GEN/1/Rev.9 (Vol. I) (8 April 1988) [4].

106 *Bordes and Temeharo v France*, above n 103, [5.9].

The Commission noted that "merely invoking risks inherent in the use of nuclear power ... is insufficient to enable the applicants to claim to be victims of a violation of the Convention, as many human activities generate risks."[107] Petitioners must show that:

> owing to the authorities' failure to take adequate precautions, the degree of probability that damage will occur is such that it may be deemed to be a violation, on condition that the consequences of the act complained of are not too remote.[108]

The complaint was inadmissible because they "failed to substantiate their claim that the French authorities failed to take all necessary measures to prevent an accident which could have occurred at any time."[109] By focusing on the causal link and remoteness of state action and individual harm, the Commission implicitly rejected a "world community interest" basis for dealing with such complaints.

In *Athanassoglu and others v Switzerland*, the ECtHR denied provisional measures to prevent a nuclear power plant operating pending judgment on ECHR violations. The petitioners, 12 Swiss nationals living near the plant, alleged violation of art 6 (right to fair trial) because the government granted an extension of the operating licence and its decision could not be challenged by judicial review.[110] By 12 votes to five, the majority judges held that art 6 was not applicable because Swiss law allowed public objections during the licensing process but did not confer any further rights once a licence was granted. The decision to extend the licence was not determinative of rights to life, physical integrity, and property. Further, "how best to regulate the use of nuclear power is a policy decision for each Contracting State to take according to its democratic processes. Article 6 § 1 cannot be read as dictating any one scheme rather than another."[111] But the dissenting judges countered that these sorts of decisions should be subject to judicial review because of "the dangers presented to the environment and the population by such installations."[112]

Although provisional measures were not ordered by the HRC or ECtHR, these cases indicate a strict approach to imminence of irreparable harm; one

---

107   *Tauira et al v France* (1995) 83-B Eur Comm HR 112, 131 (*"Tauira et al"*).

108   Ibid 132.

109   Ibid.

110   *Athanassoglou and others v Switzerland* [2000] IV Eur Court HR 173 (*"Athanassoglou and others"*).

111   Ibid [54].

112   Ibid 204.

not well-suited to capturing the long-term harm posed by nuclear radiation. Long-term harm from exposure to nuclear radiation strikes at the heart of human survival and "conceptually would be situated more towards the common core than towards the outer limits of the concept [of irreparable harm]."[113] Such problems may not arise in cases involving the use of robot weapons where there is immediacy of lethal harm and destructive capability.

6   Conclusion

Robot weapons with varying degrees of autonomy are a "world community interest" because they have the potential to aggravate or extend disputes, and violate human rights and international humanitarian law. States possessing such weapons technology can use violence against individuals/groups within other states without due process. Targeted individuals/groups are killed, and local populations may suffer collateral physical and psychological harm. This constitutes "irreparable injury"; a traditional circumstance for provisional measures. In addition, the use of robot weapons has ongoing harmful effects in forcing people and states to live in a constant state of fear and anxiety (e.g. not knowing when, where or who a UAV will strike and kill), with potential for territorial sovereignty to be violated at any time. This constitutes an "unendurable situation", which comes under the primary function of provisional measures to prevent aggravation or extension of disputes.

The *Nuclear Test Cases* set a precedent for the ICJ to consider urgent cases relating to use of new weapons technology as a "world community interest" warranting indication of provisional measures. The potential harmful effects from atmospheric nuclear tests posed a risk of irreparable prejudice to the rights of Australia and New Zealand, including aggravation or extension of the dispute. Although the Court chose not to grant an order based on New Zealand's "world community interest" claim, there is a possibility for such claims to be made in the future especially with a Court that is more cognisant of global interest issues impacting on humanity. The Court's Advisory Opinion, *Legality of the Threat or Use of Nuclear Weapons,* recognised a "world community interest" in terms of the harmful effects of nuclear weapons on humanity, yet shied away for a decisive determination of illegality. Dissenting opinions were willing to act in the interest of humanity and go behind the inter-state dimension to call for a clear determination that nuclear weapons are illegal. In recent years, the

---

113   Rieter, above n 67, 540.

Court has also focused more on the interest of humanity which makes it more receptive to "world community interest" claims.

Provisional measures to halt nuclear tests and other nuclear weapons-related matters under the HRC and ECtHR individual complaints procedures have proved more difficult. These bodies are reluctant to recognise complaints with a "world community interest" aspect, even those involving potential human rights violations. A strict approach to imminence of irreparable harm is ill-suited to capturing long-term harmful effects from nuclear radiation, and excludes consideration of "unendurable situations". Still, such problems may not arise in cases involving the use of robot weapons where there is immediacy of lethal harm and destructive capability.

All states should have standing to bring a claim before the ICJ on the basis that the continued use of robot weapons constitutes an "unendurable situation", although it is more likely to be made from a state directly affected by "irreparable injury". Pakistan, among several states subjected to UAV strikes, is the only one with a reasonable prospect of establishing prima facie jurisdiction for the ICJ to exercise incidental jurisdiction and indicate provisional measures. Pakistan would have to institute proceedings against the US alleging UAV strikes violate customary international law and treaty law on territorial sovereignty, prohibition on the use of force, right to life, and right to due process. It would then have to simultaneously request a provisional measures order obliging the US to halt any further UAV strikes until such time that the Court delivers final judgment on their legality. This would resolve the interstate dispute and, in the interest of humanity, place a type of robot weapon under closer judicial scrutiny.

Democracy in International Law-making: An Unfilled Lacuna

Salar Abbasi[*]

1 Introduction

In this paper, the ideal of democracy in international law-making is accepted as valid. Despite conceptual skepticism on the very existence of international law, it is undeniable that a very specific model of governance is carried out by international law-making and norm-identification apparatuses.[1] The importance of democracy and democratic law-making processes is crucial and preliminary[2] in providing governance and the law-making apparatus with the requirements of legitimacy. But intergovernmental organisations and international instruments have failed to address the substantive concept of democracy in international law, required in order to sketch a legitimacy formula for international law-making. In fact, conceptualisation of democracy in international law-making has almost been a non-issue in the evolution of international law. In international law scholarship, references to democracy are most commonly made with tenets of procedural democracy in mind with an inseparable connection to the notion of government. The discourse on the scope and application of democracy in national constitutions has been transferred to international legal parlance, insofar as the treatment by a government of its people is concerned, such as the cases of recognition of a state, human rights

---

[*] PhD candidate in International Law & Jurisprudence, Catholic University of Portugal, Lisbon, Global School of Law. FCT (Foundation for Research & Technology sponsored by the Ministry of Science & Education of Portugal) Scholar. And Visiting Doctoral Researcher at the Nathanson Centre for Transnational Human Rights, Crime and Security, Osgoode Hall Law School of the York University, Toronto, Canada. I am deeply thankful to Prof Hengameh Saberi for her encouraging and enlightening comments. I especially thank my dear friend and colleague Jing Geng Howard for her meticulous proof-reading of this article. I am also very much grateful to the anonymous reviewers for their enlightening comments on my paper.

1 See Philippa Webb, *International Judicial Integration and Fragmentation* (Oxford University Press, 2013).
2 See James Feibleman, *Positive Democracy* (University of North Carolina Press, 1940).

concerns,[3] and the international law of statehood in general. That stated, what about the scope and application of democracy in international law-making which applies irrespective of any government and the existence of a political structure?

According to Western legal thinkers and political philosophers, definitions of democracy rely either on procedural processes or the substantive axiom of participation for all.[4] Under the influence of Western ideas of liberal representative democracy, the electoral and adversarial model of democracy has been pervasively adopted as representative of the will of the people living in a given territory. The representative perspective of democracy lends weight to the formal process of accountability through the authorisation of representatives by the different groups or entities in a legal system including international law and indirect participation of actors in the law-making process.[5] Bentham held that representative authority "secures its members against oppression and depredation at the hands of those functionaries which it employs for its defense".[6] On the other hand, based on the substantive participatory concept, direct governance of people over people is rendered a core tenet or axiom of any given definition of democracy. Proponents of the participatory perspective of democracy argue that "democracy etymologically means governance by the people"[7] or the governance of many over many. This standpoint is best characterised by Rousseau when he criticised the representative perspective of democracy:

> Will cannot be represented; will either is or is not, your own; there is no intermediate possibility ... Deputies of the people are not, and cannot be, its representatives; they are merely its agents, and can make no final decision. Any law which the people has not ratified in person is null and void; it is not a law...[8]

---

3   These include establishing a criterion for legitimate and lawful government, giving form to the right of peoples to political self-determination, providing a context for the enjoyment of human rights and fundamental freedom.

4   See, in general, Jure Vidmar, *Democratic Statehood in International Law: The Emergence of New States in Post-Cold War Practice* (Bloomsbury Publishing, 2013).

5   See Ruth W Grant and Robert O Keohane, "Accountability and Abuses of Power in World Politics" (2005) 99 *American Political Science Review* 29.

6   David Held, *Democracy and the Global Order: From the Modern State to Cosmopolitan Governance* (Stanford University Press, 1995) 10.

7   Jan Wouters, Bart De Meester and Cedric Ryngaert, "Democracy and International Law" (2003) 34 *Netherlands Yearbook of International Law* 139, 146.

8   Jean-Jacques Rousseau, *Political Writings* (Fredrick Watkins, trans and ed, The University of Wisconsin Press, 1986) 103.

All in all, this article aims to make sense of a new inquiry on the implication of democracy for international law-making. The arguments of this article are based upon universally well-known Iranian philosophers; the idea of Global Democratic Unification by *Jalāl ad-Dīn Muhammad Balkhī,* known as *Rūmi* (1207–73), inspired preliminarily by the idea of Egalitarian Law developed by *Shahab al-Din Suhrawardi* (1155–91). This article is structured in the following order: Part 2 elaborates on conceptual skepticism regarding the existence and effectiveness of international law as a legal system. Part 3 discusses the evolutionary notion of democracy in international law. Part 4 stresses an unfilled lacuna in the discourse on the implications of democracy in international law-making. Additionally, the theoretical backbone of this article – the idea of Egalitarian Law and the idea of Global Democratic Unification – is touched upon in this Part. Part 5 grapples with a pragmatic skepticism on the applicability of these aspirational global governance models and introduces the idea of fragmented democracy for intrinsically fragmented international law as a preliminary response. Part 6 highlights the final remarks of this article and opens horizons for further elaborations in this regard.

2   International Law and a Conceptual Skepticism

Through a world order based on realism and human needs, European monarchies ruled much of the world for centuries under colonialism and the annexation of territories. In Europe, the anarchists, sometimes in alliance with the socialists, emerged as a terrifying enemy for monarchies.[9] The anarchists believed in equality of political power and called for shared wealth and political participation of many in policy and law-making. Their anarchist means established the foundation of what would then become an extremely dreadful phenomenon called terrorism. In the late 19th and early 20th centuries, the assassination of European monarchs was indicative of a tempest of change in the world order as these upheavals were, mostly, the invasion of ideas rather than the invasion of anarchy.[10]

Amidst these intellectual revolutions, international law remained dysfunctional in coping with instant and unpredictable political will-formation of its actors. This led to literary impropriety, indeterminacy, and customary uncertainty of international law which obliterated any settled methodology for identifying recognised norms based on the contradictory preferences of

---

9   See Geoffrey Blainey, *A Short History of the Twentieth Century* (Penguin UK, 2007).
10   Ibid 31.

international actors. Likewise, the proper functioning of international courts, tribunals, and intergovernmental organisations in seeking to give weight and effect to identified values has seriously been under debate. For instance, the voluntary jurisdiction of International Court of Justice "is undoubtedly a major flaw of the international legal order, since it gives leeway for states to act as judges in their own cause".[11] Given this perplexity, international norm identification is frequently marked by conflicting interpretations and is increasingly composed of co-operative and competing elements willing to participate in the norm-making process. Generally speaking, the unresponsiveness of international law to instant political will-formation on the international plane formed conceptual skepticism towards the existence and effectiveness of international law. This argument was mostly influenced by "the general realist thesis that based upon that, political morality does not reach beyond the boundaries of the state, or that only a very minimalist morality does".[12] Based on this school of thought, international legal norms are made through what actors do or consent to do, not what they morally ought to do or comply with independent of content.

The conceptual skepticism towards international law stems, firstly, from assessing international legal theory within the terms and scope of the traditional concept of law theorised for domestic legal systems that are of a centralised hierarchical political power, and secondly, due to sidelining philosophical normative inquiries pertinent to the fluid nature of international law. Legal theory developed for domestic legal systems is inherently influenced by legal standards developed for a domestic society. Typical elements are the courts and a legislature that both are, on the basis of a traditional legal theory, regarded as the creators of law. The intrinsic ingredients of such a legal system are: hierarchical distribution of political power, unilateralism, and obligation backed by either threats[13] or moral reasons for the governed people living in a given territory to comply with the rules issued by the ruler. In other words, the synthesis of unilateral rules imposed by the ruler and content-independent obedience of the people have been the constitutive elements of governance. But it is crucial to note that there is no reason to thoroughly apply typical elements of the domestic legal system to international law, for they are, to a large extent,

---

11   Gonçalo de Almeida Ribeiro, "Judicial Activism and Fidelity to Law" in Luís Pereira Coutinho, Massimo La Torre, Steven D Smith (eds), *Judicial Activism* (Springer, 2015) 31, 39.

12   Samantha Besson and John Tasioulas, *The Philosophy of International Law* (Oxford University Press, 2010).

13   That is the unpleasant consequence of refusal, or what Austin labelled "the key to the science of jurisprudence". See Herbert Lionel Adolphus Hart et al, *The Concept of Law* (Oxford University Press, 2012) 6.

distinct from each other. Domestic societies are a vertical structure marked by hierarchical centralised political power, while international law is a non-compulsory jurisdiction where political power is decentralised and horizontally distributed. According to Besson and Tasioulas, "[a]s a result, if international law does not fit the criteria of the concept of law used at the domestic level it may not (only) be a problem for the legality of international law, but (also) for those criteria themselves".[14]

International law is a very special field of legal studies. Given its horizontality, indeterminacy, and instant political will formation of its actors, a unique jurisprudence pertinent to its inherent specificities is to be inferred and developed. International law is a fluid field of law for international law-making apparatus, enjoying cognitive advantages over its subjects in determining what the latter have reasons to do.[15] Crawford persuasively described international law in practice as intellectual activities carried out for practical purposes. Given his ideas, the structure of international law is intellectual rather than material.[16] International law-making is as fluid as human intellect. Therefore, a dynamic concept of democracy pertinent to its special legal character is a preliminary step towards sketching a dynamic legal theory for international law. In other words, a fluid stream of law-making necessitates a fluid democracy to dynamically and pragmatically deal with the instant intellectual will-formation of its actors. The basic step to march dynamically with the fluidity of international law is to define a dynamic theory of democracy which effectively submits itself to a developing international law. In practice, strengthened transnational bonds and partial fusions have overtly necessitated extension of the reach of the principle of democracy beyond the notion of nation-states or the governance of the states.[17]

3 Existing Literature on the Implications of Democracy in International Law

3.1 *Democracy and the International Law of Statehood*
In order to resolve the inevitable conflict of interests of individuals in a plural society, a central government's role is to establish institutions and

---

14   Besson and Tasioulas, above n 12, 8.

15   See John Tasioulas "The Legitimacy of International Law" in Samantha Besson and John Tasioulas, *The Philosophy of International Law* (Oxford University Press, 2010).

16   See James Crawford, "Democracy and International Law" (1994) 64(1) *British Yearbook of International Law* 113.

17   See Held, above n 6.

provide mechanisms to sketch a shared interest and a common good, and to channel the conflicts into a place for discourse and compromise without recourse to violence and violation of political rights.[18] Democracy appeared as a means of protecting the rights, mostly political, of the minorities and most vulnerable strata of society. Likewise, the discourse on democracy has been dominated by the idea of human rights for minorities and also the right of self-determination for groups.[19] The principle of self-determination, championed by Woodrow Wilson after the First World War, was a revolutionary step towards de-colonisation and a building block of democratic entitlements of statehood, human rights, and freedom of expression. On the other hand, it paved the way for deep concerns of international institutions and organisations in domestic affairs of states in cases where the confirmed wishes of the governed peoples are ignored and human rights are grossly violated by the recalcitrant government.

It was after the dissolution of the Soviet Union in the early 1990s that Franck, in his work *The Emerging Right to Democratic Governance*, stressed the transformation of democratic entitlement from a moral prescription to an international legal obligation.[20] Contemporaneously, democracy began to appear as an international apparatus for granting recognition to statehood claims; it is in practice proven that granting recognition to newly evolved states which claim to have democratically constituted themselves, mostly following the post-Cold War era, has been contingent on a set of legality-based criteria, in addition to the putative criteria declared in the 1933 *Montevideo Convention on the Rights and Duties of States*.[21] These additional legality-based criteria, often considered the building blocks of democracy, include the non-violation of universally incontrovertible human rights such as the right to political participation (the right to free and fair elections), freedom of speech, and the right to self-determination.[22]

A new rhetoric loomed, mostly after the dissolution of the Soviet Union, as qualitative innovation in national law based on pro-democratic interventionism by intergovernmental organs called for the emerging right of humanitarian

---

18   See, in general, Jeremy Waldron, *Law and Disagreement* (OUP Oxford, 1999).

19   See *International Covenant on Civil and Political Rights*, opened for signature 16 December 1966, 999 UNTS 171 (entered into forced 23 March 1976) ("ICCPR"); *Universal Declaration of Human Rights*, GA Res 217A (III) UN GAOR, 3rd sess, 183rd plen mtg, UN Doc A/810 (10 December 1948) art 21.

20   See Thomas M Franck, "The Emerging Right to Democratic Governance" (1992) 86(1) *The American Journal of International Law* 46.

21   Vidmar, above n 4.

22   See Franck, above n 20.

assistance to restore democracy.[23] It was after the end of the Cold War era that international organisations culminated their efforts to help peoples of states to act on behalf of the right to self-determination and to gain democratic entitlement through participation in democratic elections.[24] From 1992–99 the United Nations Electoral Assistance Division provided various forms of electoral assistance and between 1990–95 the European Union provided electoral assistance to 44 different countries.[25] Given this, and various international covenants and instruments in this regard, the determination of the legitimacy of governments has gradually been a legalised and internationalised process.[26] The first practical pro-democratic intervention of the United Nations into the electoral monitoring of an independent state dates to 1989 when the United Nations Secretary General was asked to monitor Nicaragua's electoral process by establishing an observer mission.[27] The active, far-reaching role of the UN observers in Nicaragua clearly illustrated how much the ground rules for international election monitoring under the auspices of pro-democratic interventionism had gained legitimacy. This provided room for terms, such as interventionism, in protection of the people's sovereignty rights. According to Reisman, contemporary international law seeks to protect the people's sovereignty rather than the sovereign's sovereignty.[28] Pro-democratic interventionism experienced a huge advancement when the UN Security Council deemed coups d'état in Sierra Leone[29] and Haiti[30] as anti-democratic and "threats to

---

23   See Lois E Fielding, "Taking the next Step in the Development of New Human Rights: The Emerging Right of Humanitarian Assistance to Restore Democracy" (1994) 5 *Duke Journal of Comparative & International Law* 329.

24   See Gregory H Fox and Brad R Roth, "Democracy and International Law" (2001) *Review of International Studies* 327.

25   Ibid 330.

26   Vidmar, above n 4.

27   See The Situation in Central America: Threats to International Peace and Security and Peace Initiatives, UN Doc A/44/642 (1989).

28   W Michael Reisman, "Sovereignty and Human Rights in Contemporary International Law" (1990) 84(4) *The American Journal of International Law* 866, 869.

29   SC Res 1132, UN SCOR, 3822nd mtg, UN Doc S/RES/1132 (8 October 1997).

30   SC Res 841, UN SCOR, 3238th mtg, UN Doc S/RES/841 (16 June 1993); SC Res 861, UN SCOR, 3271st mtg, UN Doc S/RES/861 (27 August 1993); SC Res 862, UN SCOR, 3272nd mtg, UN Doc S/RES/862 (31 August 1993); SC Res 867, UN SCOR, 3282nd mtg, UN Doc S/RES/867 (23 September 1993); SC Res 873, UN SCOR, 3291st mtg UN Doc S/RES/873 (13 October 1993); SC Res 875, UN SCOR, 3293rd mtg, UN Doc S/RES/875 (16 October1993); SC Res 905, UNSCOR, 3352rd mtg, UN Doc S/RES/905 (23 March 1994); SC Res 917, UNSCOR, 3376th mtg, UN Doc S/RES/917 (6 May 1994); SC Res 933, UN SCOR, 3397th mtg, UN Doc S/RES/933 (30 June 1994); SC Pre 940, UN SCOR, 3413th mtg, UN Doc S/RES/940 (31 July 1994).

the peace", passing resolutions against the usurpation of the sovereign preroga-
tive of a population to be governed by democratically elected leaders.

Indisputably, international law is not, from a democratic perspective, capable of intervening in a specific territory when it considers a specific domestic
movement as a threat to peace. Furthermore, the principle of territorial integrity of states restricts, in scope and practice, the right of self-determination, as
well as pro-democratic interventions of international bodies, to gross violations of basic human rights.[31] It should be noted that electoral monitoring itself has room for downright undemocratic measures and does not necessarily
exhibit the true fulfillment of the right of self-determination: in some cases it
may even lead to gross violations of human rights.[32]

3.2   Cosmopolitan Democracy

States' inevitable reliance on regional and transnational commerce has incon-
trovertibly brought about ever-growing interconnectedness and interdependence among States. This is, in fact, a natural sentiment of de-bordering and
globalisation.[33] Under the overarching influence of globalisation, the very process of governance can escape the reach of the modern nation-state, as certain
domestically-made decisions and laws may influence other states in the region
and even in far regions without the political participation of the peoples of
those affected states. In this context, the meaning, scope, and applicability of
democracy have to be reconsidered in relation to overlapping local, national,
regional, and global structures and processes.[34] Under this transformationalist
literature, the modern state approach is trapped within an extensive web of
global interdependence necessitating a state's recourse to international cooperation.[35] This state of affairs necessitates a balancing between the autonomy
of the state in decision-making and the pursuit of the good of the peoples
living in the entire region. In other words, the autonomy of states is constrained by recognising the mutual dependence and democratic autonomy of
other nations. This is what Kant conceived in his "perpetual peace" under the
theory of "Ideal Deliberative Discourse". He made sense of the idea of a global
discourse within which states' conflicts of interests are considered resolvable

---

31   See Vidmar, above n 4.

32   See Steven Wheatley, "Democracy in International Law: A European Perspective" (2002)
      51(2) International and Comparative Law Quarterly 225.

33   See Armin Von Bogdandy, "Globalization and Europe: How to Square Democracy, Global-
      ization, and International Law" (2004) 15(5) European Journal of International Law 885.

34   Held, above n 6, 21.

35   Ibid 25.

through negotiation, commerce, finding mutual interests, and avoiding both war and, more importantly, preparations for war.[36]

The idea of cosmopolitan democracy, under the overall idea of cosmopolitan democratic public law, looks into processes in which the highest ideals of public law and justice could be channeled into the relations between states, as well as into the democratic governance of a state over its peoples. Central to the idea of cosmopolitan democracy is the consent and participation of the peoples of all concerned nations. Purportedly, through the implementation of cosmopolitan democratic law, states will be driven to adopt a democratic governance model and be a part of the confederation of the democratic states. In other words, through cosmopolitan democratic law, the principles of individual democratic states could come to coincide with those of the idea of cosmopolitan democratic law. Per Patomäki, "[a]s a consequence, the rights and responsibilities of people *qua* national citizens and *qua* subjects of cosmopolitan law could coincide, and democratic citizenship could take on, in principle, a truly universal status".[37] This is why Patomäki argues that democratic legitimacy for states does not seem possible without global (cosmopolitan) democracy.[38]

All in all, the discourse on democracy in international law has mostly been composed of: authority of a government or a ruler entity, liberty of the governed people, rule of obligation issued by the ruler to governed people, international watch on democratic entitlement, granting recognition to a government on the basis of compliance of the rule of obligation with human rights and the criteria of political participation and freedom of speech. In other words, the dominant political and philosophical view on the notion of democracy is strictly on the basis of governance and the rule of obligation backed by coercive mechanisms to secure compliance of the governed with the rule. However, the main concern of this article is to consider and assess democratic entitlement of international institutions in making laws. If democracy means holding the law-maker accountable through periodic electoral recognition, democracy in international law-making will continue to be a non-issue or unfeasible because there is no central political power and sovereignty in international law. In channeling into

---

36   See Immanuel Kant, *Perpetual Peace and Other Essays: On Politics, History, and Morals* (Hackett Publishing, 1983).

37   Held, above n 6, 232–233.

38   See Heikki Patomäki, "Is Democracy Possible without Global Democracy" in Tapio Kanninen and Katarina Sehm Patomäki (eds), *Building Democracy from Manila to Doha: The Evolution of the Movement of New or Restored Democracies* (Finnish Ministry of Foreign Affairs Publishing, 2005) 195.

the main concern of this article, it is necessary to touch upon the notion of democracy in international law-making, without the slightest reference to the notions of sovereignty and democratic entitlement of any given state.

3.3   Democracy in International Law-making
The international law-making apparatus is categorised in three branches: treaty-making institutions, customary international law institutions, and global governance institutions such as the WTO and the UN.[39] The two elements upon which the legitimacy assessment is made are the legitimacy of the laws made by the institutions and the legitimacy of the law-maker institutions themselves. It has been argued that "institutional legitimacy is primary in so far as the legitimacy of particular laws or of a corpus of law depends on the legitimacy of the institutions that make, interpret, and apply the laws".[40] To Buchanan, a legitimacy assessment entails moral evaluation rather than a legal realistic exegesis, which leads to the non-coercive posture of international law towards its actors. He considers legitimacy to be a less demanding criterion and draws a clear line between justice and legitimacy, giving legitimacy a contractual weight whereby parties can reach an agreement and make laws even in the absence of the requirement for justice.[41] Legitimacy assessment in international law-making is nothing but a content-independent moral reason to practically comply with the rule of obligation, or at least non-interference with it. To Raz, content-independent moral reason to comply with a rule of obligation is relevant where a ruling institution has a legitimate authority over the governed, if the governed believes that s/he could do better under the directives and rules of the ruling institution (instrumental legitimacy).[42] But the main question is whether or not international institutions have such a character as to persuade international actors to comply with their rules, independent of content.

International law is based on contradictory promises of its actors and unsettled norm-identification formulas which suffer from a considerable degree of arbitrariness and indeterminacy.[43] International law's indeterminacy, coupled with its decentralised horizontal political system, has brought about institutional illegitimacy of its organisations. For instance, the failure of the

---

39   See Allen Buchanan, "The Legitimacy of International Law" in Besson and Tasioulas, above n 12.

40   Ibid 79.

41   Ibid 80–81.

42   See, in general, Joseph Raz, *The Morality of Freedom* (Clarendon Press, 1986).

43   See Martti Koskenniemi, *From Apology to Utopia: The Structure of International Legal Argument* (Cambridge University Press, 2006).

United Nations Security Council to authorise a collective intervention to stop genocidal mass murder in a given territory is indicative of its dysfunctional posture in providing a content-independent moral obligation for its actors to comply with the rule of law. So, a critical question on the legitimacy of international law-making, which is also central to the main objective of this article, is whether or not legitimacy assessments in international law-making follows an independent substantive concept.

Given the fluidity of international law, which is based on intellectual correspondence and instant political will-formation, international law-making apparatuses enjoy cognitive advantages over its actors on how to drive the latter to remain in concert with the will of the dominant ideas. This critique is what has been called the "volitional defect" of the international law-making process.[44] Legitimacy assessments of the international law-making process have been conducted with a strict reference to structured standards such as the human rights standard or the theory of state consent. To make a long story short, international law's legitimacy has been assessed under the auspices and "dos and do nots" of independent standards, such as that of human rights or static state consent theory. Therefore, the decision-making process in international law-making has been shaped on the basis of traditional models of democracy, such as weighted voting and the majority principle. But is the electoral standard of law-making, which is based on an adversarial decision-making method, in concert with the non-hierarchical temperament of international law?

Intrinsically, "international law is universal. It is a body of law that applies to all states regardless of their specific cultures, belief systems and political organisations",[45] but in the wake of adversarial law-making methods, the geopolitical power of non-dominant member states is not of practical importance if it is not in concert with political interests of the dominant ones. In other words, while the sovereign equality of states theoretically eclipses decision-making rules in international organisations, the operation of those rules – how states behave in practice under them and the consequences of that behaviour – is not well understood.[46] Therefore, the inseparable outcome of adversarial law-making process is divisiveness, bringing with it room for almost compulsory compliance, potential hostility, and increasingly antagonistic postures of

---

44   See John Tasioulas, "The Legitimacy of International Law" in Besson and Tasioulas, above n 12.

45   Antony Anghie, "Finding the Peripheries: Sovereignty and Colonialism in Nineteenth-Century International Law" (1999) 40 *Harvard International Law Journal* 1, 2.

46   See Richard H Steinberg, "In the Shadow of Law or Power? Consensus-Based Bargaining and Outcomes in the GATT/WTO" (2002) 56(2) *International Organization* 339.

member states and international actors towards each other. In fact, through adversarial international law-making methods, the concern of inequality of actors in the international law-making process, on the basis of inequality in terms of political powers, has led to an unpleasant figure of particularism on the international plane.[47] This outcome is in contrast with the "doctrine of the legal equality of states [that] is an umbrella category for it includes within its scope the recognised rights and obligations which fall upon all States".[48]

It has been argued that the pure notion of democracy in international law-making requires fulfillment of the idea of cosmopolitan democracy.[49] Cosmopolitanism in its very nature, as stated above, characterises the necessity of equal advancement of the interests of all – pursuit of the good of all persons instead of a common good.[50] Christiano put forward two other criteria in addition to the criterion of cosmopolitanism: publicity and balancing of interests.[51] Publicity requires attachment to the principle of cosmopolitanism once it is implemented in actual institutions, and balancing of interests, which is of a reciprocal character, requires equal balancing of proposals during a course of negotiation. In the latter, once a party admits a proposal rendered by the counterpart, there is a right to have the proposal admitted. Again, this idea is a three-pronged standard of legitimacy assessment without, however, rendering a substantive concept of democracy for international law-making. In fact this, again, does not provide a response to conceptual inquiry on sketching an independent substantive concept of democracy in international law-making. So, the conceptual lacuna remains unfilled. What this research argues is that in the light of the fluidity of international law, where intellectuality is the focal tenet of its legal structure, a dynamic concept of democracy pertinent to fluidity of international law is of critical importance for the upcoming international law agenda. A well-structured concept of democracy in international law can bestow an aura of legitimacy on international law-making itself, independent of traditional ingredients of democracy already established for its application based on domestic legal and political theories.

---

47   See Nico Krisch, "International Law in Times of Hegemony: Unequal Power and the Shaping of the International Legal Order" (2005) 16(3) *European Journal of International Law* 369.

48   Malcolm Nathan Shaw, *International Law* (Cambridge University Press, 2014) 155.

49   See Held, above n 6.

50   See Thomas Christiano, "Democratic Legitimacy and International Institutions" in Besson and Tasioulas, above n 12.

51   Ibid.

4   The Unfilled Lacuna: The Main Concern of This Research

Given the traditional template of democracy that is rooted in notions of governance, governed peoples, and the government, there is a conceptual skepticism of its relevance and applicability in the international law-making process and any legitimacy assessment in this regard.[52] It must be kept in mind that international law-making apparatuses, institutions of treaty-making, institutions of customary international law, and global governance institutions such as the WTO and the UN, as well as its direct and indirect obligatory regulatory mechanisms, are indicative of a very unique sort of governance with no *demos* (governed) and no government. Without a doubt, "when there is governance it should be legitimated automatically".[53] As elaborated above, democracy is intrinsically the indispensable normative component for the legitimacy of the international legal order.

But there has been no conceptual theory of democracy pertinent to the very fluid nature of international legal theory. In detail, some writers have touched upon the necessity of sketching a new meaning of democracy for international law but have failed to render one. Therefore, there is a huge unfilled lacuna in international legal scholarship in this regard. This research aims to sketch a structured concept of democracy for international law-making and the legitimacy of international law itself. This new concept of democracy is based upon the idea of Egalitarian Law put forward in the philosophy of Illumination or *hikmat-i ishrāq* founded by *Shahab al-Din Suhrawardi* (1155–91). Central to the argument of this article is the idea of Global Democratic Unification put forward by the *Jalāl ad-Dīn Muhammad Balkhī* known as *Rūmi* (1207–73).

Before elaborating on the above-stated matters, it is important to note what I mean by calling this discourse an "unfilled lacuna". The main concern of this study is not an untouched field. Many writers have devoted their thoughts to the possibility of linking the idea of democracy to international law-making. But there has been no ordered and well-structured work on conceptualisation of democratic identity for international law-making. Some scholars have emphasised standards in assessing the democratic legitimacy of international law-makers[54] without elaborating on conceptual inquiries on democracy in international law-making, and some scholars, on the other hand, have found

---

52   See Joseph HH Weiler, "The Geology of International Law – governance, Democracy and
       Legitimacy" (2004) 64(3) *Zeitschrift für ausländisches öffentliches Recht und Völkerrecht*
       547.
53   Ibid 560.
54   See Buchanan, above n 39.

this discourse "less than optimal".[55] So, this research is new because it offers a structured, substantive notion of democracy for international law-making with no central reference to its traditional base in Western literature and, instead, makes sense of a new literature and understanding of democracy for international law on the basis of well-known Iranian philosophers: *Shahab al-Din Suhrawardi* (1155–91) and *Jalāl ad-Dīn Muhammad Balkhī* known as *Rūmi* (1207–73).

4.1   The Idea of Egalitarian Law

According to Nasr, "[a]fter the early period of Islamic history, during which the major intellectual and religious perspectives were crystallized and delineated, there is no figure in Islamic intellectual life who has left as much influence upon the later theosophical and philosophical schools of Islam as *Suhrawardi*".[56] His philosophy made a tie between intellectuality and mysticism which was deeply influenced by ancient pre-Islamic Iranian wisdom called Zoroastrianism.[57] Based on his philosophy of "Illumination" or *hikmat-i ishrāq*, the existence and occurrence of all incidents in our universe are lights of the supernatural lawgiver: God. Incidents and creatures also radiate light on each other with different degrees of intensity and weakness. Man's light – our intelligence and existence in general – is bestowed upon us by the greatest of lights: God. Similarly, law (including international law), in its very essence, is a light bestowed on mankind, and it comes into practice through man's own reasoning, on the basis of a set of motives and intellectual purposes.[58]

The other important principle of this philosophy is the principle of "sufficient reason": all incidents occurring in the world are driven by human intellect and follow a causal set-up. Given the sufficient reason principle, evil incidents as well as pleasant ones are all results of man's light – free will and reason – under the overwhelming supreme light of the lawgiver, God. Given these two principles, *Suhrawardi* agrees with the former Iranian philosopher *Avicenna* (980–1037) in considering law as a rational process of discovering norms through reasoning, analogy, co-operation and correspondence of human intellect.

---

55   Weiler, above n 52, 552.

56   Seyyed Hossein Nasr, "The Spread of the Illuminationist School of Suhrawardi" (1970) 14(3) *Islamic Quarterly* 111.

57   See Henry Corbin, *The Voyage and the Messenger: Iran and Philosophy* (North Atlantic Books, 1998).

58   Ibid.

Suhrawardi considered law nothing but democracy: political participation of all in the decision-making process. To him, law means equality. Equality, which is based on a mystical uptake adopted by *Suhrawardi* in his philosophy of Illumination, is nothing but an innate perception that emerges in people's minds when they find room to make their voices heard and participate in any course of negotiation and norm-making. In order to structure a blissful global community, law (equality to *Suhrawardi*) should be created through participation of the lights – people (global actors) living in that community – to intensify the light of their community.[59] Central to his perception of law is egalitarianism in the very process of law-making.

So, *Suhrawardi* was pretty much influenced by Athenian understanding of democracy whereby the Athenian city-state was ruled by its citizen-governors until it was eclipsed by the rise of empires, and military regimes, a shared feature with republican Rome.[60] In Western literature, the participatory perspective of democracy loomed central in the idea of "Substantive Definition of Democracy" that if "public decision-making is the business of all citizens equally, then all must be not just entitled, but also enabled, to undertake it for political equality depends on overcoming material deprivation".[61]

4.2   The Idea of Inter-cultural Global Democratic Unification by Rūmi

The most advanced concept of democracy for international law-making and conflict resolution was brilliantly put forward by *Jalāl ad-Dīn Muhammad Balkhī* known as *Rūmi* (1207–73) in his idea of Inter-Cultural Global Democratic Unification.[62] *Rūmi* proposed a structured concept of democracy for global governance and international law-making. He very intelligently demonstrated that the only path to solve very complicated international issues and conflicts is participation of all, negotiation of all, and agreement of all. What he proposed is a common decision-making model leading to the establishment of common democratic identity for international law on the basis of inter-cultural conversation, collective understanding and collective wisdom. To *Rūmi*, unification is the central core of our world. And particularism is the most ominous hurdle in providing law or equality for the people of the world.

---

59   Ibid.
60   See Held, above n 6, 5–6.
61   Susan Marks and Andrew Clapham, *International Human Rights Lexicon* (Oxford University Press, 2005) 64–65.
62   See Mevlana Jalaluddin Rumi, *Maṭnawīye Ma'nawī-Spiritual Couplets*-مثنوی معنوی – Verses Read Out (Homa Publishers, 1987).

He stressed that for the world to remain peaceful, it must be structured on the basis of participation and inter-culturalism in law-making.

Rūmi's concept consists of three pillars: connection (participation), absorption, and attraction that, if fulfilled, will potentially lead to collective wisdom, deliberative multilateralism based on egalitarianism, and content-independent legitimacy for any corpus of law in the global plane. By "connection", he means that parties to multilateral negotiation of a convention must directly participate in the law-making and decision-making process and flesh out the agreement itself through collective wisdom. By "absorption" and "attraction", he puts emphasis on balancing the interests during a course of conversation through hearing and respecting opponent proposals and at the same time making everyone's voice heard. He bases his idea of global democracy on the kernels of coexistence of different cultures, political ends, and mutual understanding of diverse ideologies. In detail, he structures a universal religion based on universalism, coexistence, and collective faith. He stresses that in order to achieve this, a participatory perspective of democracy is the only workable solution for perpetual global peace.

It is interesting to note that Christiano's criteria of cosmopolitanism, publicity, and balancing of interests for democratic legitimacy of the international law-making process have overlapping notations with the criteria put forward by *Rūmi*. By cosmopolitanism, Christiano refers to the necessity of equal advancement of interests of all – pursuit of the good of all persons instead of a common good. By the criterion of publicity, he requires attachment to the principle of cosmopolitanism once it is implemented in actual institutions. Through balancing of interests, which is reciprocal in character, once a party admits a proposal rendered by the counterpart the party holds a right to have its proposal admitted.

4.3 The Practical Implications of the Idea of Democratic Unification in International Law-making

In today's international law-making, manifestations of representative democracy in the international norm-making process include different degrees of adversarial law-making methods, such as the veto procedure, weighted voting, the majority principle, and unanimity, whereby minorities or non-dominant international subjects are not voiced determinatively and rarely find room to deliberatively pursue their interests and participate in making norms on the international plane.[63] Even when an agreement is reached by unanimity

---

63   See Suren Movsisyan, "Decision Making by Consensus in International Organizations as a Form of Negotiation" (2008)1 (3) *21st Century* <www.noravank.am/upload/pdf/337_en.pdf>.

on a resolution, via adversarial decision-making methods, it is reached "on a wording which enabled the minority to abstain rather than vote against the resolution".[64] In other words, through adversarial norm-making, there is room for dominant state actors to practically compel non-dominant ones to keep pace with their proposals. This is why Tammes likened the abstention of minorities in voting procedure to the case in medieval communities.[65] In other words, given the bilateral nature of the adversarial international law-making process, representative democracy is an instrument of assuring a statist/hegemonic structure of a world order that has precedence in thought and practice in a medieval conception that is intrinsically associated with various heterogeneous forms of political control.[66] This is why within representative democracy in the transnational arena, the basic notion of democratic governance – which is participation – is wiped out.[67] Hence it has been argued that international law suffers from, and grapples with, the democratic deficit of its normative processes.[68]

On the other hand, a participatory perspective of democracy requires public participation of all personalities of the entire international community,[69] whether it be states, non-state actors or individuals, in the law-making process, and it seeks an egalitarian multilateralism – governance of many. That is, where substantively unequal actors can have the equal opportunity to participate in and discuss not only the *modus operandi* of decision-making but also every minute detail of the negotiation of a convention.[70] Based on this, all parties to a multilateral convention hold the same right and opportunity to discuss, negotiate, and balance their proposals and reach an agreement rather than just vote for or against a proposal. This is why participatory democracy is an ideal sense of a democratically legitimate international legal order, whereby

---

64   Louis B Sohn, "Introduction: United Nations Decision-Making: Confrontation or Consensus" (1974) 15 *Harvard International Law Journal* 438, 440.

65   See Arnold Jan Pieter Tammes, *Decisions of International Organs as a Source of International Law* (Martinus Nijhoff Publishers, 1958).

66   See Richard Falk, "The Post-Westphalia Enigma" in Björn Hettne and Bertil Odén (eds), *Global governance in the 21st century: alternative perspectives on world order* (Almkvist & Wiksell International, 2002) 147.

67   See J Patrick Kelly, "Twilight of Customary International Law, The" (1999) 40 *Virginia Journal of International Law* 449.

68   See Wouters, De Meester and Ryngaert, above n 7.

69   See Nicole Roughan, "Democratic Custom v International Customary Law" (2007) 38 *Victoria University of Wellington Law Review* 403.

70   See Barry Buzan, "Negotiating by Consensus: Developments in Technique at the United Nations Conference on the Law of the Sea" (1981) 75(2) *The American Journal of International Law* 324.

inequality of actors in international norm-making is challenged and not tolerated. In Western literature it has rightly been argued that egalitarian multilateralism in international law-making can only be based on participation of all to generate a democratic character, beyond the governmental sphere, upon which more formal democratic processes then rely.[71] This objective is best backed by the "Rousseaurian premise that through participation, there is likely to be greater acceptance of collective decisions".[72]

Under the auspices of this understanding, for example, it is extremely urgent for international law to set up obligatory norms or even incentives for violent political entities, controversial leaders, and even dictators to participate in intensive negotiations in regional and international law-making processes. Once negotiation starts, all parties must be guaranteed the advancement of their balanced political interests to the extent they accept the counterparties' proposals. If the interests of the parties are literally contradictory, their interests must be balanced. This method, though seemingly aspirational, is a preliminary step towards a new international agenda based on collectivism, universalism, and global democratic unification. In detail, if the parties find their balanced interests more likely to be achieved through international law, they will respect the terms simply because they have interests in complying with them. This will grant an inherent institutional legitimacy to intergovernmental organisations convening negotiations of a convention. If cosmopolitanism, publicity, and balancing of interests become the criteria of democratic entitlement for law-making negotiations, a contractual consensus will be drawn out as a model of democratic negotiations based on participation, egalitarianism, and cosmopolitanism.[73]

One may seriously question whether the above-stated model means international law must give voice to highly controversial leaders such as those of North Korea or Syria. The answer is *yes*. International law has no alternative other than proactively negotiating with controversial leaders who are battling with internal protests and external terroristic troops, and even guaranteeing them the preservation of their balanced interests. Undeniably, the controversial leaders, dictators, and even violent protestors are a part of our cosmos, and if we argue in favor of cosmopolitan democracy, we need to make their voices heard. But does this leave room for compliance with international law rules in

71   See Iulian Moraru, David G Andersen and Michael Kaminsky, "There Is More Consensus in Egalitarian Parliaments" in *Proceedings of the Twenty-Fourth ACM Symposium on Operating Systems Principles* (ACM, 2013) 358.

72   Roughan, above n 69, 408.

73   See Geoff R Berridge, *Diplomacy: Theory and Practice* (Palgrave Macmillan, 2010).

accommodating the political ends of the controversial leaders and dictators? The answer is *of course not*. This is, in fact, a pragmatic workable model of coping with instant political will-formation and the fluidity of the international law-making process. A subtle, though extremely important, long-term harvest of this model is the marginalisation of potential dictators who normally base their ideological axiom on expansionism and annexation of other territories. In other words, by giving a voice to such leaders, international law can, in the long run, to some extent, marginalise dictators from igniting potential wars against their neighbours or other opponents. Moreover, last but not least, the lives of countless innocent people will be saved from manslaughter and ethnic cleansing.

Without a doubt, passing unilateral, heavy-handed resolutions and sanctions against a given state does not prevent but rather encourages hostility, hatred, and war-creation in the long term. Although it may seem that in the short term the preventive role of such sanctions has worked, in the long term, these actions will succumb to war-creation or at least deep conflicts. And after this hatred converts into a war, the United Nations Security Council with its post-war posture[74] finds itself only capable of discussing the conflict, enumerating the death tolls, threatening the already well-determined belligerents with further sanctions, with no proactive pre-war intervention. This article firmly argues that now is the time for international law to change its approach. This literature and law-making methods provide a workable mechanism to ensure the direct participation of its actors in fleshing out the laws rather than to vote for or against it or to abstain. Through bringing political tensions into a democratic negotiation process and guaranteeing the pursuit of their balanced political desires, in the short term, the lives of countless people will be saved. Moreover, in the long term, war-creators will be marginalised. In sum, the marginalisation of controversial political entities is not possible unless their participation in law-making is guaranteed. This is exactly the preliminary building block of a world order based on global democratic identity.

There is a serious practical skepticism as to the feasibility and implementation of such a democratic law-making model in international law, since there is no central enforcement mechanism to ensure the compliance of a wide range of actors with its normative directives. This in fact stems from the fluidity and indeterminacy of international law which, based on the argument made in this article, is to be addressed through the idea of international domain fragmentation. By domain fragmentation, it is recognisable that the sense and notion of democracy needed for a particular domain of public international law does

---

74   See Besson and Tasioulas, above n 12.

not necessarily follow the same pattern in other domains. The next part elaborates upon a dynamic fragmented notion of democracy for an intrinsically fragmented international law. Such fragmentation, to a large extent, makes the idea of global democratic unification pragmatically feasible for the upcoming international law agenda.

5   Fragmented Democracy for Fragmented International Law:
         A Pragmatic Solution

Based on Kelsen's monistic theory, any legal system is intrinsically composed of a normative hierarchy of values[75] whereby the applicability and validity of substantive norms shall be determined in accordance with their rank in this hierarchy. In domestic legal systems, due to a constitution and a centralised political structure, legislature, and court, written laws or court decisions function as a legitimate authoritative organ to give superiority to a specific norm in cases of conflicting norms. In legal literature, any attempt to cope with inconsistency and conflict of norms through integration of norms can be characterised as "constitutionalisation". In the international legal realm, idealists have considered the United Nations and its Charter as the embryonic form of a world government with the hope to enforce the rule of law at the international level – the constitutionalisation of international law.[76] Some have considered constitutionalism as a basic means of reaching collective identity and have argued that the intrinsic application of constitutionalism is "emphasising the good or proper functions that a constitution is alleged to perform, such as limiting government, embodying political ideals, and expressing collective identity".[77] But the failure of the United Nations as a reconciliatory regime and also the voluntary jurisdiction of International Court of Justice, discussed earlier, are all indicative of the dysfunctional posture of international institutions and organisations with regard to ever developing international legal theory.

Any attempt to integrate conflicting norms in international law will fail since instant political will-formation and ever-changing intellectual correspondence of its actors is, by its nature, the jurisprudential pillar of international law. In other words, the applicability or feasibility of any concept of international

---

75   See Hans Kelsen, *Pure Theory of Law* (University of California Press, 1967).
76   See Bardo Fassbender, *UN Security Council Reform and the Right of Veto: A Constitutional Perspective* (Martinus Nijhoff Publishers, 1998).
77   Alec Stone Sweet, "Constitutionalism, Legal Pluralism, and International Regimes" (2009) 16(2) *Indiana Journal of Global Legal Studies* 621, 628.

constitutionalisation is under a conceptual skepticism since international law is naturally tied with literary impropriety or the indeterminacy critique. Therefore, developing jurisprudence of international law is intrinsically fragmented. Consequently, international law must be perceived through fragmented lenses. Accordingly, this research adopts a fragmented lens in defining a substantive concept of democracy for fragmented international law-making. Given this, it is recognised that the sense and notion of democracy needed for a particular domain of public international law does not necessarily follow the same pattern in other domains. For example, democracy required for law-making in the matters of laws of war, and perhaps also military intervention of intergovernmental organisations, is not the same as the democracy needed for the World Trade Organisation or decision-making methods in international financial institutions. So, it must be noted that the idea of domain fragmentation is a kernel in conceptualising a dynamic notion of democracy for the international law-making process to coincide with the ever-developing international law.

The discourse on international law's fragmentation is categorised into two branches: judicial fragmentation and domain fragmentation. Judicial fragmentation involves the incongruent and divergent scenarios in international court decisions in different but similar or the same cases and is transparently undesirable because it will potentially lead to a high degree of indeterminacy and arbitrariness in international law.[78] Domain fragmentation is often associated with conflicts between substantive bodies of international law, such as international criminal law, environmental law, and so on. The latter branch is a significant focus of this study. Domain fragmentation of international law does not lead to divergence in reasoning or interpretation of a legal fact in the same legal issues, but rather highlights the stratification of international law as an inevitable specificity of international law. "What once appeared to be governed by 'general international law' has become the field of operation for such specialist systems as 'trade law', 'human rights law', 'environmental law', 'law of the sea', 'European law' and even such exotic and highly specialised knowledge as 'investment law' or 'international refugee law' etc. – each possessing their own principles and institutions".[79]

Central to the main objective of this article, which is the conceptualisation of a substantive notion of democracy for international law-making, is the

---

78   See Webb, above n 1, 5–6.

79   The UN International Law Commission Report, 58th Session, A/CN.4/L.682 (13 April 2006) on "Fragmentation of International Law: Difficulties Arising from the Diversification and Expansion of International Law: Report of the Study Group of the International Law Commission" 11.

fragmentation of democracy parallel to the fragmented fluid jurisprudence of international law – or to Weiler, stratified international law.[80] According to this, negotiations between parties to a war do not necessarily follow the same rules in negotiations held among parties to a financial, economic, or environmental pact. Parties to a war are mentally persuaded and driven to sacrifice the lives of thousands or even millions, including themselves, to successfully reach their political desires. In cases of the laws of war, a participatory perspective of democracy with the attainment of the *Rumi's* account of connection, absorption and attraction, and on the basis of a consensual contract, can provide content-independent legitimacy for a given set of international rules. On the other hand, in the cases of, for example, fleshing out trade laws in international law, a reference to traditional voting procedures may make sense.

Fragmentation of democracy in international law-making enhances the feasibility of the implementation of the ideal notion of democracy – participatory democracy – in some fragments of international law where political tension reaches a climax between potential belligerents. This upheaval in the discourse on democracy in international law-making may provide room for the emergence of a new literature in the legitimacy of international laws on the basis of egalitarianism, participation, and the idea of global democratic unification.

6   Conclusion

International law is intrinsically fluid and therefore entails a dynamic legal theory to correlate pragmatically with instant political will-formation of its actors and the cognitive advantages of its law-making institutions. Therefore, it is highly critical that international law adopt a substantive notion of democracy for the international law-making process.

This article advocates a participatory perspective of democracy, as international law is a decentralised legal system and democratic legitimacy of its law-making apparatus is intrinsically tied with egalitarianism or, according to *Rūmi*, connection, attraction, and absorption. Under the auspices of such an understanding of democracy, parties to a potential agreement in international law may flesh out the agreement or law itself, rather than vote for or against it, or abstain. This provides a content-independent legitimacy for the laws made by international institutions because it is made through the equal participation of its actors.

---

80   Weiler, above n 52, 151.

The other kernel of this new concept is the fragmentation of democracy for a fragmented international law. International law, which is an intellectual and ever-developing field of law, is intrinsically fragmented. The concept of democracy for international law-making must be malleable enough in order to dynamically develop with a fluid fragmented international law. Given this, democracy as it relates to matters of laws of war and, perhaps, also military intervention by intergovernmental organisations is not the same for that of the World Trade Organisation or the decision-making methods of international financial institutions.

Given the idea of Global Democratic Unification, international law has no alternative other than to set up obligatory norms or even incentives for violent political entities, controversial leaders, and even dictators to participate in intensive negotiations in regional and international law-making processes.

The necessity for sketching a substantive notion of democracy for international law-making had not been touched upon until the very end of the 20th century and the beginning of the 21st century. The advancement and culmination of this discourse on democracy and the international law-making process in the upcoming international law agenda in the 21st century provides the field with a remarkable theoretical upheaval leading to the democratic legitimacy of international law and international law-making institutions. This article is a map to provide readers with some clues for further studies in this regard.

Environmental Disputes from Regional Sea Programmes before ITLOS: Its Potential Role, Contribution, and the Challenges it Would Face in a Land-based Pollution Case

*Naporn Popattanachai**

1   Introduction

The *United Nations Convention on the Law of the Sea* (*"LOSC"*) has long been acknowledged by the international community as the Constitution of the oceans in that it establishes "a legal order for the seas and oceans" which facilitates inter alia "the peaceful use of the seas and oceans", the utilisation of resources, and "the protection and preservation of the marine environment."[1] It acts as a framework convention and is further implemented by other related international agreements;[2] therefore, as Wolfrum points out, there is a plurality

---

*   Lecturer in Law, Faculty of Law, Thammasat University, Thailand; PhD Candidate, Nottingham Law School, Nottingham Trent University, UK; Former ITLOS/Nippon Fellow at the International Tribunal for the Law of the Sea, Hamburg, Germany. The author would like to express his sincere gratitude to Judge Tafsir Malick Ndiaye, and Ms. Ximena Hinrichs, of the International Tribunal for the Law of the Sea, Hamburg, Germany; Professor Elizabeth Kirk of Nottingham Law School, Nottingham Trent University, UK; Dr. Krisdakorn Wongwuthikun of the Graduate School of Law, National Insitute of Development Administration, Thailand and; two anonymous reviewers who kindly read this paper and provided some thoughtful and constructive comments. The views expressed hereinafter are those of the author and do not necessarily reflect the views of the International Tribunal for the Law of the Sea, the Nippon Foundation of Japan, the Government of Thailand, and/or the authority of the country or institution that made their facilities available for use by the author during the 2016–2017 ITLOS-Nippon Capacity-Building and Training Programme on Dispute Settlement under the LOSC. Anv remaining errors solely rest on the author.

1   *United Nations Convention on the Law of the Sea,* opened for signature 10 December 1982, 1833 UNTS 3, (entered into force 16 November 1994) preamble (*"LOSC"*). For the "Constitution of the Oceans", see Tommy Koh, "Constitution of the Oceans", United Nations <http://www.un.org/depts/los/convention_agreements/texts/koh_english.pdf>.

2   Robin Churchill, "The LOSC Regime for Protection of the Marine Environment – Fit for the Twenty-first Century?" in Rosemary Rayfuse (ed), *Research Handbook of International Marine Environmental Law* (Edward Elgar, 2015) 3–30; Robin Churchill and Vaughan Lowe, *The Law of the Sea* (Manchester University Press, 3rd ed, 1999) 24–25.

of international norms that cover the same topic or rights and treaty parallelism exists in both substance and dispute settlement provisions.³

In the field of the protection of the marine environment, action has been taken at various levels to further implement the obligation to protect and preserve the marine environment under the LOSC. For example, states cooperate at the regional level by establishing Regional Sea Programmes ("RSPS") to prevent, reduce, and control all sources of marine pollution.⁴ RSPS are governed by both binding and non-binding instruments and they further implement the obligations under Part XII of the LOSC. Land-based pollution ("LBP") is no exception and most of these RSPS have protocols, or at least a provision in their convention, dealing with this source of pollution. Based on this example, it is inevitable that parallel rights and obligations between the LOSC and those RSPS conventions and protocols exist in both the substantive and dispute settlement provisions.

To settle a dispute under the LOSC, Article 287 provides for the choice of procedure under which states may choose a forum for cases to be adjudicated and settled, which includes the International Tribunal for the Law of the Sea ("ITLOS"). It is a specialised Tribunal established by the LOSC with the jurisdiction to adjudicate any dispute concerning the interpretation and application of the Convention submitted to it in accordance with the LOSC and all matters specifically provided for in any other agreement which confers jurisdiction on it.⁵ So far, the ITLOS has had the opportunity to adjudicate twenty-five cases, two of which were advisory opinions.⁶ Regarding the protection of the marine environment through the RSPS, only one RSPS-related case has been brought to the ITLOS, namely, the MOX Plant case.⁷ This begs the question of why, in this context and according to its record, has the service of this Tribunal been so little utilised? Are there any legal obstacles that prevent an environmental case of the RSPS reaching the ITLOS? Also, what are the potential roles,

---

3   *MOX Plant* case (*Ireland v. United Kingdom*) (*Provisional Measure*), (International Tribunal for the Law of the Sea, Case No 10, 3 December 2001) [60] ("*MOX Plant* (*Provisional Measures*)") (Judge Wolfrum) 1.

4   At present, there are 18 RSPS across the globe. See, UNEP Regional Seas Programmes <http://web.unep.org/regionalseas/>.

5   *LOSC*, above n 1, art 288 and Annex VII at art 21. Another three procedures are the International Court of Justice (ICJ), Arbitral Tribunal under Annex VII, and Special Arbitral Tribunal under Annex VIII of the *LOSC*. See *LOSC* art 287.

6   See further, *List of Cases*, ITLOS (23 July 2017) <https://www.itlos.org/cases/list-of-cases/>.

7   *Mox Plant* (*Provisional Measures*), (International Tribunal for the Law of the Sea, Case No 10, 3 December 2001).

contribution, and challenges of the ITLOS regarding an environmental case from the RSPs?

Therefore, the focus of this article are these questions concerning the Tribunal with the aim of assessing the potential roles, contribution, and challenges the ITLOS would face in handling an environmental case from the RSPs. The fact that the focus is on the ITLOS is not intended to downplay the importance of the other possible procedures specified in the LOSC. However, since the ITLOS has been established as a standing specialised Tribunal with a high level of commitment to ensuring the consistent interpretation or application of the LOSC,[8] the aim of this article is to explain its under-utilisation. In so doing, LBP is used as a case study and the reason for this is twofold. Firstly, almost all of the RSPs have a provision in their convention or protocol that specifically deals with LBP. Inevitably, the rights, obligations, and dispute settlement provision of the RSPs instruments are parallel to those of the LOSC. Apart from being chosen as the dispute settlement forum, the ITLOS has to decide in accordance with Part XV of the LOSC whether it can adjudicate a case from an RSP in view of this treaty parallelism. The second part of the reason is the severity of the problem, since LBP accounts for 80 percent of marine pollution.[9] It was recognised as continuing to be the biggest contributor to the deterioration of the marine environment at the recent United Nations Ocean Conference.[10] However, despite this recognition, it remains largely unregulated and the LOSC is the only global legal instrument that obliges states to prevent, reduce, and control this source of pollution. However, the LOSC has long been criticised for its lack of clarity and failure to compel states to address LBP.[11] Therefore, understanding the likelihood of an LBP case being brought to

8   Robin Churchill, "Some Reflections on the Operation of the Dispute Settlement System of the UN Convention on the Law of the Sea During its First Decade" in David Freestone, Richard A Barnes and David M Ong (eds), *The Law of the Sea Progess and Prospects* (Oxford University Press, 2006) 398.

9   *The State of the Marine Environment*, UNEP GESAMP Reports and Studies No. 39 (UNEP, 1990); *Protecting the Ocean From Land-Based Activities: Land-based sources and activities affecting the quality and uses of the marine, coastal and associated freshwater environment*, UNEP GESAMP Reports and Studies No. 71 (UNEP, 2001); *Report of the Secretary General: Ocean and the Law of the Sea*, UN GAOR, 59th sess, Agenda Item 50(a), UN Doc. A/59/62 /Add.1 (18 August 2004) [97].

10   *Concept Paper Partnership Dialogue 1: Addressing Marine Pollution (Advance Unedited Version)* (5–9 June 2017) UN Ocean Conference <https://oceanconference.un.org/documents> 1.

11   David VanderZwaag and Ann Powers, "The Protection of the Marine Environment from Land-based Pollution and Activities: Gauging the Tides of Global and Regional

the ITLOS will facilitate an assessment of the potential roles, contribution, and challenges of the ITLOS in clarifying the ambiguities in Article 207 of the LOSC dealing with LBP.

The proposition presented in this article is that the role of the ITLOS in an environmental dispute related to RSPs is limited in that it can only address contentious proceedings if the prerequisites of the LOSC are met. Secondly, the Tribunal will face both challenges and opportunities if an RSP environmental case reaches the ITLOS. As will be shown by the LBP case, the challenges of the ITLOS are: (i) the need to determine the content of Article 207 of the LOSC; and (ii) the need to establish a causal link between the polluting states and the damage to the marine environment. As for opportunities, the ITLOS can benefit from the subsequent practice of states from RSPs to prevent, reduce, and control LBP. RSPs contain certain parameters related to the monitoring and assessment of LBP, which can support the adjudication of the ITLOS.

The article begins with an outline of Part XV of the LOSC. The prerequisites contained in Articles 281 and 282 of the LOSC will be particularly emphasised in order to highlight their significance in deciding if an environmental case brought by an RSP can be resolved by the compulsory dispute settlement procedure of the LOSC. Secondly, the dispute settlement provisions of RSP conventions will be categorised and the likelihood of a case falling foul of Articles 281 and 282 of the LOSC will be assessed, as well as the possible involvement of the ITLOS in adjudicating an RSP environmental dispute. Thirdly, the potential challenges and contribution of the ITLOS will be illustrated with a case study of LBP, before drawing a formal conclusion.

2   Compulsory Dispute Settlement Procedure under Part XV of the LOSC

2.1   Overview of Part XV

The jurisdiction of the ITLOS covers both advisory and contentious proceedings, provided that the application for an advisory opinion or contentious case is submitted according to the LOSC, Statute, and Rules of the ITLOS. Although the application for an advisory opinion is not clarified in the LOSC, it can be

---

Governance" (2008) 23 *International Journal of Marine and Coastal Law* 423; Yoshifumi Tanaka, "Regulation of Land-Based Marine Pollution in International Law: A Comparative Analysis Between Global and Regional Legal Frameworks" (2006) 66 *Heidelberg Journal of International Law* 535.

found in Article 138 of the ITLOS Rules. In addition, based on the *Request for an Advisory Opinion submitted by the Sub-Regional Fisheries Commission*,[12] the jurisdiction for an advisory opinion is inherent in the ITLOS Statute, which forms an integral part of the *LOSC*,[13] and is based on the condition that "an international agreement related to the purposes of the Convention specifically provides for the submission to the Tribunal of a request for an advisory opinion" and "the request must be transmitted to the Tribunal by a body authorised by or in accordance with the agreement mentioned above, and such an opinion may be given on "a legal question"."[14] Referring to the ICJ *Advisory Opinion on Legality of the Use by a State of Nuclear Weapons in Armed Conflict*, the ITLOS finds that legal questions are not limited to the interpretation or application of any specific provision of the convention in question; it is "enough if these questions have, in the words of the ICJ, a 'sufficient connection' with the purposes and principles of the Convention."[15] Therefore, the ITLOS is likely to find its advisory jurisdiction and conduct the advisory proceedings if these two conditions are met.

The ITLOS may entertain a contentious case provided that the prerequisites contained in the *LOSC* are fulfilled.[16] This means that the case must accord with the procedural requirements in Section 1 and not be precluded by the

---

12   *Request for Advisory Opinion submitted by the Sub-Regional Fisheries Commission (Advisory Opinion)*, (International Tribunal for the Law of the Sea, Case No 21, 2 April 2015) [37]–[69] ("SRFC *Advisory Opinion*").

13   Ibid [54]–[8]. See also *LOSC* art 288; Statute of the ITLOS art 21; and Rules of the ITLOS (17 March 2009) art 138, ITLOS website <https://www.itlos.org/fileadmin/itlos/documents/basic_texts/Itlos_8_E_17_03_09.pdf>. The ITLOS found in the advisory opinion in relation to Article 21 of the ITLOS Statute is that "…[t]he words all 'matters' ('toutes les fois que cela' in French) should not be interpreted as covering only 'disputes', for, if that were to be the case, Article 21 of the Statute would simply have used the word 'disputes'. Consequently, it must mean something more than only 'disputes' and that something more must include advisory opinions, if specifically provided for in 'any other agreement which confers jurisdiction on the Tribunal.'"

14   SRFC *Advisory Opinion*, (International Tribunal for the Law of the Sea, Case No 21, 2 April 2015) [60].

15   Ibid [67]–[8]. In this advisory opinion, the ITLOS entertains its advisory function over the Convention on the Determination of the Minimal Conditions for Access and Exploitation of Marine Resources within the Maritime Areas under Jurisdiction of the Member States of the Sub-Regional Fisheries Commission (MCA Convention).

16   *LOSC*, above n 1, art 286. It reads: "Subject to Section 3, any dispute concerning the interpretation or application of this Convention shall, where no settlement has been reached by recourse to Section 1, be submitted at the request of any party to the dispute to the court or tribunal having jurisdiction under this section."

limitations or exceptions in Section 3 of Part XV of the LOSC. Based on the procedural requirements in Section 1 Part XV of the LOSC, state parties are required to settle any dispute concerning the interpretation or application of the LOSC peacefully, by the means provided in Article 33 of the *Charter of the United Nations*.[17] They also have the right to choose and agree the means of settling the dispute at any time.[18] More complex requirements are provided in Articles 281–283 of the LOSC, which contain: (i) a procedure where no settlement has been reached by the parties; (ii) obligations under general, regional or bilateral agreements; and (iii) obligations to exchange views.

According to Article 281 of the LOSC, if the parties to a dispute on the interpretation or application of the LOSC choose and agree to settle the dispute by peaceful means and still fail to settle the dispute by such agreed means, the dispute may be referred to the compulsory dispute settlement procedures in Section 2 of Part XV of the LOSC if the agreement made between the parties does not exclude any further procedure, and, if any, the agreed time-limit has expired. For Article 282 of the LOSC, it is stated that if the state parties have agreed, through multilateral, regional, or bilateral agreement or otherwise, the dispute relating to the interpretation or application of the LOSC shall be submitted to a procedure entailing a binding decision at the request of any party to the dispute, and that procedure will be applicable in lieu of Section 2, Part XV of the LOSC. As for Article 283, which relates to the obligation to exchange views, state parties to the dispute are required to "proceed expeditiously to an exchange of views regarding its settlement by negotiation or other peaceful means." However, a party is not "obliged to pursue procedures under Part XV, Section 1 of the Convention when it concludes that the possibilities of the settlement have been exhausted" and this includes the obligation to exchange views.[19]

The ITLOS may entertain cases in which the prerequisites specified in Section 1 have been satisfied if the dispute is not subject to any of the limitations or exceptions set out in Section 3, Part XV of the LOSC. The limitations to the applicability of the LOSC compulsory dispute settlement procedures can be found in Article 297. These include disputes concerning the interpretation or

---

17   Ibid art 279.
18   Ibid art 280.
19   *Southern Bluefin Tuna* case (*New Zealand v. Japan*) (*Provisional Measures*), (International Tribunal for the Law of the Sea, Case No 3, 27 August 1999) [60] (*"Southern Bluefin Tunas (Provisional Measures)"*); MOX *Plant* (*Provisional Measures*), (International Tribunal for the Law of the Sea, Case No 10, 3 December 2001).

application of the Convention related to, inter alia: (i) the exercise by a coastal state of its sovereign rights or jurisdiction in the Exclusive Economic Zone ("EEZ"); (ii) marine scientific research; and (iii) fisheries. In addition, states are entitled to refuse to accept the LOSC compulsory dispute settlement procedures in Section 2 for the matters specified in Article 298 of the LOSC.[20] Having cleared the prerequisites, limitations, and exceptions, the judicial institution identified in Article 287 of the LOSC can entertain the dispute provided that it concerns the interpretation or application of the LOSC or an international agreement related to the purposes of the LOSC, which is submitted to it in accordance with the agreement.

2.2 International Jurisprudence Concerning Articles 281 and 282 of the LOSC

A literal reading of Part XV of the LOSC appears to be straightforward in terms of explaining how a dispute can qualify for the compulsory dispute settlement procedure specified therein, as well as how, and by whom, the case will be adjudicated. However, in practice, it is a difficult task for the relevant judicial institutions to determine if these preconditions have been satisfied, especially those provided in Articles 281 and 282 of the LOSC. Therefore, the focus of this article is the prerequisites provided in Part XV, Section 1 of the LOSC, especially Articles 281 and 282, simply because they are the precursors for determining the potential involvement of the ITLOS in the settling of marine environment disputes of an RSP. Three cases, namely, *Southern Bluefin Tuna,*[21] *MOX Plant,*[22] and the *South China Sea Arbitration,*[23] which contribute to the assessment of the fulfilment of Articles 281 and 282 of the LOSC, are discussed below in order to demonstrate the current jurisprudence of these provisions.

---

20   *LOSC*, above n 1, art 298 (1)–(2).

21   *Southern Bluefin Tuna (Provisional Measures)*, (International Tribunal for the Law of the Sea, Case No 3, 27 August 1999); *Southern Bluefin Tuna (New Zealand v. Japan) (Jurisdiction and Admissibility)* (2000) RIAA 13 (*"Southern Bluefin Tuna (Jurisdiction and Admissibility)"*).

22   *MOX Plant case (Provisional Measures)*, (International Tribunal for the Law of the Sea, Case No 10, 3 December 2001). For the later stage of the case, see *MOX Plant case (Ireland v. United Kingdom)*, <https://www.pcacases.com/web/view/100>.

23   *The South China Sea Arbitration case (Republic of the Philippines v The People's Republic of China) (Jurisdiction and Admissibility)* (Permanent Court of Arbitration, 2015) (*"South China Sea Arbitration (Jurisdiction and Admissibility)"*); *The South China Sea Arbitration case (Republic of the Philippines v The People's Republic of China) (Award)* (Permanent Court of Arbitration, 2016) <http://www.pcacases.com/web/view/7> (*"South China Sea Arbitration (Award)"*).

2.2.1   Article 281 – *Southern Bluefin Tuna* Formula vs. *South China Sea Arbitration* Formula?

Southern Bluefin Tuna and *South China Sea Arbitration* both related to Article 281 of the LOSC. The dispute in the *Southern Bluefin Tuna* case[24] concerned the conservation of the Southern Bluefin tuna stock and the alleged violation by Japan of several LOSC provisions based on its undertaking of the unilateral experimental fishing of Southern Bluefin tuna in 1998 and 1999.[25] During the provisional measures phase, Japan argued that, in terms of fulfilling the prerequisite in Article 281, Article 16 of the 1993 *Convention for the Conservation of Southern Bluefin Tuna* ("CCSBT")[26] provided a dispute settlement mechanism to which the parties had agreed within the meaning of Article 281 of

---

24   For general comments on this case, see Robin Churchill, "International Tribunal for the Law of the Sea The Southern Bluefin Tuna Cases (*New Zealand v. Japan; Australia v. Japan*): Order for Provisional Measures of 27 August 1999" (2000) 49(4) *International & Comparative Law Quarterly* 979–990; Alan E Boyle, "The Southern Bluefin Tuna Arbitration" (2001) 50(2) *International & Comparative Law Quarterly* 447–452; Malcolm D Evans, "The *Southern Bluefin Tuna* Dispute: Provisional Thinking on Provisional Measures?" (2000) 10(1) *Yearbook of International Environmental Law* 7–14; Bernard H Oxman, "Complementary Agreement and Compulsory Jurisdiction" (2001) 95(2) *American Journal of International Law* , 277–312; David A Colson and Peggy Hoyle, "Satisfying the Procedural Prerequisites to the Compulsory Dispute Settlement: Mechanisms of the 1982 Law of the Sea Convention: Did the *Southern Bluefin Tuna* Tribunal Get It Right?" (2003) 34 *Ocean Development & International Law* 59–82; Barbara Kwiatkowska, "The *Southern Bluefin Tuna* Arbitral Tribunal Did Get It Right: A Commentary and Reply to the Article by Daid A. Colson and Dr. Peggy Hoyle" (2003) 34 *Ocean Development & International Law* 369–395.

25   New Zealand and Australia claimed that Japan allegedly violated articles 64 and 116–119 of the LOSC.

26   *Convention for the Conservation of Southern Bluefin Tuna*, opened for signature 10 May 1993, 1819 UNTS 360 (entered into force 20 May 1994). Article 16 reads as follows:

"1. If any dispute arises between two or more of the Parties concerning the interpretation or implementation of this Convention, those Parties shall consult among themselves with a view to having the dispute resolved by negotiation, inquiry, mediation, conciliation, arbitration, judicial settlement or other peaceful means of their own choice.

2. Any dispute of this character not so resolved shall, with the consent in each case of all parties to the dispute, be referred for settlement to the International Court of Justice or to arbitration; but failure to reach agreement on reference to the International Court of Justice or to arbitration shall not absolve parties to the dispute from the responsibility of continuing to seek to resolve it by any of the various peaceful means referred to in paragraph 1 above.

3. In cases where the dispute is referred to arbitration, the arbitral tribunal shall be constituted as provided in the Annex to this Convention. The Annex forms an integral part of this Convention."

the LOSC and that this precluded New Zealand and Australia from resorting to the compulsory dispute settlement procedure under Section 2 of Part XV of the LOSC.[27] Instead, the Parties were required to continue the negotiation (the chosen means under the CCSBT) "until they either resolve the substance of the dispute or agree on a mechanism for third-party intervention to help resolve it."[28]

Finding its prima facie jurisdiction, the ITLOS rejected Japan's argument related to Article 281, holding that the records of the negotiations and consultations were considered by both applicants to be under both the CCSBT and the LOSC and that the LOSC provisions had been invoked by the applicants in their diplomatic notes sent to Japan. The ITLOS took the view that "a State Party is not obliged to pursue procedures under Part XV, Section 1 of the Convention when it concludes that the possibilities of settlement have been exhausted."[29] For these reasons, it found that "the requirements for invoking the procedures under Part XV, Section 2 of the Convention have been fulfilled."[30] In a separate opinion, Judge Ad-Hoc Shearer declared that the CCSBT is a treaty that aims to "give effect to the prospective obligations of the parties" under the LOSC; therefore, the dispute had arisen under the LOSC. With respect to Article 281, he found that the terms in the dispute settlement provision of the CCSBT could "be regarded as establishing a parallel, but not exclusive, dispute resolution procedures" and that Part XV, Section 1 of the LOSC "does not give primacy to provisions such as Article 16 of the CCSBT." Even if it could be regarded to do so, Judge Shearer perceived that this provision did not exclude any of the procedures as required by Article 281 of the LOSC.[31]

However, in *Southern Bluefin Tuna (Jurisdiction and Admissibility)*,[32] the Annex VII Tribunal rendered a view contrary to that of the ITLOS in relation to Article 281 of the LOSC. Finding that it lacked the jurisdiction to entertain the case, it declared that Article 16 of the CCSBT precluded the applicability of the compulsory dispute settlement set out in Part XV, Section 2 of the LOSC.

27   "Response and Counter-Request for Provisional Measures submitted by Japan", *Southern Bluefin Tuna (Provisional Measures)*, (International Tribunal for the Law of the Sea, Case No 3, 27 August 1999) [56]–[58].

28   Ibid.

29   *Southern Bluefin Tuna (Provisional Measures)*, (International Tribunal for the Law of the Sea, Case No 3, 27 August 1999) [57]–[60].

30   Ibid [62].

31   *Southern Bluefin Tuna (Provisional Measures)*, (International Tribunal for the Law of the Sea, Case No 3, 27 August 1999) (Judge Ad Hoc Shearer).

32   *Southern Bluefin Tuna (Jurisdiction and Admissibility)*, (2000) RIAA 13.

In arriving at this decision, the Annex VII Tribunal viewed that Article 16 of the CCSBT fell within the terms and intent of Article 281 of the LOSC,[33] which contains a list of "various named procedures of peaceful settlement". It further viewed that the first element of Article 281 of the LOSC had been satisfied because no settlement had been reached by the Parties since the record showed that the negotiation had been prolonged, intense, and had later become futile.[34] However, in terms of another requirement of Article 281, namely, whether or not the agreement between the parties excluded any further procedure, it found that "the absence of an express exclusion of any procedure in Article 16 is not decisive."[35]

Based on the construction of Article 16 of the CCSBT, the Annex VII Tribunal was of the view that because Article 16 of the CCSBT requires the consent of "all parties" to the dispute for the adjudication by the International Court of Justice ("ICJ") or arbitration, the dispute is precluded from being referred to the adjudication procedure of the said judicial institution.[36] In addition, it ruled that the phrase, "failure to reach an agreement on reference to the International Court of Justice or to arbitration shall not absolve the parties to the dispute from the responsibility of continuing to seek to resolve it by any of the various peaceful means referred to in paragraph 1 above", not only "stressed the consensual nature of any reference of a dispute to either judicial settlement or arbitration", but also that "the intent of Article 16 is to remove proceedings under that Article from the reach of the compulsory procedures of Section 2 of Part XV of UNCLOS; in other words, to exclude the application for the specific dispute of any procedure of dispute resolution that is not accepted by all the parties to the dispute."[37] Therefore, it concluded that Article 16 of the CCSBT "exclude[s] any further procedure" within the meaning of Article 281 of the LOSC.[38] Justice Sir Kenneth Keith appended a separate opinion of this particular jurisdictional issue that disagreed with the majority of the Annex VII Tribunal. According to Justice Keith, the Tribunal should have found its jurisdiction, since Article 16 of the CCSBT did not exclude a further procedure; therefore, the requirement of Article 281 of the LOSC had been satisfied. From his perspective, the fact that the Parties had agreed to

---

33   Ibid [55].
34   Ibid.
35   Ibid [57].
36   Ibid.
37   Ibid.
38   Ibid [58].

"exclude any further procedure" required opting out[39] for which clear wording was needed.[40]

However, Article 281 of the LOSC, again, became one of the jurisdictional issues considered in the recent *South China Sea Arbitration (Jurisdiction and Admissibility)* case,[41] in which the Annex VII Tribunal reversed what had been decided by the former Annex VII Tribunal in the *Southern Bluefin Tuna (Jurisdiction and Admissibility)*. The moot point in the *South China Sea Arbitration* case was whether or not Article 281 required an express exclusion of any further procedure for settling the dispute under the LOSC. While the Philippines argued that an express exclusion was required in order to bar the recourse to Part XV, Section 2 of the LOSC, China agreed with the Annex VII Tribunal in the case of *Southern Bluefin Tuna (Jurisdiction and Admissibility)* that an express exclusion was not decisive, thus, it was unnecessary.[42] Judging that the relevant documents did not bar its jurisdiction by virtue of Article 281, the Annex VII Tribunal in *South China Sea Arbitration (Jurisdiction and Admissibility)* found that "the better view is that article 281 requires some clear statement of exclusion of further procedure." There are two arguments that support this conclusion, one of which is the text and context of Article 281 and the other is the structure and overall purpose of the LOSC.[43]

The first supporting argument is that the language of Article 281 of the LOSC shows that "Part XV dispute procedures 'will apply' where the parties' agreement 'does not exclude any further procedure.'" This requires an "opting out" of the Part XV procedure. This is contrary to Article 282, in which it is suggested that "the chosen binding procedure will apply 'in lieu of' the Part XV procedures 'unless the parties to the dispute otherwise agree.'" In other words, the Part XV procedures are excluded by the alternative compulsory binding

---

39   Ibid (Justice Keith) 53–54 [17].

40   Ibid [18]–[19], [22].

41   For general comments of this case, see Yoshifumi Tanaka, "Reflections on the *Philippines/ China* Arbitration" (2016) 15(2) *The Law and Practice of International Courts and Tribunals* 305–325; Natalie Klein, "The Limitation of UNCLOS Part XV Dispute Settlement in Resolving South China Sea Disputes: The South China Sea" (Paper presented at An International Law Perspective Conference, Vrije Universiteit Brussel, Brussel Belgium, 9 March 2015) <https://ssrn.com/abstract=2730411>.

42   *South China Sea Arbitration (Jurisdiction and Admissibility)*, (Permanent Court of Arbitration, 2015) [204], [210], [223]; *South China Sea Arbitration (Award)* (Permanent Court of Arbitration, 2016) [159].

43   *South China Sea Arbitration (Jurisdiction and Admissibility)*, (Permanent Court of Arbitration, 2015) [223].

procedure, and the only way to make them available is for the parties to opt back into them by "agreeing otherwise."[44] The Annex VII Tribunal added that this distinction between Articles 281 and 282 "is consistent with the overall design of the Convention as a system in which a compulsory dispute resolution is the default rule and any limitations and exceptions are carefully and precisely defined in Section 3 of Part XV."[45]

Secondly, the requirement of an express exclusion of a further procedure is consistent with "the overall object and purpose of the LOSC as a comprehensive agreement" based on the fact that, since Part XV of the LOSC is "an integral part and essential element of the Convention", "it is difficult to accept that the Parties may remove a pivotal part of the Convention without clearly expressing an intention to do so."[46] Ultimately, the Annex VII Tribunal found its jurisdiction for this case after considering several instruments that did not create an agreement to exclude any further procedures under the LOSC.

Apart from these two cases, no other case has directly related to Article 281 of the LOSC. However, as things stand at present, it may be possible to say that the interpretation of Article 281 is akin to the one that was used to decide the *South China Sea Arbitration* case.

2.2.2   Article 282 – *MOX Plant* Formula?

The *MOX Plant* case,[47] which involved Article 282 of the LOSC, concerned the potential discharge of radioactive waste and substances into the Irish Sea as a result of the operation of the Mixed Oxide Fuel ("MOX") Plant on the western coast of Sellafield in the United Kingdom. The case was brought before the ITLOS to prescribe provisional measures and before the Annex VII Tribunal, which was constituted later, and Ireland argued that the United Kingdom had

---

44   Ibid [224].

45   Ibid.

46   Ibid [225].

47   For comments on the case, see, Barbara Kwiatkowska, "The *Ireland v United Kingdom* (MOX Plant) Case: Applying the Doctrine of Treaty Parallelism" (2003) 18(1) *International Journal of Marine and Coastal Law* 1–58; Donald R Rothwell and Tim Stephens, "Dispute Resolution and the Law of the Sea: Reconciling the Interaction Between the LOS Convention and Other Environmental Instruments" in A.G. Oude Elferink and D.R. Rothwell (eds), *Ocean Management in the 21st Century: Institutional Frameworks and Responses* (Martinus Nijhoff, 2004) 209–230; Robin Churchill, "Some Reflections on the Operation of the Dispute Settlement System of the UN Convention on the Law of the Sea During its First Decade" in David Freestone, Richard A Barnes and David M Ong (eds), *The Law of the Sea Progress and Prospects* (Oxford University Press, 2006) 388–416.

violated several obligations provided for by the LOSC.[48] Among its counter-arguments, the United Kingdom raised the issue of Article 282 to the ITLOS as one of its jurisdictional objections to determine the provisional measures before proceeding to argue that the matter Ireland was complaining of was subject to other regional agreements that contained an alternative and binding means of dispute settlement. These included the 1992 *Convention for the Protection of the Marine Environment of the North–East Atlantic* ("OSPAR Convention"), the *Treaty establishing the European Community* ("EC Treaty") and the *Treaty establishing the European Atomic Energy Community* ("Euratom Treaty").[49]

With respect to Article 282 of the LOSC, the decision of the ITLOS on the relevant parts in the *MOX Plant (Provisional Measures)* case was based on the fact that Article 282 concerns "general, regional, or bilateral agreements, which provide for the settlement of disputes concerning what the Convention refers to as 'the interpretation or application of this Convention.'"[50] The dispute settlement procedures of the OSPAR Convention, EC and EURATOM treaties were only concerned with disputes related to the interpretation and application of those treaties and "not with disputes arising under the Convention".[51] The ITLOS further added that, although those treaties may contain "similar or identical" rights and obligations under the LOSC, they have a separate existence from those under the LOSC and their interpretation "may not yield the same result" as one of the LOSC based on "*inter alia*, differences in contexts, objects and purposes, subsequent practice of parties, and *travaux préparatoires.*"[52] For these reasons, for the purpose of establishing prima facie jurisdiction, the ITLOS found that Article 282 of the Convention was "not applicable to the dispute submitted to the Annex VII Tribunal"[53] since the dispute brought to the Tribunal only concerned the interpretation and application of the LOSC and no other Convention; therefore, the prima facie jurisdiction was established.

However, the relevance of regional agreements was not without doubt, as can be seen from the subsequent order suspending the proceedings by the

---

48   *MOX Plant (Provisional Measure)*, (International Tribunal for the Law of the Sea, Case No 10, 3 December 2001) [26]. This includes articles 123, 192–194, 197, 206–207, 211, and 213 of the LOSC.

49   Ibid [39]–[43]. *OSPAR Convention*, opened for signature 22 September 1992, 2354 UNTS 67 (entered into force 25 March 1998).

50   *MOX Plant (Provisional Measures)*, (International Tribunal for the Law of the Sea, Case No 10, 3 December 2001) [48].

51   Ibid [49].

52   Ibid [50]–[51].

53   Ibid [52]–[53].

MOX Plant Annex VII Tribunal,[54] when the Tribunal agreed with the finding of the ITLOS in relation to the prima facie jurisdiction. In terms of the relevance of an international agreement, namely, the OSPAR Convention, according to the Annex VII Tribunal, this Convention "is relevant to some at least of the question in issue between the Parties", but it was not considered to "alter the character of the dispute as one essentially involving the interpretation and application of the Convention."[55] It further noted that it was not "persuaded that the OSPAR Convention substantially covers the field of the present dispute so as to trigger the application of Article 281 or 282 of the Convention."[56]

Nevertheless, the more acute issue of concern at that time was the relevance of European Community Law and the Annex VII Tribunal found several legal difficulties that may affect its adjudication of both the jurisdiction and merits of the case.[57] This led to the suspension of the proceeding for the "considerations of mutual respect and comity which should prevail between judicial institutions both of which may be called upon to determine rights and obligations of the two States, in this case the European Court of Justice ('ECJ')".[58]

However, at this stage, it is unfortunate that the *MOX Plant* case never reached the merit phase where the interpretation and application of Article 282 of the LOSC could have been clarified. As things stand, it may be possible to conclude that the OSPAR Convention does not trigger the prerequisites set out in the said provision, which may be why Judge Wolfrum stated in his separate opinion that he accepted the reality of the plurality of international norms covering the same topic or right and the existence of treaty parallelism in substance and their dispute settlement provision. Having said so, "a dispute under one agreement, such as the OSPAR Convention does not become a dispute under the *Convention on the Law of the Sea* by the mere fact that both instruments cover this issue", due to their separate existence from the LOSC.[59] Alternatively, as provided by Judge Jesus in his separate opinion, the OSPAR Convention is not applicable for triggering Article 282 of the LOSC because "the issues covered by that regional Convention and the claims made by Ireland before the OSPAR Tribunal are different from and narrow than those brought

---

54   *MOX Plant case (Ireland v. United Kingdom) (Order Suspension of Proceeding on Jurisdiction and Merits, and Request for Further Provisional Measures)*, (LOSC Arbitral Tribunal, 24 June 2003) <https://pcacases.com/web/view/100> (*"Mox Plant (Suspension Order)"*).

55   Ibid [18].

56   Ibid.

57   Ibid [20].

58   Ibid [27].

59   *Mox Plant (Provisional Measures)*, (International Tribunal for the Law of the Sea, Case No 10, 3 December 2001) (Judge Wolfrum) 1.

before the Annex VII arbitral Tribunal of the Law of the Sea Convention."[60] In addition, whether or not a dispute concerns the interpretation or application of the LOSC, and whether or not Article 282 will be triggered, of course, depends on how the Applicant State frames its argument before the relevant judicial institution. To this end, time is needed for more cases to be brought before the judicial institution set out in Article 287 and to test Article 282 of the LOSC in order to assess the maturity of the application of this provision.

2.2.3   Why are Articles 281 and 282 so important to the Marine
          Environment Dispute of the RSP?

Articles 281 and 282 are very important to a marine environmental dispute from an RSP because fourteen of the eighteen RSPs are governed by regional conventions and protocols that are directly related to Part XII of the LOSC concerning the protection of the marine environment. As noted by Judge Wolfrum, this obviously illustrates the treaty parallelism in relation to both the substance and dispute settlement provisions of the LOSC vis-à-vis regional agreements.[61] In terms of LBP, not only is the execution of environmental rights and obligations in relation to LBP at the regional level enshrined in the LOSC,[62] but the subsequent practice of states suggests that Article 207 of the LOSC should be implemented at a regional level. This has been reaffirmed by various international instruments in which LBP is discussed, including Agenda 21,[63] the Washington Declaration[64] and the GPA.[65] All the existing regional conventions regulate LBP, and as of 2016, nine RSPs contain specific protocols to deal with it. In a case where an LBP dispute arises under an RSP that contains either a regional convention or protocol, or both, the substance of the dispute unavoidably concerns the interpretation and application of Articles 207 and 213 of the LOSC. For this reason, the application of the compulsory dispute settlement procedure under Part XV, Section 2 of the LOSC would clearly depend on the interpretation of Articles 281 and 282. Different readings of these two

---

60   Ibid (Judge Jesus) [6]–[7].
61   *Mox Plant (Provisional Measures)*, (International Tribunal for the Law of the Sea, Case No 10, 3 December 2001) (Judge Wolfrum) 1.
62   LOSC, above n 1, arts 197, 207 and 213.
63   *Report of the United Nations Conference on Environment and Development (Vol I)*, UN GAOR 47th sess, UN DOC A/CONF.151/REV.1 (Vol I) (12 August 1993) Annex II [17.25].
64   *Washington Declaration on Protection of the Marine Environment from Land-Based Activities*, UNEP(1995)<http://unep.org/gpa/documents/meetings/Washington/Washington Declaration.pdf>preamble[7].
65   *Global Programme of Action for the Protection of the Marine Environment from Land-based Activities*, UNEP, Doc UNEP(OCA)/LBA/IG.2/7 (5 December 1995) Ch III.

provisions can result in completely different scenarios when taking the dispute settlement provisions in regional conventions and protocols into account, and this is discussed below by analysing the dispute settlement provisions of the RSP agreements concerning potential LBP disputes.

3   Categorisation and Analysis of the Dispute Settlement Provisions of the Regional Sea Programmes Agreements

3.1   *Categorisation of RSPs' Dispute Settlement Provisions*
Having reviewed the dispute settlement provisions across RSPs, it can be argued that they can be divided into five categories. These are: (i) RSPs with a dispute settlement provision that only requires the dispute to be settled by negotiation or any other peaceful means of the parties' choice; (ii) RSPs with a dispute settlement provision that requires the consent of all parties for a third-party adjudication; (iii) RSPs providing for compulsory third-party adjudication on the request of any party; (iv) RSPs with a dispute settlement provision with the automatic referral of an unsettled dispute to a third-party for adjudication; and (v) RSPs that contain no dispute settlement provision.

3.1.1   RSPs with a Dispute Settlement Provision that only Requires the Dispute to be Settled by Negotiation or Any Other Peaceful Means of Parties' Choice
The first category concerns the dispute settlement provisions of those RSPs that contain no compulsory dispute settlement mechanism, but merely require the dispute to be settled by negotiation or any other peaceful means chosen by the parties. These include the Black Sea,[66] North–East Pacific,[67] and the Caspian Sea programmes.[68] An example can be drawn from the 1992 *Bucharest Convention of the Black Sea Region*, in which the settlement of dispute provision reads as follows;

---

66   *Convention on the Protection of the Black Sea against Pollution,* opened for signature 21 April 1992, 1764 UNTS 3 (entered into force 15 January 1994) art 25 ("Bucharest Convention").

67   *Convention for Cooperation in the Protection and Sustainable Development of the Marine and Coastal Environment of the North–East Pacific,* opened for signature 18 February 2002 (not yet in force) <http://drustage.unep.org/regionalseas/north-east-pacific#> art 25 ("Antigua Convention").

68   *Framework Convention for the Protection of the Marine Environment of the Caspian Sea,* opened for signature 4 November 2003 (entered into force 12 August 2006) <http://www .tehranconvention.org/spip.php?article4> art 30 ("Tehran Convention").

In case of a dispute between Contracting Parties concerning the interpretation and implementation of this Convention, they shall seek a settlement of the dispute through negotiations or any other peaceful means of their own choice.[69]

The dispute settlement provisions of the North–East Pacific and Caspian Sea programmes are almost identical to those of the Black Sea programme. It can be seen from the above that this formulation of the dispute settlement provision does nothing more than reiterate what is enshrined in Article 33 of the *Charter of the United Nations.* In addition, it suggests that there is no compulsory dispute settlement within the RSPs nor an exclusion of any further procedures of state parties to those RSPs under the *LOSC.*

3.1.2   RSPs with a Dispute Settlement Provision that Requires the
              Consent of All Parties for a Third-party Adjudication
The second category consists of those that not only provide the pacific means stipulated in Article 33 of the Charter of the United Nations, but also allow a third-party to adjudicate the dispute based on the common consent of the disputed parties. The RSPs in this category are the Wider Caribbean,[70] Eastern Africa,[71] Pacific,[72] Baltic,[73] and Mediterranean Sea programmes.[74] Noting

---

69   Bucharest Convention, above n 66, art 25.

70   *Convention for the Protection and Development of the Marine Environment of the Wider Caribbean Region,* opened for signature 24 March 1983, 1506 UNTS 157 (entered into force 11 October 1986) art 23 ("Cartagena Convention").

71   *Convention for the Protection, Management and Development of the Marine and Coastal Environment of the Eastern African Region,* opened for signature 21 June 1985 (entered into force 30 May 1996) in Kenneth R. Simmonds, *New Directions in the Law of the Sea* (Looseleaf) Doc. J. 26 (Oceana Publications, 1986) art 24 ("Nairobi Convention"); *Amended Nairobi Convention for the Protection, Management and Development of the Marine and Coastal Environment of the Western Indian Ocean* opened for signature 31 March 2010 (not yet in force) <http://web.unep.org/nairobiconvention/who-we-are/structure/legal-and-policy-instruments> art 25 ("Amended Nairobi Convention").

72   *Convention for the Protection of the Natural Resources and Environment of the South Pacific Region,* opened for signature 24 November 1986, [1990] ATS 30 (entered into force 22 August 1990) art 26 ("Noumea Convention").

73   *Convention on the Protection of the Marine Environment of the Baltic Sea Area,* opened for signature 9 April 1992, 1507 UNTS 167 (entered into force 17 January 2000) art 26 ("Helsinki Convention").

74   *Convention for the Protection of the Marine Environment and the Coastal Region of the Mediterranean,* opened for signature 16 February 1976, 1102 UNTS 27 (amended 10 June 1995; entered into force 9 July 2004) art 28 ("Barcelona Convention"); *Protocol to Barcelona*

some nuances, an example of this category can be seen from the *Cartagena Convention of the Wider Caribbean* programme, the dispute settlement clause of which contains the following stipulation;

1. In case of a dispute between Contracting Parties as to the interpretation or application of this Convention or its protocols, they shall seek a settlement of the dispute through negotiation or any other peaceful means of their own choice.

2. If the Contracting Parties concerned cannot settle their dispute through the means mentioned in the preceding paragraph, the dispute *shall upon common agreement*, except as may be otherwise provided in any protocol to this Convention, be submitted to arbitration under the conditions set out in the Annex on Arbitration. However, failure to reach common agreement on submission of the dispute to arbitration shall not absolve the Contracting Parties from the responsibility of continuing to seek to resolve it by the means referred to in paragraph 1...[75]

Arbitration is the common third-party choice of adjudication in this category if the dispute fails to be settled using the pacific means. It is also worth noting that a permanent arbitral tribunal or the ICJ is also among the available third-party choices of adjudication in some regions.[76] In view of the jurisprudence discussed above, it is important to note the similarity of this provision in the *Cartagena Convention* and that of the CCSBT. The formulation in the *Southern Bluefin Tuna (Jurisdiction and Admissibility)*[77] case excluded the compulsory dispute settlement procedure in Part XV, Section 2 of the *LOSC*; however, the same formulation was not considered to exclude the operation of Part XV, Section 2 of the *LOSC* according to the *South China Sea Arbitration (Jurisdiction and Admissibility)* case.[78] Therefore, different interpretations of Article 281 of the *LOSC* can result in very different scenarios in relation to the judicial

---

  Convention on Land-Based Sources, opened for signature 17 May 1980 (entered into force 17 June 1983) replaced by *Protocol for the Protection of the Mediterranean Sea against Pollution from Land-Based Sources and Activities*, opened for signature 7 March 1996 (entered into force 18 May 2006) <http://web.unep.org/unepmap/who-we-are/legal-framework> art 12 ("LBP Protocol to Barcelona Convention").

75 Cartagena Convention, above n 70, art 23 (emphasis added).

76 Helsinki Convention, above n 73, art 26.

77 *Southern Bluefin Tuna (Jurisdiction and Admissibility)*, (2000) RIAA 13.

78 *South China Sea Arbitration (Jurisdiction and Admissibility)*, (Permanent Court of Arbitration, 2015).

institution that entertains the case and the dispute settlement regimes that can be applied to environmental disputes in RSPs.

3.1.3   RSPs Providing for Compulsory Third-party Adjudication on the Request of Any Party

The RSPs in this category are the North–East Atlantic Sea programmes and the relevant part of the dispute settlement of the *OSPAR Convention* reads as follows;

1.   Any disputes between Contracting Parties relating to the interpretation or application of the Convention, which cannot be settled otherwise by the Contracting Parties concerned, for instance by means of inquiry or conciliation within the Commission, shall *at the request of any of those Contracting Parties*, be submitted to arbitration under the conditions laid down in this Article...[79]

This provision is similar to the first two categories in that it also employs the pacific means of dispute settlement, those of Article 33 of the *Charter of the United Nations*. However, it is different from the second category in terms of the way in which a dispute can be adjudicated by a third-party. While the common agreement of the disputed parties is required in the previous category, this category allows the dispute to be heard by third-party adjudication *upon the request of any party to the dispute*. In view of Part XV of the *LOSC*, an analysis of this formulation suggests that the OSPAR Convention provides for a compulsory dispute settlement by arbitration when the parties to the dispute fail to settle it by other means. This enables one of the parties to resort to third-party adjudication with or without the consent of the opposing party. Indeed, it can be said that the contracting parties to the OSPAR Convention have provided their prior consent to this compulsory settlement of an unresolved dispute by arbitration with their ratification or accession to the Convention. This category will not trigger Article 281 of the *LOSC* because, as ruled in *Southern Bluefin Tuna* and *South China Sea Arbitration (Jurisdiction and Admissibility)* cases, the dispute settlement of the OSPAR Convention requires a mere request from any parties to the dispute for the case to be submitted to arbitration. Therefore, it does not exclude any further procedure required in Article 281. However, in the light of Article 282 of the *LOSC* and the *MOX Plant (Provisional Measures)* case, although the OSPAR Convention shares the same rights and obligations as those of the *LOSC* to a certain extent, it has a separate existence. Thus, as

---

79   OSPAR Convention, above n 49, art 32 (emphasis added).

the ITLOS notes, the interpretation of the OSPAR Convention may not yield the same conclusion given the different context, objects and purposes as well as subsequent practice of states parties to the Convention.[80] Depending on the applicant state's framing of the claims and arguments, the chosen judicial institution provided under Article 287 of the LOSC may be able to entertain the case should they find that the application submitted concerns the interpretation or application of the LOSC.

3.1.4   RSPs with a Dispute Settlement Provision with the Obligation to Refer an Unsettled Dispute to a Third-party Adjudication

This category is arguably the most onerous dispute settlement provision compared to the earlier categories. The pacific means of dispute settlement are still the starting point to settle the dispute; however, if the disputing parties cannot resolve their dispute using those standard means, it requires the dispute to be referred and settled by the institutions designated within the RSP. The RSPs in this category are the the Regional Organisation for the Protection of the Marine Environment and the Coastal Areas of Bahrain, Islamic Republic of Iran, Iraq, Kuwait, Oman, Qatar, Saudi Arabia and the United Arab Emirates ("ROPME Sea"),[81] Red Sea and Gulf of Aden Sea ("PERSGA"),[82] and the West and Central African regions.[83] An example can be drawn from Article 25 of the *Kuwait Convention* of the ROPME Sea region, which contains the following provision;

(a)   In case of a dispute as to the interpretation or application of this Convention or its protocols, the Contracting States concerned shall seek a settlement of the dispute through negotiation or any other peaceful means of their own choice.

(b)   If the Contracting States concerned cannot settle the dispute through the means mentioned in paragraph (a) of this article, ***the dispute shall***

---

80   *Mox Plant (Provisional Measures)*, (International Tribunal for the Law of the Sea, Case No 10, 3 December 2001) [48]–[51].

81   *Kuwait Regional Convention for Cooperation on the Protection of the Marine Environment from Pollution* opened for signature 24 April 1978, 1140 UNTS 133 (entered into force 1 July 1979) art 25 ("Kuwait Convention").

82   *Regional Convention for the Conservation of the Red Sea and Gulf of Aden Environment,* opened for signature 14 February 1982, 9 *Environmental Policy and Law* 56 (1982) (entered into force 10 August 1985), <www.persga.org/inner.php?id=62> art 24 ("Jeddah Convention").

83   *Convention for Co-operation in the Protection and development of the Marine and Coastal Development of the West and Central African Region,* opened for signature 23 March 1981, 20 ILM 746 (entered into force 5 August 1984) art 16(2)(c), 24 ("Abidjan Convention").

be submitted to the Judicial Commission for the Settlement of Disputes
referred to in paragraph (b) (iii) of Article xvi. (Emphasis added)

Based on the above provision, the dispute settlement is compulsory, in the
sense that not only will the dispute be adjudicated by a third-party institution,
in this case the Judicial Commission of the Settlement of Disputes established
by the *Kuwait Convention*, but the state parties also have no choice of forum to
hear their dispute except the one provided by the Convention. In addition, it
is interesting to note that there are some nuances among these RSPs and this
is the case for the PERSGA Sea programme. Under the *Jeddah Convention*, the
dispute can be taken to the Judicial Committee to be settled if two conditions
have been satisfied. The first is that the disputing parties have failed to resolve
the issue by amicable means, while the second is that the dispute has been
referred to the Council, which is a political organ of the RSP, and it has still
not been able to be settled.[84] In view of Article 281 and the above-mentioned
jurisprudence, this formulation of the dispute settlement provision, arguably,
more obviously reflects the exclusion of the dispute settlement mechanism of
other regimes, such as the *LOSC*, than that of the above-mentioned categories
and may be caught under the prerequisites in Article 281 of the *LOSC*.

3.1.5   RSPs that Contain No Dispute Settlement Provision
The last category of the RSPs is the one that does not provide a dispute settlement provision in the regional Convention or Protocol. The RSPs in this
category are the South–East Pacific Sea programme and the *Convention for
the Protection of the Marine Environment and Coastal Zones of the South–East
Pacific* ("Lima Convention").[85] Firstly, it can be seen that the RSPs in this category contain no agreement that excludes any further procedures within the
meaning of Article 281, and secondly, there is no provision that indicates that
the States are bound to the compulsory dispute settlement, which entails a

---

84   Jeddah Convention, above n 82, art 24. The Council is a political organ of the Regional
       Organisation for the Conservation of the Red Sea and Gulf of Aden comprising a repre-
       sentative from each party. Its duties and functions are manifold. One of the duties and
       functions, inter alia, is "to endeavour to settle any differences or disputes between the
       Contracting Parties as to the interpretation or implementation of this Convention or its
       protocols or annexes". See, art 18.
85   *Convention for the Protection of the Marine Environment and Coastal Zones of the South–
       East Pacific,* opened for signature 12 November 1981, (entered into force 19 May 1986) in
       Kenneth R. Simmonds, *New Directions in the Law of the Sea* (Looseleaf) Doc. J. 18 (Oceana
       Publications, 1984) ("Lima Convention").

binding decision under Article 282 of the LOSC. Therefore, it is possible for a dispute to be submitted to the procedure under Part XV, Section 2 of the LOSC if the other prerequisites provided in Part XV, Section 1 are fulfilled, and it is not subject to any of the limitations or exceptions set out in Section 3 of Part XV of the LOSC.

3.2 Analysis of the above Categories in View of Part XV of the LOSC and the Jurisprudence of Articles 281 and 282

3.2.1 ITLOS Advisory Jurisdiction in Relation to RSP Agreements

The first observation can be made from the categorisation of the dispute settlement provisions of RSPs concerning the ITLOS advisory jurisdiction. It can be argued from this categorisation that no RSP agreement provides a basis for the ITLOS jurisdiction to render its advisory opinion, should any issue concerning the interpretation or application of the RSP Conventions or Protocols require one.[86] This could have several potential effects, as shown below.

One of the possible effects is that the lack of advisory jurisdiction may lead to the fragmentation of the law of the sea, since the ITLOS is the only judicial institution available in Article 287 of the LOSC that is empowered to provide an advisory opinion regarding the interpretation or application of the LOSC.[87] Considering the rapid growth of the international legal order, a prominent scholar notes that "the more evolved and sophisticated the legal system becomes, with competing or even conflicting sets of obligations, the more the subjects of international law need the help of an independent third-party".[88] This is the case for the protection of the marine environment of the LOSC and RSPs Conventions and Protocols regulating the same matters, sharing the same objectives given their different scope and application. The lack of an avenue for states or regional marine environmental bodies to seek an ITLOS advisory opinion runs the risk of inconsistent interpretations of their agreements vis-à-vis the LOSC, leading to its fragmentation.

Another possible effect of the lack of the ITLOS advisory jurisdiction is that there is no judicial impetus to stimulate states to cooperate in the protection and preservation of the marine environment. The advisory opinion of

---

86 LOSC, above n 1, art 288, Annex IV at art 21; Rules of the ITLOS, above n 13, art 138.

87 States cannot directly resort to the ICJ for its advisory jurisdiction. See, *Charter of the United Nations* art 96; *Statute of the ICJ*, art 65.

88 Pierre-Marie Dupuy, "The Danger of Fragmentation or Unification of the International Legal System and the International Court of Justice" (1999) 31(3) *International Law and Politics* 806.

international judicial institutions has the effect of clarifying legal ambiguities, thus further guiding the actions of states. It also sometimes has the effect of directly or indirectly settling a dispute, relieving the tension between states and bringing them back to cooperate to achieve a meaningful solution.[89] In addition, the openness of the advisory proceeding allows for the wider participation of states that find their interests affected to put forward their propositions.[90] From this perspective, the lack of the possibility to resort to the advisory opinion of the ITLOS can create legal stagnation and further complicate the relationship between states where a solution or clarity is needed to eliminate the legal deadlock caused by an environmental dispute of RSPs.

It may be argued that the lack of an express provision by the RSPs' conventions for the advisory jurisdiction of the ITLOS is an impediment for states seeking an advisory opinion. However, the member states of the RSPs may be able to request an ITLOS advisory opinion if Article 138 of the Rules of the ITLOS is examined more closely. Under this provision, the ITLOS "may give an advisory opinion on a legal question if an international agreement related to the purposes of the Convention specifically provides for the submission to the Tribunal of a request for such an opinion." The term "agreement" is wider than treaty and it may not necessarily be part of a treaty.[91] Such an international agreement may be reached by consensus among the states of the RSPs in the form of a decision during the Conference of the Parties ("COP"). Provided that the subject matter concerns the RSP's convention, the international agreement consensually agreed by states during the COP is sufficient to provide the basis for the ITLOS advisory jurisdiction, despite there being no explicit provision in the RSPs' conventions. Therefore, states can arguably make a recourse to the ITLOS and the advisory opinion should they agree to do so based on a consensual agreement at the COP.

---

89   Rüdiger Wolfrum, "Advisory Opinions: Are they a Suitable Alternative for the Settlement of International Disputes?" in Rüdiger Wolfrum and Ina Gätzschmann (eds), *International Dispute Settlement: Room for Innovations?* (Springer, 2013) Panel II 35–77.

90   Ibid 65.

91   For the meaning of the term "treaty", see *Vienna Convention on the Law of the Treaties*, opened for signature 23 May 1969, 1155 UNTS 331 (entered into force 27 January 1980) art 2 ("VCLT"); See also, Richard Gardiner, *Treaty Interpretation* (Oxford University Press, 2011) 483; Anthony Aust, *Modern Treaty Law and Practice* (Cambridge University Press, 3rd ed, 2013) 211; Jean-Marc Sorel and Valerie Bore Eveno, "1969 Vienna Convention: Article 31 General Rule of Interpretation" in Oliver Corten and Pierre Klein (eds), *The Vienna Convention on the Law of Treaties: A Commentary* (Oxford University Press, 2011) vol I, 823–825.

3.2.2   ITLOS Jurisdiction for Contentious Cases that Arise from RSP
          Agreements

The second observation concerns the contentious jurisdiction of the ITLOS.
It is proposed in this article that the potential role of the ITLOS is rather lim-
ited in this respect as a result of: (i) the possibility of the RSP's environmental
case being caught by the prerequisites set out in Part XV, Section 1 of the LOSC.
In this case, two points need to be substantiated, namely, the prerequisites in
Articles 281 and 282 of the LOSC; and (ii) the state's decision to accept the
ITLOS as its dispute settlement forum.[92] These two main hurdles are discussed
in turn below.

     In terms of Article 281, it can be said that, based on the *South China Sea
Arbitration (Jurisdiction and Admissibility)* case,[93] almost all the dispute settlement provision categories discussed above would not trigger the application
of Article 281 of the LOSC because they do not provide an "express exclusion"
of any further procedure showing that the states that are party to the relevant
RSP have opted out from "any further procedure", including those in Part XV,
Section 2 of the LOSC. However, the expressiveness of this exclusion may be
questionable. Basically, the remaining question relates to how express an
agreement needs to be to fulfil the requirement of Article 281. The ambiguity
of the expressiveness of the exclusion causes procedural uncertainty for states
that are party to one specific dispute settlement provision category, namely,
Category (IV) in which the unresolved dispute is automatically referred to the
judicial institution established by the RSP.[94] In this category, the dispute settlement provision of the RSP Convention instructs that the unresolved dispute be
submitted either to the judicial commission/committee established by the RSP
Convention or arbitration. If the reasoning in the *South China Sea Arbitration
(Jurisdiction and Admissibility)* case was strictly applied, this category would
not fall foul of Article 281 of the LOSC. However, it can be equally argued that
the way in which the dispute settlement provision of this category is structured,
clearly illustrates that it excludes the settlement of a dispute outside the RSPs
by: (i) the prior consent of the states for the dispute to be settled by the judicial
commission/committee or arbitration under the RSPs; and (ii) the effect of the
obligation to settle the unresolved dispute to those regional institutions. Unfortunately, the jurisprudence of Part XV of the LOSC provides no clear answers. In
addition, much would depend on the way in which the applicant state frames

---

92   *LOSC*, above n 1, art 287.
93   See, Section 2.2 above.
94   See, Section 3.4 above.

its argument concerning the jurisdiction of Part XV judicial institutions should it wish to utilise the compulsory dispute mechanism in Part XV of the *LOSC*.

Turning to the possible implications of Article 282, based on this provision and the *MOX Plant* case, most of the dispute settlement provisions categorised above would not fall short of this article. Category (III)[95] above was ruled out by the ITLOS in the *MOX Plant (Provisional Measures)* case, when the ITLOS ruled that "similar or identical" rights and obligations in the *LOSC* and other agreements have a separate existence and their interpretation "may not yield the same result" as that of the *LOSC* "having regard to, *inter alia*, differences in contexts, objects and purposes, subsequent practice of parties, and *travaux préparatoires*" and that the dispute before it only concerned the *LOSC*.[96] However, the ITLOS reasoning needs to strictly take account of the fact that it essentially depended on the way in which the applicant state framed its argument within the ambit of the term "interpretation or application" of the *LOSC*.[97] Article 282 of the *LOSC* is also not applicable to Categories (I), (II), and (V) discussed in the previous section simply because those categories do not fulfil the requirements of the said provision. Categories (I) and (V) do not contain the dispute settlement procedure that entails a binding decision, whereas Category (II) requires the common consent of the disputing parties for the dispute to be submitted to third-party adjudication. Therefore, these three Categories cannot trigger Article 282 of the *LOSC*.

The most interesting case is that of Category (IV), which pertains to RSPs with a dispute settlement provision in which an unsettled dispute is required to be referred to third-party adjudication. The fact that the dispute settlement mechanism in this Category entails a binding decision fulfils one of the requirements of Article 282.[98] However, in terms of the submission of the dispute for settlement, while it is stipulated in Article 282 that "any party" to the dispute shall be entitled to submit the case to a mechanism agreed by States through a general, regional, or bilateral agreement, the dispute settlement provision of this Category obliges them to submit their dispute to the judicial settlement commission/committee or arbitration. In this situation, it is *a fortiori* stricter than Article 282 in that it does not accord the states that are party to these RSPs the "right" to seek a judicial settlement; instead, it assigns

---

95   See, Section 3.3 above.

96   *Mox Plant (Provisional Measures)*, (International Tribunal for the Law of the Sea, Case No 10, 3 December 2001) [48]–[51].

97   The Judicial institution chosen in Article 287 has jurisdiction over a dispute concerning the interpretation or application of the *LOSC*. See, *LOSC*, above n 1, art 288.

98   The decision of the judicial commission/committee or arbitral award is final.

them the "duty" to settle their dispute within the RSPs through the means identified in the RSP Conventions. In effect, the dispute settlement provision of this Category prevents states from submitting the case elsewhere, apart from those provided for in the RSP Conventions or Protocols. Arguably, the effect produced by this Category resembles what is referred to by respected scholars as "general, regional, or bilateral agreements" within the meaning of Article 282.[99] Therefore, it seems convincing that an environmental dispute that arises from RSPs in this Category will not reach the compulsory dispute procedure of the *LOSC*, since it will be barred by Article 282 of the *LOSC*.

The last possible hurdle of this discussion is the match between the choice of states having the ITLOS as their dispute settlement forum. So far, only thirty-nine states across eighteen RSPs have chosen the ITLOS as their dispute settlement forum.[100] Unless the disputing states agree otherwise, the ITLOS jurisdiction will be limited to those cases from the thirty-nine states that choose it as their dispute settlement forum, provided that: (i) the disputing states are from the same RSP; and (ii) the dispute is related to the RSP Conventions and/or LBP Protocols. Thus, it can be said that the possibility of the ITLOS to entertain environmental disputes from RSPs will be further limited by the choice made by states under Article 287 of the *LOSC*.

4   **Potential Challenges and Contributions of the ITLOS in Settling Marine Environmental Disputes of RSPs: A Case of Land-based Pollution**

Having discussed the possibility of the ITLOS to entertain environmental disputes that arise from RSPs, it can be said that the ITLOS may face other potential challenges, as well as being able to make a potential contribution to

---

99   Myron H Nordquist, Shabtai Rosenne and Alexander Yankov, *United Nations Convention on the Law of the Sea 1982 A Commentary* (Martinus Nijhoff Publishers, 1991) 26; See also, *Treaty of the Functioning of the European Union*, opened for signature 7 February 1992, [2009] OJ C 115/199 (entered into force 1 November 1993) art 344; Barbara Kwiatkowska, "The *Ireland v United Kingdom* (MOX Plant) Case: Applying the Doctrine of Treaty Parallelism" (2003) 18(1) *International Journal of Marine and Coastal Law*, 1–58.

100   This information is correct as of 18 January 2017. Among these states, Belarus, Russian Federation, and Ukraine only accept the jurisdiction of the ITLOS for the prompt release of detained vessels or their crews under Article 292. For more information concerning the declarations of States in relation to the *LOSC*, see United Nations website <https://treaties.un.org/pages/ViewDetailsIII.aspx?src=TREATY&mtdsg_no=XXI-6 &chapter=21&Temp=mtdsg3&clang=_en>.

the development of the law of the sea should the case be referred either by the application of Article 287 of the *LOSC* or the agreement of the parties. Those possible challenges and contribution are specifically considered in turn below based on a case of an environmental dispute of RSPs concerning LBP.

4.1   Potential Challenges of the *ITLOS*

In terms of the potential challenges, the difficulty in solving an LBP dispute is that there is no international regulation specifically designed to deal with this source of pollution at the international level apart from the *LOSC*.[101] Although some international instruments, such as *the Montreal Guidelines for the Protection of the Marine Environment Against Pollution from Land-based Sources* ("Montreal Guidelines"),[102] part of Agenda 21 and the GPA, deal with LBP, they are non-binding. In addition, it is criticised in literature that Article 207 of the *LOSC* contains very general terms, which makes it difficult for states to implement and fulfil their obligation.[103] The fact that the *LOSC* was never intended to impose a detailed obligation in relation to the governance of the sea[104] makes the lack of substance of an international regulation on LBP quite challenging for the ITLOS if a case is brought before it.

---

101   *LOSC* is the only international agreement at the global level that regulates LBP, albeit generally.

102   UNEP Governing Council Decision 13/18/II (24 May 1985), <http://web.pnuma.org/gobernanza/cd/Biblioteca/Derecho%20ambiental/28%20UNEPEnv-LawGuide&PrincNo7.pdf>.

103   General criticism of the problem can be seen, inter alia, in the following literature: Patricia Birnie, Alan E Boyle and Catherine Redgwell, *International Law and the Environment* (Oxford University Press, 3rd ed, 2009) 451–54; P. Sands et al, *Principles of international environmental law* (Cambridge University Press, 2012) 372–377; Yoshifumi Tanaka, "Regulation of Land-Based Marine Pollution in International Law: A Comparative Analysis Between Global and Regional Legal Frameworks" (2006) 66 *Heidelberg Journal of International Law* 535; Thomas Mensah, "The International Legal Regime for the Protection and Preservation of the Marine Environment from Land-based Sources of Pollution" in Alan E Boyle and David Freestone (eds), *International Law and Sustainable Development* (Oxford University Press, 1999) 297–324; David VanderZwaag and Ann Powers, "The Protection of the Marine Environment from Land-based Pollution and Activities: Gauging the Tides of Global and Regional Governance" (2008) 23 *International Journal of Marine and Coastal Law* 423; Alan E Boyle, "Marine Pollution under the Law of the Sea Convention" (1985) 79 *American Journal of International Law* 347.

104   Robin Churchill, "The *LOSC* Regime for Protection of the Marine Environment – Fit for the Twenty-first Century?" in Rosemary Rayfuse (ed), *Research Handbook of International Marine Environmental Law* (Edward Elgar, 2015) 3–30; Robin Churchill and Vaughan Lowe, *The Law of the Sea* (Manchester University Press, 3rd ed, 1999) 24–25.

Secondly, in a case where the ITLOS agrees to entertain an LBP case from any RSP, another challenge is the difficulty in establishing a causal link between the damage caused by LBP and the state(s) responsible for the pollution. LBP is multi-sectorial, since it not only involves a variety of industries, but also various polluters and states.[105] Thus, any attempt to establish a causal relationship requires a huge effort and abundant financial resources. Since scientific and technological research is also inevitably required in the process of establishing this relationship, it raises the question of whether science and technology are sufficiently advanced enough to conclusively resolve this issue. Therefore, the ITLOS would find it challenging to assess this issue based on the complexity of LBP.

4.2   Potential Contribution of the ITLOS

In the event that an RSP case, especially the one concerning LBP, reaches the ITLOS, it can contribute to the development of the LOSC by interpreting Article 207 of the LOSC in accordance with the rule of treaty interpretation provided in Article 31 of the *Vienna Convention on the Law of Treaties*. Unfortunately, the task of interpreting this provision is outside the scope of this article. Given this limitation, the reason the ITLOS should do so is highlighted in this section by examining the subsequent practice of states through their RSPs. Secondly, this will also show that common parameters existing across RSPs, which can support the interpretation of Article 207 of the LOSC if there is a case before the ITLOS. These will be discussed below.

4.2.1   Regional Cooperation Concerning LBP through RSPs

In view of the above challenges, the ITLOS could interpret Article 207 of the LOSC and benefit greatly from examining the practice of states across the RSPs. The idea that the prevention, reduction, and control of LBP under Article 207 of the LOSC can be best achieved through implementation at the regional level has been recognised both in the literature, and through the practice of states.[106] The significance of regional cooperation for the management of LBP

---

105   Yoshifumi Tanaka, "The Practice of Shared Responsibility in relation to Land-based Marine Pollution" (2016) *SHARES Research Paper Series 100* <www.sharesproject.nl> 11–15. Tanaka also notes that it will be extremely difficult for the relevant judicial institution to establish and allocate responsibility to the polluting states.

106   Phillipe Sands et al, *Principles of international environmental law* (Cambridge University Press, 2012) 372–377; Patricia Birnie, Alan E Boyle and Catherine Redgwell, *International Law and the Environment* (Oxford University Press, 3rd ed, 2009) 451–454; David Vander-Zwaag and Ann Powers, "The Protection of the Marine Environment from Land-based Pollution and Activities: Gauging the Tides of Global and Regional Governance" (2008)

has been increasingly observed over the past three decades in various international conferences and instruments, including the Montreal Guidelines,[107] Agenda 21,[108] and the 1994 *Programme of Action for the Sustainable Development of Small Island Developing States* ("Barbados Programme of Action"). The latter requires Small Island Developing States ("SIDS") to take action against LBP at a regional level.[109] For example, in the case of point-source pollution from industrial waste and sewage,[110] it suggests the development of pollution prevention programmes at a regional level, and "supporting measures to assist small island developing States in improving their capacity for the negotiation, follow-up and implementation of international conventions or arrangements' in relation to LBP."[111] This demonstrates the increased significance of regional cooperation for the management of LBP.

The focus on regional cooperation has become most apparent under the GPA. Recognising the need to further implement Agenda 21, as well as the Barbados Programme of Action, the GPA implementation "requires new approaches by, and new forms of collaboration among, Governments, organisations and institutions with responsibilities and expertise relevant to marine and coastal areas, *at all levels national, regional and global.*"[112] One chapter in the GPA is devoted to regional cooperation, containing a framework of how, and in what form, regional cooperation should be developed. It especially shows the need to adopt regional programmes of action in line with the recommended approaches, targets and methodology specified,[113] as well as the other environmental tools and considerations adopted by states in their

---

23 *International Journal of Marine and Coastal Law* 423; Yoshifumi Tanaka, "Regulation of Land-Based Marine Pollution in International Law: A Comparative Analysis Between Global and Regional Legal Frameworks " (2006) 66 *Heidelberg Journal of International Law* 535; Thomas Mensah, "The International Legal Regime for the Protection and Preservation of the Marine Environment from Land-based Sources of Pollution" in Alan E Boyle and David Freestone (eds), *International Law and Sustainable Development* (Oxford University Press, 1999) 297–324; Alan E Boyle, "Marine Pollution under the Law of the Sea Convention" (1985) 79 *American Journal of International Law* 347.

107   Montreal Guidelines, above n 102.

108   Agenda 21, above n 63 [17.3–17].

109   *Report of the Global Conference on the Sustainable Development of the Small Island Developing States*, UN DOC GA/CONF.167/9 (October 1994) Annex II, III (*"Barbados Programme of Action"*).

110   Ibid [23].

111   Ibid [24 (B), (i)–(ii)] [(C), (v)].

112   The GPA, above n 65, [15] (emphasis added).

113   Ibid [32].

respective regions.[114] In fact, regional programmes of action or action plans had been implemented by states before the adoption of the GPA (even before the *LOSC*!),[115] and seventeen of eighteen regional sea programmes currently have their own regional programme of action or action plan.[116] Some regions have already renewed, revised, or adopted a new regional programme of action or action plan.[117] To this end, it can be said that state practice has developed at the regional level regarding the prevention, reduction, and control of LBP. States have taken several actions to combat LBP through RSPs, as can be seen from the adoption of regional programmes or plans of actions as part of the implementation and fulfilment of their obligations under Article 207 of the *LOSC*. Hence, the ITLOS could potentially take advantage of this regional practice to clarify the substance of the provision, if it needs to interpret Article 207 of the *LOSC* to settle the LBP case of the RSPs.

4.2.2   Common Parameters across RSPs Concerning Monitoring and
         Assessment of LBP

As mentioned above, the regional cooperation of states through RSPs is the place to examine state practice regarding the prevention, reduction, and control of LBP at the regional level. Having preliminarily examined the RSPs, there are two common parameters that could be helpful for the ITLOS to interpret Article 207 of the *LOSC* if an LBP case is brought before it. These parameters concern the procedural aspects of Article 207 of the *LOSC*, namely, the monitoring and assessment of LBP at the regional level. The parameters identified for the monitoring and assessment of LBP are: (i) the state of the marine environment; and (ii) information about LBP. It should be noted that the subsequent practice of states through RSPs concerning the monitoring and assessment of LBP is not thoroughly examined in this article. Instead, it is a preliminary review that points out the possible common state practice and the possibility of making a further examination to interpret Article 207 of the *LOSC*. The two common parameters are discussed below.

---

114   Ibid [33]–[34].

115   For example, the Mediterranean and OSPAR regional sea programmes predates the adoption of the *LOSC*.

116   The Antarctic is a regional sea programme with no regional programme of action or action plan to deal with LBP. This may be explained by the fact that the focus of this regime is the conservation of marine living resources and the Antarctic is not the origin of land-based activities to cause pollution. Therefore, this may be outside the scope of the regional sea programme. See, <https://www.ccamlr.org/>.

117   For example, the Mediterranean region. See UNEP website <http://www.unepmap.org /index.php?module=content2&catid=001001002>.

The first is the monitoring and assessment of the state of the marine environment. The instruments of eleven of the eighteen RSPs requires the monitoring and assessment of the state of the marine environment in their conventions, protocols, and/or programme of actions.[118] However, two observations should be made at this point. Firstly, although these RSPs include this requirement in their instruments, the action taken in practice is different across the RSPs. Some of the eleven RSPs have developed a concrete monitoring and assessment programme to support the requirement. An example can be drawn from the Black Sea programme where an Advisory Group on Pollution Monitoring and Assessment has been established to perform this task.[119] The same can be seen from the Northwest Pacific programme, in which a Special Monitoring & Coastal Environmental Assessment Regional Activity Centre ("CEARAC") was established for this purpose.[120] However, such a programme cannot be seen clearly in the RSPs like the East Asian or South Asian Seas programmes.

Another observation is that the term, "state of the marine environment", is not consistently employed across these eleven RSPs. However, where the term is not used, the same kind of information is required by using other terms.[121] Examples include the monitoring and assessment of "data on the natural conditions of the Protocol Area as regards its physical, biological and chemical characteristics",[122] "information and data on the condition of the

---

118   These are the Pacific, ROPME, PERSGA, Black Sea, Caspian Sea, Wider Caribbean Sea, OSPAR, East Asian Seas, South Asian Seas, NOWPAP, and North–East Pacific programmes.

119   For more information, see, The Commission on the Protection of the Black Sea Against Pollution website <http://www.blacksea-commission.org/_bssap1996.asp#Annex I>.

120   For more information, see, Special Monitoring & Coastal Environmental Assessment Regional Activity Centre website, <http://cearac.nowpap.org/about/index.html>.

121   This term is used in the Pacific Sea and South Asian Sea programmes. For the Pacific programme, see, *Pacific Regional Environmental Programme Strategic Plan 2011–2015*, Secretariat of the Pacific Regional Environment Programme <http://www.sprep.org/attachments/000921_SPREPStrategicPlan2011_2015.pdf> EMG 4.1 ("Pacific Strategic Action Plan"); For South Asian Seas Programme, see *Action Plan for the Protection and Management of the Marine and Coastal Environmental of the South Asian Seas Region* (1995), Secretariat of the Pacific Regional Environment Programme <http://www.sacep.org/pdf/SAS%20Action%20Plan.pdf> [9.2]–[9.3] ("SAS Action Plan").

122   ROMPE programme, see *Protocol for the Protection of the Marine Environment Against Pollution from Land-based Sources*, opened for signature 21 February 1990 treaty series? (entered into force 1 February 1993), <http://ropme.org/1_KAP_LEGAL_EN.clx> art 7 ("LBP Protocol to Kuwait Convention"); An almost identical term can be seen in PERSGA programme. See *Protocol Concerning the Protection of the Environment from Land-Based*

marine environmental and coastal areas concerning its physical, biological, and chemical characteristics",[123] "the quality of the marine environment and each of its compartments, that is, water, sediments, and biota",[124] "patterns and trends in the environmental quality of the Convention area",[125] "quality of the marine and coastal environment",[126] "status of the ecosystem",[127] or "environmental quality".[128]

Another set of information requirements concern LBP itself. This differs from the information on the state of the marine environment in that it specifically refers to substances, energy, or activities that pollute the marine environment. Eight of the fourteen RSPs with binding instruments generally require the monitoring and assessment of pollution, including LBP. Examples include the requirement to cooperate directly or through relevant organisations for "monitoring programmes concerning pollution"[129] or "monitoring related to

---

Activities in the Red Sea and Gulf of Aden, opened for signature 25 September 2005 (not yet in force) <http://www.persga.org/Documents/Doc_62_20090211124355.pdf> art 12(3)(a) ("LBP Protocol to Jeddah Convention").

123   For the Black Sea programme, see, *Protocol on the Protection of the Marine Environment of the Black Sea From Land Based Sources and Activities*, opened for signature 17 April 2009 (not yet in force), <http://www.blacksea-commission.org/_convention-protocols.asp> art 11(1)(a) ("The 2009 LBP Protocol to Bucharest Convention"). An almost identical term is adopted by the Caspian Sea programme. See *Protocol for the Protection of the Caspian Sea against Pollution from Land-based Sources and Activities,* opened for signature 12 December 2012 (not yet in force) art 13(a) ("LBP Protocol to Tehran Convention").

124   OSPAR Convention, above n 49, Annex IV, art 1.

125   Cartagena Convention, above n 70, art VI(1)(a).

126   UNEP, *Plan of Action for the Protection and Sustainable Development of the Marine and Coastal Areas of the North–East Pacific* (2002), <https://wedocs.unep.org/bitstream/handle/20.500.11822/11137/nep_action_plan_en.pdf?sequence=1&isAllowed=y>,III,[15(a)] ("North–East Pacific Action Plan"); *Action Plan for the Protection and Development of the Marine and Coastal areas of the East Asian Region* (1983), <http://www.cobsea.org/documents/action_plan/ActionPlan1983.pdf> [11] ("1983 EAS Action Plan").

127   *Action Plan for the Protection and Sustainable Development of the Marine and Coastal Areas of the East Asian Region* UNEP(OCA)/EAS IG5/6 (1994) Annex IV, [7] ("1994 EAS Action Plan").

128   *Action Plan for the Protection, Management, and Development of the Marine and Coastal Environment of the Northwest Pacific Region* (1994), NOWPAPA CEARAC <http://www.nowpap.org/> [12] ("NOWPAP Action Plan").

129   Kuwait Convention, above n 81, art 10(1); Lima Convention, above n 85, art 7(1); Abidjan Convention, above n 83, art 14 (1); Jeddah Convention, above n 82, art 10 (1); Nairobi Convention, above n 71, art 14(2); Bucharest Convention, above n 66, art 15(4); Tehran Convention, above n 68, art 9; Barcelona Convention, above n 74, art 12.

all types of pollution".[130] This is also the case for the RSPs with non-binding instruments.[131]

Specifically, in terms of LBP, all nine of the RSPs with an LBP Protocol commonly require two sets of LBP information that are common across the RSPs. These are: (i) the level, nature, extents, sources, pathways, risks and effects of LBP pollution to the marine environment of the RSPs;[132] and (ii) data regarding the input of priority LBP substances or energy that cause, or are likely to cause, significant harm to the marine environment.[133] If it is not determined in the Annex or Protocol to the Convention, states will agree and make a list of the priority substances, which will be included in the Action Plan of their RSPs.

130   Kuwait Convention, above n 81, art 10(2); Abidjan Convention, above n 83, art 14(2); Jeddah Convention, above n 82, art 10(2).

131   SAS Action Plan, above n 121, [9.3]; EAS 1983 Action Plan, above n 126, [14.1–3]; 1994 EAS Action Plan, above n 127, [7], [14].

132   LBP Protocol to Jeddah Convention, above n 122, art 12(1)(a); LBP Protocol to Barcelona Convention, above n 74, art 8(a); *Protocol for the Protection of the South East Pacific Against Pollution from Land – Based Sources*, opened for signature 22 July 1983 (entered into force 23 September 1986) <http://www.cpps-int.org/index.php/principal> art 8(1) ("LBP Protocol to Lima Convention"); *Protocol on Protection of the Black Sea Marine Environment Against Pollution from Land Based Source*, opened for signature 21 April 1992, 1764 UNTS 18 (entered into force 15 January 1994) art 5 ("1992 LBP Protocol to Bucharest Convention"); *Protocol Concerning Pollution from Land-based Activities*, opened for signature 6 October 1999 (entered into force 13 August 2010) <http://cep.unep.org/cartagena-convention /lbs-protocol/protocol-concerning-pollution-from-land-based-sources-and-activities> art 6(1)(5) ("LBP Protocol to Cartagena Convention"); *Protocol for the Protection of the Marine and Coastal Environment of the West Indian Ocean from Land-based Sources and Activities*, opened for signature 31 March 2010 (not yet in force), <http://www.unep.org /nairobiconvention/protocol-protection-marine-and-coastal-environment-western -indian-ocean-land-based-sources-and> Annex III ("LBP Protocol to Nairobi Convention"). The same information is also required under the monitoring requirements for the RSPs that operate only on a conventional-basis without a Protocol. See, Helsinki Convention, above n 73, art 24(2); OSPAR Convention, above n 49, art 6 and Annex IV.

133   1992 LBP Protocol to Bucharest Convention, above n 132, art 5; 2009 LBP Protocol to Bucharest Convention, above n 113, art 11(1)(b); Kuwait Convention, above n 75, art 7(1) (b); LBP Protocol to Jeddah Convention, above n 112, art 12 (3)(b); LBP Protocol to Tehran Convention, above n 123, art 1 (1)(b); Additional Protocol to the Abidjan Convention Concerning Cooperation in the Protection and Development of Marine and Coastal Environment from Land-Based Sources and Activities in the Western, Central and Southern African Region, opened for signature 22 June 2012 (not yet in force) <http:// abidjanconvention.org/media/documents/protocols/LBSA%20Protocol-Adopted.pdf> art 14 ("LBP Protocol to Abidjan Convention").

The question arises as to how the ITLOS can benefit from these parameters. Firstly, these common parameters are not hypothetical, but they exist based on state practice to deal with marine pollution, especially LBP, at a regional level. As discussed above, states have agreed that LBP can be best tackled by regional cooperation. Against this background, it reflects how states perceive the content and the implementation of Article 207 of the LOSC in terms of what has to be monitored and assessed to protect the marine environment. Therefore, these parameters assist the ITLOS in the assessment of the suitability, severity, and seriousness of states' conduct related to LBP and can guide the ITLOS to interpret and/or assess the application of Article 207 of the LOSC as well as their RSP agreements. Secondly, these parameters help the ITLOS to assess the magnitude and severity of the environmental conditions of the RSP's marine environment and hence, enable the Tribunal to decide if provisional measures to protect the marine environment should be granted.

5   Conclusion

It can be seen from the above analysis that the potential involvement of the ITLOS in environmental disputes of the RSPs is rather limited. On its face, the ITLOS cannot participate in advisory proceedings, since none of the RSP conventions or protocols provide the basis for the Tribunal's advisory jurisdiction. However, the possible avenue may be opened through the interpretation of Article 138 of the Rules of the ITLOS. The plurality of judicial institutions results in a potentially fragmented and inconsistent interpretation of the LOSC. In addition, although it is possible that the ITLOS may entertain a contentious jurisdiction over an environmental dispute of an RSP, especially in the case of LBP, the possibility of the Tribunal exercising its jurisdiction is constrained by two essential factors.

Firstly, the interpretation of Articles 281 and 282 plays an influential role to deciding whether or not the ITLOS has jurisdiction over an environmental dispute from an RSP. Based on the RSPs' dispute settlement provisions and current jurisprudence, it is likely that the ITLOS may find its jurisdiction in most RSP environmental disputes, provided that the case is framed and presented to the Tribunal as one related to the interpretation or application of the LOSC. However, it is uncertain if disputes arising from RSPs such as ROPME Sea, PERSGA, and the West and Central African regions will be barred by the application of their dispute settlement provision, which obligates the disputing states to refer an unresolved dispute to the judicial body within those RSPs. This is due to the ambiguity over the interpretation of Articles 281 and 282 of the LOSC. The way in which these two provisions are applied requires further clarification by the judicial institution provided in Part XV, Section 2 of the *LOSC*.

The matching of the state's choice of procedure under Article 287 of the *LOSC* is another factor as to whether or not the ITLOS can entertain an environmental dispute from the an RSP. So far, 39 States have accepted the ITLOS as a forum for the settlement of disputes. Not only must the disputing states be two of these 39 States, but they must also both belong to the same RSP. This unavoidably reduces the possibility of an RSP case reaching the ITLOS. Indeed, not only does awareness need to be raised among the *LOSC* state parties, but states also need to be informed of the utilities and advantages of the ITLOS compared to other judicial forums. In time, this may raise the profile of the Tribunal and its service in the international community.

The ITLOS will face both challenges and opportunities in handling the LBP cases from the RSPs. The challenges include, inter alia, the lack of international regulations related to LBP. The *LOSC* is the only international agreement that over-archingly deals with LBP.[134] Article 207 has been criticised as too general and has not helped states to fulfil their *LOSC* obligation. In the event that an LBP case reaches the ITLOS, determining the substantive content of Article 207 of the *LOSC* will be extremely challenging due to the difficulty in establishing the causal link between the polluting states and the related damage caused by LBP. When considering the multi-sectoral nature of LBP, the multiplicity of the polluting states, and the scientific, technological and financial factors that need to be put into the equation to establish the causal link, this is arguably the biggest challenge of the Tribunal in deciding the LBP disputes of RSPs.

In terms of the potential contribution of the ITLOS, the practice of states demonstrates that they have agreed, through various conferences and instruments, that LBP can be tackled more effectively at the regional level. The preliminary review of state practice through the RSPs suggests that there are useful parameters the ITLOS could take into account if it interprets Article 207 of the *LOSC*. The state of the marine environment and information about LBP are the two parameters identified across the RSPs for monitoring and assessing LBP at the regional level.

These two sets of information are a useful baseline for the ITLOS to not only decide whether or not provisional measures should be granted to protect the marine environment, but also to inform the ITLOS if a state excessively pollutes the marine environment with LBP. Therefore, if the ITLOS has to interpret Article 207 of the *LOSC*, this provides a promising opportunity to not only clarify the ambiguity that stems from Article 207 of the *LOSC*, but

---

134   *LOSC*, above n 1, arts 207–213.

also to guide and direct states' actions toward a better implementation of this provision. If an environmental case of the RSPs reaches the ITLOS, despite all the above-mentioned difficulties, it is hoped that the Tribunal would take the opportunity to contribute to the development of international law of the sea and ensure a consistent interpretation of the *LOSC*.

The Nascent Law of Cyber Blockades and Zones

*Ana Lenard**

1   Introduction

Technology has allowed humans to conduct war and intervene in the affairs of other states in every realm possible. In addition to fostering human expansion into new realms (from land, to sea and air), technology has provided for the development of new means and methods by which warfare and intervention can be conducted. With the creation of the cyber realm, cyber warfare and intervention using cyber tactics have become possible, and indeed, commonplace. Each realm of expansion has raised difficult legal questions that states have often dealt with by relying on existing international law, with appropriate adjustments to accommodate the unique attributes of each realm. Many international lawyers have also approached the task of ascertaining the law of cyber warfare and intervention in this way, seeking appropriate analogies in existing international law.

Following this method, this article seeks to add to the scholarship on cyber warfare and intervention by considering whether the law of conventional blockades and zones can apply to the same cyber tactics, and if not, what the law of cyber blockades and zones otherwise ought to be. This is an area where there is not yet much scholarship, although international lawyers have touched on it. For example, in the Tallinn Manual 2.0 on the International Law Applicable to Cyber Operations, released on 8 February 2017, cyber blockades and zones receive a passing mention.[1]

There are two reasons why ascertaining the law of cyber blockades and zones is important. First, in the late 2000s, cyber operations appearing to be cyber blockades were conducted against Estonia and Georgia.[2] This confirms that such tactics exist and can be used against states. Secondly, it is foreseeable that tactics such as cyber blockades and zones will become more prevalent in the future as states look for low-risk, low-cost ways to conduct or support war efforts, or intervene in the affairs of other states.

---

*   LLB(Hons)/BSc. Associate at Gilbert Walker. I would like to thank Dr Caroline Foster and Jack Oliver-Hood for their support and guidance in writing this article.
1   Michael N Schmitt (ed), *Tallinn Manual 2.0 on the International Law Applicable to Cyber Warfare* (Cambridge University Press, 2017) (*"Tallinn Manual"*).
2   See Section 4.2.1 below.

This article canvasses the topic of cyber blockades and zones in three parts. Part 2 is about blockades and details what they are, their purpose, the law, and the function that blockade law serves – or the "mischief" to which it is directed. Part 3 will follow the same structure in respect of exclusion zones, with a focus on no-fly zones in particular. Part 4 involves a discussion of cyber blockades and zones, their purpose, the mischief inherent in such cyber tactics that requires regulation by law, and whether the law of blockades and zones can be the basis of the law regulating the same cyber tactics.

2   Blockades

2.1   *What is a Blockade?*
A blockade is a method of warfare involving "the blocking of the approach to the enemy coast, or a part of it, for the purpose of preventing ingress and egress of vessels or aircraft of all States".[3] Aerial blockades became possible with the expansion of warfare into air space.[4] An aerial blockade is defined as "a belligerent operation to prevent aircraft ... from entering or exiting specified airfields or coastal areas belonging to, occupied by, or under the control of the enemy."[5] A blockade might be close or distant, partial or total, porous or tight, and limited or unlimited. Traditionally, warships would organise themselves into a cordon around the enemy coastline,[6] but in modern times, distant blockades have become possible with developments in technology such as

---

3   Louise Doswald-Beck (ed), *San Remo Manual on International Law applicable to Armed Conflicts at Sea* (Cambridge University Press, 1995) (*"San Remo Manual"*) 176; Terry D Gill and Dieter Fleck (eds), *The Handbook of the International Law of Military Operations* (Oxford University Press, 2015) [20.17]; Natalie Klein, *Maritime Security and the Law of the Sea* (Oxford, 2011) 292.

4   Alison Lawlor Russell, *Cyber Blockades* (Georgetown University Press, 2014) 34. See also Michael N Schmitt, "Chapter 6: Aerial Blockades in Historical, Legal and Practical Perspective" in Michael N Schmitt, *Essays on Law and War at the Fault Lines* (Asser Press, 2012) ("Aerial Blockades") 209.

5   "Manual on International Law Applicable to Air and Missile Warfare" (Programme on Humanitarian Policy and Conflict Research at Harvard University, 2009) (*"Harvard Manual"*) r 147.

6   Horace B Robertson, "Interdiction of Iraqi Maritime Commerce in the 1990–1991 Persian Gulf Conflict" (1991) 22(3) *Ocean Development and International Law* 289, 290; DP O'Connell, *The International Law of the Sea* (Clarendon Press, 1984) 1150–1; Klein, above n 3, 292.

missiles, mines and submarines.[7] Offensive blockades focus on preventing ingress, whereas defensive blockades aim to prevent egress.[8]

There can easily be confusion between blockades and other types of operations that are similar, such as exclusion zones, sieges, sanctions and embargoes.[9] The difference between blockades and exclusion zones is canvassed below in Section 3.1. A siege is a land operation that cuts supplies off to an encircled area so as to force surrender, whereas a blockade is a less harsh and more flexible operation – it is part of the broader goal of weakening the enemy economically, and it can be expansive or narrow.[10] Sanctions and embargoes involve cutting trade with another state so as to condemn certain actions by that state and put pressure on the government to act differently. They do not involve any physical coercion or encirclement.[11]

The purpose of the two forms of modern blockade – naval and air blockades – will now be considered. Examination of these purposes is critical for understanding their relevance (or irrelevance) to the emergent legal framework applying to the same cyber tactics.

2.2   Purpose of Blockades

2.2.1   Naval Blockade

The goal of a blockade is to weaken the enemy state, denying it items and communications of value.[12] A blockade can isolate a nation[13] and "suspend the entire commerce of that place".[14] Historically, naval blockades were often used strategically in conjunction with other methods of warfare,[15] and contributed to the war effort by putting economic pressure on the enemy.[16] Economic

---

7   Klein, above n 3, 292; Robert E Morabito, "Maritime Interdiction: Evolution of a Strategy" (1991) 22 *Ocean Development and International Law* 301, 304; *San Remo Manual*, above n 3, [96].

8   Russell, above n 4, 20.

9   Ibid 36.

10   Hersch Lauterpacht (ed), *Lassa Oppenheim – International law: a treatise* (Longmans Green, 7th ed, 1952) 768.

11   Schmitt, "Aerial Blockades", above n 4, 212.

12   Russell, above n 4, 20; Maurice Parmelee, *Blockade and Sea Power: The Blockade, 1914–1919, and Its Significance for a World State* (Thomas Y Crowell, 1924) 8.

13   Parmelee, above n 12, 8.

14   James Farrant, "Modern Maritime Neutrality Law" (2014) 90 *International Law Studies* 198, 252, quoting *The Vrouw Judith* (1799) 1 C Rob 150, 151–152, per Sir William Scott.

15   Wolff Heintschel von Heinegg, "The Current State of The Law of Naval Warfare: A Fresh Look at the San Remo Manual" in Anthony M Helm (ed), *The Law of War in the 21st Century: Weaponry and the Use of Force* (Naval War College, 2006) 269, 276.

16   Russell, above n 4, 22.

pressure can be exercised in a broad or narrow fashion.[17] It may be aimed at preventing the flow of military goods or at weakening the enemy's military power through undermining the economy.[18] There is, however, a limit to economic pressure: a naval blockade must not be established if its sole purpose is to deny essentials to civilians.[19] If that requirement is discharged, a naval blockade is a perfectly legitimate military tactic.[20]

An example demonstrating the purpose of a naval blockade is the blockade of Gaza by Israel in 2007. The blockade was imposed by Israel against Gaza following Hamas's success in the Gaza elections. Hamas, a political organisation in Gaza, had regularly antagonised Israel, including by firing rockets into its territory. Israel hoped to use the blockade to force regime change.[21] The blockade continues today,[22] with Hamas remaining in power.[23] The Gaza blockade is an example of the broad purpose of weakening the enemy. Another example is the blockade of Libya established in 2011 pursuant to United Nations Security Council Resolution ("UNSCR") 1973. The resolution authorised the use of all necessary force in ensuring compliance with the arms embargo against Libya.[24] The goal was to limit the influx of military supplies that could be used by Colonel Gaddafi against Libyan rebels.[25] This example demonstrates the narrow purpose of limiting enemy military capabilities.

---

17   Ibid 19.

18   *Tallinn Manual*, above n 1, 195; Gill and Fleck, above n 3, [20.17]; Klein, above n 3, 292; "The Commander's Handbook on the Law of Naval Operations – NWP 1–14M" (Department of the Navy, 2007) ("US Commander's Handbook") [7.7.1]–[7.7.5]; Russell, above n 4, 37.

19   *San Remo Manual*, above n 3, [102].

20   Jon Van Dyke, "The Disappearing Right to Navigational Freedom in the Exclusive Economic Zone" (2005) 29 *Marine Policy* 107, 114.

21   Susan de Muth, "Israel's Own Goal: Susan De Muth Looks at the Truth behind the Israeli Media Hype Concerning the Gaza Flotilla Blockade, the Action That Saw a Turning of the Tide of World Opinion", *The Middle East* (online), 1 August 2010 <https://www.highbeam.com/doc/1G1-234998165.html>; "Emergency Appeal" (United Nations Relief and Works Agency for Palestinian Refugees, 2012).

22   Belal Aldabbour, "Gaza: '100,000 hours of isolation'", *Al Jazeera* (online), 1 February 2017 <http://www.aljazeera.com/indepth/features/2017/01/gaza-100000-hours-isolation-170131070726612.html>.

23   Ali Younes, "Fatah and Hamas to form unity government", *Al Jazeera* (online), 19 January 2017 <http://www.aljazeera.com/news/2017/01/fatah-hamas-form-unity-government-170118031339203.html>.

24   SC Res 1973, UN SCOR, 6498th mtg, UN Doc S/RES/1973 (17 March 2011).

25   Tamir Eshel, "NATO Takes Control – Coordinating Air and Naval Blockade on Libya", *Defense Update* (online), 27 March 2011 <http://defense-update.com/20110327_libya_report.html>.

2.2.2   Aerial Blockade

The purpose of aerial blockade is the same as that of naval blockade, being to "deny the enemy the use of neutral aircraft to transport personnel and goods to or from the blockaded area".[26] Aerial blockades have several additional benefits. First, they can interfere with shipping at ports of origin and destination, whereas naval blockades focus only on the blockaded territory. Secondly, aircraft are much faster than vessels and so can interfere with more ships over time. Thirdly, aircraft can coordinate with ships to enhance the effectiveness of a naval blockade. Finally, unlike naval blockades, aerial blockades can also affect internal supply and communication lines.[27] Aerial blockades are therefore a good example of how developments in technology provide states with more flexibility in conducting warfare.

When aerial blockade emerged as a military tactic, it seemed "destined to be the only effective type of blockade".[28] Subsequently, aerial blockades have not proven to be as common as naval blockades. They have also been used in a different manner, for example mostly to support naval blockades or to enforce sanctions and embargoes. Since the Second World War, the most prominent use of air power has been in relation to exclusion zones, discussed below.[29] More recently, an aerial blockade was established over Lebanon during the war with Israel in 2006 (in conjunction with a naval blockade). This was to restrict ingress and egress of aircraft carrying arms to Hezbollah. Aircraft carrying humanitarian goods and refugees were given free passage.[30]

Having determined the common purpose of aerial and naval blockade, namely blocking the movement of communications and goods, this article will now detail the modern law of blockade before turning to the historical development of that body of law. This is relevant for discussing what the law of cyber blockade ought to be, because it is necessary to ascertain whether the same mischief is inherent in both types of blockade.

2.3   *The Modern Law of Blockade*
2.3.1   Naval Blockade

The Definition of Aggression (the "Definition") adopted by the United Nations General Assembly states that "[a]ggression is the use of armed force by

---

26   "Commentary on the HPCR Manual on International Law Applicable to Air and Missile Warfare" (Programme on Humanitarian Policy and Conflict Research at Harvard University, 2010) ("Harvard Manual Commentary") 287.

27   Alexander P De Seversky and Rouben Mamoulian Collection (Library of Congress), *Victory through Air Power* (Simon and Schuster, 1942) 128–129.

28   Ibid 128.

29   Russell, above n 4, 47–48.

30   Ibid 50.

a State against the sovereignty, territorial integrity or political independence of another State".[31] Under art 3 of the Definition, a "blockade of the ports or coasts of a State by the armed forces of another State" is an act of aggression. This suggests that the international community views a blockade as a use of force prohibited by art 2(4) of the *Charter of the United Nations* (the "*Charter*"). This is supported by the fact that *Charter* art 42 lists blockade as an "action by ... sea" that may be used to "maintain or restore international peace and security" if measures not involving the use of armed force in art 41 are inadequate. The contrary view is that blockade is not a use of force because it "lacks any physical action" against a state's territory.[32] Ultimately, the weight of authority suggests that blockade is a use of force. Therefore, a blockade can only be justified if authorised by the United Nations Security Council pursuant to *Charter* art 42 or if established in self-defence pursuant to *Charter* art 51 or customary international law.[33] As such, a blockade cannot be a lawful countermeasure because a countermeasure can only be lawful if it does not breach the prohibition on the use of force in *Charter* art 2(4).[34]

Once the requirements for the use of force have been met, a blockade must also comply with the law of naval blockade as detailed in the San Remo Manual on International Law Applicable to Armed Conflicts at Sea ("San Remo Manual").[35] The genesis and authority of the San Remo Manual is discussed in Section 2.4 below. The rules are canvassed here, initially, to provide a framework for the discussion below on the purpose of the law.

First, a blockade must be declared and notified (including specification of its location, size, duration and commencement).[36] Secondly, a blockade must

---

31   *Resolution on the Definition of Aggression*, GA Res 3314 (XXIX), UN GAOR, 29th sess, 2319th
       plen mtg, UN Doc A/Res/29/3314, (14 December 1974) (*"Definition of Aggression"*) art 1.

32   Oxford Public International Law, *Max Planck Encyclopaedia of Public International Law*
       (September 2015), "Prohibition on the Use of Force" [23].

33   *Military and Paramilitary Activities in and against Nicaragua (Nicaragua v United States of
       America) (Merits)* [1984] ICJ Rep 392, [176]; *Caroline* case 29 BFSP 1137, 30 BFSP 195; Mal-
       colm N Shaw, *International Law* (Cambridge University Press, 7th ed, 2014) 820, 827; Ian
       Brownlie, *International Law and the Use of Force by States* (Clarendon Press, 1963) 279, n 2.

34   *Draft Articles on Responsibility of States for Internationally Wrongful Acts*, UN GAOR, 53rd
       sess, Supp No 10, UN Doc A/56/83 (2001) art 50.

35   *San Remo Manual*, above n 3, 196; and US Commander's Handbook, above n 18,
       [7.7.2]–[7.7.2.5].

36   *Final Protocol of the Naval Conference* opened for signature 26 February 1909, 208 Parry's
       TS 338 ("London Declaration 1909") arts 8–13, 16; *San Remo Manual*, above n 3, [93]–[94].

be effective, which is a question of fact.[37] Effectiveness is achieved when it is dangerous to attempt to enter or exit a blockaded area.[38] Thirdly, the distance of stationed forces from the coast is determined by military requirements.[39] The question of distance goes to effectiveness. While there has been debate about adequate distance to prevent egress from blockaded waters, the aim of the rule is to preserve the fundamental requirement that a blockade is effective when it actually prevents entry into and exit from blockaded waters.[40] Fourthly, neutral coasts and ports should not be blocked.[41] Fifthly, enforcement and maintenance of the blockade may be by a combination of legitimate methods of warfare so long as the effect is not inconsistent with the rules of naval warfare generally.[42] Sixthly, changes to a blockade (including cessation and re-establishment) must be notified.[43] Finally, application to vessels and aircraft must be impartial as between states.[44]

In terms of enforcement, vessels entering the blockaded zone without authorisation may suffer attack.[45] Aircraft can be used to enforce naval blockades and can prevent the entry and exit of other aircraft into the blockaded area.[46] Neutral aircraft and vessels and relief consignments for the civilian population may be granted permission to enter or exit the blockaded area.[47] However, merchant vessels of all states believed on reasonable grounds to be breaching a blockade may be captured, and if they clearly resist capture after prior warning, may be attacked.[48]

The rule that a blockade must not be established if its sole purpose is to deny essentials to civilians[49] also includes situations where the damage to

---

37   *Declaration Respecting Maritime Laws* opened for signature 30 March 1856, 115 Parry's TS 1 ("Paris Declaration 1856") r 4; London Declaration 1909, arts 2–3; *San Remo Manual*, above n 3, [95]. In the San Remo Manual, this paragraph fuses rule 4 of the Paris Declaration and art 3 of the London Declaration. The latter specifies how to determine whether or not a blockade is effective, that is, "a question of fact".

38   Gill and Fleck, above n 3, [20.17].

39   *San Remo Manual*, above n 3, [96].

40   Ibid 177.

41   Ibid [99]. This is a modernised version of art 18 of the London Declaration 1909: at 178.

42   Ibid [97].

43   Ibid [101].

44   Ibid [100]. This reflects art 5 of the London Declaration 1909: at 178.

45   Klein, above n 3, 295.

46   *San Remo Manual*, above n 3, 177–178.

47   London Declaration 1909, art 6.

48   *San Remo Manual*, above n 3, [98].

49   Ibid [102].

civilians is disproportionate relative to the anticipated military advantage.[50]
If the civilian population of a blockaded area does not have adequate
food or essentials for survival, the blockading party must provide for free
passage of essential supplies subject to the right to prescribe technical arrangements and supervise the passage.[51] This requirement comes from art
54(1) of Additional Protocol I to the Geneva Conventions of 1949 (AP I).[52]
A difficulty faced by the drafters of the Manual ("San Remo Round Table")
when including this requirement was that it is arguable that AP I renders
all blockades unlawful. The Round Table debated the question extensively,
and by majority view, decided that blockades with the sole purpose of
starving the population are unlawful, but blockades with the same effect
trigger the obligation to provide free passage.[53] Finally, passage for medical
supplies to the civilian population and wounded or sick members of the
armed forces must also be allowed subject to the right to prescribe technical arrangements.[54]

As noted above, the 2007 Gaza blockade is an example of the application
and operation of blockade law. The blockade was found by four separate inquiries to be governed by the law of naval warfare.[55] The United Nations
Secretary-General's report also found that Israel had acted in self-defence in
the context of an armed conflict.[56]

---

50   Ibid [102].

51   Ibid [103].

52   *Protocol Additional to the Geneva Conventions of 12 August 1949, and relating to the Protec-
      tion of Victims of International Armed Conflicts (Protocol I)*, opened for signature 8 June
      1977, 1125 UNTS 3 (entered into force 7 December 1978).

53   *San Remo Manual*, above n 3, 179–180. The wording of the free passage paragraph comes
      from art 70 of AP I, although the language has been simplified to make clear that there
      is an obligation on the blockading power to allow transit, which is an otherwise hotly
      debated issue under AP I.

54   *San Remo Manual*, above n 3, [104].

55   Farrant, above n 14, 251; Jacob Turkel et al., "The Public Commission to Examine the Mari-
      time Incident of 31 May 2010" (2011); "Report on the Israeli Attack on the Humanitarian
      Aid Convoy to Gaza on 31 May 2010" (Turkish National Commission of Inquiry, 2011); Geof-
      frey Palmer et al., "Report of the Secretary-General"s Panel of Inquiry on the 31 May 2010
      Flotilla Incident" (2011) ("Palmer report"); *Report of the international fact-finding mission
      to investigate violations of international law, including international humanitarian and hu-
      man rights law, resulting from the Israeli attacks on the flotilla of ships carrying humanitar-
      ian assistance*, UN GAOR, 15th sess, Agenda Item 1, UN Doc A/HRC/15/21 (27 September
      2010).

56   Palmer report, above n 55, 40–41.

2.3.2 Aerial Blockade

The law of naval blockade has been treated as extending to aerial blockades.[57] In so far as those rules are necessarily modified for the aerial sphere, state practice over time will tell precisely what the customary international law of aerial blockade is.[58] As an act of aggression, aerial blockade is subject to the same requirements discussed above for the use of force. The Programme on Humanitarian Policy and Conflict Research at Harvard University Manual on International Law Applicable to Air and Missile Warfare 2009 ("Harvard Manual") sets out the law applicable to aerial blockades (borrowing, in many respects, from the San Remo Manual). The status of the Harvard Manual is the same as that of the San Remo Manual, discussed in Section 2.4 below.

The party seeking to instigate the blockade must declare and notify the blockade[59] (including changes and cessation)[60] with the usual specifications.[61] An additional requirement is to issue a Notice to Airmen whenever feasible at the establishment of the blockade.[62] Further, access to the airspace of neutrals must not be barred,[63] plus the blockade must be effective.[64] This means that civilian aircraft believed on reasonable grounds to be breaching or attempting to breach the blockade are forced to land, inspected, and captured or diverted. Resistance to interception or an order to land gives rise to a risk of attack with prior warning.[65] Effectiveness also requires equal enforcement of the blockade against unmanned aerial vehicles.[66] The distance of forces,[67] impartial enforcement,[68] and civilian suffering requirements are all the same as for the law of naval blockade.[69] The Harvard Manual adds that aircraft in distress must be allowed to enter the blockaded area when necessary.[70] An aerial blockade may be enforced and maintained by a combination of lawful means of warfare, provided the result is not inconsistent with the law of international

---

57 See, e.g., *Harvard Manual*, above n 5, rr 150, 153, 157.
58 Schmitt, "Aerial Blockade", above n 4, 255–256.
59 *Harvard Manual*, above n 5, r 148(a).
60 Rule 149.
61 Rule 148(b).
62 Rule 148(c).
63 Rule 150.
64 Rule 151.
65 Rule 156.
66 Harvard Manual Commentary, above n 26, 287.
67 *Harvard Manual*, above n 5, r 152.
68 Rule 155.
69 Rules 157–159.
70 Rule 153(b).

armed conflict.[71] Finally, to the extent the blockade is maintained and enforced exclusively by military aircraft, the condition of effectiveness[72] requires a sufficient degree of air superiority.[73]

The history and purpose of the law of blockade will now be considered with a view to determining the "mischief" at which the law is directed. This is critical for understanding whether the law of blockade provides a sound analogy for the emergent legal framework applying to the same cyber tactics.

2.4   History and Purpose of the Law of Blockade

The law of naval blockade has its genesis in ancient times. When naval blockades emerged as a method of warfare, they were a seaward extension of land sieges, with belligerents declaring that any party attempting to trade with the enemy would be treated as such.[74] This conflicted with the freedom of the seas, itself a developing principle of international law in the 16th century.[75] Over time, the law of naval blockade developed largely in response to the need of neutral states to secure their rights in wartime.[76] For neutral states, there were two problems with how blockade was being used as a tactic by belligerents. First was the fact that belligerents were declaring that neutral states attempting to trade with the enemy would be treated as such.[77] Secondly, and relatedly, was the fact that belligerent states declared excessive blockades that they could not possibly enforce. So, neutral states would not easily be able to ascertain whether they were breaching a blockade (due to poor enforcement) and they would have excessively restricted use of the seas (unless willing to breach a blockade and suffer the consequences).[78]

Striking the right balance between neutral and belligerent rights dominated legal discourse about the emerging law of blockade through to the 18th century. Blockades that were imposed but not enforced, known as "paper blockades", were continuing to be used by the British.[79] Concerns about the balance between neutral and belligerent rights drove the codification of the law, which

---

71   Rule 153(a).

72   Rule 151.

73   Rule 154.

74   Schmitt, "Aerial Blockades", above n 4, 218–219; Russell, above n 4, 38–39.

75   Schmitt, "Aerial Blockades", above n 4, 220.

76   Parmelee, above n 12, 19; Schmitt, "Aerial Blockades", above n 4, 218–219; *Oppenheim*, above n 10, 775.

77   Schmitt, "Aerial Blockades", above n 4, 218–219; Russell, above n 4, 38–39.

78   Schmitt, "Aerial Blockades", above n 4, 220.

79   Ibid 221–222.

began in 1780 when Russia proposed a set of rules.[80] Driven by the desire to eliminate paper blockades, states decided that effectiveness should be a prerequisite for a lawful blockade. Various countries, such as Russia, Denmark, Sweden and Prussia then entered into bilateral agreements requiring breach of a blockade to be "dangerous" so as to curtail the imposition of excessive boundaries.[81]

In spite of this development, neutral states' rights to freely use the high seas continued to be violated by Britain and France who declared over-inclusive and ineffective blockades throughout the Napoleonic wars.[82] The issue was finally addressed again at the Congress of Paris in 1856 through the Declaration of Paris.[83] England, France, Russia, Turkey, Austria, Sardinia and Prussia agreed that effectiveness would be a key requirement before a blockade could be considered lawful. Eventually, 42 other nations acceded to the treaty, although not the United States.[84] By the 19th century, the rules of naval blockade had crystallised into customary international law.[85]

The 1909 London Declaration was another attempt at codification of the law by ten naval powers. The Declaration came about because an International Prize Court, which was to be an appellate court for national prize courts, was proposed at the 1907 Hague Peace Conference.[86] In order for the International Prize Court to be effective, Great Britain initiated a conference to create a code for the court to use. This code was the London Declaration.[87] The major naval powers – Britain, Russia, the United States, France, Germany, Italy, Japan, the Netherlands and Spain – signed the Declaration. However, the House of Lords in Britain never enacted legislation to support the International Prize Court, so the Declaration was never put to use.[88] The Declaration is, however, regarded as a good record of customary law at the time.[89]

---

80   Parmelee, above n 12, 19; Russell, above n 4, 37.

81   Schmitt, "Aerial Blockades", above n 4, 222.

82   Parmelee, above n 12, 20; Russell, above n 4, 37.

83   Parmelee, above n 12, 20–21.

84   Schmitt, "Aerial Blockades", above n 4, 223.

85   Parmelee, above n 12, 35; Palmer report, above n 55, 82.

86   A prize is "property captured at sea under the laws of war". Such property would have to be brought before a national prize court which would rule on its fate: Oxford Public International Law, *Max Planck Encyclopaedia of Public International Law* (December 2009), "Prize Law" [1], [8].

87   Schmitt, "Aerial Blockades", above n 4, 225.

88   Ibid 226.

89   Parmelee, above n 12, at 35; Palmer report, above n 55, 82; Oxford Public International Law, *Max Planck Encyclopaedia of Public International Law* (October 2015), "Blockade", [10] (*"Max Planck*, "Blockade"").

The customary status of the law of naval blockade is supported by the fact that states relied on it throughout the 20th century.[90] A reference to blockade also found its way into *United Nations Charter* art 42, and blockade is referred to in modern naval manuals.[91]

In 1994, 87 years after the London Declaration was drafted, naval law experts came together in order to enunciate the international law applicable to armed conflicts at sea. They wrote the San Remo Manual, which included the law of blockade and modernised the non-binding 1909 London Declaration and 1856 Paris Declaration "where appropriate".[92] The assumption at the heart of the San Remo Manual is that the London Declaration is an accurate record of customary international law.[93]

There are no comprehensive treaties dealing with the law of naval blockade.[94] The 1982 United Nations Convention on the Law of the Sea only deals with peacetime uses of the seas.[95] The 1949 Geneva Convention for the Amelioration of the Condition of Wounded, Sick and Shipwrecked Members of Armed Forces at Sea, which governs naval warfare in the modern day,[96] does not touch on the law of naval blockade.[97] There has been considerable state practice in the area of naval warfare over time, with the result that "demands on a new rule of custom may be considerably higher".[98] Additionally, once established, it will be difficult to negate custom because "it is not to be expected that [state] practice ... should have been perfect".[99] Inconsistency might be treated as a breach of the rule rather than abandonment of it.[100] In saying that, the law of naval blockade has, over time, adapted to changing technology, state priorities and international legal standards.[101] In recent times, the customary

---

90   *Max Planck*, "Blockade", above n 89, [15]–[22].

91   Ibid [23].

92   *San Remo Manual*, above n 3, 176.

93   Ian Kennedy, "Practice makes custom: a closer look at the traditional law of naval blockade" (2012) 70 *University of Toronto Faculty of Law Review* 10, 18.

94   J Ashley Roach, "The Law of Naval Warfare at the turn of two centuries" (2000) 94 *American Journal of International Law* 64 ("The Law of Naval Warfare at the turn of two centuries"), 65.

95   Opened for signature 10 December 1982, 1833 UNTS 3 (entered into force 16 November 1994).

96   Opened for signature 12 August 1949, 75 UNTS 85 (entered into force 21 October 1950).

97   Roach, "The Law of Naval Warfare at the turn of two centuries", above n 94, 65.

98   Jan Klabbers, *International Law* (Cambridge University Press, 2013) 27.

99   *Nicaragua*, above n 33, [186].

100   Klabbers, above n 98, 32.

101   Russell, above n 4, 39; Schmitt, "Aerial Blockades", above n 4, 236.

nature of the law of naval blockade has been referred to in four reports on the 2007 Gaza blockade (discussed above).[102]

While it is generally accepted that the San Remo Manual encapsulates the customary law of blockade, a minority of the San Remo Round Table thought that the traditional rules were in desuetude[103] and that state practice had not aligned with those rules for nearly 100 years.[104] The London Declaration has been referred to as having a legacy of "neglect and rejection", and as being the "over-ripe product of 'parties' calculations of moral advantage and material self-interest".[105] It has also been said that the Declaration went further than stating customary international law at the time and sought to define uniform rules that had previously been used in divergent ways. Some contemporary prize tribunals described the Declaration as a "sweeping change" of international law and so they did not rely on it heavily as an accurate record of the law.[106] In addition, certain post-Second World War legal academics variously described the law as "confused, irrelevant, and non-existent".[107] These views, however, do not come through in the San Remo Manual as it was the result of a majoritarian process. But the provisions have, nonetheless, been adopted in military manuals,[108] thus establishing *opinio juris*.[109] In addition, the fact that all four Gaza blockade reports rely on the law of blockade is telling.[110]

In conclusion, whilst there is some criticism of the customary basis of the law of naval blockade, generally speaking the San Remo Manual is regarded as good authority.[111] It has been referred to as the "most comprehensive statement

---

102   See above n 55.

103   *San Remo Manual*, above n 3, 176; von Heinegg, above n 15, 278; *Max Planck*, "Blockade", above n 89, [23].

104   Kennedy, above n 93, 13.

105   Ibid 19, quoting Geoffrey Best, *Humanity in Warfare: The Modern History of International Laws in Armed Conflict* (Weidenfeld and Nicolson, 1980) 247.

106   Ibid 19.

107   Ibid 21.

108   *Max Planck*, "Blockade", above n 89, [23]; *San Remo Manual*, above n 3, 176. This includes manuals from the United States (US Commander's Handbook, above n 18, [7.7]), Germany ("Humanitarian Law in Armed Conflicts Manual" (Federal Ministry of Defence, 1992) [1051]) and Britain ("The Joint Service Manual of the Law of Armed Conflict – JSP 383" (Joint Doctrine and Concepts Centre, 2004) [12.56]).

109   *North Sea Continental Shelf* (*Germany v Denmark*) [1969] ICJ Rep 3, [77].

110   Farrant, above n 14, 269.

111   Jeremy Rabkin and Ariel Rabkin, "Navigating Conflicts in Cyberspace: Legal Lessons from the History of War at Sea" (2013) 14(1) *Chicago Journal of International Law* 197, 208.

on [the] customary law" of naval warfare.[112] As noted above, the law of naval blockade has been treated as extending to aerial blockades by the authors of the Harvard Manual.[113] Any modification of those rules encapsulated in the Manual will be accepted, or not, over time through state practice.[114]

2.5   Summary of the Law of Blockade

The law of blockade emerged to resolve the tension between the rights of belligerent and neutral states to the seas. That tension gives rise to a series of requirements that must be met in order for a blockade to be lawful, including effectiveness and notification. Other requirements for a lawful blockade reflect modern humanitarian law. The law of aerial blockade is, at its core, the same as naval blockade law but is modified to suit the unique attributes of the aerial sphere.

3   Zones

3.1   What is a Zone?

Amongst various other types of zones,[115] warring parties can create exclusion zones, which are defined as:[116]

> ... a three dimensional space beyond the territorial sovereignty of any State in which a Belligerent Party claims to be relieved from certain provisions of the law of international armed conflict, or where that Belligerent Party purports to be entitled to restrict the freedom of aviation (or navigation) of other States.

If a person or object enters a zone, they can be considered a lawful target, however, a zone can never lawfully be "free fire".[117]

Like with blockades, there are both naval and aerial exclusion zones. A naval exclusion zone is an area where a belligerent state exercises control over parts

---

See also, for example, Gill and Fleck, above n 3, [20.01], [20.06], [20.07], [20.17] and Klein, above n 3, 285, 292, who cite the San Remo Manual.

112   Rabkin and Rabkin, above n 111, 208.

113   See, e.g., *Harvard Manual*, above n 5, rr 150, 153, 157.

114   Schmitt, "Aerial Blockade", above n 4, 255–256.

115   Gill and Fleck, above n 3, [20.18]; *Tallinn Manual*, above n 1, 507.

116   Harvard Manual Commentary, above n 26, 235.

117   *Harvard Manual*, above n 5, r 105(b).

of the sea and excludes shipping.[118] The focus in this article is on the most common type of aerial exclusion zone, the no-fly zone ("NFZ"). A NFZ is "a three dimensional airspace by which the Belligerent Party restricts or prohibits aviation in its own or in enemy national territory".[119] In practical terms, a NFZ is a "de facto aerial occupation of sovereign air space in which ... only aircraft of the enforcement forces may fly".[120]

It is important for legal purposes to differentiate between blockades and zones – the two are often conflated.[121] Zones can be distinguished from blockades because their purpose is not to interfere with enemy exports, and their focus is on the internal area of the zone rather than the boundary.[122] Contrastingly, the focus of blockades is on the horizontal line that marks the limits of the blockaded area.[123] In addition, the prevention of enemy exports can only lawfully be carried out by a blockade.[124] Clear strategic articulation is important by parties conducting blockades or zones so that the applicable law can be ascertained.[125]

The purpose of zones will now be considered. Examination of these purposes is critical for understanding their relevance (or irrelevance) to the emergent legal framework applying to the same cyber tactics.

3.2   *Purpose of Zones*

Zones are aimed at facilitating the military goals of the establishing party. However, determining the lawful aims of zones can be difficult because of variable state practice.[126] For example, zones have been implemented to: defend high-value targets (such as in the 2003 Iraq War); delineate areas of hostility; and also for safety, search, capture and diversion purposes.[127] Some have suggested that naval zones started being used by states looking to avoid

---

118   *San Remo Manual*, above n 3, 270.

119   Harvard Manual Commentary, above n 26, 235.

120   Michael N Schmitt, "Clipped Wings: Effective and Legal No-fly Zone Rules of Engagement" (1997–1998) 20 *Loyola of Los Angeles International and Comparative Law Review* 727, 729.

121   Russell, above n 4, 36.

122   Gill and Fleck, above n 3, [20.18].

123   Harvard Manual Commentary, above n 26, 236.

124   Ibid 236.

125   Jeremiah Gertler et al., *No-Fly Zones: Strategic, Operation, and Legal Considerations for Congress* (CRS Report for Congress, 2013) 3.

126   Gill and Fleck, above n 3, [20.18].

127   Ibid.

the more tedious law of naval blockade.[128] However, as discussed above, and as noted by the San Remo Round Table, zones have different objectives from blockades.[129]

The most common purpose of zones is to protect neutral states from belligerent activity or to indicate an area where shipping or aviation may be at risk.[130] In respect of NFZs, humanitarian objectives have been central to those NFZs imposed by the United Nations Security Council. NFZs have thus been used as a tool to protect people where their own state is attempting to misuse air forces against them, in essence enforcing the "minimum requirements of humanity".[131] NFZs are sometimes used to control air space to achieve a political objective.[132]

Four recent NFZs exemplify use of the tactic for humanitarian purposes. The first two, Operation Southern Watch (1992–2003) and Operation Northern Watch (1997–2003), were implemented in Iraq.[133] The goal of both NFZs was to prevent the Iraqi government wielding airpower against civilians, as was occurring at the time. UNSCR 688 demanded Iraq immediately end its campaign against its civilians, and authorised the Secretary-General to engage in humanitarian efforts. The resolution was understood as authorisation for the establishment of a NFZ.[134] There was international support for the NFZs, which were the first since the end of the Cold War. A key feature of the NFZs was concurrent implementation with naval interdiction and economic sanctions.[135] The third NFZ was Operation Deny Flight established over Bosnia and Herzegovina between 1993 and 1995. Again, the aim was to protect civilians by preventing the use of air space for warfare. The NFZ evolved to support United Nations troops on the ground. It was a successful operation because air dominance paved the way for the North Atlantic Treaty Organisation's ("NATO") subsequent bombing campaign. That campaign effectively brought about the end of the war.[136] The final NFZ exemplifying humanitarian purposes was the zone established over Libya in 2011 in the wake of the Arab Spring. The aim of

---

128   Farrant, above n 14, 273.
129   Ibid.
130   Klein, above n 3, 58; Harvard Manual Commentary, above n 26, 235.
131   Stefan A Kaiser, "No-Fly Zones Established by the United Nations Security Council" (2011) 60 *Abhandlungen* 402, 411.
132   Schmitt, "Clipped Wings", above n 120, 742; Luisa Vierucci, "The No-Fly Zone over Libya: Enforcement Issues" (2011) 21 *Italian Yearbook of International Law* 21, 29, 35, 37.
133   Russell, above n 4, 48.
134   Ibid.
135   Ibid 49.
136   Ibid 50.

the NFZ was to protect civilians from Colonel Gaddafi's use of airpower against them. The zone was instigated by UNSCR 1973, which banned all flights except for those providing humanitarian relief.[137] The resolution authorised "all necessary means" to protect civilians and enforce the NFZ, as well as establishing an arms embargo. In furthering the goal of the resolution, NATO targeted ground forces and air defense systems. The NFZ was also used in conjunction with a naval blockade thus evidencing the broader strategic role of such tactics.[138]

Having determined the common purpose of zones, which is to protect states or indicate where aviation or shipping is at risk, this article will now detail the modern law of zones before turning to the historical development of that body of law. This is relevant for discussing what the law of cyber zones ought to be, because it is necessary to ascertain whether the same mischief is inherent in both types of zones.

3.3   *The Modern Law of Zones*

Whether a zone is a use of force is canvassed below in Section 3.4 as it relates to the history of the law of zones. Unlike blockades, there are no clear indications in the *Charter of the United Nations* or the Definition of Aggression that zones are a use of force. However, the likely view is that they are because states often cite self-defence as the basis for their establishment.[139]

3.3.1   Naval Zones

The current law of naval zones has been driven by state practice since the World Wars and so finds its source in customary international law.[140] Provisions on the establishment of zones have been included in military manuals since the 1990s as a legitimate method of warfare.[141] Some participants in the San Remo Round Table thought that zones were illegal and should not be covered in the Manual, but the majority viewed zones as a reality for which guidelines would be desirable.[142] The law as detailed in the San Remo Manual follows.

First, the same body of law applies inside and outside the zone.[143] Secondly, the extent, location and duration of the zone must not exceed what is

---

137   SC Res 1973, UN SCOR, 6498th mtg, UN Doc S/RES/1973 (17 March 2011).

138   Russell, above n 4, 51.

139   Oxford Public International Law, *Max Planck Encyclopaedia of Public International Law* (October 2015), "War Zones" [34].

140   Farrant, above n 14, 273; *San Remo Manual*, above n 3, 181.

141   Klein, above n 3, 58; Harvard Manual Commentary, above n 26, 235.

142   *San Remo Manual*, above n 2, 181.

143   Ibid [106].

strictly required by military necessity and the principles of proportionality.[144] Thirdly, due regard must be given to neutral states' rights to legitimate uses of the seas.[145] Fourthly, safe passage through the zone for neutral vessels and aircraft must be provided in certain circumstances (where the zone impedes free and safe access to ports and where normal navigation routes are affected) and notification of the details of any safe passage is required.[146] Fifthly, compliance with the measures taken by one belligerent in the zone shall not be construed as an act harmful to the opposing belligerent.[147] Sixthly, nothing in the San Remo Manual derogates from the customary belligerent right to control neutral vessels and aircraft in the immediate vicinity of naval operations.[148] Finally, a belligerent's duties under international humanitarian law continue in spite of the establishment of a zone that might adversely affect legitimate uses of defined areas of the sea.[149] This rule is targeted at the idea that a zone might be "free-fire" and create rights to attack, which was rejected by the San Remo Round Table. This is distinct from the likelihood that parties might do certain things within a zone. A zone might be established as a defence mechanism, in which case it would be assumed that vessels and aircraft entering the zone are hostile.[150]

3.3.2 Aerial Zones

The Harvard Manual details the rules for aerial exclusion zones and NFZs. The rules are broadly the same as those in the San Remo Manual applicable to naval zones. First, obligations under the law of armed conflict continue in spite of the establishment of exclusion or no-fly zones, and "free-fire" zones are prohibited.[151] Secondly, nothing in the Harvard Manual derogates from a belligerent's right to control civil aviation in the immediate vicinity of hostilities or to take appropriate measures of protection in the form of, for example, establishing warning zones.[152] Thirdly, if a belligerent establishes an exclusion zone in international airspace:[153]

---

144   Ibid.
145   Ibid.
146   Ibid.
147   Ibid [107].
148   Ibid [108].
149   Ibid [105].
150   Ibid 181.
151   *Harvard Manual*, above n 5, r 105.
152   Rule 106.
153   Rule 107.

- the same rules of the law of international armed conflict will apply both inside and outside the zone;
- the extent, location, duration of the zone and measures imposed must not exceed what is reasonably required by military necessity;
- there must be notification to all concerned of the commencement, duration, location and extent of the zone and any restrictions;
- the zone must neither encompass nor completely bar access to the airspace of neutrals; and
- due regard must be given to the lawful use by neutrals of their Exclusive Economic Zones and continental shelf.

The rules are slightly different for NFZs. First, a belligerent party may establish and enforce a NFZ in its own or in enemy national airspace.[154] Secondly, the commencement, duration, location and extent of the NFZ must be appropriately notified to all concerned.[155] Finally, subject to the rules set out in earlier parts of the Harvard Manual on attacks and precautions, aircraft entering a NFZ without specific permission are liable to be attacked.[156] Unlike exclusion zones and blockades, NFZs pertain only to airspace and aircraft.[157]

The history and purpose of the law of zones will now be considered with a view to determining the "mischief" at which the law is directed. This is critical for understanding whether the law of zones provides a sound analogy for the emergent legal framework that applies to the same cyber tactics.

3.4   *History and Purpose of the Law of Zones*

Exclusion zones in the context of war, and NFZs in particular, are a military tactic that has only recently emerged. Initially, the establishment of NFZs was on spurious legal grounds. For example, Operations Northern and Southern Watch over Iraq were justified on the basis of a UNSC resolution,[158] which did not refer to the possibility of the establishment of a NFZ (although a previous resolution which authorised operations in the Gulf War did authorise military action).[159] The states involved invoked collective self-defence, with the United Kingdom additionally relying on the doctrine of humanitarian intervention.[160]

---

154   Rule 108.

155   Rule 109.

156   Rule 110.

157   Harvard Manual Commentary, above n 26, 235.

158   SC Res 688, UN SCOR, 2982nd mtg, UN Doc S/RES/688 (5 April 1991).

159   SC Res 678, UN SCOR, 2963rd mtg, UN Doc S/RES/678 (29 November 1990).

160   Vierucci, above n 132, 44; Harvard Manual Commentary, above n 26, 236.

Subsequently, the more recent NFZ over Libya in 2011 was explicitly established in UNSCR 1973.[161]

NFZs have only ever been lawfully established pursuant to UNSC resolutions.[162] This suggests that states might view the establishment of a NFZ as a breach of the prohibition on the use of force in *United Nations Charter* art 2(4). At least one prominent scholar believes that NFZs are a use of force against the territorial integrity of a state for the purposes of military action.[163]

Well aside from establishment, it is uncontroversial that a NFZ would be implemented using force.[164] Thus any enforcement action relating to a NFZ would breach *Charter* art 2(4) (unless authorised or in self-defence).[165]

In either case, given the historical grounding of NFZs in Security Council authorisation, NFZs likely must continue to be authorised by the Security Council in order to withstand international scrutiny.[166] For these reasons, some scholars suggest that in circumstances where a NFZ is imposed without authorisation and where there has been no armed attack by the state on which the NFZ is imposed, the NFZ could be considered an armed attack.[167]

The history of, and need for authorisation of, NFZs hints at the mischief inherent in them that calls for regulation by law. The mischief is similar to the concerns that the law of blockade is designed to address. The core concern is humanitarian, with a focus on making sure that the law of armed conflict cannot be circumnavigated (culminating in a prohibition on free-fire zones and the need for notification).[168] The second concern of the law of zones relates to the rights of neutral users of airspace (including, in particular, neutral trade).[169]

3.5   *Summary of the Law of Zones*

Like blockade law, zone law addresses humanitarian concerns and the need to balance neutral and belligerent states' rights through a set of detailed and prescriptive rules. Zone law requires notification and respect for neutrality, and prohibits a free-fire approach. The mischief at which zone law is directed is

---

161   SC Res 1973, UN SCOR, 6498th mtg, UN Doc S/RES/1973 (17 March 2011).
162   Schmitt, "Clipped Wings", above n 120, 739.
163   Ibid; *Definition of Aggression*, above n 31.
164   Vierucci, above n 132, 44; Harvard Manual Commentary, above n 26, 236.
165   Michael N Schmitt, "Wings over Libya: The No-Fly Zone in Legal Perspective" (2011) 46 *Yale Journal of International Law Online* 45, 47.
166   Schmitt, "Clipped Wings", above n 132, 739.
167   Gertler et al., above n 125, 5; Schmitt, "Clipped Wings", above n 120, 743–744.
168   Harvard Manual Commentary, above n 26, 237.
169   Ibid 240–241.

therefore similar to the mischief that blockade law is concerned with. However, the nature and purposes of the two tactics are distinct.

4   Cyber Blockades and Zones

Having considered the nature of blockades and zones and the content and purpose of the law regulating them, the focus of this section is to consider whether modern blockade and zone law can extend to the same cyber tactics. The assessment involves four steps.

First, the groundwork for a discussion of the law is laid: definitions are provided, the features of cyberspace are compared with the physical realm and the operational aspects of cyber tactics amounting to a cyber blockade or zone are detailed. This is with a view to highlighting potential legal challenges in using the current law as a basis for the law of cyber blockades and zones. Secondly, consideration is given to whether the purposes of naval, aerial and cyber blockades and zones align. Thirdly, the mischief of such cyber tactics is considered to see whether it is the same mischief that is at the heart of blockade and zone law. Finally, the article details what the law of cyber blockades and zones ought to be.

The discussion on the law takes as its starting point the rules enunciated in the Tallinn Manual 2.0 on the International Law Applicable to Cyber Warfare ("Tallinn Manual").[170] The Tallinn Manual is a non-binding document aimed at examining how international law applies to cyber operations.[171] It was originally created in 2013 by an independent group of experts (the "Experts") on the instigation of the NATO Cooperative Cyber Defence Centre of Excellence. The 2.0 version was released on 8 February 2017.[172]

4.1   *What are Cyber Blockades and Zones?*
This section covers definitions relevant for a discussion on cyberspace and cyber warfare, compares attributes of cyberspace to those of the physical realm, and details how a cyber blockade or zone is conducted.

---

170   *Tallinn Manual,* above n 1.
171   Ibid 1.
172   The group was led by Professor Michael N Schmitt of the United States Naval War College and University of Exeter. Included in the group were pre-eminent experts such as Colonel (retired, United States Air Force) Gary D Brown, Marine Corps University; Professor Terry D Gill, University of Amsterdam and Netherlands Defence Academy; Professor Wolff Heintschel von Heinegg, Europa-Universität Viadrina; Professor Eric Talbot Jensen, Brigham Young University Law School and Professor Kriangsak Kittichaisaree, International Law Commission: *Tallinn Manual,* above n 1, xii–xiii.

4.1.1 Definitions

In the Tallinn Manual, cyberspace is defined as "[t]he environment formed by physical and non-physical components to store, modify, and exchange data using computer networks".[173] Cyber warfare is defined as "warfare conducted in cyberspace through cyber means and methods".[174] "Means" include cyber weapons and associated systems,[175] whilst "methods" are the cyber tactics, techniques, and procedures used to conduct hostilities.[176] Cyber operation refers to "[t]he employment of cyber capabilities to achieve objectives in or through cyberspace".[177] Cyber attack is a more specific term defined in the Tallinn Manual as a "cyber operation, whether offensive or defensive, that is reasonably expected to cause injury or death to persons or damage or destruction to objects".[178] However, cyber attack can also be defined more broadly, as has been done by NATO, as an "[a]ction taken to disrupt, deny, degrade or destroy information resident in a computer and/or computer network, or the computer and/or computer network itself".[179] Well aside from the legal challenges posed by expansion into a new realm like cyberspace, definitional difficulties have also translated into lack of clarity in scholarship in this area.[180] The different ways in which a cyber attack can be defined is a good example of how legal analyses relying on a use of force paradigm might be premature.

4.1.2 Features of Cyberspace

Cyberspace has physical and virtual elements.[181] It can be broken down into a five-layer schema: people, cyber identities (email, social media accounts, credentials), cyber objects (the logical layer: software and its settings, operating system), objects (the physical layer: hardware, routers, switches) and

---

173 Ibid 564.
174 Nils Melzer, "Cyberwarfare and International Law" (United Nations Institute for Disarmament Research, 2011) 4.
175 *Tallinn Manual*, above n 1, r 103.
176 Rule 103.
177 Ibid 564.
178 Rule 92.
179 "Glossary of Terms and Definitions – AAP-06" (NATO, 2013). The following countries canvassed in the NATO glossary define it in the latter way: Austria, Canada, Germany, Lithuania, New Zealand, the United States, Russia, Switzerland, Romania, Nigeria and the United Kingdom.
180 Gill and Fleck, above n 3, 457–458.
181 "Cyberspace Operations Concept Capability Plan 2016–2028" (The United States Army, 2010) 9.

Features	Cyberspace	Land	Sea	Air
Time	Compressed.[a]	Expanded.	Expanded.	Compressed.
Space	Compressed.[b] Self-contained, but traverses other domains.[c] Malleable boundaries.[d] Holding territory is not required.	Expansive, finite, self-contained. Fixed boundaries. Holding territory is required.	Expansive, finite, self-contained. Fixed boundaries. Holding territory may be required.	Expansive, finite, self-contained. Boundaries extend into space. Holding territory is not required.[e]
Accessibility	A function of availability of cyber capabilities, but otherwise generally high.[f]	A function of distance.	A function of availability of vessels.	A function of availability of aircraft.
Cost	Low – but can be significant in other areas (reconnaissance, planning, development, expertise).[g]	High.	Medium to high.	High.
Weapons	Near complete overlap between military and civilian weapons.[h]	Very little overlap between military and civilian weapons.	Some overlap between military and civilian weapons.	Some overlap between military and civilian weapons.
Attacks	Origin can be camouflaged (electrical or other faults can be blamed).	Attack is obvious.	Attack is obvious.	Attack is usually obvious.
Actors	State and non-state. High potential for anonymity.[i] Might have no mens rea or knowledge.[j]	State and non-state. Anonymity is difficult to achieve. Actors likely to have mens rea.	Mostly state actors. Anonymity is difficult to achieve. Actors likely to have mens rea.	Mostly state actors.[k] Anonymity is difficult to achieve. Actors likely to have mens rea.
Risk to person	Low for attackers, high for victims.	High for attackers and victims.	High for attackers and victims.	High for attackers and victims.

Features	Cyberspace	Land	Sea	Air
Advantage holder	States with cyber capabilities.	States with geographical advantages.	States with naval forces and coasts.	States with air assets.
Disadvantage holder	States with high reliance on cyberspace but poor defence systems.	States with poor defence systems.	States with high reliance on the sea but poor defence systems.	States with poor defence systems.
Determinants of success	Innovation and investment.[l]	Military resources.	Naval resources.	Aerial resources.
Effect on other domains	Can enhance and diminish actions in other domains depending on whether dominance is maintained.[m]	Dominance is often determinative.	Can enhance and diminish actions in other domains depending on whether dominance is maintained.	Can enhance and diminish actions in other domains depending on whether dominance is maintained.
Importance for communications	High.	Medium.	Medium.	Medium.

a   Russell, above n 4, 12.
b   Ibid.
c   Ibid 13.
d   Ibid.
e   Rabkin and Rabkin, above n 111, 205.
f   Russell, above n 4, 13; Melzer, above n 174, 5.
g   Russell, above n 4, 13.
h   Rabkin and Rabkin, above n 111, 254.
i   Russell, above n 4, 13; Melzer, above n 174, 5.
j   That is to say, computers can be used to perpetrate attacks without the knowledge of their users and so are "innocent".
k   Rabkin and Rabkin, above n 111, 197.
l   Russell, above n 4, 13.
m   Ibid 12.

locations (the geographical layer).[182] Cyber operations are directed at the virtual layers (cyber identities and objects) of cyberspace and can be generated through malware, viruses and direct access.[183] The various layers of cyberspace mean that there are many different entry points for potential cyber attacks by belligerent parties.

As a domain grounded in the physical realm, cyberspace is not completely distinct from the physical world. However, cyberspace has unique attributes that might necessitate adjustments to the law as it currently is.[184] It is helpful to understand the similarities and differences between operations in cyberspace and in other realms (see table on page 116–117):

The table illustrates that while there are some substantial similarities between cyberspace and other realms, cyberspace has some unique features capable of altering the traditional balance of power between states, and between states and non-state actors.[185] Non-state actors take on a more prominent role because time and space compression allows them to generate physical effects in other parts of the world with relative anonymity. Anonymity, time-space compression, and a lack of physical risk to the person create a unique incentive plane for cyber warriors to propagate attacks. Usually, the mental and physical cost of going to war is much higher. These features have led to scholars warning of the potentially catastrophic consequences of cyber operations. Anonymity also makes it easier for states to breach the principle of non-intervention through coercive cyber operations.[186]

At the same time, cyberspace is an equaliser between states. Historically, large naval forces were a prerequisite to being a world power. Now, the same might be said of states with the best cyber capabilities.[187] Investment in cyber operations might allow states to become formidable geopolitical actors in spite of having minimal physical military assets. The same is true for states that are geographically disadvantaged. A good example is Israel's role in influencing the conclusion of a framework agreement requiring Iran to redesign and reduce its nuclear facilities. Alongside the United States, Israel is widely suspected to have been involved in the Stuxnet operation from 2008 that caused physical

---

182   David Raymond et al., "Key Terrain in Cyberspace: Seeking the High Ground" in P Brangetto et al. (eds), *6th CCDCOE Proceedings* (NATO CCD COE, 2014) 287, 292.

183   *Tallinn Manual*, above n 1, 564.

184   Melzer, above n 174, 5; Russell, above n 4, 13.

185   Ibid 64.

186   Russell Buchan, "Cyber Attacks: Unlawful Uses of Force or Prohibited Interventions?" (2012) 17 *Journal of Conflict and Security Law* 211.

187   Russell, above n 4, 37.

damage to Iran's nuclear enrichment facility, Natanz. The operation was aimed at buying time for negotiations with Iran by stalling uranium enrichment.[188] Thus, amidst difficult geographical circumstances (a small land area and constant conflict in the region), Israel was able to have a strong hand in influencing outcomes of international significance through cyber attacks.

Equally, already powerful states are empowered through investment in cyber capabilities and can intervene in the affairs of other states in circumstances where the consequences of doing so are unclear. For example, Russia recently interfered in the United States election held on 8 November 2016 through the use of cyber operations.[189] Russia's actions are widely believed to have helped Donald Trump be elected President in spite of losing the popular vote to his opponent Secretary Hillary Clinton by over 2.8 million votes.[190]

The key difference between cyberspace and the physical realm relates to the fact that cyberspace has several virtual and physical layers. This gives rise to an ability to conduct cyber blockades and zones using different methods, and those varying methods have an impact on the extent to which the rights of neutral states are affected. For example, if a cyber blockade on communications is conducted in the physical realm by damaging cyber infrastructure, this might have an impact on neutral states relying on that infrastructure. If using cyber attacks in the virtual sphere, however, neutral states' rights would not be diminished if the attacks were precise in targeting the blockaded state only.

In summary, military and socioeconomic expansion into cyberspace creates new opportunities and vulnerabilities. The fact that there are some differences between the realms is not fatal to the application of blockade and zone law to cyberspace. However, whilst the core aspects of and rationale for blockade and zone law could still apply, it is likely that some adjustments will be necessary for the law to be an effective regulator of the same tactics in cyberspace. In this regard, the position is no different from how the law has developed with previous realm expansions (for example, with the expansion of blockades into airspace). The starting point should therefore be the current law, with necessary adjustments to accommodate the unique features of cyberspace.

---

188 David E Sanger, "Obama Order Sped Up Wave of Cyberattacks Against Iran", *The New York Times* (online), 1 June 2012 <http://www.nytimes.com/2012/06/01/world/middleeast/obama-ordered-wave-of-cyberattacks-against-iran.html>.

189 "Assessing Russian Activities and Intentions in Recent US Elections" (Intelligence Community Assessment, 2017).

190 David Wasserman, "2016 Popular Vote Tracker" *The Cook Political Report* (online), 2 January 2017 <http://cookpolitical.com/story/10174>.

4.1.3   Operational Aspects of Cyber Blockades and Zones

4.1.3.1   *What is a Cyber Blockade?*

A cyber blockade is a "curtain" in cyberspace blocking communications to and from an enemy state.[191] A cyber blockade can be conducted through strong distributed denial-of-service ("DDoS") attacks.[192] Using innocent computers, DDoS attacks spread malicious codes that ultimately overwhelm systems, using up their bandwidth, and causing them to crash.[193] Often DDoS attacks are used against web and mail servers, and other similar systems. Beyond public-facing systems, DDoS attacks can target access control and transportation systems in order to stop them from working. Attacks aimed at blocking communications can also be carried out through electromagnetic manipulation (electromagnetic pulse weapons and jamming devices)[194] or physical alteration of infrastructure.[195] Both types of actions can be executed with relative ease to block communications.[196] Information and communications networks are vital for states' economies and security. Interfering with such networks through cyber attacks could have a very negative impact on a state. The effects of interfering with the operation of information and communication networks are similar to that of a naval or aerial blockade.[197]

4.1.3.2   *What is a Cyber Zone?*

A cyber zone is difficult to define and, if possible, technically challenging.[198] The Tallinn Experts provide an example of what a cyber zone might look like, indicating that it would be technically possible. The example the Experts provide is that of a zone that could be set up around a sensitive military network. If an intruder hacks into the network, a clear warning could be provided that there might be an automatic "hack-back" if the intruder does not exit the zone.[199] A suggested definition, following the Harvard Manual, is a space beyond the territorial sovereignty of a state in which a state claims to be relieved from certain provisions of the law of armed conflict or purports to be entitled to restrict the freedom of the use of cyberspace of other states.[200]

---

191   *Tallinn Manual*, above n 1, 505–506.
192   Cassandra M Kirsch, "Science Fiction No More: Cyber Warfare and the United States" (2011–12) 40 *Denver Journal of International Law and Policy* 620, 627.
193   Russell, above n 4, 18.
194   Ibid 17.
195   Ibid 16.
196   Ibid 15.
197   Ibid 35.
198   *Tallinn Manual*, above n 1, 508.
199   Ibid.
200   Harvard Manual Commentary, above n 26, 235.

4.2   Purpose of Cyber Blockades and Zones

4.2.1   Cyber Blockade

A cyber blockade might be used to block communications to and from the enemy state[201] with a view to doing one of four things: negatively affecting the enemy's balance of trade; isolating the enemy; causing discomfort and suffering to put pressure on the government to capitulate to demands; or generally weakening the enemy.[202] The cyber attacks against Estonia in 2007 and Georgia in 2008 are cited as examples of cyber blockades.[203] They have been described as "politics by other means" and a mechanism by which critics can be silenced.[204] Those "blockades" will be discussed in more detail below, with a view to clearly understanding their purposes and highlighting potential legal challenges.

4.2.1.1   Estonia

Estonia experienced wide-scale DDoS attacks in April and May of 2007. The attacks targeted the government, and key services and industries. Daily business effectively came to a halt, and a significant portion of the country could not send or receive communications beyond Estonia's borders. This undermined Estonia's ability to deal with internal or external threats to security.[205]

The blockade was thought to have occurred due to the decision by the Estonian Parliament to move a Bronze Soldier monument and the remains of soldiers beneath it from central Tallinn to a military cemetery.[206] The monument commemorated Soviet soldiers who had freed Tallinn from German rule in World War Two,[207] and its relocation was perceived as an affront by the Russian minority, thus leading to riots.[208] In the years preceding 2007, there had been violent clashes between Estonians and the Russian minority as a result of political action inspired by the monument.[209] These clashes were preceded by tensions generated by a long period of Soviet rule from World War Two

---

201   *Tallinn Manual*, above n 1, 505.

202   Russell, above n 4, 133; Marco Roscini, "World wide warfare – jus ad bellum and the use of cyber force" in Armin von Bogdandy and Rüdiger Wolfrum (eds), *Max Planck Yearbook of United Nations Law* (Brill, 2010) 85, 111.

203   See, e.g., Kevin L Miller, "The Kampala Compromise and cyberattacks: can there be an international crime of cyber-aggression?" (2014) 23 *Southern California Interdisciplinary Law Journal* 217, 234 referring to the DDoS attacks on Georgia as having "similar effects to a blockade"; Russell, above n 4, 69.

204   Russell, above n 4, 18.

205   Ibid.

206   Ibid 73.

207   Ibid 74.

208   Ibid 73.

209   Ibid 74–75.

until 1991. In April 2007, the Russian government protested the shifting of the monument and warned of serious consequences if the Estonian government were to proceed.[210]

Excavations to remove the monument began on 26 April 2007, with cyber attacks commencing that evening. The DDoS attacks began with website vandalism. It became impossible to access many government and corporate websites. In the following days, the websites of newspapers, the President and the Prime Minister were brought down.[211] By the end of the month, more sophisticated attacks were employed. The largest wave of attacks was on Russia's Victory Day, 9 May 2007. This set of attacks commencing on Victory Day continued for a week, followed by a third wave from 18 May. In total, one million computers were engaged without the knowledge of their owners around the world. Only one person was held accountable and fined for the attacks. Subsequently, it was discovered that Russian websites contained instructions for executing DDoS attacks.[212] As a result of this and other findings, it is widely thought that the Russian government was responsible for, or involved in, the attacks in some way.[213] The Estonian blockade highlights the power of non-state actors in cyberspace as well as the difficulties of obtaining adequate evidence of attribution.

4.2.1.2   *Georgia*

Georgia has also had a difficult past with Russia. It was a part of the Soviet Union and gained independence in 1990. In 2008, a conflict arose about the independence of certain regions in Georgia. The regions concerned were South Ossetia and Abkhazia. In spite of newfound independence in the early 1990s, low levels of conflict continued in the regions in subsequent years.[214] Russia had a close connection with South Ossetia, and Georgia's expressed desire to more closely align itself with the European Union and NATO and move away from Russia's influence was perceived by Russia as a threat to its border security.

A series of events followed that led to tensions escalating between the two countries (more specifically: a blown up pipeline; deportation of nationals; and embargoes). Russia also bombed Georgia in 2007. The catalyst for war

---

210   Ibid 75.
211   Ibid.
212   Ibid 76.
213   Ibid.
214   Ibid 98.

between the two countries was the shooting down of a Georgian unmanned aerial vehicle over Abkhazia. The local government claimed responsibility, but footage revealed the culprit was a Russian MiG-29. As a result of the incident, Russian troops moved into Abkhazia to "repair a railway line" at the end of May 2007, but this was perceived as an act of aggression by Georgia. Military tensions increased on both sides with violence occurring in the independent regions in July 2008.[215]

On 19 July 2008, DDoS attacks targeted the Georgian President's website taking it offline for 24 hours. War broke out on 7 August 2008 with Georgian troops moving into South Ossetia (largely provoked by the movement of Russian troops into the area in preceding months). Combat on land and a naval blockade were employed. President Sarkozy of France, however, managed to negotiate a ceasefire a week later.[216]

Websites of political and financial institutions were defaced and DDoS attacks were also employed, alongside other more efficient methods of attack.[217] This significantly reduced the number of machines required to achieve the same impact as that of DDoS attacks. This suggests that the attacks might have been premeditated and supported by prior reconnaissance.[218] In terms of consequences, a total of 54 institutions were targeted including Parliament, the President, the biggest online forum in Georgia and the largest commercial bank.[219] Email addresses were spammed disrupting communication,[220] the government was hindered in its ability to provide information and report on the war,[221] and electronic banking was cut off for ten days.[222] There was no permanent damage, and the costs of the attacks have not been quantified.[223] One Georgian report referred to the attacks as a "cyber blockade"; Russian media coining them an "information blockade".[224] As with Estonia, instructions for conducting the attacks were posted on Russian websites and blogs.[225]

---

215 Ibid 100.
216 Ibid 102.
217 Ibid 105–106.
218 Ibid 106.
219 Ibid 103–104.
220 Ibid 106.
221 Ibid 107.
222 Ibid 108.
223 Ibid.
224 Ibid 106.
225 Ibid 105.

4.2.1.3   *Assessment of Purpose and Potential Legal Challenges*

The attacks in both countries were DDoS attacks that severed access to cyber-space. In Georgia the attacks coincided with Russian assault by land, sea and air.[226] Reasons for the attacks have been suspected to be political[227] as they came at a time of heightened tension and conflict in both countries.[228] However, neither set of attacks was thought of as an act of war at the time. This may be because the situation was unprecedented and international law has not yet developed in this area.[229]

In Estonia, the purpose of the blockade appeared to be to put psychological pressure on the populous by fostering disorder and fear at a time of unrest where it was vital to have access to information. In Georgia, there might have been four potential aims: stimulating fear at a time of crisis; interfering with the government's ability to act; isolating the country from international support; and harming the financial sector.[230]

In both cases, non-state actors conducted the attacks but Russia was suspected to have been ultimately responsible.[231] In Estonia, one individual was fined. In Georgia, nobody has been held responsible.[232] Neither of the blockades targeted neutrals such as neighbouring or distant states, and so their rights were preserved (although access to information hosted in Estonia and Georgia and communication with nationals would have been affected).[233]

In conclusion, these two incidents evidence that cyber blockade is possible, and for broadly similar purposes as naval or aerial blockade. Key legal challenges emerging from these events are whether a cyber blockade amounts to a use of force giving rise to the right to engage in self-defence and difficulties with evidence of attribution.

4.2.2   Cyber Zones

There has been considerably less thought regarding the possibility of cyber zones and there are no historical examples. However, there are several possible purposes for which cyber zones could be used. Like with physical exclusion

---

226   Ibid 131.
227   Ibid 129.
228   Ibid 132.
229   Ibid.
230   Ibid 134–135.
231   Ibid 130.
232   Ibid 129–130.
233   Ibid 133.

zones, they can be used to defend high-value targets[234] or for humanitarian purposes.[235] One example of the former is that given by the Tallinn Experts – a zone around a sensitive military network aimed at protecting information.[236] Cyber zones could also be used in the same way NFZs are for humanitarian purposes to protect hospitals, emergency services providers and others from cyber attacks on their infrastructure by their own government.[237]

These purposes align with the purposes for which zones are used in the physical realm. Key legal challenges involve a lack of state practice in this area, whether a cyber zone amounts to a use of force (either in its establishment or enforcement), and difficulties in obtaining evidence of attribution.

4.2.3   Conclusion

Cyber blockades and zones have broadly the same purposes as blockades and zones in the physical realm. On that basis, it is appropriate to consider whether the same "mischief" calling for regulation by law is inherent in cyber blockades and zones as is inherent in the same tactics in the physical realm. Legal challenges posed by cyberspace are addressed below.

4.3   *The Mischief Inherent in Cyber Blockades and Zones*

The mischief inherent in blockades is the need to regulate the balance between the rights of neutral and belligerent states, as well as to address humanitarian concerns and reduce the impact of blockades on civilians. A similar mischief is inherent in the establishment of zones. What is unique about cyber operations is the unprecedented ability to design targeted operations that could virtually eliminate civilian suffering or an impact on neutral states. But that is ultimately only a difference in the potential scope – and not nature – of the mischief. Therefore, the mischief inherent in cyber blockades and zones is similar to that of the same physical tactics and it is useful to consider blockade and zone law as a starting point. Individual rules can then be assessed to see whether they are necessary or useful in the cyber context.

4.4   *The Law of Cyber Blockades and Zones*

In respect of both cyber blockades and zones, there is no customary international law that has developed, nor is there an applicable treaty. Therefore, the question is whether the customary international law underpinning the law of

---

234   Gill and Fleck, above n 3, [20.18].
235   Kaiser, above n 131, 411.
236   *Tallinn Manual*, above n 1, 508.
237   *Harvard Manual*, above n 5, r 108.

blockades and zones could and should be extended to cyber blockades and zones.

4.4.1   Cyber Blockade
4.4.1.1   *The Tallinn Manual Experts*

How the requirements of the law of blockade would work in the cyber realm was only touched on briefly by the Tallinn Manual Experts. The Experts were divided between the applicability of the current law of blockade and the need for new law.[238] A majority of the Experts were of the view that the current law could be applied to a cyber blockade.[239] However, a minority of the Experts thought that electronic jamming was a more appropriate analogy. But, when examining the effect of aerial and naval blockades, it becomes evident that a similar effect would arise using a cyber blockade as for traditional blockades, such as a negative impact on the enemy's economy. In addition, the scale of economic activity conducted through the internet evidences a qualitative difference between a cyber blockade and the mere jamming of communications.[240]

Finally, the Experts were of the view that the law of blockade, assuming it could apply in the cyber realm, could be extended to landlocked land. It is otherwise not possible to have a naval blockade of landlocked land as this would impact on the neutrality of neighbouring countries by requiring the use of their land in order to be effective.[241]

In summary, there was debate amongst the Experts as to the conceptual possibility of having a cyber blockade. The Experts who accepted the possibility diverged as to how the law of blockade might apply in the cyber context, or they had concerns about the practical difficulties of satisfying the legal requirements. Given that there was no consensus, the Experts did not enunciate any rules, but merely reinforced the idea that cyber means could be used to assist in the execution of a traditional naval or aerial blockade.[242] In respect of neutrality, the majority of Experts (accepting the possibility of cyber blockade) noted that a cyber blockade could not prevent access to, or interfere with, neutral cyber infrastructure and communications.[243]

---

238   *Tallinn Manual*, above n 1, 505.
239   Ibid.
240   Ibid.
241   Ibid 506.
242   Ibid 507, r 128.
243   Ibid 509.

4.4.1.2   *What Should the Law be?*

On its face, the assertion by the majority of Experts that the current law of blockade can apply to cyber blockade appears to make sense. However, that is a big leap without considering what the respective purposes of the tactics are and why blockade law emerged. The aim of this article has been to do that.

The core purposes of blockades are similar to those of cyber blockade. In particular, there are similarities in terms of the aims of undermining enemy commerce and blocking communications.[244] Additionally, inherent in both types of blockade is mischief that requires regulation by law: harm to civilians and the undermining of the rights of neutral states. Therefore, the purposes and mischief of physical and cyber blockades being the same, the traditional law of blockade is a natural starting point for a discussion on the potential law of cyber blockade.

The key legal challenge relates to whether a cyber blockade would be a use of force. The definition of aggression and *United Nations Charter* art 42 indicate that blockades are a use of force, however, this cannot be said to extend to cyber blockades, which are not contemplated by these instruments. Unless a cyber blockade is effected using physical force (such as by damaging property so as to create the effect of a cyber block on communications), a standard DDoS cyber blockade conducted entirely in the cyber realm does not have the indicia of a tactic involving the use of force – military armed force and physical damage are absent.[245] So, the applicable legal regime would appear to differ according to the nature of the tactic, and would not be dictated by its form as a blockade. If, on the spectrum between the principle of non-intervention[246] and the law on the use of force, a cyber operation falls closer to the former, then it will give rise to a right to rely on the doctrine of counter-measures, but not self-defence.[247] If a cyber operation involves the use of force, then self-defence

---

244   Rabkin and Rabkin, above n 111, 197 and 203.

245   Bruno Simma (ed), *The Charter of the United Nations: A Commentary* (Oxford University Press, 2nd ed, 2002) 118. Although, Simma's treatise was published in 2002. Whilst reliance on the use of cyber operations in warfare and in interfering with the affairs of other states would have been reasonably commonplace by then, it would not have been anywhere near as developed as it is now, 15 years later. It would be interesting to know how Simma would approach the interpretation of the use of force in 2017. Nevertheless, it is doubtful that the longstanding interpretation of the Charter as requiring some *physical* use of force would be looked at in a new light because of the proliferation of cyber operations.

246   *Nicaragua*, above n 33, [205]; Buchan, above n 186.

247   Buchan, above n 186, 226; *Gabčíkovo-Nagymaros Project* (*Hungary v Slovakia*) [1997] ICJ Rep 7, [83].

might be a legitimate response. Other states might also take different perspectives as to where an operation falls along the spectrum, thus compounding the confusion. Against this backdrop is the reality that blockades are traditionally considered a use of force, meaning that states might be likely to treat cyber blockades in the same way. This lack of clarity could neutralise the potential benefits of cyber blockades, like the ability to avoid the use of physical force. In the future, the law ought to be clarified so that it is fit for purpose. If a feature of cyber blockade is minimal or non-existent use of force, then the applicable legal regime should support that feature and not negate it by creating uncertainty and tension.

Whether a blockade is a use of force is not, however, fatal to a conclusion that the framework for regulating blockades could nonetheless apply. The law of blockade is self-contained, and seeks to remedy the mischief that has been identified above as largely being common to both cyber and physical blockades.

Another legal challenge is the fact that it is easy for states to camouflage the instigation of a cyber blockade through the use of non-state actors (as appeared to be the case with the Estonian and Georgian cyber blockades, with rumours that Russia was ultimately responsible). So, whilst it might seem wise for a law of cyber blockade to be developed, states might easily avoid having to comply with that law because of the ease with which non-state actors can be employed to conduct a cyber blockade. This is a problem of adequate evidence of attribution. For some states this will not be as significant a problem depending on the level of sophistication of their cyber capabilities and their ability to obtain evidence of responsibility. Other states, like Estonia and Georgia, will only be left with remedies against non-state actors, short of having proof of state involvement. All that states can really do in those circumstances is take preventive measures before any attacks occur and steps in self-defence post-attack.[248]

While acknowledging the force of these challenges, the remainder of this section is focused on what the law of cyber blockade ought to be. The following aspects of the traditional law of blockade should apply to cyber blockade. First, there should be a declaration and notification, including specification of the extent, duration and commencement of the blockade.[249] Changes should also

---

248   See, e.g., Michael Hayden, "The battlefield of cyberspace: the inevitable new military branch – the cyber force" (2008) 18 *Albany Law Journal of Science and Technology* 293; Erica Hauck, "The Cloud of War: Securing the Operational Domain of Cyberspace With a Robust Military Command" (2014) 41 *North Kentucky Law Review* 515.

249   London Declaration 1909, above n 36, arts 8–13 and 16; *San Remo Manual*, above n 3, [93]–[94]; *Harvard Manual*, above n 5, rr 148–149.

be notified.[250] An equivalent to a Notice to Airmen is not necessary because there is no risk to life in the same way that there is with an aerial blockade.[251] The requirement of notification generally is directed at both protecting the rights of neutral states and humanitarian concerns, and so should apply to cyber blockade.

Secondly, the requirement of effectiveness should remain.[252] This also stems from a concern for striking the right balance between the rights of belligerent and neutral states. A minority of Tallinn Experts were of the view that a cyber blockade could not be effective because blockaded communications could be routed through other lines of communication, such as phone and radio.[253] But the majority conducted their analysis by reference to the effect of expansion into air space on naval blockade, noting that the expansion did not render naval blockade ineffective and vice versa only because a blockade targeted a single realm as opposed to all available realms. Effectiveness might also be enhanced by other means such as electronic and kinetic warfare.[254] The question is always "[d]oes [the blockade] impose ... such risks as to give a considerable chance of either stopping or crippling [the enemy] if [s/]he attempt[s] [to breach] it?"[255] Relatedly, the rule that neutral states should not be affected should apply to cyber blockades so as to effect the right balance between belligerent and neutral states' rights.[256]

The third requirement, that the distance of stationed forces from the coast is determined by military requirements, does not apply in cyberspace because the concept of distance is not comparable between the realms.[257]

Fourthly, the requirement that enforcement and maintenance of a blockade may be by a combination of legitimate methods of warfare, so long as the effect is not inconsistent with the rules of warfare generally, can apply to a cyber blockade.[258] However, the specific rules that address humanitarian concerns may need some elaboration.[259] A cyber blockade can be established and

---

250   *San Remo Manual*, above n 3, [101].

251   *Harvard Manual*, above n 5, r 148(c).

252   Gill and Fleck, above n 3, [20.17]; Paris Declaration 1856, above n 36, r 4; London Declaration 1909, above n 36, arts 2–3; *San Remo Manual*, above n 3, [95].

253   *Tallinn Manual*, above n 1, 506.

254   Ibid 506.

255   Captain Mahan, "Blockade in Relation to Naval Strategy" (1895) 39(213) *Royal United Services Institution Journal* 1057, 1066.

256   *San Remo Manual*, above n 3, [99]; *Harvard Manual*, above n 5, r 150.

257   *San Remo Manual*, above n 3, [96]; *Harvard Manual*, above n 5, r 152.

258   *San Remo Manual*, above n 3, [97]; *Harvard Manual*, above n 5, r 153(a).

259   *Harvard Manual*, above n 5, rr 157–159.

enforced by way of cyber attacks conducted on networks within a state's borders. So, whilst a cyber blockade can be very targeted and minimise its impact on civilians, the potential for civilian suffering is also much greater if, for example, a cyber blockade led to a loss of control of infrastructure like nuclear facilities or dams. While it is likely that cyber blockades that have an impact on such facilities would be illegal, by virtue of being disproportionate to their anticipated military advantage, it is not clear that that would always be the case. Rules sensitive to the possibilities of the cyber realm may emerge in time, but for now, reliance on the general application of humanitarian law will have to suffice in the absence of relevant case studies.[260]

In saying that, there is room for improvement to the more specific rules of blockade law relating to passage of food, essentials and medical supplies. Those rules provide that if a civilian population of a blockaded area does not have adequate food or essentials for survival, the blockading party must provide for free passage of such supplies subject to the right to prescribe technical arrangements and supervise the passage.[261] This is also the case for medical essentials.[262] The difficulty with these rules as they currently stand relates to the difference in how physical versus cyber blockades are effected. A naval or aerial blockade stops supplies and communications from exiting or entering a country, but a cyber blockade could stop the supply and transportation of the same within a state's borders just by blocking cyber communications generally. The rules therefore might need to be more carefully worded to cover situations that give rise to a negative impact on a state's internal flow of essential supplies. Moreover, given the reliance on cyberspace in modern medical treatment, the concept of "medical supplies" needs to be broadened to factor in the administration of treatment using the cyber realm.

Finally, application to communications and transactions should be impartial as between states, as it is in the traditional law of blockade.[263]

In conclusion, the two key challenges to the applicability and usefulness of the law of blockade in cyberspace are: whether a cyber blockade constitutes a use of force; and the ability of states to mask their responsibility through the use of non-state actors. Both are considerable challenges, but do not negate the value of having a legal framework by which to assess the legality of a cyber blockade for those states that openly use the tactic.

---

260   *San Remo Manual*, above n 3, [102].

261   Ibid [103].

262   Ibid [104].

263   *San Remo Manual*, above n 3, [100]; *Harvard Manual*, above n 5, r 155.

4.4.2 Cyber Zones

4.4.2.1 *The Tallinn Manual Experts*

The Tallinn Experts considered that cyber zones are difficult to define. The Experts were also concerned about the practical difficulty of compliance with a zone by cyber actors where actors may have no control of the cyber infrastructure over which communications travel.[264] Bearing those concerns in mind, the Experts did not come to a decision on potential rules for cyber zones. They did, however, affirm the legality of the use of cyber operations to support naval or aerial zones.[265]

4.4.2.2 *What Should the Law be?*

A cyber zone is even less likely to be a use of force than a cyber blockade because there is a lack of physical harm. A cyber blockade, on the other hand, might cause considerable suffering in the physical world by blocking access to vital services such as banking. So, on an effects-based approach, a cyber blockade would more likely be a use of force than a cyber zone. There would also, in all likelihood, be a lack of physical harm in the enforcement of a cyber zone. The prospect of hack-back is an entirely different consideration from enforcing a NFZ, which may permit or require the shooting down of aircraft. Like with cyber blockades, a zone is only likely to be a breach of the principle of non-intervention. Again, this does not mean that the law of zones has no role to play. Borrowing from the legal framework for zones, regulating the same cyber tactic need not hinge on whether there has been a use of force. The traditional rules and how they could apply to cyber zones is discussed below.

The first question is whether it should be permissible for a belligerent to establish a cyber zone in enemy territory. Following the law of NFZs, this should be permissible on the basis of humanitarian concerns or the need to protect one's own military assets in enemy territory.[266]

The next issue is whether the same body of law should apply inside and outside the zone.[267] Given humanitarian concerns are still present with cyber zones (a hack-back could involve causing physical damage depending on how it is programmed), this rule should continue to apply. There is still an inherent risk that the idea of a zone, cyber or otherwise, involves the creation of a space that allows free fire.[268] The presumption that a vessel or aircraft is hostile when

---

264 *Tallinn Manual*, above n 1, 508.
265 Ibid.
266 Rule 108.
267 *San Remo Manual*, above n 3, [106]; *Harvard Manual*, above n 5, rr 105 and 107.
268 *San Remo Manual*, above n 3, [105].

entering a physical zone is strengthened in the cyber realm whereby any cyber attack that hinges on a hacking operation is obviously hostile.[269] In those circumstances, automatic hack-back should be permissible.[270] In circumstances where a cyber operation appears innocent but may actually be hostile, a warning mechanism should be in place so as to make sure that any response is proportionate. Warning mechanisms are used in the law of naval and aerial zones.[271]

Thirdly, the rules that attempt to balance the rights of neutral and belligerent states must be considered. Those rules are:[272]

- a limit on the extent, location and duration of a zone as a function of what is required by military necessity and proportionality;
- notification of the commencement, duration, location and extent of the zone and any restrictions;
- due regard for neutral states' rights to legitimate uses of the seas and airspace;
- provision for and notification of safe passage routes for neutral vessels and aircraft;
- compliance with a zone is not to be taken as an act harmful to the opposing belligerent;[273] and
- aircraft entering a NFZ without specific permission are liable to be attacked.[274]

As discussed above, cyber operations can be targeted so as to minimise impact on neutral states. But some cyber zones may have more of an impact on neutral states than others. For example, a zone around a sensitive military network would have little impact on neutral states because a cyber assailant would need to intend to hack into the closed network in the first place in order to breach it. In those circumstances, there would be no need to notify a zone because anybody breaching the zone would be knowingly doing so. On the other hand, a zone around an open network, or a cyber operation involving damage to physical infrastructure might have more of an impact on neutral states. Therefore,

---

269   Ibid 181.
270   *Harvard Manual,* above n 5, r 110.
271   *San Remo Manual,* above n 3, [108], *Harvard Manual,* above n 5, r 106.
272   *San Remo Manual,* above n 3, [106]–[107]; *Harvard Manual,* above n 5, rr 107 and 109.
273   *San Remo Manual,* above n 3, [107].
274   *Harvard Manual,* above n 5, r 110.

rules that aim to strike a balance between the rights of neutral and belligerent states are still relevant to what the law of cyber zones ought to be.[275]

5   Conclusion

This article has canvassed the nature of blockades and zones, the law that regulates them, and how that law might apply to the same cyber tactics. The analysis has centred on what the purposes of the respective tactics are, and the mischief that the law of blockades and zones is directed at. This has been with a view to understanding whether the current law (with or without adjustment) or new law is necessary in a world where cyber blockades and zones are a possibility.

In conclusion, the current law should be the basis of the law of cyber blockades and zones, with adjustments to reflect the idiosyncrasies of cyberspace. It is not necessary for cyber blockades and zones to be a use of force in order for the current law to be a useful analogy – they are still a breach of the principle of non-intervention, entitling victim states to employ countermeasures.

Presently, cyber blockades and zones are not prevalent. However, should the Tallinn Manual authors decide to produce a third version, a clearer discussion of what the law ought to be is desirable – the Manual will undoubtedly be a useful tool for drafters of domestic military manuals, thus going on to inform state practice and eventually customary international law. More research is needed as to what circumstances cyber blockades and zones might be used in and how, with further consideration of what the exact scope of the modified law of blockade and zones would be. It is desirable for states to develop clear rules because it is anticipated that they will otherwise take advantage of a lacuna in the law to use low-cost, low-risk tactics like cyber blockades and zones without proper regard for humanitarian concerns or the rights of neutral states.

---

275   *Harvard Manual,* above n 5, r 107; *San Remo Manual,* above n 3, [106].

Determining Modes of Liability in International Criminal Law: Why the Common Purpose Doctrine is the Strongest Legal Response to Mass Atrocity Crimes

*Selma Kafedžić**

We know that often holding those who have carried out mass atrocities accountable is at times our best tool to prevent further atrocities[1]

∴

1 Introduction

Determining responsibility for collective criminality is one of the most contentious areas of international criminal law.[2] The reality of mass atrocities[3] makes the task of establishing *who* is accountable for *what* especially challenging.[4] The lack of evidence in circumstances of utter destruction, as is the case in most post-conflict societies, is one of the most paradoxical aspects of international criminal law and adds a unique challenge to international prosecutions.[5] The evolution of this body of law has accelerated in the last few decades, regrettably as a result of a number of devastating conflicts on continents across the

---

* Selma Kafedžić, Judicial Support Advisor, High Court, Christchurch, New Zealand. Views expressed are naturally the author's own.

1 Samantha Power and David Pressman, "President Obama Directs New Atrocity Prevention Measures" (press release, 6 August 2011).

2 Jens D. Ohlin, "Joint Intentions to Commit International Crimes" (2011) 11 (2) *Chicago Journal of International Law* 693, 694.

3 "The terms mass atrocity or mass atrocity crimes are used to refer to genocide, war crimes, ethnic cleansing and crimes against humanity." For a full description of the etymology of this term see Gareth Evans, *The Responsibility to Protect: Ending Mass Atrocity Crimes Once and for All* (Brooks Institution Press, 1st ed, 2009) Ch 1.

4 Neha Jain "Individual Responsibility for Mass Atrocity: In Search of a Concept of Penetration" (2013) 61 *The American Journal of Comparative Law* 831, 835.

5 For a discussion on challenges of access to evidence see, Eric Stover, *The Witness* (University of Pennsylvania Press, 1st ed, 2011) Ch 3.

globe. The establishment of the ad-hoc tribunals, including the International Criminal Tribunal for the former Yugoslavia ("ICTY"), the International Criminal Tribunal for Rwanda ("ICTR") and the Special Court for Sierra Leone ("SCSL"), amongst others, has resulted in a large volume of jurisprudence concerning modes of liability in international criminal law. Likewise, the formation of the International Criminal Court ("ICC") has also added to this area of law, albeit through a different doctrinal approach.

The way in which the ad-hoc tribunals and the ICC have approached modes of co-perpetrator liability can be categorised into two diverging normative methodologies. The tribunals, and in particular the ICTY, have focused predominantly on the common purpose/intent theory,[6] applied via the doctrine of joint criminal enterprise ("JCE").[7] The ICC, which has more limited jurisprudence due to its shorter tenure, has conversely adopted the doctrine of co-perpetration based on the control over crime theory.[8] This article argues that, in the context of international crimes, JCE[9] is the superior mechanism in ascribing criminal liability to perpetrators of mass atrocities. The emphasis this doctrine places on the shared intent of a collective provides a stronger response to the unique complexities of mass atrocity crimes. It enables international law to capture all those responsible for such crimes and not just the direct perpetrators. JCE is also more established in international criminal law than the control theory and is a more developed, and therefore a more useful, theory. Finally, impunity for mass atrocity crimes can no longer be accepted. Whilst some of the more notorious war criminals have been tried and prosecuted for their part in mass atrocity crimes, countless others have escaped justice; a wrong permitted in part by a prohibitively narrow construction of criminal liability in international law.

This article is comprised of three parts: the first part provides a brief summary of how the concept of criminal liability in international law has evolved from the aftermath of World War II to its current state. The second part provides a closer analysis of the ad-hoc tribunals and the ICC and considers some of the case law that has established the respective doctrines in the

---

6   The terms common purpose/common intent are often used interchangeably. The remainder of this paper will refer to common purpose.

7   The application of JCE as the doctrinal approach at the ICTY was established in *Prosecutor v Tadić* (*Judgement*) (ICTY Appeals Chamber IT-94-I-A, 15 July 1999) ("*Tadić Appeal*").

8   The control over crime approach was established in *Prosecutor v Thomas Lubanga Dyilo* (*Judgement*) (ICC Trial Chamber I 01/04-01/06-2842, March 2012) ("*Lubanga Appeal*").

9   The author in this article refers to the common purpose theory and supports its application via the doctrine of JCE. References to JCE are made on this basis.

jurisprudence of these courts. Even the most fervent supporters of JCE cannot ignore obvious inconsistencies with the application of JCE. Some of the most obvious contradictions are addressed in this part. The final part of this article recommends that the common purpose doctrine (via JCE) should be the doctrinal basis in establishing individual criminal liability for mass atrocity crimes in future international criminal prosecutions. Refinements of some aspects of JCE would ensure the doctrine is applied appropriately and within the parameters of international law.

2   The Raison D'être of International Criminal Law

2.1   *Individual Criminal Liability for Mass Atrocities*
The history of humans is unfortunately filled with the persistence of mass atrocities.[10] Although the prosecution of war criminals at the domestic level dates back to the ancient Greeks,[11] international prosecutions are a relatively modern development.[12] Consequently, this area of international law is still in its adolescence.[13] The modern state system's Westphalian roots has meant that, traditionally, international law has only governed relations between states.[14] Formerly, the prosecution of individuals fell within the realm of domestic legal systems.[15] When it came to abuses of power, more often than not, government officials in despotic states were immune from punishment as they were either protected by sovereign immunity or came before biased national courts. Beigbeder explains that in order for national trials to be successful, they require an independent judiciary and an impartial justice system. In many countries, however, the separation of powers is blurred during conflicts and governments are reluctant to prosecute their own leaders or members of the military, especially if the regime is still in place.[16]

There were attempts after World War I to establish an international tribunal in order to try those responsible for the offences committed during that war:

---

10   Jain, above n 4, 831.

11   William Schabas, *An Introduction to the International Criminal Court* (Cambridge University Press, 4th ed, 2011) 1.

12   Jain, above n 4, 831.

13   Anio Cassese and others, *Cassese's International Criminal Law* (Oxford University Press, 3rd ed, 2013) xii.

14   Yves Beigbeder, *International Criminal Courts* (Palgrave Macmilllan, 1st ed, 2008) 1.

15   Ibid 2.

16   For an excellent analysis of where national courts have failed to successfully prosecute individuals for international crimes see: Yves Beigbeder, *International Justice Against Impunity* (Brill, 1st ed, 2005) Ch 1.

in particular, officials and soldiers from Turkey, Germany, Austria-Hungary and Bulgaria.[17] No such tribunal was ever realised and although Germany and Turkey did establish domestic trials, these were ineffective and resulted in numerous acquittals of those who had committed criminal acts and very light sentences for those who had been convicted.[18] In Turkey, trials were particularly challenging given that Turkey denied (and continues to deny) that any crimes against humanity had been perpetrated against the Armenians.[19]

The majority of scholarly literature identifies the aftermath of World War II as the catalyst for legal change as millions of people throughout the world struggled to comprehend and recuperate from the atrocities and unprecedented destruction of World War II.[20] The International Military Tribunal of Nuremberg ("Nuremberg Tribunal"),[21] established to prosecute members of the Nazi party for the persecution of Jews and other minority groups during the Holocaust, abandoned the previously sacrosanct principle of sovereign immunity for military and political leaders.[22] In his opening speech, the Chief Prosecutor at Nuremberg, Supreme Court Justice Robert Jackson, proclaimed that the concept that a state commits crimes was a fallacy, insisting that crimes are always committed by people and that it would be absurd if such people were protected by immunity.[23] Consequently, the individuals on trial

---

17   Theodor Meron, "Reflections on the Prosecution of War Crimes by International Tribunals" (2006) 100 (3) *American Society of International Law* 551, 555.

18   M. Cherif Bassiouni, "World War I: The War to End All Wars and the Birth of a Handicapped International Criminal Justice System" (2002) 30(3) *Denver Journal of International Law and Policy* 244–353.

19   Meron, above n 17, 558.

20   See, e.g., Harmen van der Wilt, "Joint Criminal Enterprise: Possibilities and Limitations" (2007) 5 (1) *Journal of International Criminal Justice* 91, 93; Alison Mars Danner and Jenny S. Martinez, "Guilty Associations: Joint Criminal Enterprise, Command Responsibility and the Development of International Criminal Law" (2005) 93 *California Law Review* 75, 85; Douglas Guilfoyle, "Responsibility for Collective Atrocities: Fair Labelling and Approaches to Commission in International Criminal Law" (2011) 64 *Current Legal Problems* 255, 258; Mark A. Summers, "The Problem of Risk in International Criminal Law" (2014) 13(4) *Washing University Global Studies Law Review* 667, 668.

21   The International Military Tribunal for the Far East (Tokyo Tribunal) was also established with the purpose of prosecuting war criminals in the Far East. This essay will not refer to the Tokyo Tribunal as the relevant jurisprudence for this essay stems from the Nuremberg Tribunal.

22   Geoffrey Robertson, "Ending Impunity: How International Criminal Law Can Put Tyrants on Trial" (2005) 38(3) *ell International Law Journal* 649, 654.

23   Robert Jackson, *Opening Statement Before the International Military Tribunal* (10 January 2017) <roberthjackson.org>.

at Nuremberg were denied the refuge of immunity and the responsibility for their criminal actions was determined on an individual basis.[24] Since then the idea of individual liability under international criminal law has been part of general international law.[25]

The concept of humanitarianism in armed conflict gained momentum after Nuremberg and segued into the codification of the laws of war, now termed international humanitarian law ("IHL").[26] *The four Geneva Conventions of 1949* and their *Additional Protocols ("Geneva Conventions")* embody the rules of war[27] and seek to minimise the effects of armed conflict by establishing rules protecting those not involved in, or no longer involved in, conflict.[28] The *Geneva Conventions* offer protection to civilians, aid workers, medics, wounded, sick or shipwrecked soldiers and prisoners of war in instances of international armed conflict and, to a lesser extent, in instances of non-international armed conflict.[29]

---

24   The Charter of the Nuremberg Tribunals states that "the official position of defendants, whether as Heads of State or responsible officials in Government Departments, shall not be considered as freeing them from responsibility or mitigating punishment". See *Charter of the International Military Tribunal – Annex to the Agreement for the Prosecution and Punishment of the Major War Criminals of the European Axis,* opened for signature 8 August 1945, 82 UNTS 279 (entered into force August 8 1945) art 7.

25   Edoardo Greppi, "The Evolution of Individual Criminal Responsibility Under International Law" (1999) 835 International Review of the Red Cross (5 March 2017) <www.icrc.org accessed>.

26   Steven R. Ratner, Jason S. Abrams and James L. Bischoff, *Accountability for Human Rights Atrocities in International Law: Beyond the Nuremberg Legacy* (Oxford University Press, 3rd ed, 2009) 4.

27   It should be noted that although the Geneva Conventions of 1949 and their Additional Protocols ("*Geneva Conventions*") are considered the most important treaties pertaining to international humanitarian law, they incorporate law that was existing, in part, in other treaties such as the *Hague Conventions* of 1899 and 1907, which aimed to regulate methods of warfare and war crimes. Whilst the terms "laws of war" and "international humanitarian law" are often used interchangeably, the latter is more focused on humanitarian principles.

28   *The Geneva Conventions of 1949 and their Additional Protocols* (15 February 2017) The International Committee of the Red Cross <www.icrc.org>.

29   The *Geneva Conventions* apply to armed conflicts of an international character with the exception of Common Article 3 which provides some protection in instances of non-international armed conflict. The *Protocol Additional to the Geneva Conventions* of 12 August 1949 and relating to the *Protection of Victims of Non-International Armed Conflicts (Second Additional Protocol)* extended the protections within Common Article 3 since the majority of the victims of armed conflict were those within conflicts not of

2.2   The Complexity of Modern Conflicts

Notwithstanding the normative shift that occurred in international law post World War II, there are certain features of mass atrocities that are unique to collective crimes. The very essence of group criminality is founded upon a shared intention or goal to pursue a particular plan or seek a specific outcome.[30] The implementation of such objectives relies on a collective division of responsibilities necessary to the success of the endeavour. The undertaking is only effective because of the coordinated efforts of all of the co-perpetrators.[31] In international criminal proceedings, ascertaining *who* exactly did *what* can be extremely difficult, particularly given that despite prolific and obvious destruction in post-conflict zones, the gathering of evidence can be a Herculean task.[32]

Furthermore, although the nature of collective crimes does rely on a plurality of individuals to carry out the criminal acts, the precise contribution or role of individuals is not always the same. For example, in a collective of individuals who plan to kill X, where A plans the murder, B supplies the murder weapon, C, D and E apprehend and beat the victim before E delivers the final shot, there are multiple modes of liability at play for the crime of murder. If E had carried out the murder alone, then E would be liable under direct perpetration as the conduct would be attributed solely to E.[33] However, since the murder involved a number of people, tasked with carrying out different aspects of the murder, the crime was carried out by joint perpetrators or co-perpetrators. Just as domestic criminal law requires conformity with the principle of individual criminal responsibility, international tribunals, and more recently the ICC, are also required to establish *precisely* how an accused or co-accused was involved with the crimes with which they are charged.[34]

Of course, a truism of warfare is that the individuals most responsible for offences (such as senior members of governments or militaries) are often

---

an international character. However, non-international armed conflict rules are generally more limited.

30   Jain, above n 4, 831.

31   Neha Jain, "The Control Theory of Co-Perpetration in International Criminal Law" (2011) 12(1) *Chicago Journal of International* Law 159, 167.

32   Meron, above n 17, 561.

33   Steffen Wirth, "Co-perpetration in the *Lubanga* Trial Judgement" (2012) 10 *Journal of International Criminal Justice* 971, 971.

34   Kai Ambos, Hector Olásolo and Adrian Fulford, *Criminal Responsibility of Senior Political and Military Leaders as Principals to International Crimes* (Bloomsbury Publishing, 1st ed, 2009) 2.

remote from the scenes of crimes and are rarely the physical perpetrators.[35] When facing trial, such perpetrators can, and do, use their lack of proximity to the crimes as a defence or in an attempt to distinguish themselves from a perpetrator as an aider or abettor.[36] In this context, international tribunals are faced with the dilemma of ascertaining how those who did not contribute to the *actus reus* of a crime can be held responsible as perpetrators.[37]

The most obvious distinction between the approaches taken by the ad-hoc tribunals and the ICC in attempting to respond to this dilemma is that, JCE is more focused on the common intent of the participants and the control theory, as the term suggests, is more focused on the level of control an accused exercised over the crime.[38] The following section provides a closer analysis of these approaches.

3   The Doctrinal Evolution of Criminal Culpability in International Criminal Law

3.1   *Extending Liability: The Approach of the Ad-Hoc Tribunals: ICTY, ICTR and SCSL*

It was almost fifty years after the Nuremberg trials that war criminals were, again, indicted under international law for serious violations of IHL committed during conflicts in the former Yugoslavia, Rwanda, Cambodia, Sierra Leone, East Timor/Timor Leste and the Lebanon.[39] The ICTY paved the jurisprudential path and established early on, in the now prolifically analysed *Tadić* case, that the basis to determine criminal liability for co-perpetration would be founded on the common purpose concept via the doctrine of JCE.[40] This approach has received a plethora of criticism. Nevertheless, it has remained

---

35   Ibid 3.

36   For example, in *Prosecutor v Charles Ghankay Taylor*, Charles Taylor was found liable for aiding and abetting (as opposed to having direct responsibility for) international crimes, partly because he was remote from the scene of the crimes and therefore could not be deemed as a co-perpetrator. *Prosecutor v Charles Ghankay Taylor (Judgement)* (SCSL Trial Chamber SCSL-03-01-T, 18 May 2012) ("*Taylor Trial*").

37   Jain, above n 31, 162.

38   James G. Stewart, "The End of "Modes of Liability" for International Crimes" (2012) 25 *Leiden Journal of International Law* 165, 166.

39   The Hon. David Hunt, "The International Criminal Court: High Hopes, "Creative Ambiguity" and an Unfortunate Mistrust of Judges" (2004) 2 *Journal of International Criminal Justice* 56, 57.

40   *Tadić Appeal* (ICTY Appeals Chamber IT-94-I-A, 15 July 1999).

the overriding mode of criminal liability for the ICTY Office of the Prosecutor in issuing indictments.[41]

Joint Criminal Enterprise apportions equal criminal liability upon individuals who share a common intention to carry out a common plan, regardless of which member is the actual perpetrator of the crime.[42] Central to this doctrine is the mental state of each of the co-accused.[43] Much has been written about *Tadić*, but it is necessary to briefly revisit the facts of that case in order to highlight how the ICTY arrived at its conclusion and why the application of JCE was the correct approach in that case.

3.1.1   International Criminal Tribunal for the Former Yugoslavia

The ICTY's jurisdiction extends to prosecuting individuals responsible for serious violations of IHL committed in the Former Yugoslavia.[44] One of the first persons accused of such violations was Duško Tadić, a former café owner, and a member of the Serbian paramilitary during the conflict.[45] He was charged with 34 counts of crimes against humanity and violations of the laws and customs of war.[46] Tadić faced a specific charge of the wilful killing and murder of five Muslim men in the town of Jaskići in Bosnia.[47] Tadić was one of a number of men who had entered the village, beaten the villagers and forcibly removed them from their homes. After the group left the village five Muslim men, who had been alive when the group entered, were dead.[48]

The Trial Chamber found Tadić guilty of 11 counts of crimes against humanity and violations of the laws and customs of war,[49] and not guilty of 20 others,

---

41   Cliff Farhang "Point of No Return: Joint Criminal Enterprise in *Brđanin*" (2010) 23 *Leiden Journal of International Law* 137, 138.

42   In *Tadić Appeal* the Appeals Chamber states that "when two or more persons act together to further a common criminal purpose, offences perpetrated by any of them may entail the criminal liability of all the members of the group", *Tadić Appeal* (ICTY Appeals Chamber IT-94-I-A, 15 July 1999) [195].

43   Stephen Ranieri, "Extended Joint Criminal Enterprise in International Criminal Law: From Foreseeability, to Intention to Control over the Crime" (2016) 80(6) *The Journal of Criminal Law* 436, 439.

44   SC Res 827, UN SCOR, 48th sess, 3217th mtg, UN Doc S/RES/827 (25 May 1993), as amended by SC Res 1877, UN SCOR, 64th sess, 6155th mtg, UN Doc S/RES/1877 (7 July 2009) SC Res 827, art 1 ("*ICTY Statute*").

45   *Prosecutor v Tadić (Judgement)* (ICTY Trial Chamber IT-94-1-T, 7 May 1997) [181]–[182] ("*Tadić Trial*").

46   Ibid [36]–[51].

47   Ibid [51].

48   Ibid [759].

49   Ibid [285].

including the murder of the Muslim men in Jaskići.[50] Whilst the Trial Chamber was satisfied that Tadić had been a part of the group of Serb men who had entered Jaskići, it could not be satisfied, beyond reasonable doubt, that Tadić had actually killed, or taken part in the killing of, the Muslim men.[51] The Trial Chamber, having found insufficient evidence that Tadić had carried out the objective elements of this particular offence, did not enter into a *mens rea* assessment.

The Appeals Chamber re-examined this approach and found that the Trial Chamber had erred in its ruling and in its application of the beyond reasonable doubt test. The Appeals Chamber found that the only reasonable conclusion, based on the evidence, was that Tadić and his group of men were responsible for the killings.[52] Indeed, as the Trial Chamber itself had found, the evidence showed that the armed group of men that entered the town, including Tadić, had forcibly separated the men in the village and removed them to an undisclosed location, firing shots as they entered and departed from the village. Five Muslim men were dead after the group departed. There was no other explanation as to how else the men might have been killed. The Appeals Chamber, contrary to the Trial Chamber, was satisfied that the evidence established Tadić's guilt.[53]

The necessary elements for JCE were outlined as being comprised of the objective elements, which included: a plurality of persons; the existence of a common plan, which amounted to the perpetration of a crime within the *ICTY Statute*; and participation of the accused in the common plan.[54] This is an aspect of JCE that many critics of the doctrine overlook[55] – in order to be deemed criminally liable, the accused must already be involved in a common plan that constitutes a violation of the *ICTY Statute*. This will be addressed further below.

---

50   Ibid [373].

51   The Trial Chamber found that whilst it was not irrelevant that the men had died on the same day as the group entered their village, "it is accordingly a distinct possibility that it may have been the act of a quite distinct group of armed men, or the unauthorized and unforeseen act of one of the force that entered [another village] for which the accused cannot be held responsible, that caused their death", ibid.

52   *Tadić Appeal* (ICTY Appeals Chamber IT-94-I-A, 15 July 1999) [183].

53   Ibid.

54   Ibid [227].

55   This is an understandable oversight since the decision of the Appeals Chamber in *Prosecutor v Radoslav Brđanin* created controversy by extending JCE liability to those not party to the JCE. This decision and recommendations for future application of the doctrine are considered in further detail later in the article. *Prosecutor v Radoslav Brđanin (Judgement)* (ICTY Appeals Chamber ITT-99-36-A, 3 April 2007) ("*Brđanin Appeal*").

In addition, the Chamber ruled that JCE applies in three distinct instances. Firstly, where there is evidence of the same criminal intent to commit a crime.[56] Secondly, where there is awareness of the nature of the system of ill-treatment coupled with the intent to further the ill-treatment.[57] Finally, where there is evidence that the accused intended to take part in a common criminal plan in order to progress the criminal purpose, and where it was foreseeable that a member of the group may commit an offence outside the object of the common purpose.[58] These categories of JCE are termed in the literature as basic JCE for the first category, systemic JCE for the second and extended JCE for the third.

The *mens rea* requirements differ for each category. Basic JCE requires intent to commit a certain crime, that is, shared intent of all of the co-perpetrators. Systemic JCE requires personal knowledge of the system of ill-treatment, coupled with the intent to perpetuate the ill-treatment. Extended JCE requires intention to participate in and further the criminal purpose of the group.[59] Liability under this category was extended to include crimes other than the one that was agreed upon in the common purpose, if it were foreseeable that a crime of that sort might be perpetrated by someone in the group and the accused willingly took that risk.[60] This extension proved to be a critical juncture in the jurisprudence of the ICTY as it meant that an accused could be held responsible as a co-perpetrator for a crime in the absence of any direct evidence that demonstrated the accused had in fact committed the crime themselves.[61] This is the aspect of JCE that has been vehemently opposed and will be addressed further in Section 3.

It was on this extended basis that Tadić was found to have willingly taken part in the common criminal plan to rid the town of Jaskići of the non-Serb population. The Appeals Chamber conceded that, whilst the common criminal plan was not to murder the men, frequent killings and inhumane treatment of non-Serbs had been taking place in other areas where there were expulsions of non-Serbs, and Tadić was aware of this.[62] He was aware that he was a member of a group of men taking part in acts where such killings were likely to occur

---

56   *Tadić Appeal* (ICTY Appeals Chamber IT-94-I-A, 15 July 1999) [196].

57   Ibid [202].

58   The references to JCE in the remainder of this article will be referring to extended JCE unless otherwise stated.

59   *Tadić Appeal* (ICTY Appeals Chamber IT-94-I-A, 15 July 1999) [204].

60   Ibid [229].

61   Ibid [185].

62   Ibid [232].

and he nevertheless participated.[63] In other words, it was foreseeable that the forcible, armed expulsion of people, in these circumstances, might eventuate and Tadić willingly took that risk. This was the basis of his guilt for the murder of the men in Jaskići.[64]

This aspect of the judgment has attracted significant controversy but many of the criticisms tend to be superficial. The critics argue that it is counterintuitive to principles of criminal law, (which should uphold the standard that individuals shall only be liable for their own actions and contributions to a crime)[65] to impose liability upon individuals who may not have committed, or even contributed to, the *actus reus*. Upon a closer consideration of the particular characteristics of mass atrocity crimes, however, the Appeal Chamber's reasoning is wholly justified. It responds to the very essence of mass atrocity crimes; holding co-perpetrators liable as aiders or abettors negates their level of criminal culpability.[66]

The Appeals Chamber examined post-World War II national military cases and customary international law and stated that it would be unjust to hold responsible only those who perform the physical act whilst ignoring all of the co-perpetrators who made it physically possible for the perpetrator to commit the crime.[67] The case law relied on by the Appeals Chamber included examples of mob violence where the exact contribution to the eventual harm was impossible to ascertain and where all those who participated in the criminal acts were found guilty as co-perpetrators. This included instances where the eventual consequence, for example death, may not have been the direct intention of the common criminal design but where it occurred as a result of the ill-treatment.[68] Despite criticism after *Tadić*, the JCE doctrine has continued to be applied by the ICTY in subsequent cases, though not without some

---

63   Ibid.

64   Ibid [233].

65   The principle of *nulla poena sine culpa* is cited by the Appeals Chamber as being the foundation of criminal responsibility; that is, nobody may be held criminally liable for acts which they have not committed, ibid [186].

66   Ibid [192].

67   Ibid.

68   The Appeals Chamber provides the example of the *Essen Lynching* case in which a group of German citizens were charged with the murder of three British prisoners of war, in violation with the laws of war. The British military tribunal adjudicating the case found the accused guilty of murder, even though none of them had directly killed the POWs. The Tribunal found since they had all participated, in various ways, in the ill-treatment of the POWs, they were all concerned with the killing. From this case, the Appeals Chamber in *Tadić* made the inference that "the court assumed that the convicted persons who simply

confusion and inconsistency. The discrepancy of the application of JCE has done the ICTY no favours in terms of harnessing support for the doctrine.[69] The following section highlights some of these inconsistencies.

In *Prosecutor v Stakić* the Trial Chamber rejected JCE and introduced the doctrine of co-perpetration based on the control theory to the ICTY.[70] The Trial Chamber reasoned that JCE was one form of perpetrator liability but that other forms of co-perpetration should also be taken into consideration.[71] The analysis was centred around the word "commission" under *ICTY Statute* art 7(1) and the attempt to direct its interpretation towards what the Chamber termed more traditional approaches to determining liability.[72] It found that co-perpetration was more akin to "commission" in most legal systems and that employing co-perpetration, instead of JCE, addressed the "misleading impression that a new crime not foreseen in the *Statute* of this Tribunal has been introduced through the backdoor".[73] This was an obvious rebuttal to all of the criticism targeted at the legal basis of JCE. Stakić's involvement in the alleged crimes was subsequently analysed through Roxin's doctrine of control over the crime.

This attempt to distinguish the ICTY from applying JCE as an exclusive form of perpetrator liability was short-lived as the Appeals Chamber overruled the Trial Chamber's judgment and, in particular, its rejection of JCE.[74] The key justification of the Appeals Chamber was that co-perpetration was not supported by customary international law, unlike JCE, which they claimed was firmly established.[75]

Multiple cases since *Stakić* have relied on JCE and judges have attempted to clarify problematic aspects of this doctrine. For example, in *Prosecutor v*

---

    struck a blow or implicitly incited the murder could have foreseen that others would kill the prisoners; hence they too were found guilty of murder." Ibid.

69   For an in-depth analysis of the ICTY's application of JCE and the issues this doctrine has raised at the ICTY see, Attila Bogdan, "Individual Criminal Responsibility in the Execution of a 'Joint Criminal Enterprise' in the Jurisprudence of the ad-hoc International Tribunal for the Former Yugoslavia" (2006) 6 *International Criminal Law Review* 63, 120.

70   *Prosecutor v Milomir Stakić* (*Judgement*) (ICTY Trial Chamber IT-92-24-T, 31 July 2003) [438] ("*Stakić Trial*").

71   Ibid [428].

72   Ibid [438].

73   Ibid [441].

74   *Prosecutor v Milomir Stakić* (*Judgement*) (ICTY Appeal Chamber IT-92-24-A, 22 March 2006) ("*Stakić Appeal*").

75   Ibid [62]. There was negligible discussion as to why the Appeals Chamber found co-perpetration was unsupported in customary international law.

Brđanin, the Trial Chamber had to consider whether an accused could be held liable under JCE for the conduct of persons not party to the JCE.[76] Radoslav Brđanin, the President of a Serbian political group in Bosnia, was accused of being party to a JCE, the purpose of which was the removal of Bosnian Muslims and Bosnian Croats from the planned Bosnian Serb state.[77]

The Prosecution did not submit that Brđanin had perpetrated any of the crimes. It was alleged that crimes against humanity and war crimes has been committed by paramilitary groups in the implementation of the JCE. It was pleaded these were a natural and foreseeable consequence of the implementation of the deportation of Bosnian Muslims and Croats.[78] The Trial Chamber rightly held that the scope of the JCE in this case rendered Brđanin too remote from the crimes to be liable under JCE.[79]

The Appeals Chamber[80] cited earlier ICTY jurisprudence in support of its new ruling, which found that the Trial Chamber had erred in declaring that the perpetrator must be a member of the JCE in order to be criminally liable as a principal. This re-scoping of JCE to include those who were not party to the JCE was criticised as an irreconcilable parting from *Tadić* and from the fundamental principles of individual criminal liability.[81] This author agrees with that criticism. One of the pre-conditions of liability under JCE must be that the prosecution establishes, beyond reasonable doubt, that the accused was party to the JCE. To impose liability upon perpetrators of mass atrocity crimes under JCE, when it cannot be established that they were even party to the JCE, is nonsensical at best and legal over-reaching at worst. This article provides further recommendations on this aspect of the doctrine in Part IV (A).

Undoubtedly, one of the most perplexing decisions from the ICTY was in one of its most prominent cases, *Prosecutor v Šešelj*. This trial involved one of

---

76   *Prosecutor v Radoslav Brđanin (Judgement)* (ICTY Trial Chamber IT-99-36-T, 1 September 2004) [345] (*"Brđanin Trial"*).

77   Ibid [10]–[19].

78   Ibid [345].

79   Ibid [355]–[356].

80   It should be noted that although the Appeals Chamber did consider some of the legal issues pertaining to JCE, and in doing so, it overruled the Trial Chamber's findings, it did not examine the consequences of the new findings. In other words, it did not convict Brđanin since it was deemed to be unfair to Brđanin to enter new convictions based on the fact that Brđanin may have explored different defences on the basis that principal perpetrators need not be JCE members. For further discussion see *Brđanin Appeal* (ICTY Appeals Chamber ITT-99-36-A, 3 April 2007) [361].

81   Cliff Farhang, "Point of No Return" Joint Criminal Enterprise in Brđanin" (2010) 23 *Leiden Journal of International Law* 137, 139.

the highest ranking Serbian politicians, Vojislav Šešelj, who was the President of the Serbian Radical Party and who was charged with nine counts of war crimes and crimes against humanity.[82] Šešelj was specifically charged with participating in a JCE (along with other prominent Serbian politicians, including former Serbian President Slobodan Milošević) to deport the non-Serb population within parts of Croatia and Bosnia, in order to create ethnically-separate territories in Bosnia and Croatia.[83] Šešelj's specific role was the recruitment and organisation of volunteers, nicknamed "Šešeljevci" or "Šešelj's men", who carried out the alleged crimes which included murder, torture, forcible displacement and destruction of villages.[84]

Having accepted the basis for the JCE as being the deportation of non-Serb civilians, instead of assessing whether there was sufficient evidence to establish that Šešelj was a party to the JCE, and whether the perpetrated crimes were a natural and foreseeable consequence of that JCE, the majority engaged in analysis of the scope of the JCE itself.[85] Quoting at length from the *Prosecutor v Milošević* case (Milošević being alleged to be a part of the JCE), the majority criticised the prosecution's approach[86] in *that* case. The majority stated that the proposition that the JCE was based on the political goal of creating a Greater Serbia would involve simplifying the recognition of states and the complex consequences that ensued.[87] Here, the majority needlessly waded perilously close to the political. In any event, the creation of a Greater Serbia was not the alleged JCE in *Šešelj*. Unfortunately, the prosecutor, who might have directed the majority to their error, did not assist the Chamber sufficiently and Šešelj was acquitted of all counts.[88]

Aside from inaccurately questioning the prosecution's basis for the JCE itself, there were very few reasons given for the majority's findings. This point was raised by Judge Lattanzi in a highly disapproving dissenting opinion in the *Šešelj* judgment.[89] Judge Lattanzi criticised the majority's approach and in particular their misrepresentation of the basis for the JCE. The Judge stated

---

82   *Prosecutor v Vojislav Šešelj (Judgement)* (ICTY Trial Chamber IT-03-67-T, 31 March 2016) [8] ("*Šešelj Trial*").

83   Ibid [222].

84   Ibid [409].

85   Ibid [265].

86   Ibid [280].

87   Ibid [265].

88   Ibid [280].

89   *Prosecutor v Vojislav Šešelj (Partially Dissenting Opinion of Judge Flavia Lattanzi – Amended Version Volume 3)* (ICTY Trial Chamber IT-03-67-T, 31 March 2016) (*Šešelj Dissenting Opinion*).

that the Chamber had already accepted the basis for the JCE as being the permanent and forced removal of the non-Serb population, through the commission of crimes. These crimes included persecution, murder, torture, deportation and forcible transfer, amongst others.[90] The majority's misconstruction of the JCE permeated the rest of their reasoning which failed to properly consider the "abundant evidence" pointing to a JCE.[91] Judge Lattanzi was in such disagreement with the majority that she ended her opinion by stating that:[92]

> with this Judgement we have been thrown back centuries into the past, to a period in human history when we used to say *Silent enim leges inter arma* (in times of war, the law is silent).

The Šešelj decision was particularly surprising as it was released shortly after the *Prosecutor v Karadžić* judgement which concerned the prosecution of a high ranking Serb politician, similar to Šešelj. In *Karadžić*, the Trial Chamber found the accused guilty of membership in four separate JCEs which were even broader than those pleaded by the prosecution in *Šešelj*. These included permanently removing Bosnian Muslims and Croats from Bosnia, the sniping and shelling of Sarajevo and the elimination of Bosnian Muslims from Srebrenica.[93] A comparison of these two decisions, and how and why the ICTY reached such diverging verdicts, could be the subject of an altogether different article. The prosecutor in *Šešelj* regrettably failed to convince the international tribunal that Šešelj had committed these crimes. The *Šešelj* verdict has been appealed and it remains to be seen whether the Appeals Chamber will overturn the acquittal and in particular how it will analyse the issues regarding JCE.

3.1.2 International Criminal Tribunal for Rwanda

A year after the establishment of the ICTY, the tribunal to prosecute individuals for gross violations of IHL in Rwanda was also created.[94] JCE has been less frequently invoked by the Office of the Prosecutor at the ICTR than at the ICTY and, hence, there are fewer judgments where JCE is analysed in any depth.[95]

---

90   Ibid [75].
91   Ibid [77]–[87].
92   Ibid [50].
93   *Prosecutor v Radovan Karadžić (Public Redacted Version of Judgement)* (ICTY Trial Chamber IT-95-5/18-T, 24 March 2016) [3].
94   SC Res 955, UNSCOR 49th sess, 3453rd mtg, UN Doc S/RES/955 (8 November 1994) annex ("*ICTR Statute*").
95   *ICTR Statute* arts 2(3)(a) and (2)(3)(b) include genocide and conspiracy to commit genocide as punishable offences. These have been the basis of the majority of the Prosecutor's

Prosecutor v Ntakirutimana was one of the first cases where the Appeals Chamber had to consider JCE.[96] The Chamber examined the *ICTR Statute* and compared it with the *Statute of the ICTY*. It found that since both statutes had exactly the same provisions pertaining to individual criminal liability,[97] and since JCE was part of the jurisprudence of the ICTY,[98] the ICTR would apply JCE.[99] The reasons JCE was not applied in *Ntakirutimana* was not due to any resistance to the doctrine itself but was due to the fact that the prosecution had not specified that the accused were all charged under JCE.[100] Similarly, in *Prosecutor v Rwamakuba*, the Trial Chamber confirmed that JCE existed in customary international law but that it was not required to apply it in the case, as the accused was charged for his direct participation in the alleged crimes and hence, co-perpetration was not at issue.[101]

In a landmark decision regarding mass rape and sexual assault, the Appeals Chamber found Édouard Karamera and Matthieu Ngirumpatse, two of the highest ranking politicians during the Rwandan genocide, guilty of mass rape, sexual assault and mutilation of thousands of Tutsi women and girls during the Rwandan genocide.[102] Although there was an absence of evidence to prove that Karamera and Ngirumpatse had committed the sexual crimes themselves, or that they had ordered their soldiers to commit them, the Trial Chamber found, and the Appeals Chamber confirmed, that both of the accused had

---

indictments. For some examples see *Prosecutor v Michel Bagaragaza* (*Amended Indictment*) (ICTR-2005-86-I, 1 December 2006); *Prosecutor v Simon Bikindi* (*Amended Indictment*) (ICTR-2001-72-I, 20 May 2005); *Prosecutor v Kayishema et al.* (*First Amended Indictment*) (ICTR-95-1-I, 29 April 1996).

96   *Prosecutor v Elizaphan Ntakirutimana and Gérard Ntakirutimana* (*Judgement*) (ICTR Appeals Chamber ICTR-96-10-A and ICTR-96-17-A, 13 December 2004) [468] (*Elizaphan Ntakirutimana and Gérard Ntakirutimana Appeal*).

97   *ICTR Statute* art 6(1) and *ICTY Statute* art 7(1) both read as follows: "A person who planned, instigated, ordered, committed or otherwise aided and abetted in the planning, preparation or execution of a crime referred to in articles 2 to 4 of the present Statute, shall be individually responsible for the crime."

98   *Elizaphan Ntakirutimana and Gérard Ntakirutimana Appeal* (ICTR Appeals Chamber ICTR-96-10-A and ICTR-96-17-A, 13 December 2004) [462].

99   Ibid [468].

100   Ibid [474].

101   *Prosecutor v André Rwamakuba* (*Judgement*) (ICTR Trial Chamber ICTR-98-44C-T, 20 September 2006) [27].

102   *Prosecutor v Édouard Karamera and Matthieu Ngirumpatse* (*Judgement*) (ICTR Trial Chamber ICTR-98-44-1, 2 February 2012) [1490] (*"Édouard Karamera and Matthieu Ngirumpatse Trial"*).

participated in a widespread, common criminal enterprise, whose purpose was to destroy the Tutsi ethnic population in Rwanda. It was a natural and foreseeable consequence that rape and sexual violations would occur as part of this common criminal plan to annihilate an entire ethnic group.[103] Specifically, the Trial Chamber stated that:[104]

> during a campaign to destroy, in whole or in part, a national, ethnic, racial, or religious group, a natural and foreseeable consequence of that campaign will be that soldiers and militias who participate in the destruction will resort to rapes and sexual assaults ... rape and sexual assault of Tutsi women and girls was a natural and foreseeable consequence of the JCE to destroy the Tutsi ethnicity because the perpetrators were participating in the campaign to exterminate Tutsis in Rwanda.

Haffajee states that the use of JCE to hold those responsible for rape as a war crime in Rwanda to account "holds great promise" since it contextualises the crime of rape as part of a larger plan that motivated the violence in Rwanda.[105] Despite these widespread rapes that occurred in Rwanda, the challenge of gathering evidence had previously rendered it impossible for the prosecution to secure convictions. JCE enabled the ICTR to respond to these evidentiary difficulties as prosecutors no longer had to prove the *precise* connection between the accused and the rapes, on the condition that the rapes were a natural and foreseeable consequence of the JCE.[106]

3.1.3   Special Court for Sierra Leone

The SCSL was established in 2002 in order to address grave violations of IHL perpetrated during Sierra Leone's civil war.[107] JCE has featured at the SCSL but

---

103   The Chamber noted that there was a "heightened risk that the strong will abuse the weak during a war and ... especially that soldiers and other combatants, if not restricted by their superiors, will commit rapes against women and girls of the opposite party to the conflict", ibid [1475], [1477].

104   Ibid [1476].

105   Rebecca L. Haffajee, "Prosecuting Crimes of Rape and Sexual Violence at the ICTR: The Application of Joint Criminal Enterprise Theory" (2006) 29(1) *Harvard Journal of Law and Gender* 201, 202.

106   Ibid.

107   SC Res 1315, UN SCOR, 4186th mtg, UN Doc S/RES/1315 (14 August 2000) ("*Agreement Between the United Nations and the Government of Sierra Leone on the Establishment of a Special Court for Sierra Leone*") art 1.

less so than the ICTY and ICTR.[108] In *Prosecutor v Taylor* (the first international trial to prosecute a Head of State since the Nuremberg trials)[109] Charles Taylor, the former President of Liberia, was charged with five counts of crimes against humanity, violations of Common Article 3 to the *Geneva Conventions* and *Additional Protocol II*, and one count of conscripting and enlisting child soldiers.[110] It is an indication of how far international criminal law has progressed that Taylor was even able to be prosecuted, since he did not commit these crimes in his own country but in Sierra Leone.[111]

Taylor was found guilty, on the basis of individual criminal responsibility, of aiding and abetting on all 11 counts but the Trial Chamber ruled that the prosecution had failed to prove beyond reasonable doubt that Taylor's actions were in pursuit of a common plan that was part of any JCE.[112] The Chamber's reasoning noted the following distinction between JCE and aiding/abetting:[113]

> Joint criminal enterprise, as a unique form of enterprise or common purpose liability, is particularly characterised by the legal requirement of a common criminal purpose. This common criminal purpose justifies holding an accused liable not only for his own contribution to the commission of crimes, but also for the contributions of those with whom he shares a common purpose. [Aiding and Abetting] are distinct from joint criminal enterprise in their legal elements and the consequent assignment of criminal liability, as for aiding and abetting an accused is only held liable for his own contributions to the commission of the crimes.

Although the Trial Chamber found that there was evidence to confirm that Taylor had participated in providing significant political and military support for the invasion of Sierra Leone, and that he had accepted diamonds from certain rebel groups in exchange for arms, this was deemed as evidence of their quid pro quo relationship, rather than evidence of a common plan and JCE.[114]

---

108   Gideon Boas, James L. Bischoff and Natalie L. Reid, *International Criminal Law Practitioner Library: Volume 1, Forms of Responsibility in International Criminal Law* (Cambridge University Press, 1st ed, 2008) 128.

109   *Lessons from the Trial of Charles Taylor* (31 January 2017) Human Rights Watch <www.hrw.org>

110   *Taylor Trial* (SCSL Trial Chamber SCSL-03-01-T, 18 May 2012) [12].

111   Taylor was elected President of Liberia in 1997. He was charged with committing crimes in violation of international humanitarian law in Sierra Leone between 1996–2002, during the time of Sierra Leone's civil war.

112   *Taylor Trial* (SCSL Trial Chamber SCSL-03-01-T, 18 May 2012) [621].

113   Ibid.

114   Ibid [6852]–[6900].

Jalloh suggests that the prosecution exaggerated the level of Taylor's involvement in the conflict in Sierra Leone,[115] a claim that was not able to be established on the evidence. The Appeal Chamber's judgment essentially upheld the Trial Chamber's judgment finding that the Trial Chamber's findings were reasonable in light of the evidence.[116] The fact that the SCSL did not find Taylor guilty on the basis of JCE is not in itself a rejection of the doctrine but a failure by the Office of the Prosecutor to establish beyond reasonable doubt that Taylor was guilty on this basis. Failure to satisfy any Court of an accused's liability on the evidence must rightly result in a failure to secure a conviction *on that basis.*

3.1.3.1   *Common Purpose: Reliable Doctrine or Flawed Theory?*
The approach of the ad-hoc tribunals, in particular the ICTY, has received some support and much criticism for varying reasons.[117] One of JCE's most prominent supporters was the jurist and scholar Antonio Cassese. For Cassese, JCE was a very important doctrine that guaranteed the culpability of individuals would not be concealed in the "fog of criminality."[118] Cassese contended that impunity for group criminality was morally wrong and breached the principles of criminal law, to protect individuals and communities from acts that cause irreparable damage.[119] Indeed, the Appeals Chamber in *Tadić*, the body responsible for introducing JCE to the jurisprudence of international criminal law, cited similar justifications for the application of JCE. The Chamber stated that international crimes committed during times of war do not stem from the tendencies of individuals but constitute expressions of group criminality. It went on to state that, although it is possible that perpetrations of the criminal

---

115   Charles Chernor Jalloh, "The Law and Politics of the Charles Taylor Case" (2015) 43(3) *Denver Journal of International Law and Policy* 229, 233.

116   *Prosecutor v Charles Ghankay Taylor (Judgement)* (SCSL Appeals Chamber SCSL-03-01-A, 26 September 2013) ("*Taylor Appeal*").

117   See Danner and Martinez, above n 20; Jens David Ohlin, "Joint Criminal Confusion" (2009) 12 (3) *New Criminal Law Review* 406–419; Gunel Guliyeva, "The Concept of Joint Criminal Enterprise and ICC Jurisdiction" (2008) 5(1) *Eyes on the International Criminal Court* 49–79; Mark J. Osiel, "Modes of Participation in Mass Atrocities" (2005) 38(3) *ell International Law Journal* 793–822; Linda Engvall. "The Future of Extended Joint Criminal Enterprise – Will the ICTY's Innovation Meet the Standards of the ICC" (2007) 76 *Nordic Journal of International Law* 241–263.

118   Anio Cassese and others. "Amicus Curiae Brief of Anio Cassese and Members of the Journal of International Criminal Justice on Joint Criminal Enterprise' (2009) 20 *Criminal Law Forum* 289, 294.

119   Ibid 294.

acts may be limited only to some members of the group, the other members are often indispensible in facilitating the implementation of the crime. The moral gravity is no less, and no different, for those than it is for the physical perpetrators.[120]

Others have highlighted that JCE, as applied by the ICTY, is appealing in that it is able to extend to those who perpetrate crimes outside any formal chain of command. This was particularly prescient in the ICTY trials, as many of the accused were civilians who took up fighting or belonged to various paramilitary groups.[121] Such groups are common in mass atrocities, especially given the reality that often, though everyone has a part to play in carrying out the task, no one person can be said to have ultimate control over any other or over the commission of the crime.[122]

The general consensus from critics is that JCE is akin to guilt by association and infringes on the principle of individual criminal responsibility.[123] This is mostly targeted at the *mens rea* requirement for extended JCE.[124] Olasolo suggests that the extended form of JCE, in particular, imposes a standard akin to advertent recklessness as it does not require the accused to have knowledge that there is a likelihood, or even a strong likelihood, that the foreseeable consequences are a part of implementing the common purpose.[125] In fact, Olasolo argues that in some instances it is irrelevant whether or not the accused even foresaw that the consequences might occur, but it is sufficient that the accused was simply in a position to be able to foresee that crimes may occur.[126] The central issue for Olasolo, and others, is that such an approach conflicts, and even breaches, the principles of individual culpability, a concept that is central to criminal law.[127]

---

120   *Tadić Appeal* (ICTY Appeals Chamber IT-94-I-A, 15 July 1999) [191]. The Chamber goes on to say that only holding the physical perpetrators liable would disregard the role of the co-perpetrators and that, basing their responsibility on aiding and abetting may understate their level of responsibility for the criminal acts.

121   Osiel, above n 117, 797.

122   Ibid.

123   Danner and Martinez, above n 20, 134.

124   Ibid 109. Danner and Martinez argue that the foreseeability requirement in extended JCEs lowers the *mens rea* assessment from that of intention to knowledge or recklessness.

125   Hector Olasolo, "Joint Criminal Enterprise and its Extended Form: A Theory of Perpetration Giving Rise to Principal Liability, A Notion of Accessorial Liability, or a Form of Partnership in Crime?" (2009) 20 *Criminal Law Forum* 263, 280.

126   Ibid 281.

127   Ibid 284.

Danner and Martinez extend this critique and suggest that the ICTY's application of JCE could threaten the legitimacy of international law and undermine human rights.[128] This is partly due to the fact that there is limited jurisprudential direction on how the scope of a JCE should be defined.[129] Critics argue that this lack of a doctrinal framework has resulted in very broad indictments and has permitted the ICTY, in particular, to hold individuals such as Tadić liable for serious international crimes without any evidence that he in fact committed them.[130] The risk with this form of JCE, according to critics, is that it may result in unjust convictions for individuals who may indeed have been guilty of *some* crimes but who did not deserve the level of culpability attributed to them.[131]

Concerns regarding the foreseeability requirement within JCE can be responded to in the following ways. Foreseeability within the *mens rea* element of JCE is not unique. Numerous domestic legal systems accommodate for group-type offending with similar legal doctrines.[132] The author is acutely aware of the significant differences between domestic and international crimes, and the legal systems underpinning the laws that seek to punish offenders for such crimes. Comparisons of JCE with domestic law are made with great caution. It is, however, important to highlight that there is a similar principle to JCE within domestic legal systems. This principle holds that criminal law should capture those who participate in group criminality and who perpetrate crimes beyond those that are strictly part of the criminal purpose but where they are a foreseeable extension of the initial crime.

One example is *New Zealand Crimes Act 1961* s 66(2) which renders everyone a party to, and guilty of, an offence if they commit the offence or help or encourage its commission. The provision extends liability to offences outside the common purpose and states that "where two or more persons form a common intention to prosecute any unlawful purpose ... each of them is a party to every offence committed by any one of them in the prosecution of the common purpose if the commissions of that offence was known to be a

---

128   Danner and Martinez, above n 20, 132. The authors attribute this to the fact that it is common for international courts to wish to restore some sort of justice to victims but warn that permitting such an extended form of liability infringes on the human rights of the accused, who deserve the right to a fair trial.

129   Danner and Martinez, above n 20, 134–135.

130   Shane Darcy "Imputed Criminal Liability and the Goals of International Justice" (2007) 20 *Leiden Journal of International Law* 377, 386.

131   Ibid 386.

132   Ibid.

probable consequence of the prosecution of an unlawful common purpose."[133] The Supreme Court of New Zealand has defined probable consequence to mean "could well happen."[134] Additionally, an inference of foresight may be drawn from "voluntary participation in a criminal enterprise."[135] In establishing liability under s 66(2), the Crown must prove that the accused knew (a subjective standard) that the commission of the incidental offence could well happen in the pursuit of the initial offence but intention as to the incidental offence is not required.[136] This is not dissimilar from liability under JCE which requires intention for the common purpose offence but not for the incidental offence.

The policy reasoning behind such provisions was eruditely expressed by Lord Steyn in *R v Powell and another*:[137]

> It is just that a secondary party who foresees that the primary offender might kill with the intent sufficient for murder, and assists and encourages the primary offender in the criminal enterprise on this basis, should be guilty of murder. He ought to be criminally liable for harm that he foresaw and that in fact resulted from the crime he assisted and encouraged. ... The criminal justice system exists to control crime. A prime function of that system must be to deal justly but effectively with those who join with others in criminal enterprise. Experience has shown that joint criminal enterprises only too readily escalate into the commission of greater offences.

This principle equally applies in international criminal law. Individuals who participate in the perpetration of JCE, in the context of mass atrocity crimes, should be guilty of the crime in question if they foresee it.

Cassese described the incidental crime as "the outgrowth of previously agreed or planned criminal conduct for which each participant in the common plan is already responsible."[138] Contrary to the Appeal Chamber's decision in *Brđanin*, when JCE is properly applied, an accused can never be charged with the incidental crime without firstly being party to the common criminal plan.

---

133   *New Zealand Crimes Act 1961*, s 66(2).

134   *Ashin v R* [2014] NZSC 153, [2015] 1 NZLR 493, (2014) 27 CRNZ 314 [100]–[101].

135   *R v Ma'u* [2008] NZCA 117.

136   *Uhrle v R* [2016] NZSC 64 [5].

137   *Regina v Powell and another* [1999] 1 AC 1 HL.

138   Anio Cassese, "Proper Limits of Individual Responsibility under the Doctrine of JCE" (2007) 5 *Journal of International Criminal Justice* 10, 119.

An accused becomes criminally culpable for the incidental crime because they willingly engaged in the commission of a specific crime, were in a position where they could foresee that the incidental crime would occur, and they willingly took the risk and did nothing to oppose or disengage from the criminal conduct.[139] Each of these elements must be established by the prosecution, to the very high standard of beyond reasonable doubt, before an accused can be charged.

Finally, as in domestic criminal systems, varying degrees of criminal perpetration can be addressed at sentencing. In *Prosecutor v Erdemović*, the ICTY addressed different levels of involvement in a JCE through sentencing. Dražen Erdemović was charged with, and pleaded guilty to, murder as a crime against humanity for his part in the killing of approximately 1200 Muslim men during the genocide of Srebrenica.[140] He argued, in part, that he was forced to participate in the crimes under duress as he felt there was a threat to his life, and the lives of his wife and children, if he did not.[141] Nonetheless, Erdemović partook in the killings and personally killed between 10–100 Muslim men.[142]

The Trial Chamber of the ICTY rightly reasoned that, given the nature of the crimes, the threat he felt to his own life could not absolve him from the crime he had committed, particularly as the duress he felt was not proven beyond reasonable doubt and could not be verified by independent evidence.[143] The Chamber found Erdemović was guilty of murder as a crime against humanity. Due to his guilty plea, his cooperation with the ICTY, and the remorse he demonstrated, he was issued a relatively light sentence of ten years imprisonment.[144]

Given some of the unfavourable reviews of JCE, it is not unexpected that the ICC rejected the common purpose approach and commenced its tenure with a

---

139   Cassese, above n 137, 120.

140   *Prosecutor v Dražen Erdemović (Sentencing Judgement)* (ICTY Trial Chamber IT-96-22-T, 29 November 1996) [3] (*"Erdemović Sentencing"*).

141   Ibid [114].

142   Darryl Robinson, "The Identity Crisis of International Criminal Law" (2008) 21 *Leiden Journal of International Law* 925, 931.

143   *Erdemović Sentencing* (ICTY Trial Chamber IT-96-22-T, 29 November 1996) [19].

144   The Appeals Chamber discusses how the moral gravity of participation in group criminality is no different between those who physically perpetrate the crime and those who participate and contribute in some other way. The Chamber was of the view that to hold the non-perpetrators liable as accessories would discount the fact that those individuals made it possible for the crime to be implemented, *Tadić Appeal* (ICTY Appeals Chamber IT-94-I-A, 15 July 1999) [192].

doctrinal distinction which, in this author's view, was erroneous. The following section explores the chosen doctrine of the ICC.

3.2   Narrowing the Scope of Liability: The International Criminal Court

The *Rome Statute* was concluded before the ICTY had commenced the majority of its trials. It entered into force amidst heated debates regarding modes of liability in international law.[145] Article 25 sets out modes of criminal liability[146] but the *Statute* is silent on whether the ICC must apply any particular theory of criminal responsibility.[147] One of the first indictments issued by the ICC's Office of the Prosecutor was for Thomas Lubanga Dyilo, who was charged under art 25(3)(a) for the crime of enlisting, conscripting and using children to participate in armed hostilities.[148]

The Prosecution elected to plead that Lubanga was guilty under the doctrine of co-perpetration and was careful to distinguish art 25(3)(a) from co-perpetration in the form of JCE. The prosecutor stated that the *Rome Statute* did not proscribe as broad definitions of criminal liability as the *ICTY Statute*.[149] Instead, the prosecution submitted that co-perpetration under the

---

145   The *Rome Statute of the International Criminal Court* opened for signature 17 July 1998, 2187 UNTS 3 (entered into force 1 July 2002) ("*Rome Statute*") was adopted in 1998 and entered into force 2002. Most of the trials at the ICTY commenced after 1998.

146   The wording of the relevant provisions of art 25(3)(a)-(d) is: "in accordance with this Statute, a person shall be criminally responsible and liable for punishment for a crime within the jurisdiction of the Court if that person: (a) Commits such a crime, whether as an individual, jointly with another or through another person, regardless of whether that other person is criminally responsible; (b) Orders, solicits or induces the commission of such a crime which in fact occurs or is attempted; (c) For the purpose of facilitating the commission of such a crime, aids, abets or otherwise assists in its commission or its attempted commission, including providing the means for its commission; (d) In any other way contributes to the commission or attempted commission of such a crime by a group of persons acting with a common purpose."

147   *Rome Statute* art 1.

148   *Situation in the Democratic Republic of the Congo in the case of the Prosecutor v Thomas Lubanga Dyilo (Warrant for Arrest)* (ICC Pre-Trial Chamber I ICC-01/04-01/06, 10 February 2006) [4] ("*Lubanga Warrant for Arrest*"). Lubanga, the former leader of the paramilitary group Union of Congolese Patriots, was accused of conducting massacres against civilians during the conflict between various rebel and paramilitary groups in the Congo from 1998–2005. Lubanga was personally charged with co-perpetration under *Rome Statute* art 25(3)(a), for the war crime of conscripting children under the age of fifteen to his army and using them in conflicts.

149   *Decision on the Confirmation of Charges in the Case of the Prosecutor v Thomas Lubanga Dyilo (Judgement)* (ICC Pre-Trial Chamber I ICC 01/04-01/06-803, 29 January 2007) [323] ("*Lubanga Pre-Trial*").

Rome Statute was based on the control over crime theory and, in particular, it held individuals liable as co-perpetrators when they had joint control over a crime through their essential contribution to the commission of that crime.[150]

It was at this point that the Pre-Trial Chamber reiterated the three approaches to determining criminal liability. Firstly, the objective approach held that principals to a crime were those who had physically contributed to the criminal act, by carrying out one or more elements of the offence.[151] For example, in a murder, the individuals who physically committed one or more acts which killed the victim would be liable as principals.[152] Those who may have been involved with the murder in some way behind the scenes, but who did not physically commit the *actus reus*, were found to be accomplices.[153] The subjective approach (adopted by the ad-hoc tribunals) held as principals all those who shared a common intent to commit a crime, regardless of their level of individual contribution to the realisation of the objective elements of the offence.[154] The Pre-Trial Chamber then set out a third approach, which it adopted in *Lubanga*: the control over crime approach. This approach deems that principals are all those who control the commission of the crime and not just those who commit the physical acts. Namely, those in control who determine whether and how such crimes will be conducted and realised.[155] This approach is addressed in more detail in the following section.

3.2.1 Control over the Crime

The control over crime theory has its roots in German criminal law and in the writings of the legal scholar, Claus Roxin.[156] Roxin wrote in the early 1960s (during the time of some of the Nazi war crimes trials in the domestic courts of Germany) in opposition to the approach taken by West German courts at the time, which had found many former Nazis guilty as accomplices, and not as principals, to crimes.[157] The position of other German legal scholars supported

---

150   Ibid [322]. The Prosecutor did not reference any specific cases from the ICTY in this submission.
151   Ibid [328].
152   Ibid.
153   Ibid.
154   Ibid [329].
155   Ibid [330].
156   Claus Roxin, "Crimes as Part of Organised Power Structures" (2011) 9 *Journal of International Criminal Justice* 191, 205.
157   One particular case Roxin mentions is the trial of Bogdan Stashynsky, a member of the KGB, who had murdered two exiled Ukranian leaders. The weapon of murder was a spray gun that contained crushed cyanide and was intended to make the murders look like

Germany's courts. It affirmed that those who did not directly participate in the commission of a crime, but who were behind the scenes, could never be deemed to be perpetrators themselves but only abettors.[158] This approach was unacceptable to Roxin who argued that the corollary of this was that even Hitler himself – the man most responsible for initiating the Nazi crimes – was excluded as a perpetrator of these crimes,[159] a result which was preposterous to him.

These objections stem from Roxin's principle argument: in the context of group criminality, such as that of the Holocaust, crimes can never be carried out by a single offender but are committed by a large number of people acting in various roles, with varying degrees of participation.[160] Through his theory of *Organisationsherrschaft*, Roxin attempted to create a concept whereby Nazi leaders could be held responsible as perpetrators for the crimes committed during the Nazi era.[161] This required an "unprejudiced understanding of the concept of control"[162] as Roxin suggested that organisational structures, such as the one that the Third Reich had established, did not depend on the actions of specific individuals but functioned automatically. Those directing the orders to kill could be expected to have their orders obeyed and carried out.[163] These perpetrators behind perpetrators, those in the highest echelons of an organisation, who ordered or directed the commission of crimes, were just as guilty for those crimes as the direct perpetrators.[164] This did not free direct perpetrators of their guilt (assuming they were not coerced or under duress) but acknowledged the reality of systemic criminality and apportioned equal blame to those who controlled the crime, even if they did not themselves perform the *actus reus*.

---

heart attacks. Stashynsky later confessed and was tried at the Federal Supreme Court in Germany. The Court applied the subjective approach in establishing perpetrator/accessory liability and found Stashynsky guilty of abetting the murders, ibid.

158   Roxin refers to the German scholars Welzel and Gallas who posited that those who were behind the scenes of a crime could never be deemed as perpetrators but instead as instigators or abettors, ibid.

159   Ibid 198.

160   Ibid.

161   Jens David Ohlin, Elies Van Sliedregt and Thomas Weigend, "Assessing the Control Theory" (2013) 26 *Leiden Journal of International Law* 725, 726.

162   Roxin, above n 157, 198.

163   Ibid.

164   Roxin discusses how the inverse of normal organisation control is true in instances of mass criminality as usually the more remote an individual is from the victim of the crime, the less control they are deemed to have, whereas distance from the crime in mass criminality equates to greater organisational control, ibid.

The control theory focuses on the unlawfulness of the elements of an offence rather than the mind-set of the accused at the time.[165]

3.2.1.1   *A Note on Command/Superior Responsibility*

A note must be made here in order to clarify why, in such instances, the doctrines of command or superior liability are rarely invoked. Liability under command or superior responsibility is itself a contested area of international criminal law, and in particular the issue of whether an accused charged under command/superior responsibility is charged as a principal or as an accessory is an ongoing debate.[166] Additionally, it should be noted that command responsibility applies to military commanders. Superior responsibility is not limited to those within the military but attaches to military *and* civilian individuals, who exercise control over subordinates.[167] The threshold for establishing responsibility for superiors is higher than that for command responsibility under the *Rome Statute*, as it requires evidence that the superior had information regarding the acts of his subordinates and that the superior chose not to act upon this information.[168] Command responsibility requires that the commander knew or should have known their forces were committing or about to commit crimes.[169] There is no scope within this article to discuss the details of this separate doctrine, however, it is necessary to highlight how command/superior responsibility differs from co-perpetration.

Rome Statute art 28 outlines the elements of command and superior responsibility.[170] To reiterate, co-perpetration is a form of liability that is dependent on the co-accused contributing in some way to the realisation of the objective elements of the crime. An accused charged under command/superior responsibility can be found liable for failing to act; in other words, there is no one physical act that is required, but omitting to act is sufficient to establish liability.[171] It must be proven that the accused had actual or constructive

---

165   Jain, above n 31, 165.

166   For further reading on this subject, see G. Mettraux, *The Law of Command Responsibility* (Oxford University Press, 1st ed, 2009).

167   René Värk, "Superior Responsibility" (2012) 15 *Esian National Defence College Proceedings* 143, 144.

168   Jamie Allan Williamson, "Some Considerations on Command Responsibility and Criminal Liability" (2008) 90 (870) *International Review of the Red Cross* 303, 308.

169   Ibid.

170   *Rome Statute* art 28(1) (a)-(c) and art 28(2)(a)-(c).

171   Elies van Sliedregt, "Article 28 of the ICC Statute: Mode of Liability and/or Separate Offense?" (2009) 12(3) *New Criminal Law Review: An International and Interdisciplinary Journal* 420, 422.

knowledge and that he or she failed to take all reasonable and necessary steps within their power to prevent or punish the crimes.[172] This doctrine has been employed in instances where there is insufficient evidence to prove that the accused directly participated in the commission of crimes but where they facilitated the crime indirectly, either by enabling the crimes or failing to act in order to prevent the crimes.[173] There have been few convictions under superior/command responsibility as typically it is established that the accused was a direct participant in the crime.[174]

3.2.1.2   *Returning to Lubanga*

The ICC held that the concept of control could be interpreted in three ways. Having control over the crime included direct perpetration where individuals physically carry out the objective elements of the offence.[175] It also included indirect perpetration, where the individual had control over the mind of those carrying out the physical elements of the offence, even if they did not participate in the actual commission of the crime.[176] Finally, this mode of liability encompasses co-perpetration where the individual has, along with others, control over the offence by virtue of an "essential" task assigned to them.[177]

The components of co-perpetration are further segregated into objective and subjective elements. The objective elements require the existence of an agreement between two or more persons[178] and a coordinated essential contribution by each co-perpetrator to the realisation of the objective elements of the crime.[179] The *mens rea* requirements are: the fulfilment of the subjective elements of the particular crime; the mutual awareness and acceptance amongst the co-perpetrators that the implementation of the agreement may result in the fulfilment of the objective elements of the crime; and, that the accused must be aware of the factual circumstances enabling him or her to jointly control the crime.[180] The essential contribution requirement is the

---

172   *Rome Statute* art 28(1)(a)-(c) and art 28(2)(a)-(c).

173   Värk, above n 166, 159.

174   Ibid. There has only been one case at the ICC concerning this mode of responsibility: *Prosecutor v Jean-Pierre Bemba Gombo* (*Judgement*) (ICC Pre-Trial Chamber II ICC-01/05-01/08, 15 June 2009).

175   *Lubanga Pre-Trial* (ICC Pre-Trial Chamber I ICC 01/04-01/06-803, 29 January 2007) [332].

176   Ibid.

177   Ibid.

178   Ibid [342].

179   Ibid [345].

180   Ibid [349].

aspect of co-perpetration, based on the control over crime doctrine, which has proven to be problematic and is considered in further detail in the following section.

3.2.2   Essential Contribution

The determinative factor of the essential contribution test, as framed by the Pre-Trial Chamber in *Lubanga,* is whether the co-perpetrator had sufficient power to be able to frustrate the commission of the crime.[181] A co-accused can only be found liable as a co-perpetrator when they could frustrate the crime by failing to carry out their task.[182] Some scholars have reframed this requirement as a form of "negative control".[183] That is, the co-perpetrator bears the power to disrupt the commission of the crime, which is distinct from having the ability to ensure the crime is committed.[184] The complexity of this requirement becomes immediately apparent when courts are burdened with the overwhelming task of determining what *exactly* constitutes an essential contribution. This intricacy is evident even in the judgment of the Trial Chamber in *Lubanga* itself. The prosecution attempted to convince the Trial Chamber that, in order to establish co-perpetrator liability, as provided for in art 25(3)(a), it was not necessary that the contribution of the accused be deemed essential but rather "substantial".[185] This submission was rejected on the basis that it was contrary to how art 25(3)(a)-(d) operates as a whole, as explained by the Trial Chamber. Since both arts 25(3)(a) and 25(3)(d) address group criminality, the difference is that the former is focused on *commission* and the latter on *contribution*.[186] Thus, the Chamber reasoned that art 25(3)(a) was of greater significance since it focused on direct co-perpetration without really explaining how art 25(3)(d) operates or what its significance is. The second reason the "substantial" submission was rejected was due to the overlap with art 25(3)(c) which encompasses aiding and abetting and which requires a "substantial

---

181   Ibid [347].

182   Thomas Weigend, "Intent, Mistake of Law, and Co-Perpetration in the *Lubanga* Decision on Confirmation of Charges" (2008) 6(3) *Journal of International Criminal Justice* 471, 476.

183   Héctor Olásolo and Ana Pérez Cepeda, "The Notion of Control of the Crime and its Application by the ICTY in the *Stakić* Case" (2004) 4 *International Criminal Law Review* 475, 502.

184   Ibid.

185   *Lubanga Pre-Trial* (ICC Pre-Trial Chamber I ICC 01/04-01/06-803, 29 January 2007) [991].

186   Ibid [996]. The Chamber explained that in art 25(3)(a) the co-accused commits the crime whereas under 25(3)(d), the co-accused contributes "in any other way" to the implementation of the crime by a group of individuals, pursuant to a common purpose.

contribution".[187] The conclusion was that since art 25(3)(a) was concerned with the highest mode of liability, it had to impose a higher burden than for aiding and abetting – hence, the level of contribution for commission had to be "essential."[188]

The facts of *Lubanga* made it very clear for the Trial Chamber to establish that there was sufficient evidence of an agreement, the purpose of which was to construct an army and ensure the domination of Ituri.[189] The next point of analysis was whether the essential contribution requirement had been met, with the Trial Chamber establishing at the outset that there was no requirement within the *Rome Statute* that the essential contribution of the co-perpetrator must occur contemporaneously with the commission of the crime.[190] Additionally, the Chamber stated that an assessment of whether an accused's contribution was essential was to be determined on a case-by-case basis since it required an adaptable approach, thereby rejecting any notion of a standardised legal test.[191]

The prosecution then argued that Lubanga was party to a common plan to build an army and commence a political movement and that he, in turn, coordinated and approved the military's movements, which resulted in the recruitment of child soldiers.[192] This submission was accepted by the Chamber. It found that the enlistment and use of child soldiers did form part of the common plan, since a common plan did not have to have been directed at the specific crime in question.[193] This finding raises a contentious issue within the control theory as interpreted by the ICC in that it is unclear whether the accused's essential contribution must be made towards the common goal in general, or the specific crime in question. It is necessary at this juncture to outline the exact wording with respect to the essential contribution requirement, which is: "that the accused provided an essential contribution to the *common plan*[194] that resulted in the commission of the relevant crime."[195]

In *Lubanga*, according to the prosecution, Lubanga's contribution was essential to the realisation of the common plan, since he had control over

---

187   Ibid [991]. A substantial contribution was defined as when "the crime might still have occurred absent the contribution of the Accused but not without great difficulty."

188   Ibid [997].

189   Ibid [1045].

190   Ibid [982].

191   Ibid [1001].

192   Ibid [1019].

193   Ibid [1021].

194   Emphasis added.

195   Ibid [1006].

the military and this role of controlling the military was sufficient in itself to establish that Lubanga's contribution to the recruitment of child soldiers was essential.[196] The defence challenged this line of argument by stating that Lubanga's logistical and organisational role of providing weapons and ammunition to the FPLC was irrelevant when it came to the charge of enlisting child soldiers and that the recruitment of child soldiers was not dependent on Lubanga's contribution.[197]

The Chamber found Lubanga guilty of enlisting child soldiers but the way it arrived at this conclusion is riddled with contradictions and confusion. Having outlined that the contribution had to be specific to the common plan, the Trial Chamber assessed Lubanga's involvement with the specific crime of recruiting and enlisting child soldiers rather than the common plan, which was to create an army and a political movement.[198] The evidence which proved determinative in finding Lubanga liable as a co-perpetrator was the fact that he visited and addressed soldiers and recruits at a training camp[199] and that he had child soldiers acting as his bodyguards.[200] Unfortunately, the Trial Chamber did not enter into an analysis of whether the recruitment of child soldiers would have occurred had it not been for Lubanga's contribution, and did not consider whether Lubanga had the power to frustrate the crimes,[201] so the threshold for this test remains elusive.

This line of reasoning has been criticised with some scholars suggesting that, other than Lubanga's overall co-ordinating role, there was scant evidence to suggest he had directly participated in the recruitment of child soldiers and therefore his contribution could not be regarded as essential.[202] Put another way, without Lubanga's contribution the plan would have still succeeded.[203] The Chamber's proclamation of the undisputed role Lubanga enjoyed as President and Commander in Chief is more reflective of the sort of analysis required to establish liability under *Rome Statute* art 28 for command or superior responsibility than it is for co-perpetration.

The analysis of evidence by the Chamber is predominantly centred on Lubanga's authority to issue orders or directives and the level of his

---

196   Ibid [1138].
197   Ibid [1139].
198   Ibid [1224].
199   Ibid [1245].
200   Ibid.
201   Steffen Wirth, "Co-perpetration in the *Lubanga* Judgement" (2012) 10 *Journal of International Criminal Justice 971*, 987.
202   Weigend, above n 181, 476.
203   Ibid 476.

involvement in military operations, in order to establish that Lubanga had ultimate authority.[204] This line of enquiry was unnecessary to the issue before the
Chamber, since co-perpetration, as applied by the Trial Chamber in *Lubanga*, is
not focused on the hierarchical ranking of a co-accused within an organisation
but superior and command responsibility – one of the elements under that
mode of liability is the establishment that the accused had "effective control"
of their subordinates.[205] The current author is not alone in objecting to some
of the Trial Chamber's analysis and approach. The following section considers
some additional points of critique.

3.2.2.1   *The Complications with "Essential" Contribution*

Disagreements regarding the appropriate approach to establish co-perpetration
liability were present within the Trial Chamber in *Lubanga*. Judge Fulford de-
viated from the approach taken by the majority for several reasons. His most
pressing concern with the essential contribution requirement is the fact that it
requires judges to enter into the realm of the counterfactual and conduct analyses based on hypothetical constructions of what may have resulted, were it
not for the contribution of the accused.[206] Judge Fulford posits that this hypothetical exercise places too high a threshold on the Prosecution, which would
be required to present counterfactuals to the court.[207] Instead, Judge Fulford
submits the correct application of art 25(3)(a) only requires the prosecution
to establish the contribution of the individual to the commission of the crime,
with one or more persons, and not whether the contribution was essential.[208]

Much of the literature on this point supports Judge Fulford's dissent. Yanev
and Koojimans refer to the East Timor Tribunal's decision in *João Sarmento* to
highlight the practical impact of such an approach.[209] Sarmento was found to

---

204   See the line of enquiry taken in *Lubanga Pre-Trial* (ICC Pre-Trial Chamber I ICC 01/04-
01/06-803, 29 January 2007) [1141]–[1223].

205   Article 28(a) states that:
"A military commander or person effectively acting as a military commander shall be
criminally responsible for crimes within the jurisdiction of the Court committed by *forces
under his or her effective command and control,* or effective authority and control as the
case may be.
The provision for superior responsibility is virtually the same except for the fact that it
refers to 'effective authority and control' rather than command and control."

206   *Prosecutor v Thomas Lubanga Dyilo (Judgement – Dissenting Opinion of Judge Fulford)* (ICC
Trial Chamber I 01/04-01/06-2842, 14 March 2012) [10] ("*Lubanga Dissenting Opinion*").

207   Ibid [10].

208   Ibid [15].

209   L. Yanev and T. Koojimans, "Divided Minds in the Lubanga Trial Judgement: A Case
Against the Joint Control Theory" (2013) 13(4) *International Criminal Law Review* 789, 799.

be a member of a militia group in Samu, in East Timor, and was accused of the murder of three men.[210] He was charged under Section 14(3)(a)[211] of the *United Nations Transitional Administration in East Timor Regulation*, which is identical in wording to *Rome Statute* art 25(3)(a).[212] The Tribunal found Sarmento guilty of murder as a co-perpetrator, even though he was one of a number of persons who had taken part in the beating and killing of the victim.[213] The Tribunal made this ruling despite any evidence that he had committed the fatal act.[214]

An application of the essential contribution requirement in this case would have required the judges to enter into the realm of the counterfactual.[215] And where does such an enquiry end? Under the essential contribution requirement, Sarmento, who shared the intention to kill the victim, and participated in beating the victim, but whose lack of contribution would not have frustrated the crime (since there were a number of others who would have ensured the completion of the crime) would not have been found liable under the control theory. It could not be proven that his contribution was essential to the crime. At best, he may have been liable as an accessory to the crime. This begs the question raised by Yanev and Koojimans: how can it be just if an individual is deemed to be an accessory due to the fact that, despite his shared intention, a retrospective assessment of the counterfactual renders his contribution to be less than his partners in crime?[216] Yanev and Koojimans argue that if the essential contribution standard were to be followed strictly, and if the standard of power to frustrate the crime guided the interpretation of art 25(3)(a), proving co-perpetration would be a never-ending task.[217]

Judge Van Den Wyngaert directed similar criticism of the control theory approach in her opinion in the *Ngudjolo* decision. Ngudjolo Chui, a former nurse who became a colonel in the armed forces of the Democratic Republic of the Congo ("DRC"), was charged under art 25(3)(a) with seven counts of

---

210   Ibid.

211   Ibid.

212   *United Nations Transitional Administration in East Timor Regulations* s 14(3)(a) reads that a person shall be criminally responsible if they: commit such a crime, whether as an individual, jointly with another or through another person, regardless of whether that other person is criminally responsible.

213   Yanev and Koojimans, above n 208, 799.

214   Ibid.

215   Jens D. Ohlin, "Joint Intentions to Commit International Crimes" (2011) 11(2) *Chicago Journal of International Law* 693, 733.

216   Yanev and Koojimans, above n 208, 824.

217   Ibid 822.

war crimes and three counts of crimes against humanity that had allegedly taken place during an attack against the Bogoro village in the DRC on 24 February 2003.[218] The prosecution argued that Ngudjolo was party to a common plan which resulted in the commission of various crimes against humanity of which he had joint control. He had allegedly made an essential contribution to the commission of these crimes.[219] Ngudjolo was acquitted on all counts as the Trial Chamber could not be satisfied, beyond reasonable doubt, that there was sufficient evidence to prove that Ngudjolo was guilty of the alleged crimes.[220]

Whilst Judge Wyngaert agreed with the acquittal of Ngudjolo, she did not agree with the majority's interpretation of art 25(3)(a). Judge Wyngaert failed to see any legal basis for the requisite of essential contribution in the control theory.[221] Essential contribution, according to Judge Wyngaert, is not within the purview of the *Rome Statute* and forces the ICC to engage in academic analyses of whether crimes would still have been committed if one of the accused had not made exactly the same contribution.[222]

Another weakness with the essential contribution requirement highlighted by scholars is its redirection of the focus of enquiry away from the mental state of the co-perpetrators and their shared intentions to their objective role in the implementation of the crime.[223] Ohlin rightly opines that the very nature of collective criminality makes this predominant focus on contribution problematic, as it is the *common intention* to pursue some sort of plan or agreement and the *intention* to coordinate efforts to ensure the successful implementation of that plan or agreement, which makes group criminality unique.[224] Indeed, the collective nature of mass crimes is critical in determining individual criminal liability.[225] The control over crime theory risks acquitting individuals with the

---

218 *Situation in the Democratic Republic of the Congo in the Case of the Prosecutor v Germain Katanga and Mathieu Ngudjolo Dyilo* (*Decision on the Confirmation of Charges*) (ICC Pre-Trial Chamber I ICC-01/04-01/07, 30 September 2008) [8] ("*Katanga Confirmation of Charges*").

219 Ibid [35].

220 *Prosecutor v Mathieu Ngudjolo Dyilo* (*Judgement*) (ICC Trial Chamber II ICC-01/04-01/06, 14 March 2012) [110].

221 *Prosecutor v Mathieu Ngudjolo Dyilo* (*Concurring Opinion of Judge Christine van den Wyngaert*) (ICC Trial Chamber II ICC-01/04-02/12, 18 December 2012) [6] ("*Ngudjolo Concurring Opinion*").

222 Ibid [42].

223 Ohlin, above n 214, 725.

224 Ibid.

225 Beatrice I. Bonafe, *The Relationship Between State and Individual Responsibility for International Crimes* (Brill, 1st ed, 2009) 167.

requisite *mens rea*, the intention to commit the crime, if their contribution is not deemed to have been essential. To demonstrate the incongruity that can result from such an approach, let us consider a hypothetical example.

A group of soldiers enters a village inhabited by a minority ethnic group and all agree that they will each enter a block of houses and kill any occupants. The majority of soldiers kill a number of people, whilst some find "their" blocks of houses to be empty and therefore do not kill any people. After the conflict ends, all of the soldiers are prosecuted at the ICC under art 25(3)(a) for murder as a crime against humanity. The Chamber, in application of the control over crime theory, finds that it cannot be satisfied beyond reasonable doubt that all of the soldiers were co-perpetrators of murder as some did not kill any individuals and their contribution cannot be said to have been essential to the crime. This is despite the fact that the soldiers who found the empty houses had equal intention to kill anyone they encountered, as long as they belonged to the ethnic minority.

This is the central aspect of group criminality. In the above example, the intention did not simply extend to themselves but also to the group; they shared a commitment to achieve the overall outcome (evacuate the village) which meant that they were intending to kill and they intended for their colleagues to kill as well.[226] Were it not for the intention of all of the men, and not just those who did in fact commit the acts which resulted in the killings, the overall objective would not have been achieved. Hence, all of the individuals are equally guilty. The control over crime theory, however, cannot encompass all of their guilt as the doctrine is limited to those who had the power to frustrate the crimes. In the above example, which one of the soldiers can be said to have exercised such control? The answer is that not one of them alone had such power. Examples of actual cases highlight this point further.

3.2.2.1.1   Prosecutor v Muthaura et al.

In the ICC case, *Prosecutor v Muthaura et al.*, Muthaura and Kenyatta were charged under art 25(3)(a) for murder, deportation, rape, persecution and other inhumane acts, as crimes against humanity, which they allegedly carried out post the 2007–2008 election in Kenya.[227] The prosecution alleged that Muthaura, Kenyatta and Hussein Ali were party to a common plan to

---

226   Ohlin, above n 214, 728.

227   *Prosecutor v Frances Kirimi Muthaura, Uhuru Muigai Kenyatta and Mohammed Hussein Ali* (*Decision on the Confirmation of Charges*) (ICC Pre-Trial Chamber II ICC-01/09-02/11, 23 January 2012) [21].

commit widespread and systemic attacks against the supporters of the Kenyan government's opposition.[228] The allegation included the submission that Kenyatta and Muthura exercised authority over the Mungiki (pro-government group) and directed them to commit the crimes.[229] Ali, the Commissioner of the Kenyan Police, was charged with instructing Kenyan police forces not to get in the way of the attacks and once the attacks began Ali prevented the police force from responding adequately and from arresting the perpetrators of the attacks.[230]

These attacks resulted in many brutal deaths (some victims were beheaded and others burned alive), severe injuries suffered by survivors, sexual violence and substantial displacement of people.[231] The prosecution alleged that all three co-accused were aware of the factual circumstances enabling them to exercise joint control over the crime.[232] Despite his involvement in the common plan, Ali was charged under art 25(3)(d) instead of art 25(3)(a). Yanek and Koojimans argue that the reason the prosecution elected to charge Ali under art 25(3)(d) was due to the excessive burden of meeting the essential contribution requirements.[233] This was so despite the fact that Ali shared every intention of the common plan.

The stringent requirement established in *Lubanga* deterred the prosecution from charging Ali under art 25(3)(a) who, even with evidence to prove that his contribution was paramount to the implementation of the common plan, was deemed unlikely by the Prosecutor to meet the burden of essential contribution.[234] Under JCE, there would have been a much higher likelihood that Ali would have been found to be a co-perpetrator, since he shared the same intention as the others. This case serves to demonstrate that there is a very real risk that individuals will be charged under a lower standard of liability, as Judge Fulford correctly observed. The standard for essential contribution is too difficult for the prosecution to meet, not because of insufficient evidence to prove that the co-accused made a contribution and possessed a shared intent, but because of the impossibility of convincing a Trial Chamber of a plethora of hypotheticals, as demanded by the power to frustrate the crime test.

---

228   Ibid [102].
229   Ibid [404].
230   Ibid [420]–[430].
231   Ibid [49].
232   Ibid.
233   Yanev and Koojimans, above n 208, 824.
234   Ibid.

3.2.2.1.2   Prosecutor v Omar Hassan Ahmad Al Bashir

The power to frustrate the crime within essential contribution was also discussed in the *Prosecutor v Omar Al Bashir Decision on the Prosecution's Application for a Warrant of Arrest* by Judge Ušacka. Al-Bashir was charged under art 25(3)(a) as an indirect perpetrator or indirect co-perpetrator for committing war crimes, crimes against humanity and genocide through the Sudanese Armed Forces and their allied Militia and the Sudanese Police Force.[235] The Chamber found that Al-Bashir's contribution as President of the State of Sudan and Commander-in-Chief of the Sudanese Armed Forces had been essential.[236] Judge Ušacka was not convinced that co-perpetration can exist when a plan, such as in the *Al-Bashir* case, is dominated by one individual.[237] This objection came as a result of the legal test established by the court in *Lubanga* of having the power to frustrate the crime.[238]

It was not clear to Judge Ušacka whether Al-Bashir held sole control and as such would have been able to frustrate the crime, or whether this control was held by others who also had the power to frustrate the crime.[239] This issue is imperative in the context of mass crimes. Establishing that a co-accused had the ability to disrupt the commission of the crime suggests that the co-accused

---

235   *Prosecutor v Omar Al Bashir (Decision on the Prosecution's Application for a Warrant of Arrest against Omar Hassan Ahmad Al Bashir)* (ICC Pre-Trial Chamber I, ICC-02/05-01/09, 4 March 2009) [221] (*"Al Bashir Warrant of Arrest"*). The Pre-Trial Chamber references the *Katanga* and *Ngudjolo* cases to explain that indirect perpetration requires the leader to use his power of control over the apparatus to execute the crimes; that as the behind the scenes perpetrator, the leader mobilises his authority and role within the organisation to ensure his orders are obeyed. The Pre-Trial Chamber then refers to *Lubanga, Katanga* and *Ngudjolo* to explain that co-perpetration requires a division of all the essential tasks necessary for the implementation of the crime and the mutual dependence on all the members of the common plan to carry out their tasks since each of them, though lacking the overall control of the crime, has the power to frustrate the crime by not undertaking their essential tasks.

236   *Al Bashir Warrant of Arrest* (ICC Pre-Trial Chamber I, ICC-02/05-01/09, 4 March 2009) [220]. Once again, the Chamber came to this finding based on Al Bashir's *de jure* and *de facto* control.

237   *Prosecutor v Omar Al Bashir (Decision on the Prosecution's Application for a Warrant of Arrest against Omar Hassan Ahmad Al Bashir – Separate and Partially Dissenting Opinion of Judge Anita Ušacka)* (ICC Pre-Trial Chamber I, ICC-02/05-01/09, 4 March 2009) [104] (*"Al Bashir Warrant of Arrest Dissenting Opinion"*).

238   Ibid [220].

239   Judge Ušacka stated that, given the absence of evidence that Al Bashir had the power to frustrate the crimes, the warrant of arrest should have been based on indirect perpetration since indirect perpetration did not contain any such requirement, ibid.

enjoyed a level of autonomy to render to them the power to put a stop to the crime simply by not performing their task.[240] The consequence of this is that the legal test under art 25(3)(a) may be so stringent that only very few individuals at the highest level, for example leaders or highly ranked members of the military, would have the power to frustrate a crime. The result, therefore, would be that other members of the common plan, or individuals who had participated in the commission of the crime and played an important role in it, would be deemed only as accessories and not principals.[241]

This focus on the co-accused's position in the group or organisation as being determinative of whether the individual had the requisite power to frustrate the commission of the crime is counterintuitive to Roxin's definition of co-perpetration, which the ICC has relied on in grasping elements of the doctrine.[242] Roxin's explanation of co-perpetration was not centred on the accused's ranking in an institutional hierarchy but was centred on the group's synchronised collaboration and joint control over a crime.[243] The ability to prevent the occurrence of the crime was not attributed to one individual; instead they each had the power to prevent the crime if either one or the other did not perform their particular act.[244] Hence, it can be deduced that the control over crime theory, as developed by Roxin, did not distinguish between acts that were essential and those that were significant or important, and did not do so on the basis of rank.

3.2.3   Lack of Legal Basis for Control over Crime Theory

In addition to the objections based on the substantive elements of the control over crime approach, the legal basis of this theory has also been called into question. The following section considers some of the most pertinent arguments in further detail.

---

240   In *Lubanga Pre-Trial* (ICC Pre-Trial Chamber I ICC 01/04-01/06-803, 29 January 2007) [220] the Trial Chamber cites Roxin as the principal authority for the control theory of co-perpetration.

241   Yanev and Koojimans, above n 208, 826.

242   *Lubanga Pre-Trial* (ICC Pre-Trial Chamber I ICC 01/04-01/06-803, 29 January 2007) [220].

243   *Stakić Trial* (ICTY Trial Chamber IT-92-24-T, 31 July 2003) [440].

244   Ibid. The Trial Chamber provides an example given by Roxin of how co-perpetration operates. If there are two people who rule a country – they are deemed as "joint rulers" – and it is typical that the acts of each one depend on the co-perpetration of the other. The inverse of this is that if they refuse to participate, each one can frustrate the action.

3.2.3.1   The Intention of the Drafters of the Rome Statute

Sadat and Jolly claim to represent the view of observers of early ICC case law in voicing their trepidation with the way in which the ICC has interpreted art 25, partly due to its inconsistency with the plain meaning of the *Rome Statute*.[245] Similarly, Judges Fulford and Wyngaert have both expressed their concern over the lack of a statutory legal basis in adopting the control over crime approach in application of art 25(3)(a).[246] These will be considered briefly.

Judge Fulford contends that it is unnecessary to employ superfluous words in order to give effect to the *Statute* as the plain meaning of art 25(3) is very clear on how the provision should be interpreted.[247] Particular attention is paid to the word "commits" within art 25(3); Judge Fulford states that there is no additional statutory requirement for the commission to be direct or otherwise. It simply requires an operative link between the involvement of the accused and the commission of the crime.[248] Nor is there any requirement to prove that the accused's role was essential by demonstrating the accused had the power to frustrate the crime.[249] Under this approach, the prosecution would simply be required to establish, beyond reasonable doubt that the accused contributed to the crime by perpetrating it along with others.[250]

The use of the control theory to impose a hierarchy of blameworthiness between differing modes of liability contained in art 25(3)(a)-(d) is rejected by both judges[251] and both are wary of applying doctrines from national criminal jurisdictions to the approach of the ICC.[252] With respect to the hierarchy of liability, neither judge views art 25(3) as being exclusive to only one mode of criminal liability, and both state that invoking the control theory to enforce the

---

245   Leila Nadya Sadat and Jarrod M. Jolli "International Criminal Courts and Tribunals: Seven Canons of ICC Treaty Interpretation: Making Sense of Article 25's Rorschach Blot" (2014) 27 *Leiden Journal of International Law* 755, 757.

246   *Lubanga Dissenting Opinion* (ICC Trial Chamber I 01/04-01/06-2842, 14 March 2012); *Ngudjolo Concurring Opinion* (ICC Trial Chamber II ICC-01/04-02/12, 18 December 2012).

247   *Lubanga Dissenting Opinion* (ICC Trial Chamber I 01/04-01/06-2842, 14 March 2012) [13].

248   Ibid [15].

249   Ibid.

250   Ibid.

251   Ibid. Judge Fulford argues that the wording of art 25(3) does not require the modes of liability under art 25(3)(a)–(d) to be mutually exclusive.

252   *Lubanga Dissenting Opinion* (ICC Trial Chamber I 01/04-01/06-2842, 14 March 2012) [10]–[11] and *Ngudjolo Concurring Opinion* (ICC Trial Chamber II ICC-01/04-02/12, 18 December 2012) [15].

higher blameworthiness of an accused under art 25(3)(a) is unnecessary.[253] The control theory's Germanic roots are problematic in that the context of jurisdiction at the ICC differs so greatly from national criminal systems.[254] The Germanic importation of the control theory extends the mode of liability under art 25(3)(a) beyond what the *Statute* permits.[255]

Critics often point to the fact that there is little support for the control over crime theory in the *Rome Statute* by referencing the *travaux préparatoires* of art 25(3).[256] In preparation of the drafting of the *Rome Statute*, the Preparatory Committee on the Establishment of an International Criminal Court produced a draft article regarding criminal liability following their first session in April 1996.[257] The *travaux préparatoires* do not contain any specific reference to the doctrine of control over crime – rather, the wording of the early draft of art 25(3)(a) seems to indicate that the definitive aspect of co-perpetration is a common intent.[258]

The exact wording of this early draft provides that "where two or more persons jointly commit a crime under this *Statute* with a *common intent* to commit such a crime, each person shall be criminally responsible and liable to be punished as a principal."[259] As Yanev and Koojimans argue, nothing in the wording or preparatory works of art 25(3)(a) suggests that the drafters of the *Rome Statute* intended to employ any requirement of an essential contribution

---

253   *Lubanga Dissenting Opinion* (ICC Trial Chamber I 01/04-01/06-2842, 14 March 2012) [6]–[9]; *Ngudjolo Concurring Opinion* (ICC Trial Chamber II ICC-01/04-02/12, 18 December 2012) [22]–[25].

254   Judge Fulford in his Dissenting Opinion in *Lubanga* explains that, in German law, the sentencing is determined by the mode of liability under which an accused is convicted, a feature that is absent from the ICC but the application of the German doctrine did not take this factor into account, *Lubanga Dissenting Opinion* (ICC Trial Chamber I 01/04-01/06-2842, 14 March 2012) [10]–[11].

255   See *Ngudjolo Concurring Opinion* (ICC Trial Chamber II ICC-01/04-02/12, 18 December 2012) [18]. Judge Wyngeart discusses the importance of *Statute* art 22(2) which prohibits the ICC from defining crimes by analogy. The Judge views the import of the control theory as equivalent to analogising in order to establish a higher level of blame under art 25(3)(a) which the Judge finds unnecessary.

256   See Yanek and Koojimans, above n 208, 826; Sadat and Jolly, above n 244, 774; *Ngudjolo Concurring Opinion* (ICC Trial Chamber II ICC-01/04-02/12, 18 December 2012) [13].

257   Yanev and Koojimans, above n 208, 807.

258   Ibid.

259   *Report of the Preparatory Committee on the Establishment of the International Criminal Court, Vol. II (Compilation of Proposals)*, UN GAOR, 51st sess, UN Doc A/51/22[VOL-II] (SUPP) (14 September 1996) 81–82.

into this article, but rather placed emphasis on the importance of common intent as the determining factor in establishing co-principal liability.[260]

3.2.3.2   Lack of Support for the Control Theory in International Law

As discussed earlier, the Trial Chamber of the ICTY did attempt to incorporate co-perpetration based on the control theory into its jurisprudence in *Stakić* but this was rejected by the Appeals Chamber approach for various reasons. Firstly, the Appeals Chamber found that there was no evidence of the existence of this mode of liability in customary international law.[261] Similarly, the Special Tribunal for Lebanon agreed with the Appeal Chamber's finding in *Stakić* and asserted there was no support for co-perpetration via the control theory approach in customary international law.[262] In *Lubanga,* the Pre-Trial Chamber declared that the control over crime approach to co-perpetration was applied in numerous legal systems.[263] This relied on the separate opinion of Judge Schomburg in the ICTR case of *Sylvestre Gacumbitsi v Prosecutor*, where the learned judge disagreed with the majority and expressed his support for co-perpetration based on Roxin's theory.[264] This reliance on Judge Schomburg's opinion is erroneous for two reasons.

Firstly, as Ohlin points out, Judge Schomburg relied on a scholarly authority based on a normative analysis of what international criminal law should be and not what the law was. Indeed, there was little or no support for the control theory amongst common law scholars until the decision in *Lubanga*.[265] Secondly, the authorities upon which Judge Schomburg relied referenced domestic legal systems which rely on various modes of perpetration, such as indirect perpetration. Yanev and Koojimans highlight the discrepancy in relying on authorities from domestic legal systems that simply use the same terms as art 25(3)(a) but do not apply those terms via the control theory.[266]

---

260   Yanev and Koojimans, above n 208, 807.

261   *Stakić Appeal* (ICTY Appeal Chamber IT-92-24-A, 22 March 2006) [62].

262   *Interlocutory Decision on the Applicable Law: Terrorism, Conspiracy, Homicide, Perpetra-
       tion, Cumulative Charging Special* (Tribunal for Lebanon Appeals Chamber STL-11-01/I, 16
       February 2011) [256].

263   *Lubanga Pre-Trial* (ICC Pre-Trial Chamber I ICC 01/04-01/06-803, 29 January 2007) [330].

264   *Sylvestre Gacumbitsi v The Prosecutor (Judgement – Separate Opinion of Judge Schomburg
       on the Criminal Responsibility of the Appellant for Committing Genocide)* (ICTR Appeals
       Chamber ICTR-2001-64-A, 7 July 2006) [16].

265   Jens David Ohlin, "Co-Perpetration: German *Dogmatik* or German Invasion?" in Carsten
       Stehn (ed) *The Law and Practice of the International Criminal Court: A Critical Account of
       Challenges and Achievements* (Oxford University Press, 1st ed, 2015) 7.

266   Yanev and Koojimans, above n 208, 813.

Likewise, Judge Wyngaert warns that domestic legal systems use comparable words to denote a divergence of differing modes of criminal liability and that these vary from one system to another.[267] In other words, the same words do not carry the same meaning in different jurisdictions.

The absence of analysis of the application of co-perpetration in domestic legal systems by Judge Schomburg, and subsequently by the majority in *Lubanga*, ignores the fact the control theory is not applied in many national systems.[268] The authorities that do apply Roxin's approach are unsurprisingly all found within the works of German legal scholars; German courts have at times relied on the control over crime approach but it cannot be said with any conviction that this has been the dominant approach.[269] Put bluntly, the ICC relied on unpersuasive authorities to establish its doctrinal approach to criminal liability.

Due to the very nature of international crimes, not all scholars are convinced that the approach of the ICC vis-à-vis modes of liability pays enough credence to intention. Yanek and Koojimans call for the overhaul of co-perpetration by abandoning the control over crime theory in favour of the common intent requirement. The authors suggest the ICC employ co-perpetration based on common intent via the JCE doctrine or a re-construction of co-perpetration by a renewed focus on the intention element.[270] Ohlin likewise argues that intention, and not control, should be at the centre of any group crime enquiry. Ohlin is critical of the ICC's profuse emphasis of the control requirement and dismissiveness of the mental component of joint crimes.[271] Individuals who share an intention for the group to commit the crime should be liable as principals and those who do not share the intention but do make a contribution to the crime should be liable as accomplices.[272] There are a number of reasons why the common purpose doctrine is superior to the control over crime doctrine in determining criminal liability for international crimes. That stated, improvements could be made to the doctrine in order to ensure its correct application in future international criminal proceedings.

---

267 *Ngudjolo Concurring Opinion* (ICC Trial Chamber II ICC-01/04-02/12, 18 December 2012) [12].

268 Yanev and Koojimans, above n 208, 813.

269 Ibid.

270 Yanev and Koojimans encourage a revision of the JCE doctrine, if co-perpetration were to be based on it, in order to address the problems within JCE, ibid 813.

271 Ohlin, above n 214, 746, qualifies his statement by arguing that the aspect of control over a crime is not altogether irrelevant but that it has simply been the basis of too much focus by the ICC.

272 Ibid.

4   Recommendations for Determining Perpetrator Liability

4.1   Defining JCE

As this article has repeatedly stated, one of the key concerns with the common purpose doctrine through JCE is the inconsistency of approach with defining the scope of a JCE. Unhelpfully, the ICTY's own application of the common purpose doctrine via JCE has been inconsistent and, at times, perplexing. In order for JCE to serve as a reliable tool for future international courts, the doctrine should only extend to those who knowingly and willingly participate in the common criminal plan. An individual accused of a crime, where it cannot be established that the individual was party to the common criminal plan, rightly falls outside the JCE. This is the *sine qua non* condition without which a charge under JCE cannot be brought. It must be at the forefront of any international criminal prosecution purporting to charge an accused under JCE that the onus of the prosecution is to establish, beyond reasonable doubt, the existence of a JCE and the accused's involvement in that JCE.

4.2   Returning to the Principles of International Criminal Law in the
Context of Mass Atrocity: The Role of the ICC

The ICC is responsible for protecting humanitarian ideals by ensuring the punishment of those perpetrating acts that constitute crimes under IHL. Schiff states that "the ICC soars with the loftiest ideals as it grapples with the basest of human acts."[273] Revisiting these lofty ideals within the *Rome Statute* itself serves as a reminder of the very essence of the ICC's purpose.

Human history serves to remind us that the road to ending impunity for international crimes has been an arduous one.[274] The establishment of the ICC brings with it a renewed responsibility to ensure that those who have perpetrated international crimes are held accountable and that those who may be involved in such crimes are dissuaded by the law itself. Damaška suggests that suasion should be one of the purposes of international criminal law and that international courts should aim their judgments at increasing the sense of responsibility for international crimes by divulging and denouncing such inhumanity.[275]

---

273   Benjamin N. Schiff, *Building the International Criminal Court* (Cambridge University Press, 1st ed, 2008) 1.

274   Robertson, above n 22, writes an excellent summary of the path to ending impunity.

275   Mirjan Dimaška, "What is the Point of International Criminal Justice?" (2008) 83(1) *Chicago-Kent Law Review* 329, 345.

The most prevailing feature within mass atrocity crimes is the shared intent, coupled with shared commitment, to pursue some sort of policy or plan through the commission of acts that amount to serious breaches of IHL.[276] Individuals like Tadić, Karadžić, Lubanga and Al Bashir do not operate in isolation of an overarching, systemic policy. The shared intent, the belief in achieving the objective of ethnic cleansing, or genocide, or building an army in order to invade a country, is the driving force behind such mass criminality. This ethos of criminality very often includes all and every level of governments and militaries, and in some conflicts extends beyond official organisations to civilians-turned-paramilitaries, who all participate in the criminal endeavours in pursuit of a common plan.[277] One well-documented example was the genocide carried out in Srebrenica in July 1995, which was completely calculated, highly organised and relied on a multitude of people in its implementation.[278] The importance of the common purpose to pursue a criminal plan has been reflected in the jurisprudence of the ICTY through its focus on the shared intention of the perpetrators of collective criminality and its adoption of the common purpose doctrine via JCE. The control theory is dismissive of the very nature of mass criminality and has no mechanism to capture the common intention of the group.

The reality in many cases of conflict is that there is often a scarcity of evidence as to who exactly did what.[279] The difficulties of trying to establish each individual's *precise* contribution within a JCE are unlikely to result in many convictions. Even in instances where there is evidence to prove the individual was both involved in and shared an intention to commit the crime but whose contribution may not have been deemed essential to the commission of the crime.[280] The control theory, as discussed above, unnecessarily imposes too high a threshold for the prosecution. It virtually ignores the element of intent amongst a group and does not defend the international community from collective criminality.[281]

---

276   Mark J. Osiel, "Modes of Participation in Mass Atrocity" (2005) 38 *ell International Law Journal* 793, 798.

277   Anio Cassese, "The Proper Limits of Individual Responsibility under the Doctrine of Joint Criminal Enterprise" (2007) 5 *Journal of International Criminal Justice* 109, 110.

278   Herman van der Wilt, "Srebrenica: On Joint Criminal Enterprise, Aiding and Abetting and Command Responsibility" (2015) 62(2) *Netherlands International Law Review* 229, 230.

279   Christopher Cowley, "To What Degree is the Concept of Joint Criminal Enterprise Coherent? A Discussion with Regard to the International Criminal Tribunal of the Former Yugoslavia" (2015) 79(4) *The Journal of Criminal Law* 270, 271.

280   Ibid.

281   Cassese, above n 276, 112.

4.3   Elements of the Common Purpose Doctrine

The common purpose doctrine, properly understood, is not intent on extending its legal tentacles in order to convict as many individuals as possible. Rather, it is the only doctrine that is capable of reaching all of those who intentionally engage in and contribute to international crimes but who may not have the power to frustrate the crimes. These individuals would otherwise either escape justice or be labelled as accessories, thereby understating the extent of their individual criminal responsibility.

An added advantage of the common purpose doctrine is that it does not focus on hypotheticals, such as how circumstances might have turned out had it not been for the participation of some members of the group. Rather, it assesses the contribution and participation in a criminal endeavour based on what did eventuate.[282] This avoids all of the complications associated with the power to frustrate test within the control theory, of having to consider what a co-accused did not do but may have done,[283] a task that has been criticised by international criminal judges.[284] Additionally, the weight of practice supports the common purpose doctrine to a greater degree than it supports the control theory, the latter being more limited and less developed. Even if critics disagree with elements of the common purpose doctrine, the reality is that there is now a comprehensive body of law regarding this theory, which adds credibility to the common purpose doctrine that is not equalled by the control theory.

Finally, as a matter of policy, the international criminal system exists in order to control international crimes. Countless cases from the tribunals and the ICC have demonstrated that where there exists a collective of people who share an intention to engage in a common criminal purpose, this often results in ancillary crimes that may not have been strictly intended but that are not outside the realm of foreseeability. International criminal law must discourage individuals from engaging in criminal enterprises, and it must reprimand those who willingly pursue criminal endeavours and where greater crimes are foreseeable. Whilst it may seem utopian to suggest that the ICC contains the power to influence people's actions and the choices individuals make, history has proven that when the law is sluggish, great atrocities are committed.

---

282   There is no equivalent "power to frustrate" test in the common purpose doctrine.

283   Osiel, above n 275, 798.

284   Judge Fulford and Judge Wyngaert in their separate opinions in *Lubanga* and *Ngudjolo* respectively voiced their disapproval of judges having to enter into the realm of the hypothetical, *Lubanga Dissenting Opinion* (ICC Trial Chamber I 01/04-01/06-2842, 14 March 2012); *Ngudjolo Concurring Opinion* (ICC Trial Chamber II ICC-01/04-02/12, 18 December 2012).

The control theory is not without merit, but it does not assist the ICC in honouring its mandate to hold perpetrators of mass atrocities accountable while at the same time condemning the repetition of such brutal acts of inhumanity.

5   Conclusion

The predicament of ascribing criminal liability for perpetrators of mass crimes has challenged the ad-hoc tribunals and continues to challenge the ICC. It is an unenviable task to be the adjudicator of international crimes. Credence must be paid to long established principles of criminal law but, equally, the law must respond to violations of IHL. Unfortunately, the very essence of mass atrocities, with their dependency on a large number of participants to implement the crimes, is such that it is very difficult to ascertain each individual's liability. International criminal law has attempted to address this challenge through the doctrines of common purpose (via JCE) and control over the crime.

Whilst both doctrines have supporters and critics, the common purpose doctrine is a more appropriate mechanism to ensure that international criminal law does not permit perpetrators of war crimes to slip through the doctrinal gaps. This is by virtue of the fact that the common purpose doctrine places the majority of the emphasis on what the group intended to do as a collective. Although the *actus reus* of each individual is also assessed, less emphasis is placed on the physical contribution to the commission of the crimes since in many instances those most guilty are remote from the scene of the crime. Unlike the control theory, the common purpose doctrine does not require Prosecutors to construct hypothetical alternatives as to what may have eventuated had the accused in question not performed their act, a feature of the control theory that has been criticised by international judges and scholars. Another advantage of the common purpose doctrine is its ability to extend beyond the confines of a military hierarchy and include everyone who may have contributed to the violation of IHL.

More important than any of these factors, however, is the ICC's responsibility to condemn, in the strongest possible terms, the sorts of inhumane acts that commonly prevail in modern conflict – acts that have shaken humanity and reinstated terms such as genocide, ethnic cleansing and crimes against humanity into the modern lexicon. By focusing on the common intent of the collective, the common purpose doctrine ensures that all those who participate in any way in the commission of the grossest violations of IHL are made accountable for their actions. Whilst in many ways international criminal trials are too late for many of the victims of mass atrocities, the only greater injustice is if those who are liable escape responsibility.

Challenging Cultural Backgrounds and Vernacularizing Human Rights

*Sami Thamir Alrashidi**

1   Introduction

International law scholars, lawyers and legal feminists need to continue to find ways to address the persistence of cultural and social norms, which are frequently cited by governments as reasons for their failure to achieve gender equality.[1] One of the obligations placed on states parties in the international human rights law system is the obligation to conduct human rights education. In 2000, the Human Rights Committee in its General Comment No 28 pointed out that public education should be included as one of the measures that states should take to achieve gender equality.[2] In 2010, the *Convention on the Elimination of All Forms of Discrimination Against Women* ("*CEDAW*") Committee in its general recommendation No 28 on the core obligations of states parties under *CEDAW* art 2, stated that states parties should adopt measures that make sure of "the practical realization of the elimination of discrimination against women and women's equality with men". One of these measures is promoting "education and support for the goals of the Conventions throughout the education system and in community".[3]

However, it can be argued that human rights education may not be the only measure that can be used to make human rights norms and principles more understandable and acceptable for many societies, especially Islamic ones. For

---

*   Sami Thamir Alrashidi, PhD, Flinders University, Australia.

1   Yakin Erturk, "Considering the Role of Men in Gender Agenda Setting: Conceptual Policy Issues" (2004) 78 *Feminist Review* 3, 7.

2   Human Rights Committee, *General Comment No 28, Article 3 (The Equality of Rights between Men and Women)*, 68th sess, UN Doc HRI/GEN/Rev. 9/(Vol. 1) (29 March 2000); Committee on Economic, Social and Cultural Rights, *General Comment No 16, The Equal Right of Men and Women to the Enjoyment of all Economic, Social and Cultural Rights (art 3 of the International Covenant on Economic, Social and Cultural Rights)* UN ESC, 34th sess, E/C.12/2005/4 (11 August 2005).

3   Committee on the Elimination of Discrimination against Women, *General Recommendation No 28 on the Core Obligations of States Parties under Article 2 of the Convention on the Elimination of All Forms of Discrimination against Women*, UN Doc CEDAW/C/GC/28 (16 December 2010) [36].

this purpose, this article poses the following question: How can the obstacles to adoption of women's human rights in the Islamic context be addressed? The answer that I propose in this article is that some of these obstacles can be addressed by both changing the cultural background and vernacularizing human rights so they can be comprehended in the local context. It is within this context in mind that this article proposes what I call the "background-vernacularist" approach, which aims to bring together existing ideas about changing the cultural background and vernacularizing human rights norms.

The article is divided into three parts. Part 2 discusses the background-vernacularist approach, discussing in particular feminist theorist Susan Hekman's analysis of and reflections on background theories and Sally Engle Merry's vernacularist approach. Part 3 illustrates the background-vernacularist approach by looking at Arabic thinker Mohammed al-Jabri's ideas about how modernity can be achieved in the Arab-Islamic world. Part 3 concludes with an introduction to Islamic feminism by giving a brief discussion of the concept of *ijtihad*. Understanding the concept of *ijtihad* prepares the way to understanding what Islamic feminism is about. Part 4 discusses some Islamic feminists and considers briefly the main transnational advocacy networks that have adopted a strategy similar to the background-vernacularist approach.

The main conclusion that this article attempts to draw is that many Islamic feminist arguments, and the strategies proposed by transnational advocacy networks, are aligned with the methodologies that the background-vernacularist approach suggests. Hence, we will be able to understand how the legal-cultural background could be challenged in order to tell the story of international human rights law in the Islamic context.

2   The Background-Vernacularist Approach

It should be noted that there has been, in international law and international relations scholarship, considerable discussion on how international law can change states' and individuals' behaviour toward human rights practices. There are many theories proposed by some international law and international relations scholars for addressing this issue.[4] However, it is beyond the scope of

---

4   Ryan Goodman and Derek Jinks, "How to Influence States: Socialization and International Human Rights Law" (2004) 54 (3) *Duke Law Journal* 621; Kal Raustiala and Anne-Marie Slaighter, "International Law, International Relations and Compliance" in Water Carlsnaes, Thomas Risse and Beth A. Simmons (eds.), *Handbook of International Relations* (Sage Publication Ltd, 2002) 538; Ann E. Towns and Bahar Rumelili, "Taking the pressure: unpacking the

this article to discuss such theories. What is important for us in the context of the discussion in this article is that all these theories have focused on how the norms of international law regarding human rights could spread and become acceptable to states and individuals, in order to persuade them to comply with international human rights law. In this sense, it could be argued that the matter here is simply one of legitimacy.[5] In considering the legitimacy of human rights norms, I have developed an approach that is designed to be useful in practice, drawing from feminist work. The background-vernacularist approach that I develop in this article suggests that in order to legitimize human rights norms, we need to work on changing the cultural background that challenges the legitimacy of human rights norms and then we need to vernacularize human rights norms in a language that could be understandable and acceptable for certain societies. On the one hand, such an approach could be useful because the language of this approach provides idioms and concepts that enable us to understand the elements of the cultural background. On the other hand, it also enables us to understand the procedures used to challenge the cultural background in existing literature and the intellectual history.

My main aim in this article is not to develop the theory in depth. Rather, it is to articulate an approach, which has a theoretical justification that can be used to understand history and to promote change in practical situations.

In order to advance my argument, this part attempts to answer the question "what is the background-vernacularist approach"? This part is divided into two sections. The first section of this part discusses Susan Hekman's arguments about the background. Although, Hekman's work – as well as that of other feminist theorists mentioned in this article, such as Sandra Harding and Donna Haraway – on this topic is now over a decade old, it has a great deal to offer towards understanding the process of cultural change. The second section in this part discusses the arguments about vernacularization of human rights norms and principles proposed by legal anthropologist Sally Engle Merry.

2.1 The Background Approach

The main purpose of Hekman's argument about feminist background theory is to reshape the feminist standpoint so that it can assist in deep cultural change.

---

relation between norms, social hierarchies, and social pressures on states" (2017) 23 *European Journal of International Relations* 1.

5   Ian Hurd, "Legitimacy and Authority in International Politics" (1999) 53 (2) *International Organization* 379; Oona A. Hathaway, "Do Human Rights Treaties Make a Difference?" (2002) 111 (8) *The Yale Law Journal* 1935; Seyla Benhabib, "The legitimacy of human rights" (2008) 137 (3) *Daedalus* 94.

Hekman's aim is to ensure that feminist discourse makes sense for people in order to change background knowledge, which reinforces the inferior status of women.[6]

Hekman points out that "feminist concepts challenge the modernist epistemology of mainstream social science. Feminist concepts reveal that all concepts are partial, political, and chosen according to the interests of the investigator."[7] Yet feminist arguments are not acceptable to many social scientists because the modernist assumption that "concepts correspond to social reality is still prevalent in many social sciences".[8] Hence, as Hekman argues, making feminist arguments can be difficult because "they entail a radical definition of social science".[9]

In order to avoid the epistemological and methodological problems faced by feminists, Hekman suggests that "feminists must construct arguments that are both convincing in the terms of the hegemonic discourse and at the same time transform that discourse".[10] Instead of being preoccupied by revealing the truth, the task of feminists' is to develop "a new methodology to accommodate differences and legitimizing [sic.] more than one path to moral truth".[11] Hekman's argument is based on the following premises, reflecting the work of a number of philosophers:[12]

> Every society requires a ground for meaning that makes language intelligible, that this ground is ungrounded in the sense that it lacks universal validity, and that this ground provides a stable foundation for meaning that extends over time. It is my contention that these premises give rise to a set of unique problems for feminist theory. If feminists assume with the anti-foundationalists that truth statements are grounded in social meanings (or language games, or prejudices, or discourses), then their theories, unlike those of nonfeminists, must confront the inferiority of women that those social meanings dictate. The grounded ground of

6   Susan Hekman, "Backgrounds and Riverbeds: Feminist Reflections" (1999) 25(2) *Feminist Studies* 427, 428–429.

7   Susan J Hekman, *The Future of Differences: Truth and Methods in Feminist Theory* (Polity Press, 1999) 52, 89.

8   Ibid.

9   Ibid.

10   Ibid.

11   Ibid 120.

12   Such as Ludwig Wittgenstein, Michel Foucault, Hans-Georg Gadamer, Judith Butler and Donna Haraway, to name a few.

anti-foundational thought is synonymous with hegemonic masculinist discourse.[13]

Hekman argues that, although non-feminist anti-foundationalist epistemologists "do not offer much guidance when it comes to how those social meanings change or might be changed", they do explain "how change cannot occur".[14] She explains that, according to anti-foundational epistemologists, social meanings cannot be changed by "claiming that they are in some absolute sense 'wrong' and replacing them with understandings that are 'true' and 'right'".[15] If "social meanings define what is 'true', it follows that only other social meanings can define another truth that would, in turn, define another social structure".[16]

Hekman argues that this is not particularly helpful for feminists because of its ambiguity and because the process of presenting new foundational social meanings may reinforce the inferior status of women. In other words, Hekman suggests that it might not be helpful for feminists simply to critique the truth of negative social meanings, which already exist, in an attempt to replace them with other truths. This is because of the absence of "an independent truth or reality to which" feminists can appeal. Therefore, it would seem that it leaves "feminism in a vicious circle from which there is no escape".[17]

2.1.1   Facts as Pictures

Hekman further elaborates her main idea by appealing to the theory of the "Background", especially Wittgenstein's "Picture Theory of Language".[18] For Wittgenstein, propositions are pictures.[19] Pictures themselves are background facts. The question here is: how can pictures be described and clarified, and ultimately altered? A certain picture prevents a specific group of people from seeing an alternative picture that another group of people attempt to clarify. Wittgenstein stated that "[a] *picture* held us captive. And we could not get outside of it, for it lay in our language and language seemed to repeat it to us inexorably".[20] However, clarification of the picture may enable a mutual

---

13   Hekman, *The Future of Differences*, above n 7, 120.

14   Ibid.

15   Ibid.

16   Ibid.

17   Ibid 121.

18   I borrowed the term "Picture Theory of Language" from David Keyt, "Wittgenstein's Picture Theory of Langauge" (1964) 73 (4) *The Philosophical Review* 493.

19   David Shier, "How Can Pictures Be Propositions?" (1997) 10 (1) *Ratio* 65, 66.

20   Quoted in Hekman, "Backgrounds and Riverbeds" above n 6, 434. See also, Ludwig Wittgenstein, *Philosophical Investigations* (Macmillan. 1958).

understanding between two groups of people who start with a different point of view.

As Hekman explains, Wittgenstein's metaphor of the picture is one idea of the background. Another metaphor of Wittgenstein's that Hekman used interchangeably with his metaphor of picture was that of the "riverbed" of thoughts.[21] Wittgenstein wrote:

> It might be imagined that some propositions, of the form of empirical propositions, were hardened and functioned as channels for such empirical propositions as were not hardened but fluid; and that this relation altered with time, in that fluid propositions hardened, and hard one becomes fluid. The mythology may change back into a state of flux, the riverbed of thoughts may shift.[22]

Here, for Hekman, the picture and riverbed of thoughts refer to the cultural background. What Hekman suggests is that feminists should make efforts to change the existing picture and replace it with another picture that is related to, but is not the same as, the original picture. In other words, as Hekman suggests, one needs to change the criteria that determine intelligibility or "what makes sense" before proclaiming another truth. I will explain this further shortly.[23]

2.1.2   A Truth as a Story

As I have pointed out, Hekman suggests that feminists should make efforts to change the existing picture in order to replace it with a new picture. However, this new picture should be related in some way to the existing picture. Drawing upon Michel Foucault's concept of "insurrection of subjugated knowledge",[24] Hekman points out that feminist discourse is subjugated knowledge. Such discourse, which is based on the experience of women, has created a new picture. But, this new picture is "invisible in the present picture".[25] Hekman writes:

---

21   Hekman writes: "Wittgenstein's uses several arresting metaphors to describe what I am calling here the Background. He refers to a 'picture' that holds us captive, preventing us from seeing another picture. In his-evocation of the riverbed, the Background is the channel through which our thought flows, giving it structure and making intelligible. Implicit in both metaphors is the possibility of change." See Hekman, "Backgrounds and Riverbeds" above n 6, 440.

22   Ibid 433.

23   Ibid, 437.

24   Michel Foucault, *Power/Knowledge* (Pantheon Books, 1980) 81.

25   Hekman, "Backgrounds and Riverbeds", above n 6, 440.

The now-extensive literature on feminist epistemology elaborates the significance of this new picture of knowledge. What has not been adequately discussed in this literature, however, is how this new picture that emerges from feminist discourse relates to the Background. If the Background theorists are correct, then efforts to change the picture, to shift the riverbed of thought, must have some connection to the existing picture/riverbed. If feminist discourse is to be successful in effecting an epistemological shift, it must both make sense in the dominant discourse of the existing Background and at the same time alter that discourse. In other words, feminists must use language understandably but also subversively in order to change linguistic social practice.[26]

Hekman argues that Donna Haraway's argument is useful here.[27] Hekman is interested in Haraway's argument for two reasons. First, as Hekman points out, Haraway considered feminist experience as "a story-telling practice".[28] For Haraway, as Hekman notes, gender, race, nation, family, nature, sexuality, and class are themes that have been "written into the body of nature in Western science, since the eighteenth century".[29] For Haraway, as Hekman points out, those themes are understood as constructed categories not "prior universal social categories". This is because these themes are patriarchal stories. Thus, they should not be understood as *a priori* truths.

Second, understanding race and gender, for example, as patriarchal stories means that there is the possibility to tell another story, which is a feminist one. As Hekman argues, the new story should be related to the original story, interacting with it in particular ways. At the same time, this new story should depart from the original story. When the feminist story departs from the patriarchal story, it should change its meanings.

Changing the meanings of the original story, for Hekman, can be understood through Sandra Harding's idea of making familiar things strange. Harding writes: "[T]hinking from the perspective of women's lives makes strange what had appeared familiar, which is the beginning of any scientific inquiry".[30]

---

26   Ibid, 441.

27   Donna Jeanne Haraway, *Primate Visions: Gender, Race, and Nature in the World of Modern Science* (Routledge, 1989).

28   Hekman, "Backgrounds and Riverbeds" above n 6, 444.

29   Ibid 443.

30   Sandra Harding, *Whose Science? Whose Knowledge? Thinking from Women's Lives* (Cornell University Press, 1991) 150. See also Teri Elliot, "Making Strange What had Appeared Familiar" (1994) 77(4) *Monist* 424.

In order to fill in the gap in feminist strategies, Hekman proposes to use background theories as a guide for feminists to establish an intelligible discourse that challenges the grounded knowledge that reinforces the inferiority of women's status in the social context. This challenge enables the background, as well as its consequences, to be changed. Hekman proposes some steps to promote change in the background of grounded knowledge.

2.1.3   Changing the Background's Steps

To change the background, according to Hekman, the first step is to bring the background itself into focus to look at its familiar concepts. These concepts should be identified and their fundamental elements should be examined. When the concepts of the background are identified and their fundamental elements are examined, their implications should be explored. Bringing the background into focus in this way allows it to be the subject of critique. I find this first step useful in understanding international law's norms, such as *CEDAW* art 5(a). Article 5(a) of *CEDAW* urges state parties to "modify the social patterns of conduct of men and women". The purpose of modifying the social patterns of conduct, as art 5(a) stipulates, is to eliminate the "prejudices and customary and all other practices which are based on the idea of the inferiority or the superiority of either of the sexes or on stereotyped roles for men and women."

By applying Hekman's first step to art 5(a) briefly, we can say that "gender stereotype" is the background or the original picture/story, which holds a certain society captive and prevents them from seeing another picture or hearing another story, which is the picture/story of gender equality. In this manner, we are bringing the background into focus. By doing this, we then identify its familiar concepts. Gender stereotype's familiar concepts, for example, are identified by Rebecca Cook and Simone Cusack's argument.[31] Cook and Cusack point out that gender stereotypes are "concerned with the social and cultural construction of men and women, due to their different physical, biological, sexual, and social functions".[32] Social and cultural constructions, which reinforce the "gender stereotype", have been constructed by many familiar concepts such as religion, customary law, history, literature, and the legal system. By identifying these familiar concepts, we need then to examine their fundamental elements. For example, if a "gender stereotype" or "gender inequality" is based on the concept of "religion", we need to examine the religious elements that have justified such a stereotype or inequality. I will show

---

31   Rebecca J Cook and Simone Cusack, *Gender Stereotyping: Transnational Legal Perspectives* (University of Pennsylvania Press, 2010) 9.

32   Ibid 20.

later what Islamic feminists suggest to deal with religious elements that reinforce gender inequality. So, by identifying the familiar concepts and examining
their basic elements, we can then explore their implications. For example, gender stereotyping, as Cook and Cusack indicate, is not problematic in itself. It
becomes problematic when it operates to deny the fundamental freedoms and
human rights of individuals by creating "gender hierarchies" and ignoring the
"characteristics, abilities, needs, wishes, and circumstances" of particular individuals in law and society.[33] Rikki Holtmaat points out that gender stereotypes
mean that women are not treated as respected, dignified and equal human beings and that women's autonomy is denied as a result.[34] So, it could be argued
that exploring the negative implications of gender stereotype, for example, is
the turning point that prepares the way for the second step.

The second step is to deploy Harding's concept of making "strange what had
appeared familiar". Haraway's argument is useful in this context. As Hekman
points out, Haraway suggests that feminists' task is not to reveal the truth or
to tell a false story; the task is to tell another story and to construct an alternative story/picture. This alternative story/picture of the background does not
mean that feminists are looking to reveal the truth. Rather, it enables them to
argue for it. As I mentioned previously, exploring the negative implications of
gender stereotypes, for example, is the turning point that prepares the way for
the step of "making strange what had appeared familiar". This is because the
cultural background that constitutes the gender stereotypes does not suggest
that such stereotypes are harmful because people are used to practicing them
as a part of their familiar cultural practice. In this sense, gender stereotypes are
legitimized by many elements of cultural background such as religion, customary law, and so on. Hence, to challenge this negative familiar cultural practice,
we need to explore its implications to show how it is not legitimate and it does
not reflect the positive elements of the cultural background of a certain society. However, this does not mean that we can say that gender stereotypes are
simply "wrong". Before claiming that, we need to change the conditions that
determine what makes sense to a certain society and conditions the belief that
gender stereotypes are "right" or "true". By doing this, we are making the familiar cultural practice, such as gender stereotype, to appear strange. However,
my purpose is not to discuss the gender stereotypes in depth. Nor am I trying
to give a deep explanation of each step of the approach that I am developing

---

33   Ibid.
34   Rikki Holtmaat, "Article 5" in Marsha Freeman, Christine Chinkin, and Beate Rudolf (eds.),
      *The UN Convention on the Elimination of All Forms of Discrimination Against Women: A
      Commentary* (Oxford University Press, 2012) 142, 145.

in this article. My main purpose is to introduce the approach briefly and present the key points that enable us to think of changing the cultural background before we present international human rights norms.

According to Hekman, this strategy involves a revision to Audre Lorde's famous dictum: "the master's tools will never dismantle the master's house".[35] Hekman suggests that *only* the master's tools can dismantle the master's house. As Hekman suggested, the master's tools are the discourses that establish the background. What makes them useable is that they are not "monolithic". Those discourses include many different resources, some of which can be "turned into tools of resistance".[36] In this sense, Hekman asserts, women's marginality and silence may be preserved, if the master's tools are not employed.

Hekman's argument is not, therefore, about how international law can change states' and individuals' behaviour toward human rights practices. But, it is a useful framework for thinking about how social backgrounds can be changed to better accommodate rights. In addition, although Hekman's discussion is useful, it does not provide a practical blueprint for how another picture or story in the context of human rights can be constructed. Sally Engle Merry's theory of vernacularization is useful here for explaining some of the elements of constructing another picture, as I will discuss in the following section.

2.2   *Vernacularization of Human Rights*

Legal anthropologist Sally Engle Merry points out that, if the ideas of human rights "are to have an impact, they need to become part of the consciousness of ordinary people around the world".[37] This has relevance to Hekman's emphasis on background theories, which pay attention to the importance of common understandings that underpin human intelligibility. As Hekman argues, human social life would not be possible if there were not "a core of agreed-upon assumptions about both the social and natural worlds".[38] What Merry suggests to achieve a common understanding of the ideas of human rights is to translate them into local terms, that is, to remake these ideas of human rights in the vernacular language.

Merry points out that "considerable research on law and everyday social life shows that law's power to shape society depends not on punishment alone but on becoming embedded in everyday social practices, shaping the rules people

---

35   Audre Lorde, *Sister Outsider: Essays and Speeches* (Crossing Press, 1984) 112.

36   Hekman, "Backgrounds and Riverbeds", above n 6, 446.

37   Sally Engle Merry, *Human Rights and Gender Violence: Translating International Law Into Local Justice* (University of Chicago Press, 2006) 1, 2.

38   Hekman, "Backgrounds and Riverbeds", above n 6, 122.

carry in their heads".[39] Merry is aware of the difficulty of the task of vernacularizing human rights so that the concepts are understandable in terms of the common understandings of the local community. Merry writes:

> [R]emaking human rights in the vernacular is difficult. Local communities often conceive of social justice in quite different terms from human rights activists. They generally lack knowledge of relevant documents and provisions of the human rights system. Global human rights reformers, on the other hand, are typically rooted in a transnational legal culture remote from myriad local social situations in which human rights are violated.[40]

Merry's argument for the vernacularization of human rights norms and principles relies on "the role of activists who serve as intermediaries between different sets of cultural understandings of gender, violence, and justice". Merry explains:

> The global human rights system is now deeply transnational, no longer rooted exclusively in the West. It takes place in global settings with representatives from nations and NGOs around the world. Activists from many countries enthusiastically adopt this language and translate it for grassroots people. Vulnerable people take up human rights ideas in a wide variety of local contexts because they offer hope to subordinated groups.[41]

For Merry, human rights norms need to be taken from a universalist discourse to be adopted into the local language, much like a translation. However, this translation, as Merry points out, does not mean the basic meanings of human rights norms should be changed.

Merry indicates that making this translation effective requires three types of change in the ways the ideas are presented. Firstly, it requires that human rights norms should be framed in images, symbols, or religious or secular narratives that resonate with the local community.[42] Secondly, human rights should be framed for appropriate circumstances and conditions in specific

---

39   Merry, above n 37, 2.
40   Ibid.
41   Ibid.
42   Ibid 220.

places. Translation of human rights norms should take into account local economic, social and political systems. Thirdly, the targeted population should be defined.[43]

Merry therefore insists that translation does not mean transformation. Basic norms of human rights remain part of the modern view of good and societal justice, which emphasises independence, choice, equality, secularism and integrity. Furthermore, Merry holds the state responsible for establishing these conditions so that an individual can seek their legal rights from the government.[44]

The vernacularist approach attempts to achieve social change by suggesting that international human rights norms and principles should be translated into the local discourse, whether this is religious, traditional or secular. It rightly suggests that the translators of human rights should pay close attention to the appropriate circumstances of the places and the targeted population. My purpose here is not to criticize the vernacularist approach because I find it useful, as do many other scholars and human rights advocates. However, I believe it can be made more effective, in promoting human rights principles and norms, by supplementing it with an approach which also pays attention to changing the cultural background.

Although vernacularization is important because it seeks to make human rights norms intelligible to human beings in the local context, it does not suggest challenging the social meanings that reinforce social injustice and inequality in the society. When, for example, a customary law or religious law in a certain society supports social injustice and inequality by suggesting that there are inferior groups and superior groups in society, it might be difficult to rely only on vernacularizing equality norms and principles.[45] This is because such inequality has its background in religion, customs, history and literature. It is rooted in the background of the social construction. The basis of the vernacularization approach is that unfamiliar concepts of human rights should be transformed into the local discourse to be familiar and intelligible. It is about making strange concepts appear familiar in the local context. Clearly, however,

---

43   Ibid. Merry writes: "[V]ictims of domestic violence in the United States are typically intimate partners, not necessarily married or heterosexual, whereas in China they are typically members of an extended household of several generations but not necessarily in intimate sexual relationships."

44   Ibid 221.

45   It is beyond the scope of this article to do extensive research on what is happening in the field. This means that I am aware of the fact that my practical knowledge about the vernacularization of human rights is limited.

vernacularizers may meet with resistance from traditional or religious groups who believe in the inequality of certain groups in society and who perceive that they have legitimate arguments that derive from their religion, custom, history and literature. The background approach proposed by Hekman becomes especially applicable in such a situation. It might be appropriate, in many instances, to combine the background and vernacularist approaches to complement each other in order to improve the potential for compliance with human rights norms and principles.

3   Making Sense of the Background-Vernacularist Approach

As Hekman argues, the background approach suggests that, in order to present a different truth, it is crucial to create the criteria for that truth in the first place so that it will be intelligible. In the vernacularist approach, the new truth that human rights advocates and vernacularizers attempt to present is the transformed and translated concepts of human rights norms and principles. The question here is: Does vernacularization of human rights in specific contexts also rely on changing the cultural background so that the human rights discourse can be accepted or legitimated?

This part gives two examples to illustrate why I have combined these two approaches together to become the background-vernacularist approach. The first example relates to the environmentalization of concepts, as suggested by Mohammed Abed al-Jabri, which is similar to what I have described as the background-vernacularist approach. The second example is the concept of *ijtihad*, which is one of the main religious tools within Islamic thinking that is used to re-interpret religious texts in order to revise or produce religious rules. *Ijtihad* can be a useful tool for demanding women's human rights in Muslim-majority countries. It allows a challenge to the background of cultural norms and social meanings that constitute the inferior status of women, especially in family law.

3.1   *Environmentalization of Concepts: Secularism*
For a better understanding of how the vernacularization of concepts could take place in the Islamic-Arab world, it is useful to look at the Arabic thinker Mohammed Abed al-Jabri's argument about *Tabiyat almafaheem* (literally environmentalization of concepts). As I will explain, his argument has some parallels with the background-vernacularist approach.

First, al-Jabri asserts the importance of changing the background of the Arab-Islamic epistemological heritage so that modernist principles such as human rights, democracy and rationality can be adopted.[46] As al-Jabri argues, many Arab intellectuals attempt to discuss rationality and democracy without investigating their roots in Arab-Islamic epistemology.[47] This means, as al-Jabri argues, that those intellectuals have failed to deconstruct the dominant principles that determine the truth in Arab-Islamic epistemology in order to construct new principles. Here, as in Hekman's background approach, al-Jabri suggests that the elements that established the background of the truth in Arab-Islamic epistemology should be deconstructed before Arab intellectuals claim new truth which supports rationality and democracy.

Second, al-Jabri asserts the importance of a shared common intelligibility. He argues that the project of modernity in the Arab world has been ineffective because it has been perceived as imported from outside.[48] It created a negative reaction in Arab societies. Arab conservatives resisted modernity, portraying it as an alien invader that comes to destroy Arab-Islamic identity, values and principles. In order to avoid this, al-Jabri suggests that Arab intellectuals should practice rationality in their investigation of traditional Arab-Islamic epistemology and the prevailing roots of dictatorship and its manifestations. In doing so, Arab intellectuals will be able to establish their own modernity, enabling it to join the universal modernity. This argument is broadly similar to Hekman's ideas about promoting change in the epistemological background. Modernity for al-Jabri is about modernizing rationality and beliefs. For al-Jabri, if the predominant culture supports tradition, such as religious discourse, then the discourse of modernity should be based on investigating that tradition. There is, therefore, a parallel argument between al-Jabri's argument and the background approach. As I discussed previously, Hekman suggested that in order to replace the original story with a new story, the latter should be related to the original one. Similarly, al-Jabri suggests that Arab intellectuals – in their argument for rationality and democracy – should make their argument relevant to the discourse that the local culture supports. So, if the local culture supports tradition, Arab intellectuals should focus on tradition. Hence, tradition should be investigated, al-Jabri argues, in order to re-interpret the principles

---

46   Mohammed al-Jabri, *Arab-Islamic Philosophy: A Contemporary Critique* (Aziz Abbassi trans, University of Texas Centre for Middle Eastern Studies, 1999) [trans of: *Nahnuwa'l-Turath: al-Khitab al-'Arabi al-Mu'asir: DirasahTahiliyyahNaqdiyyah* (1982)]. Al-Jabri's arguments about modernity first appeared in the introduction of his article "Nahnuwal-Turath" (The Heritage and Us) which was published separately in 1980 and later included in this collection of his works.

47   Ibid 3–4.

48   Ibid 5.

and values of the tradition, and to present modern points of view, which is the new story or picture in Hekman's sense. In doing so, al-Jabri argues, modernity will be acceptable in the hearts and minds of all people in Arab-Islamic society. Then it will achieve its goals with less resistance than previously.[49]

Another relevant argument to the background-vernacularist approach made by al-Jabri was what he called the environmentalization of concepts of modernity, which can be compared to Merry's vernacularization approach. The environmentalization of concepts, for al-Jabri, has two steps. The first step is to bring the targeted concept into focus and explore its history and origin. The second step is to think of how the concept could be implanted in the background of the targeted epistemological environment.[50] For instance, in his attempt to environmentalize the concept of secularism in Arab thought, al-Jabri argues that the Western concept of secularism has no background in the Islamic world. Therefore, it cannot be located easily.[51] However, al-Jabri suggests that Arab intellectuals could use the concepts of democracy and rationality to replace the idea of secularism.[52] They will be more intelligible and acceptable in the Islamic-Arab world and will face less resistance.

There are, therefore, parallels between the arguments of Hekman, Merry and al-Jabri. When Hekman suggests that human intelligibility requires common shared assumptions, and that these must be changed to enable social change and the empowerment of women, she speaks of changing the background. The background that was constituted to enforce the inferior status of women cannot be changed, unless feminists change its elements. Similarly, Merry suggests that human rights norms and principles will not be effective unless they are translated into the vernacular language. Merry is suggesting using the common understandings of local people to make human rights principles familiar. Al-Jabri's discussion of modernity in the Arab world supports

---

49   Al-Jabri wrote: "This is the conception of modernity that we ought to define in light of our present. Modernity is above all rationality and democracy. A rational and critical approach to all aspects of our existence – of which tradition emerges as one of the aspects that is most present and most rooted in us – is the only true modernist option. Our concern with tradition is therefore dictated by the necessity to elevate our approach to tradition to the level of modernity, in order to serve modernity and to give it a foundation within our 'authenticity'. Ibid 7."

50   Mohammed Abed al-Jabri, "Islah Tabiyat almafaheem: al-Ilmaniah Inmothajan" [The Reform: Environmentalization of Concepts: Secularism as a Case Study] <http://hem.bredband.net/b155908/m382.htm>.

51   Saed Shabar, "Al-Ilmaniah al-Arabiah: Khitab da' im al-iltbas" [Arabic Secularism: A Lasting Confusing Discourse] <http://www.aljabriabed.net/n44_03chbbar.htm#_ednref7>.

52   Ibid.

these same arguments. I have used Hekman and Merry's arguments instead of al-Jabri's argument to frame my argument in this article because they help us to see the concepts within the context of Western theory and its efforts both to change itself and to promote human rights across the world.

3.2   The Concept of Ijtihad and Islamic Feminism

One of the main obstacles facing Islamic feminists in reforming Islamic family law or securing gender equality is the legitimacy of practicing *ijtihad*, which is the main tool of Islamic jurisprudence, what is called *fiqh*; I will come back to this later. In Islamic jurisprudence, *ijtihad* refers to "personal effort undertaken by the jurist in order to understand the source and deduce the rules or in the absence of a clear textual guidance, formulate independent judgments".[53] Discussing the definition of *ijtihad*, Wael Hallaq writes:

> As conceived by classical Muslim jurists, *ijtihad* is the exertion of mental energy in the search for a legal opinion to the extent that the faculties of the jurist become incapable of further effort. In other words, *ijtihad* is the maximum effort expended by the jurist to master and apply the principles and rules of *usul al-fiqh* (legal theory) for the purpose of discovering God's law. The activity of *ijtihad* is assumed by many a modern [sic] scholar to have ceased about the end of the third/ninth century, with the consent of the Muslim jurists themselves. This process [is] known as "closing the gate of *ijtihad*" (in Arabic: "*insidad bab al-ijtihad*").[54]

The practice of *ijtihad* is often viewed as being solely the work of jurists and religious scholars. This is because of the complicated requirements for the interpretation of theological texts in Islamic jurisprudence, as well as the fact that the results of *ijtihad* could lead to a legal decision, or at least to jurisprudential opinion, which in turn may pose a challenge to the prevailing jurisprudential views.

---

53   Tariq Ramadan, "Ijtihad and Maslaha: The Foundation of Governance" in MA Muqatedar Khan (ed), *Islamic Democratic Discourse: Theory, Debates and Philosophical Perspectives* (Lexington Books, 2006) 3, 9–10. See also Adham A Hashish, "*Ijtihad* Institutions: The Key to Islamic Democracy Bridging and Balancing Political and Intellectual Islam" (2010) 9(1) *Richmond Journal of Global Law & Business* 60, 67; Amna Arshad, "Ijtihad as a Tool for Islamic Legal Reform: Advancing Women's Rights in Morocco" (2006) 16 *Kansas Journal of Law and Public Policy* 129.

54   Wael B Hallaq, "Was the Gate of Ijtihad Closed" (1984) 16 *International Journal of Middle East Studies* 3, 3.

Examining women's status by *ijtihad* from Islamic jurisprudence and the history of Islamic religious literature is the main work of Islamic feminism. The difficulty with Islamic feminists practising *ijtihad* is that their conclusions may not be accepted or taken seriously. Therefore, the results of their *ijtihad* may not lead to a legal decision or a respected religious opinion, such as a *fatwa*. As mentioned, *ijtihad* is supposed to be practised by a recognized religious scholar, who is normally a male graduate of a prestigious Islamic university.[55] Alternatively, the scholar should have been recommended by other recognized religious scholars, which requires a proper training in *ijtihad*. Asifa Quraishi-Landes notes that, "without proper training in *ijtihad*, a scholar's *fiqh* [Islamic jurisprudence] conclusion will not garner the status of probability that gives it validity, and *ijtihad* expertise is no small accomplishment".[56] A second reason for the non-recognition of feminist practitioners of *ijtihad* is that many religious scholars have agreed that the door was closed on practising *ijtihad* a long time ago.[57] The main idea behind closing the door on *ijtihad* is the belief that scholars, prior to the third/ninth century, resolved all the issues of Islamic practices. The main basis for this belief is what is called *ijma al Ulama* (the past consensus of religious scholars or jurists). Quraishi-Landes considers that the idea of past consensus is one of the main obstacles facing the reform of Islamic family law, for example marriage law. Quraishi-Landes writes:

> The impact of past consensus – is a bit more complicated and potentially more of an obstacle. Consensus, a core idea in established Islamic legal theory, can have a drastic impact upon the staying power of individual *fiqh* rules. To put it briefly, Islamic jurisprudence is built upon the multiplicity of many different schools of *fiqh* doctrine, but if there is unanimous agreement of all qualified jurists of a given age, that agreement has a higher status than an average *fiqh* rule. According to Islamic

---

55   For example, Himat Hafez Barrazangi points out that one of the barriers that Muslim feminists face in the United States of America is that male religious scholars are still the main identified religious group who practise *ijtihad* or the interpretation of Quranic texts. In other words, male religious scholars in the United States monopolize the Islamic religious field. Himat Hafez Barrazangi, "Why Muslim Women are Re-interpreting the Qur'an and Hadith: A Transformative Scholarship-Activism" in Marie A Failinger, Elizabeth R Schiltz and Susan J Stabile (eds), *Feminism, Law, and Religion* (Ashgate, 2013) 257, 271–273.

56   Asifa Quraishi-Landes, "A Meditation on *Mahr*, Modernity, and Muslim Marriage Contract Law" in Marie et al. (eds), *Feminism, Law, and Religion* (2013) 173, 185.

57   For an interesting historical investigation and explanation of how *ijtihad* was closed, see Robert R Reilly, *The Closing of the Muslim Mind: How Intellectual Suicide Created the Modern Islamist Crisis* (ISI Books, 2011).

legal theory, consensus transforms a *fiqh* rule from mere probability to certainty – the same epistemological status as the Quranic text.[58]

Following this logic, Islamic feminist methods can be considered among the methods that the background-vernacularist approach suggests could be deployed in Muslim-majority countries. This is because Islamic feminism has deployed religious discourse to challenge and deconstruct another religious discourse. In addition, it has made strange what appeared familiar because it differentiates between Islam as a system of belief and Islam as a jurisprudence system. Furthermore, Islamic feminism challenges a "non-foundational foundation" for the inferior status of women in Islam.[59]

In a very broad sense, scholars describe Islamic feminism as centred on the effort to promote women's rights in a way which remains consistent with core Islamic values. For instance, Wendy Isaacs-Martin points out that "Islamic feminisms offer an interpretation of human rights within the contexts of western philosophy and Islamic society in accordance with Qur'anic interpretations".[60]

Rebecca Barlow and Shahram Akbarzadeh argue that advocacy for women's human rights in Muslim societies, which is the main target of Islamic feminism, does not necessarily reject Islam. Rather, it seeks the re-investigation of the historical texts of Islam in order to differentiate between God's "ordinances and the transcendental spiritual message of Islam".[61] Similarly, Riham Bahi describes the work of Islamic feminists as scholarship that articulates "a gender-sensitive discourse within an Islamic framework or paradigm".[62] It uses "*ijtihad* (independent investigation of the religious sources) and *tafsir* (interpretation of the Qur'an) as their basic methodology in order to establish a new gender-sensitive hermeneutics".[63]

However, as Bahi argues, some secular feminists have criticized the Islamic feminist methodology of re-reading religious texts in a "liberatory mode".[64]

58   Quraishi-Landes, above n 56, 186.
59   Shahrazad Mojab points out that "Islamic feminists ... demand equality in law much in the same way that" liberal feminists advocated formal equality. Shahrazad Mojab, "Theorizing the Politics of 'Islamic Feminism'" (2001) 69 *Feminist Review* 124, 138.
60   Wendy Isaacs-Martin, "Muslim Women and Human Rights: Does Political Transformation Equal Social Transformation?" (2013) 40(1) *Politikon* 113, 117.
61   Rebecca Barlow and Shahram Akbarzadeh, "Women's Rights in the Muslim World: Reform or Reconstruction?" (2006) 27(8) *Third World Quarterly* 1481.
62   Riham Bahi, "Islamic and Secular Feminisms: Two Discourses Mobilized for Gender Justice" (2011) 3(2) *Contemporary Readings in Law and Social Justice* 138, 146.
63   Ibid.
64   Ibid 147.

According to Bahi, secular feminists dismiss the alternative reading of religious texts. Bahi agrees with Jasmine Zine that some secular feminists "fall into the same trap as fundamentalists who derive only static and literal meanings from the Qur'an".[65] Ziba Mir-Hosseini points out that "all these opponents of the feminist project in Islam share one thing – an essentialist and non-historical understanding of Islam and Islamic law".[66] Mir-Hosseini differentiates between Sharia, as what Muslims believe is "the totality of God's will as revealed to the prophet Muhamed", and the science of jurisprudence, which is called *fiqh* (literally "understanding"). The Islamic science of jurisprudence, *fiqh*, "is the process of human endeavour to discern and extract legal rules from the sacred sources of Islam" such as the Quran and the Sunna (reported sayings and deeds of Prophet Muhammed).[67]

Ignorance of this difference between Islam as a religion of belief and Islamic law as a system of jurisprudence has created misunderstanding about what Islamic feminist work is about. Mir-Hosseini is aware that "religious faith and organised religion are linked, but they are not same thing, as is implied by conflating them in the label 'Islamic' or 'religious'". As Mir-Hosseini points out, *fiqh* "is often mistakenly equated with Sharia".[68] Therefore, the texts of *fiqh*, "which are patriarchal in both spirit and form, are frequently invoked as God's law, as a means to silence and frustrate Muslim's search for legal justice and equality".[69] On the basis of this, Mir-Hosseini's mission as an Islamic feminist is "to challenge the patriarchal interpretations of the Sharia at the level of *fiqh*, which is nothing more than the human understanding of the divine will".[70] This lasting confusion between Sharia and *fiqh* put religious and traditional fundamentalists and secular fundamentalists in the same position. As Mir-Hosseini explains, while Muslim traditionalists and fundamentalists confuse the two concepts as "a means of silencing other internal voices and [to] abuse the authority of the text for authoritarian purposes", secular fundamentalists do the same. Secular fundamentalists deploy the concepts of enlightenment and science as "a means of showing the misogyny of Islam". However, as Mir-Hosseini argues, secular fundamentalists ignore "the contexts in which the texts were produced, as well as the existence of alternative texts".[71]

---

65   Ibid.
66   Ziba Mir-Hosseini, "Muslim Women's Quest for Equality: Between Islamic Law and Feminism" (2006) 32(4) *Critical Inquiry* 629, 641.
67   Ibid 632.
68   Ibid.
69   Ibid 633.
70   Ibid.
71   Ibid 641.

It can be argued that the methodology of Islamic feminism is like a jurispru-dential methodology that seeks the reform of Islamic family law through de-ploying the same legal methods that Islamic fundamentalists used to produce a patriarchal Islamic law that discriminates against women and reinforces their inferior status in societies. Margot Badran points out that, while secu-lar feminism in the Arab world enabled women to participate in public life through breaking down the dichotomy between the private and public sphere, Islamic feminism is more appropriate for reforming Islamic family law.[72]

Islamic feminism can be considered a possible focal point for the background-vernacularist approach because, in its advocacy of the promo-tion of women's human rights in Muslim-majority countries, it reinterprets religious discourse to challenge anti-feminist or anti-human rights discourse. As I discussed earlier, one of the steps that enables the background of social meanings, or their riverbed of thought to be changed, is making sense of the discourse. Making sense of the discourse requires that the discourse should not be unreasonable to the dominant discourse or to ordinary people.

What many Islamic feminists are doing is deploying religious discourse that supports women's human rights, and deconstructing another religious dis-course that constitutes the inferior status of women in Islamic discourse. More-over, Islamic feminism is relevant to the background-vernacularist approach's methods because it attempts to make strange what had appeared familiar. This can be seen in its attempts to distinguish between the spirit of Islam and Is-lamic law. Instead of conflating the two, Islamic feminism separates them. This gives Islamic feminists more space to criticize the inferior status of women in Islamic jurisprudence, while they can avoid criticizing Islam *per se*. In this sense, criticizing Islamic jurisprudence, which many Islamic feminists consid-er male-made and patriarchal, is not criticizing Islam as a religion or a system of belief.

4   Transnational Feminist Networks and Challenging the Cultural Background

In this part I look at Women Living Under Muslim Laws ("WLUML"), Sisterhood Is Global Institute ("SIGI"), and Musawah. The purpose of this discussion is to show, in a brief way, how those transnational advocacy networks have attempt-ed to address the obstacles to adoption of women's human rights in Islamic

---

72   Margot Badran, "From Islamic Feminism to a Muslim Holistic Feminism" (2011) 42(1) *IDS Bulletin* 78, 80–82.

contexts. These organizations provide an illustration of efforts to change the cultural background, which can lay the groundwork for vernacularization.

Before considering how these transnational networks identified the obstacles facing securing gender equality in Muslim societies, and what they suggested for overcoming them, it might be useful to provide a brief explanation of the notion of transnational networks.

Margaret Keck and Kathryn Sikkink define transnational advocacy networks as networks that include "relevant actors working internationally on an issue, who are bound together by shared values, a common discourse, and dense exchanges of information and services".[73] For Keck and Sikkink, transnational advocacy networks aim to "change the behavior of states and of international organizations".[74] At the same time, they frame issues "to make them comprehensible to target audiences, to attract attention and encourage action, and to 'fit' with favorable institutional venues".[75] The actors in transnational advocacy networks "bring new ideas, norms, and discourses into policy debates, and serve as sources of information and testimony".[76] Networks are "communicative structures" and, in order to "influence discourse, procedures, and policy, activists may engage and become part of larger policy communities that group actors working on an issue from a variety of institutional and value perspectives".[77]

Drawing upon this brief definition of transnational advocacy networks, Valerie Sperling, Myra Ferree and Barbara Risman point out that transnational advocacy networks "typically identify themselves with social movements, such as environmentalism or feminism".[78] They do this as "a means of naming the values, discourses, and objectives that bind them together".[79] For Sperling, Ferree and Risman, transnational advocacy networks should not themselves be considered as social movements. This is because social movements involve "mass mobilization, contentious and confrontational tactics, and efforts to carry politics out of conventional venues into the streets".[80] Unlike social

---

73   Margaret E Keck and Kathryn Sikkink, *Activists Beyond Borders: Advocacy Networks in International Politics* (Cornell University Press, 1998) 2.

74   Ibid.

75   Ibid 3.

76   Ibid.

77   Ibid.

78   Valerie Sperling, Myra Marx Ferree and Barbara Risman, "Constructing Global Feminism: Transnational Advocacy Networks and Russian Women's Activism" (2001) 26(4) *Signs: Journal of Women in Culture and Society* 1155, 1156.

79   Ibid.

80   Ibid 1157.

movements, transnational advocacy networks "mobilize smaller numbers of individual activists who use more specialized resources of expertise and access to elites". These networks provide "new information to political leaders and reframe issues for elites in an attempt to gain the support of powerful institutions for their ideas".[81] This is "rather than relying on demonstrations of mass public support and overt confrontations with authorities".[82] However, the main shared principle between transitional advocacy networks and social movements is the achievement of social change.

Claudia Derichs points out that the description of transnational advocacy networks "matches with transnational Islamic women's networks".[83] Transnational Islamic women's networks are similar to other women's transnational advocacy networks because they are "organized around principles of challenging gender hierarchy and improving the conditions of women's lives".[84] In this sense, we can understand that WLUML, SIGI, and Musawah are transnational Islamic feminist networks. This is because they have identified the main challenges facing the implementation of women's human rights norms and principles. Also, they have suggested how such challenges could be addressed. In the following, I will describe, briefly, the challenges identified by these networks and what they have suggested to overcome them.

For WLUML, the religious identity imposed on women can be considered as the main challenge to women's rights because laws in Muslim societies "are characterized as Islamic, divinely ordained" and cannot be challenged.[85] In this sense, "religious laws are deemed fixed and immutable". On this basis "women and men are made to believe that the fundamentalist view is the only way imaginable for a woman unless she abandons her religion".[86] So, as WLUML notes, this religious identity, which was imposed on women, affects women even in secular states. In its attempts to address these challenges, WLUML

---

81   Ibid. See also Keck and Sikkink, above n 73, 30.

82   Ibid.

83   Claudia Derichs, "Transnational Women's Movements and Networking: The Case of Musawah for Equality in the Family" (2010) 14(3) *Gender, Technology and Development* 405, 409.

84   Sperling, Ferree and Risman, above n 78, 1157.

85   Madhavi Sunder, "Piercing the Veil" (2003) 112 *Yale Law Journal* 1399, 1436. WLUML emerged in 1984 as a response to the rise of fundamentalism in Algeria. Madhavi Sunder points out that the main strategic work of WLUML "offered an important retort to fundamentalists who depicted women's rights as 'Western' and un-Islamic". In this sense, as Sunder points out [at 1434], WLUML's approach does not only confront "fundamentalist understandings of religion, but formal legal understandings, as well".

86   Ibid, 1436.

attempt to avoid advocating women's equality on the basis of "purely secular strategies".[87] Its approach "entails both critiquing the fundamentalist claims about women's religious identity and empowering women to reshape religious identity in more egalitarian terms". WLUML recognizes that many women will resist rights "if they are only possible outside the context of religious and cultural community. Thus, it pursues strategies that would reconcile religion and rights, making it possible for women to have both."[88]

For the Sisterhood Is Global Institute, the major obstacle to the diffusion of the concepts and development of women's human rights is a "lack of work on identifying and developing culturally relevant language" to convey to Muslim women the message of international human rights documents.[89] On the basis of this idea, the SIGI members underlined the need "for developing models that could use indigenous ideas, concepts, myths, and idioms to explain and support the rights contained in international documents".[90] The main premise of this project is that "universal human rights are consonant with the spirit of Islam".[91] This statement is based on the idea that many Muslims "believe

---

87   Ibid.

88   Ibid 1441.

89   Mahnaz Afkhami and Haleh Vaziri, *Claiming Our Rights: A Manual for Women's Human Rights Education in Muslim Societies* (Sisterhood Is Global Institute, 1996) ii. The SIGI launched a pioneering program to produce a human rights manual containing Quranic verses and Hadith supporting the idea of women's rights, which is called *Claiming Our Rights: A Manual for Women's Human Rights Education in Muslim Societies*. As Afkhami and Vaziri, at ii, points out that the purpose of *Claiming Our Rights: A Manual for Women's Human Rights Education in Muslim Societies* is to provide a model of human rights education in order to "facilitate transmission of the universal human rights concepts inscribed in the major international documents to grassroots populations in Muslim societies".

90   Ibid iii.

91   Ibid v. The theoretical framework of this model of human rights education is a communication model. Such a model requires communicators, "a medium, a message, and an audience". The communicators can be "women's organizations, human rights organizations, and appropriate government agencies". In the discussion of the audience, Afkhami and Vaziri pointed out that the human rights education model is based on "interaction, reciprocity of roles, and exchange of positions between communicators and their audiences". In this sense, the audience can be "a government agency, a religious group, a village gathering, women in workshop, or family members". In discussion of the medium, Afkhami and Vaziri pointed out that there are several possibilities. They include news media, formal and informal organizations, and groups and individuals. As Afkhami and Vaziri pointed out, a good "medium allows for dialogue". Radio, TV satellites, the internet and so on make it "possible for international rights organizations and countries and corporations that control the international media to play an overwhelming role in transmitting the rights message".

that Islam contains the essentials of human rights".[92] Therefore, "human rights documents must be presented in a dialogue with Islamic tenets, if they are to succeed in Muslim societies".[93] Afkhami and Vaziri argued that the message should be designed to be appropriate in "the existing cultural, political, and technological environments".[94] Although the messages derive from the international human rights documents, they should be designed in a way that people can understand them.

For Musawah, the challenges are considered in the context of current Islamic family laws.[95] Musawah declared that the existing Islamic family laws are unjust and frequently ignore Muslim families' and individuals' experiences and lives.[96] Gender inequality is still evident inside Muslim families. What Musawah suggests for the achievement of equality in Muslim families is that such achievement is possible by considering a holistic approach that takes into account many aspects that promote the norms of equality.[97] Women's

---

92 Ibid.

93 Ibid v. As Afkhami and Vaziri points out, at viii, the main objective of this model "is not to teach a particular truth; it is to establish dialogue". It should be noted here this has parallels to Hekamn's argument of telling the alternative story, as I discussed previously. As I had indicated previously, Hekman suggested that the alternative story/picture of the background does not mean that feminists are looking to reveal the truth. Rather, it enables them to argue for it.

94 Ibid.

95 As Zinah Anwar points out, the idea of Musawah (which literally means equality in Arabic) was proposed in March 2006 in Kuala Lumpur, Malaysia at a Sisters in Islam International Consultation on "Trends in Family Law Reform in Muslim Countries". The participants at that meeting "felt a compelling need to build an international network of women's groups in Muslim world that have for decades been working on family law to share strategies". This was needed because many groups "have not made the hoped-for progress in their reform efforts because they have worked in isolation – at both national and transnational levels – and because of opposition from conservative groups within society and a lack of support from their governments". See Zainah Anwar, "Introduction: Why Equality and Justice Now" in Zainah Anwar (ed), *Wanted: Equality and Justice in the Muslim Family* (Musawah an initiative of Sisters in Islam (SIS Forum Malaysia), 2009) 2.

96 Musawah, Framework For Action (English) <http://www.musawah.org/resources/publi cations/framework_for_action_(English)>.

97 Margot Badran calls the project of Musawah "Muslim holistic feminism" because it uses Islamic feminist theories of equality and justice based on religious sources, "together with the secular discourses of democracy and human rights". So Muslim holistic feminism is a "multi-stranded discursive approach". The main purpose of Musawah is to reform Islamic family law in Muslim societies. In this sense, Badran sees the Musawah as an example of secular feminists and Islamic feminists cooperating with each other to advocate for

and men's experiences and lives, universal human rights principles, Islamic teachings, and constitutional guarantees should be brought together as a holistic approach for the strategy of the achievement of equality.[98] In its Framework for Action, Musawah points out that equality and justice in the family are possible because "Qur'anic teachings encompass the principles of justice ('adl), equality (musawah), equity (insaf), human dignity (karamah), love and compassion (mawaddah wa rahmah)".[99] As Musawah argues, these principles "reflect universal norms and are consistent with contemporary human rights standards".[100]

Transnational advocacy networks including WLUML, SIGI and Musawah share some similar strategies with the background-vernacularist approach, as I have described it above. First, they are based on the view that the religious discourse that constitutes women's inferior status cannot be challenged without adopting another religious discourse that deploys more egalitarian terms. Second, all of them agree that women's equality is possible, if the reinterpretation of religious texts is allowed.

In sum, these transnational advocacy networks are clearly trying to change the cultural background by introducing a different interpretation of religious discourse. But it should also be noted that some of these networks, such as SIGI, have used a strategy similar to vernacularization.

5   Challenging the Cultural Background and Telling the Story of
       Human Rights

This article has suggested that, in order to universalize human rights standards, these standards should be implanted in the domestic legal and cultural discourse, through the vernacularization of human rights norms. According to the background-vernacularist approach, as I have developed it, this vernacularization is unlikely to be effective without challenging or changing the background of social norms and meanings that reinforce the inferior status of women. Vernacularization, therefore, requires that those elements of the background, which may resonate with human rights, are drawn out and strengthened.

---

gender equality and social justice in Muslim countries. See Badran, "From Islamic Feminism to a Muslim Holistic Feminism", above n 72.

98   Musawah, above n 96.

99   Musawah, Musawah Framework For Action (2009) 5 <http://www.musawah.org/sites/default/files/Musawah-Framework-EN_1.pdf>.

100   Ibid.

As I discussed early in this article, challenging or changing the background suggests that the "master's tools" together with a critical re-interpretation of those tools can dismantle the master's house. The master's tools, as I mentioned previously, are the discourses that establish the background of cultural norms or social meanings. What makes the master's tools useful for the story of human rights is that they include various resources, some of which can be deployed as tools to resist an authoritative discourse. This involves constructing and using a hybrid discourse, which is building upon one social language to turn it to the advantage of another social language. This is an attempt to draw a new discursive picture based on the original discursive picture.

To understand this, it might be useful to consider a frequently used definition of culture in literature, which is a definition proposed by Edward Burnett Tylor. Although this is a very old definition of "culture", it is still relevant. Tylor defined culture as follows:

> Culture or Civilization, taken in its wide ethnographic sense, is that complex whole which includes knowledge, belief, art, morals, law, custom, and any other capabilities and habits acquired by man [sic] as a member of society. The condition of culture among the various societies of mankind, in so far as it is capable of being investigated on general principles, is a subject apt for the study of laws of human thought and action.[101]

Bronwyn Winter, Denise Thompson and Sheila Jeffreys point out that feminist anthropologists have drawn upon this definition and argued that the behaviour of men and women "can change, and that both sexes can deviate from cultural norms in working to bring about such change".[102] The Human Rights Council's *Report of the Working Group on the Issue of Discrimination against Women in Law and in Practice* (2015) points out that "[c]ulture is a broad concept encompassing all forms of conduct, organization and human behavior within society, including family, language, religion, philosophy, law, government, art and sport".[103] The report further points out that culture "is not a static or unchanging concept, although some States tend to present it as such in order to justify

---

101   Edward Burnett Tylor, *Primitive Culture: Researches into the Development of Mythology, Philosophy, Religion, Art, and Custom* (J Murray, 1871) 1.

102   Bronwyn Winter, Denise Thompson and Sheila Jeffreys, "The UN Approach to Harmful Traditional Practices" (2002) 4(1) *International Feminist Journal of Politics* 72, 78.

103   Human Rights Council, *Report of the Working Group on the Issue of Discrimination against Women in Law and in Practice*, 29th sess, Agenda Item 3, UN Doc A/HRC/29/50 (2 April 2015) [10].

inequality between men and women".[104] In this sense, since "cultures are nei-ther homogeneous nor unchanging, there are very significant differences be-tween them concerning their stages of development and the extent to which the patriarchy, misogyny and practices that are harmful to women and girls exist within them".[105]

The report of the Due Diligence Project, prepared by Zarizana Abdul Aziz and Janine Moussa, which was submitted to the United Nations Working Group on Discrimination against Women in Law and in Practice in January 2015, points out that culture is a social construct and is not static and un-changing.[106] This is so "even if presented as such by some States. Culture is ever changing; it adapts and re-creates itself in support of society's values".[107] Following this sense, culture "is constantly reproduced by both collective and individual contributions through exchanges; as such, culture is formed by con-testations between differing views. Consequently culture is a living process and is necessarily dynamic, adaptive and innovative."[108] This aspect of culture makes the background-vernacularist approach possible, because it relies upon culture being both adaptable and dynamic.

In this context, we can find that the interventions and arguments of some Islamic feminists and some transnational networks interested in promot-ing women's human rights in Islamic countries, such as WLUML, SIGI and Musawah, useful. Many such arguments focus on the idea that the religious background that supports gender inequality in Islamic jurisprudence and Islamic history is not unchangeable. For this purpose, they attempt to avoid the advocacy of the promotion of women's human rights through only the human rights discourse, which is secular. Rather, they attempted to reconcile the secular discourse with the religious discourse in order to be effective in Muslim-majority countries. Such discourses take a dual strategy because they build on an original story, which is a religious one, and then tell an alternative story, which is a religious-secular story.

Broadly, this process suggests two points. First, it suggests that the cultural background of gender inequality can be challenged by making its familiarity

---

104   Ibid.
105   Ibid [13].
106   Zarizana Abdul Aziz and Janine Moussa, *The Due Diligence Principle and the Role of the State: Discrimination Against Women in Family and Cultural Life* (United Nations Working Group on Discrimination against Women in Law and in Practice, 2015) <http://www.duediligenceproject.org/ewExternalFiles/DDP%20UNWG%20Submission%20Final%20300115_2.pdf>.
107   Ibid 5.
108   Ibid.

appear strange. In this sense, the gender inequality in Islamic jurisprudence is strange because there is no clear evidence that tells that such inequality is the totality of God's Will. For developing this claim, as I have shown previously, some Islamic feminists support this idea by using some of what could be called the "master's tools", such as *ijtihad* and *tafseer* in order to re-interpret and challenge the religious background of gender inequality. They believe that current Islamic family law is patriarchal and discriminates against women because male-biased clerics and religious scholars wrote it. So, Islamic family law is not completely derived from God's ordinances. Hence, I call this step the step of challenging the cultural background.

Second, it suggests that the alternative story is based on vernacularizing some human rights concepts. Many Muslims, as Musawah argued above, believe that human rights concepts, such as equality, justice, equity and freedom, reflect many Islamic principles. To make sense of such a claim to ordinary people, the educational model, for instance, as proposed by the SIGI, is useful. Such a model is similar to the vernacularist approach proposed by Merry. The main purpose of doing this is to make familiar what appears strange. It appeals to efforts to make sense of the alternative story or picture of the issue of equality in the Islamic context. This step is the step of telling the human rights story.

6   Conclusion

In this article, I have argued that background and vernacularist approaches are complementary to each other. I have discussed each approach in some detail to show why this is so. As I showed, the background-vernacularist approach could be considered an appropriate theoretical framework to understand how cultural strategies and discourse can be deployed in the effort to promote women's human rights.

Through the lens of the background-vernacularist approach, this article does not provide a specific blueprint for change. It suggests that in order to achieve, for example, legal and substantive equality of women, one needs to change the cultural norms that create or reinforce views about women's position in society and then translate the relevant human rights norms and principles into domestic legal and cultural norms. The task here is not to change all of the surrounding culture or to challenge the culture per se. Rather, it is an attempt to change or challenge specific cultural norms or social meanings that constitute the inferior status of women.

Through the lens of the background-vernacularist approach, this article argues that the strategy of the application of human rights norms involves

making strange what had appeared familiar in the cultural norms and practices and at the same time making familiar what had appeared strange in introducing international human rights norms and principles.

At the first stage, in order to make strange what had appeared familiar, this
approach suggests that the background of cultural norms or social meanings
that establish the inferior status of women should be challenged and deconstructed. The background of social meanings or cultural meanings are deconstructed or challenged by making them seem strange or at least by showing
that such cultural meanings or cultural norms do not produce social justice or
fairness in a certain society because there is another story of fairness and justice that can be told. Then the second stage involves telling the other story, the
story of vernacularized norms and principles of human rights. In this sense,
what had appeared strange, which is international human rights norms and
principles, should become familiar because vernacularization means that international human rights norms are transformed into domestic legal norms
and language, in order to make them familiar and intelligible for local, ordinary people.

The main examples given in this article relate to the theoretical arguments of
Islamic feminists and the practical application of such arguments, which have
been embodied in transnational advocacy networks such as Women Living
Under Muslim Law, Sisterhood Is Global Institute, and Musawah. As shown
in this article, their arguments emphasise that women's human rights can be
promoted through the deployment of religious discourse in Muslim-majority
countries and societies. They argue that this can serve two purposes. First, it
can be useful to challenge the cultural background of cultural norms that discriminate against women through deploying the same methods and discourse
deployed by religious fundamentalists. Thus, such a method provides women's
human rights advocates with tools to give an effective response and critique
to fundamentalist discourse and arguments. Second, such a method provides
a re-definition of the identity of religious women because it allows them to
advocate for their equality within their own religious discourse and terms.

The South Pacific

∴

The Pacific Islands Forum 2016

*Tony Angelo**

The 16 members of the Pacific Islands Forum gathered in Pohnpei in the Federated States of Micronesia in September 2016 for their 47th Annual Meeting. The states were represented by their Heads of State or by their Heads of Government. Niue and Palau were represented by their Ministers of Foreign Affairs, Kiribati by a special representative, and Solomon Islands by its Deputy Prime Minister. Fiji was represented by its Minister of Foreign Affairs, the Prime Minister maintaining his personal boycott of the meetings of the Forum.

Though not independent states, French Polynesia and New Caledonia were both admitted as full members of the Forum at this meeting.

Climate change, fisheries, the ocean, and the Regional Assistance Mission to Solomon Islands ('RAMSI'), which are regular items on the Forum agenda, were also important matters for the 47th Forum.[1]

1   Climate Change

Climate change and disaster risk management have long occupied the attention of Pacific island countries. The lead-up to the Paris agreement had provided the opportunity for many calls for action by Pacific leaders. For instance, the Polynesian Leaders' Group Declaration of 16 July 2015 was particularly significant in its recognising that the Pacific Ocean, which occupies one-third of the Earth's surface, was of special relevance to the small island countries of the Pacific. Every change in it has major consequences for the people of the Pacific. The Polynesian Leaders' Group Declaration states that the Polynesian Leaders' Group saw itself as the voice for the ocean. The Group also supported a limit on global warming to below 1.5C of pre-industrial levels by 2100 and the Green Climate Fund. The Group saw the need for a legally binding international document dealing with climate change. The Pacific Islands Development Forum at its September 2015 meeting called for greater funding and better legislation to deal with the demands of climate change. In the run-up to the Paris meeting the Pacific Islands Forum, on 11 September 2015,

---

* Professor, Faculty of Law, Victoria University Wellington, NZ.
1 For the official record of the meeting see, the Forum Communique PIFS(16)9 <www .forumsec.org/resources/uploads/embeds/file/2016_Forum_Com>.

reiterated its concern and calls for action. Substantially, the Paris Agreement acknowledged and answered the various Pacific calls. The 2016 Forum welcomed the Paris Agreement but also recognised that reaching the goal of limiting global temperature increases was a matter that Forum members would have to address with urgency. The Forum had before it the draft Framework for Resilient Development in the Pacific ("FRDP").[2] The leaders endorsed that document and agreed that it be finalised as soon as possible and be put into operation when the Paris Agreement came into force.

The FRDP is the product of much consultation between agencies and governments in the Pacific and was signed off by the Secretary General for the Forum, by the Director General of the SPC, by the Director General of SPREP, and also by the Special Representative of the Secretary-General for disaster risk reduction. The FRDP sets out guidelines for actions that can be taken to address climate change effects in a holistic manner and also how to deal with disaster risk management. It provides a series of strategies which relate to improving climate change adaptation actions, and to improving resilience to the effects of disaster. The FRDP also deals with strategies for reducing carbon emissions and strengthening disaster preparedness, response and recovery. The Pohnpei statement: Strengthening Pacific Resilience to Climate Change and Disaster Risk will complement the FRDP.[3] The limited personnel, finance, and infrastructure of most Pacific islands means that addressing climate change is a huge challenge and one that they cannot meet alone.

2   Fisheries

Fisheries remains a topic high on the Forum agenda. Much work had been done in the general Forum context in the previous year and, in particular, the FFA and the Forum Secretariat were commended for their work on increasing the return from the fishery resource and ensuring its sustainable management. The Forum also commented on the successful renegotiation of the Fisheries Treaty with the United States of America.

It was noted that focus on the offshore fishery had led to attention being directed away from coastal fisheries management. The Forum agreed that the inshore fishery would henceforth be included under the heading of Fisheries

---

2   Annex 1 to the Forum Communique, ibid.
3   Annex 2 to the Forum Communique, ibid.

and systems would be put in place to address matters such as ciguatera and the proper management of the harvesting of beche-de-mer. The New Zealand government announced the commitment of $12.15 million for the support of coastal fisheries and aquaculture in the Forum region.

The Forum noted that illegal fishing and the associated activities are estimated to cost the region about USD 616 million per annum.[4]

3   West Papua

The West Papua issue was again noted both as a matter of political sensitivity and one for mutual discussions with the government of Indonesia. The Forum had proposed that there be a fact-finding mission to West Papua but the Indonesian government had refused to approve such a mission. The Forum stated that an open and constructive dialogue with Indonesia was important.

4   Regional Assistance Mission to Solomon Islands

Despite the many challenges that RAMSI has faced over the years, it has been a success and so much was acknowledged by the Forum: It was seen as "a shining example of Pacific diplomacy and cooperation". The anticipated date of withdrawal of RAMSI from Solomon Islands is July 2017.

5   Business

Another significant matter of discussion was Pacer Plus. It was noted that the agreement was expected to be signed by the end of 2016. It was also noted that Papua New Guinea will not be party to the Agreement and that Fiji had reservations as to the final text. Australia and New Zealand agreed to provide resources for (1) the implementation of Pacer Plus in the area of the economic cooperation chapter of the Agreement and (2) for broader trade-related assistance for the Forum countries.[5] On the matter of private sector development in the region, the leaders repeated their support for improving

---

4 Figures provided by the FFA.

5 Pacer Plus was unlikely to change things for the smaller Pacific countries since these already have tariff-free access to the markets in Australia and New Zealand.

mobility of personnel and the processes which support business activity in the Pacific.

6   Cyber Security

Concern was expressed by the leaders about the security risks from cyber-crime. They therefore agreed to work together to establish a CERT (Computer Emergency Response Team) for the region.

The 2017 meeting of the Forum will be hosted by Samoa.

The Year in Review

∵

International Human Rights Law

Shea Elizabeth Esterling*

1 Introduction

This note reviews New Zealand's state practice concerning international human rights law in 2016. It was a notable year for New Zealand as it concluded its term as a non-permanent member of the United Nations Security Council in December 2016. During its two years on the Security Council, New Zealand considered some of the most serious threats to international peace and security that have significant human rights dimensions, including: the dismal humanitarian situation in Syria, the continued brutal attacks by Islamic State of Iraq and the Levant ("ISIL") on civilians, the continuing Israeli/Palestinian conflict, the continued instability in the eastern Congo at the hands of armed groups, as well as a host of other issues across Africa ranging from attacks in northern Mali to the crises in Somalia, Libya and the Central African Republic. Aside from its engagement with UN Charter based bodies, New Zealand continued its engagement with UN treaty based bodies as a result of its commitments under various human rights treaties. These treaty based bodies issued concluding observations and recommendations in relation to New Zealand's commitments under the *International Covenant on Civil and Political Rights* and the *Convention on the Rights of the Child* and its *Optional Protocol*, while New Zealand submitted its periodic reports as per its commitments under the *International Convention on the Elimination of All Forms of Racial Discrimination* and the *Convention on the Elimination of All Forms of Discrimination against Women* and follow-up information under the *Convention against Torture and Other Cruel, Inhuman or Degrading Treatment or Punishment*. On the domestic side, the New Zealand Human Rights Commission continued its work, much of which focused on the recovery of Christchurch and in particular the human rights aspects of residential red zones post-earthquake, as well as exploring the issue of assisted dying which was deemed the human rights debate of the year.

---

*   University of Canterbury

© KONINKLIJKE BRILL NV, LEIDEN, 2018 | DOI 10.1163/9789004345911_009

2   New Zealand and UN Human Rights Treaty Bodies

2.1   *Concluding Observations on the Sixth Periodic Report of New*
         Zealand under the International Covenant on Civil and
         Political Rights

In May 2015, New Zealand submitted its Sixth Periodic Report under the *International Covenant on Civil and Politics Rights ("ICCPR")*[1] to the Human Rights Committee ("HRC"), the body charged with overseeing the implementation of the Covenant. The report covered the period of January 2008 through March 2015. A draft of the report was circulated for public comment in December 2014, prior to its lodgement with the United Nations. Twenty non-governmental organizations ("NGOs") made submissions on the draft, with these then being considered in the preparation of the final report.[2] After submission of this report, further information was submitted by eleven Civil Society Organizations including the Aotearoa Indigenous Rights Trust ("AIR Trust"), the Monitoring Mechanism of the National Iwi Charis, Privacy International and Peace Movement Aotearoa amongst others. This information functions as a Shadow Report. A Shadow Report is a report to the HRC from a source other than the government in an effort to fill in the gaps of the "not so good" which might be minimized or overlooked by the government in its report.[3] The importance of a Shadow Report is underscored by the fact that the concluding observations of the HRC, while not formally legally binding, are authoritative interpretations of international human rights law.

At the outset of its *Concluding Observations* issued in April 2016, the HRC welcomed various legislative and institutional measures taken by New Zealand since the last periodic report in 2008, including:

· The adoption of the *Organised Crime and Anti-Corruption Legislation Act 2015*;
· The adoption of the *Harmful Digital Communications Act 2015*;

---

1 Human Rights Committee, *Consideration of Reports submitted by States parties under Article 40 of the Covenant pursuant to the Optional Reporting Procedure – Sixth Periodic Report of States parties due in 2015: New Zealand*, UN Doc CCPR/C/NZL/6 (2015) ("Sixth Periodic Report ICCPR").

2 Ibid [6].

3 See, Tony Ellis, *In the Matter of New Zealand's 6th Periodic Report: Alternative Shadow Report Filed by Dr. Tony Ellis* (14 March 2016) Office of United Nations High Commissioner for Human Rights <http://tbinternet.ohchr.org/Treaties/CCPR/Shared%20Documents/NZL/INT_CCPR_CSS_NZL_23261_E.pdf>.

- The adoption of the *Fisheries (Foreign Charter Vessels and Other Matters) Amendment Act 2014*;
- The adoption of the *Vulnerable Children Act 2014*;
- The adoption of the *Māori Disability Action Plan for Disability Support Services (Whāia Te Ao Mārama) 2012–2017*;
- The adoption of the *National Pasifika Disability Plan (Faiva Ora) 2014–2016*;
- The adoption of the *Marriage (Definition of Marriage) Amendment Act 2013*;
- The adoption of the *Youth Crime Action Plan 2013–2023*;
- The adoption of the *Māori Education Strategy, Ka Hikitia: Accelerating Success 2013–2017*.[4]

These measures roughly correspond to the key developments noted by New Zealand in its Sixth Periodic Report.[5]

However, the HRC continued, noting nineteen principle areas of concern and subsequent recommendations for remedy. Some of these areas include concern over underrepresentation of women in corporate governance and senior management in the public and private sector, the overrepresentation of women in some types of occupations, and the gender pay gap. Collectively deemed concerns in relation to equality between women and men, the recommendations here include the full incorporation of the principle of equality between women and men in all national policies,[6] the operationalization and implementation of equal pay for work of equal value across New Zealand,[7] the promotion of greater women's representation in managerial and leadership positions in the public and private sector[8] and the development and implementation of programmes to achieve general equality and empowerment for all women and girls, with particular focus on Māori and Pasifika women and girls.[9]

Indeed, the HRC called for particular focus on protecting Māori and Pasifika peoples in a number of recommendations, including those related to domestic and gender-based violence, child abuse, non-discrimination in employment and vocational training and non-discrimination in law enforcement. Regarding domestic and gender based violence, the HRC welcomed New Zealand's

---

4 Human Rights Committee, *Concluding Observations on the Sixth Periodic Report of New Zealand*, UN Doc CCPR/C/NZL/CO/6 (2016) [3] ("ICCPR Concluding Observations").
5 Sixth Periodic Report ICCPR, above n 1, [3].
6 ICCPR Concluding Observations, above n 4, [18(a)].
7 Ibid [18(d)].
8 Ibid [17(c)].
9 Ibid [18(b)].

establishment in 2014 of the Ministerial Group on Family Violence and Sexual Violence and the implementation of community based anti-domestic violence campaigns.[10] However, it remains concerned about the high prevalence of domestic violence, especially among Māori and Pasifika women and girls.[11] Its recommendations include the incorporation of programmes to combat such violence into the *National Plan of Action for Humans Rights*[12] and the development and implementation of programmes aimed at victims' rehabilitation and redress.[13] Regarding violence against children, the HRC remained concerned about the significant number of children in New Zealand who suffer physical and psychological abuse and neglect and, in particular, regretted the absence of information regarding programmes of rehabilitation, reintegration and redress for child victims, in particular Māori and Pasifika child victims.[14] It calls on New Zealand to strengthen efforts to combat child abuse including through the development and implementation of multi-stakeholder, child-friendly early detection and reporting mechanisms.[15] The HRC also requests that New Zealand provide detailed information in its next periodic report on the outcomes of the *Children's Action Plan* and the review of the Child, Youth and Family agency.[16] Aside from issues of violence, another theme that concerned the HRC, in relation to Māori and Pasifika in particular, was discrimination. Regarding discrimination in the workplace, the HRC recommended that New Zealand address the high unemployment rates among Māori and Pasifika and in particular Māori and Pasifika women and young people through the development and implementation of comprehensive employment and vocational training strategies.[17] In law enforcement, the HRC recommended the review of its policies, with the aim to reduce the incarceration rates and overrepresentation of members of Māori and Pasifika communities, particularly women and young people,[18] as well as the elimination of direct and indirect discrimination against Māori and Pasifika in the administration of justice through human rights training programmes.[19]

---

10   Ibid [29].
11   Ibid.
12   Ibid [29(b)].
13   Ibid [29(d)].
14   Ibid [31].
15   Ibid [32(a)].
16   Ibid [32(b)].
17   Ibid [22(a)].
18   Ibid [26(a)].
19   Ibid [26(b)].

The HRC also concerned itself with issues in relation to Indigenous Peoples and discrimination more broadly. As regards the former, the HRC remained concerned that since the adoption by the Waitangi Tribunal decision *WAI 262* in 2011, New Zealand has not provided the relevant human rights bodies with information regarding policies and an implementation timetable. Furthermore, it noted New Zealand's insufficient engagement with Indigenous Peoples prior to the signing of the *Trans-Pacific Partnership Agreement* in February 2016 which included provisions that may have had a negative impact on their rights.[20] The HRC recommends that to remedy these issues, New Zealand strengthens the role of the *Treaty of Waitangi* in the existing constitutional arrangements[21] and guarantees the informed participation of Indigenous Peoples in all relevant national and international consultation processes including those that affect them directly.[22] Regarding discrimination, the HRC remained concerned with prejudice against racial and religious groups in New Zealand[23] and recommended the development and implementation of a comprehensive national strategy to combat racism, racial discrimination, xenophobia and religious hatred.[24]

Finally, the HRC also expressed concern about the high number or reservations to human rights treaties in particular *ICCPR* arts 10.2 and 10.3 concerning the detention of youth and urged New Zealand to withdraw these reservations.[25] Concerns about privacy and specifically privacy in the context of anti-terrorism legislation were raised by the HRC, vis-a-vis government surveillance of communication, so it recommends the review of New Zealand's counter-terrorism legislation[26] as well as the review of the legal framework for regulating communications surveillance.[27]

2.2 Concluding Observations on the Fifth Periodic Report of New Zealand under the Convention on the Rights of the Child

In December 2015, New Zealand submitted its Fifth Periodic Report regarding the *Convention on the Rights of the Child* ("*CRC*") to the body charged with overseeing its implementation: the Committee on the Rights of the Child

---

20   Ibid [45].
21   Ibid [46(a)].
22   Ibid [46(b)].
23   Ibid [19].
24   Ibid [20].
25   Ibid [5].
26   Ibid [14].
27   Ibid [16].

(the "Committee").[28] This report included developments from February 2011 through March 2015 and aimed to update the Committee on New Zealand's progress against the *2011 Concluding Observations*.[29] After submission of this periodic report, further information was submitted by eight Civil Society Organizations including the New Zealand Global Coalition to Protect Education from Attack, the New Zealand Law Society and Stop Intersex Genital Mutilations.org amongst others. In addition, a number of National Human Rights Institutions ("NHRI") submitted shadow reports, including the New Zealand Children's Commissioner and the New Zealand Human Rights Commission.

At the outset of its *Concluding Observations* issued in October 2016, the Committee welcomed the submission of the Fifth Periodic Report and the progress achieved by New Zealand in children's rights, noting in particular its ratification of the *Optional Protocol to the Convention on the Rights of the Child on the Sale of Children, Child Prostitution and Child Pornography* in 2011.[30] However, the Committee highlighted six areas of concerns that require the adoption of "urgent" measures. These areas include: violence, abuse and neglect; children deprived of a family environment; standard of living; children belonging to minority or Indigenous groups; child labour; and juvenile justice.[31]

Regarding violence, abuse and neglect, the Committee recommends that New Zealand immediately end the use of restraints and detention in state care of children, the creation of a national database on all cases of violence against children and the development of a comprehensive strategy to combat the abuse and neglect of children in all settings, with particular attention to Māori and Pasifika children and children with disabilities. It further recommends that regarding Māori and Pasifika children and children with disabilities, New Zealand strengthens education and awareness programmes to prevent and combat child abuse.[32]

In relation to children deprived of a family environment, the Committee recommends that in reforming the care system, New Zealand needs to ensure that the best interest of the child is the pre-eminent consideration in every case and that the voice of the child is heard in matters affecting her or him. Further,

---

28   Committee on the Rights of the Child, *Consideration of Reports submitted by States parties under Article 44 of the Convention – Fifth Periodic Report of States parties due in 2015: New Zealand*, UN Doc CRC/C/NZL/5 (2015) ("CRC Fifth Periodic Report").

29   Ibid [1].

30   Committee on the Rights of the Child, *Concluding Observations on the Fifth Periodic Report of New Zealand*, UN Doc CRC/C/NZL/CO/5 (2016), [2]–[3] ("CRC Concluding Observations").

31   Ibid [4].

32   Ibid [23].

the Committee recommends ensuring that in this reformation process, there is a common understanding of a child-centred approach across the care system with regular monitoring of the implementation and impacts of reform with particular attention, again, to Māori and Pasifika children and children with disabilities. With regard to Māori children specifically, the Committee urges New Zealand to address the overrepresentation of Māori children in state care by implementing the recommendations of the Children's Commissioner 2015 report entitled *State of Care*.[33]

As regards the standard of living, the Committee recommends the introduction of a systemic approach to child poverty with particular focus on Māori and Pasifika children and establishing a national definition of poverty. The Committee also suggests that New Zealand should consider holding targeted consultations with families, children and Civil Society Organizations with the aim of strengthening strategies and measures for the reduction of child poverty.[34]

Regarding matters related to children belonging to minority or Indigenous groups, the Committee urges New Zealand to develop a comprehensive and cross-sector strategy for the full enjoyment of the rights of Māori and Pasifika children in light of the Committee's *General Comment No 11* (2009) which specifically addresses the rights of Indigenous children under the CRC. In the development of this strategy, the Committee also urges close cooperation with Indigenous communities.[35]

Concerning child labour, the Committee recommends the creation of a minimum age of entry into employment that is in line with international standards, the creation of minimum wage guarantees for working children under the age of sixteen, the ratification of the *International Labour Organization Minimum Age Convention 1973 (No 138)* and the amendment of the *Health and Safety at Work Act* to recognize and address issues affecting working children.[36]

Finally, concerning juvenile justice, the Committee laments New Zealand's lack of progress in this area and urges the Government to raise the minimum age of criminal responsibility to eighteen years old and to strengthen efforts to address the overrepresentation of Māori and Pasifika children and young people in the juvenile justice system, including through improvement of the police's cultural awareness.[37]

---

33   Ibid [28].
34   Ibid [36].
35   Ibid [42].
36   Ibid [44].
37   Ibid [45].

2.3   *Concluding Observations on the Report Submitted by New Zealand*
        under Article 12 (1) of the Optional Protocol to the Convention on the
        Rights of the Child on the Sale of Children, Child Prostitution and
        Child Pornography

As aforementioned, the Committee on the Rights of the Child welcomed New
Zealand's ratification of the *Optional Protocol to the Convention on the Rights
of the Child on the Sale of Children, Child Prostitution and Child Pornography*
("*CRC-OP-SC*") in 2011.[38] As with other international human rights treaties, the
CRC-OP-SC requires that state parties submit a periodic report. New Zealand
submitted its first report under the *CRC-OP-SC* in 2014.[39] In October 2016, the
Committee released its *Concluding Observations* on this initial report.[40]

The Committee begins by welcoming New Zealand's initial report under
the *CRC-OP-SC* and notes that the present *Concluding Observations*[41] should
be read in conjunction with New Zealand's Fifth Periodic Report regarding the
CRC.[42] It provides an overview of the positive aspects taken by New Zealand in
relation to the implementation of *CRC-OP-SC*, including the adoption of:

·   The 2015 amendment to the *Crimes Act* aimed at criminalizing domestic
    trafficking and aspects of grooming, and the 2005 amendment aimed at
    criminalizing dealing in children for the purpose of sexual exploitation, the
    removal of body parts and engagement in forced labour;
·   The *Vulnerable Children Act*, in 2014, which sets clear expectations for
    consistent safety checking across the children's workforce;
·   The *Victims' Rights Amendment Act*, the *Parole Amendment Act* and the
    Sentencing Amendment Act, in 2014, and the *Children, Young Persons and
    Their Families Amendment Act*, in 2016;
·   The *Adoption Amendment Act*, in 2011, which inserts Sections 27 (A)–(D)
    into the *Adoption Act 1955* and creates the offence to improperly induce con-
    sent for the adoption of a child.[43]

---

38   See, Committee on the Rights of the Child, *Concluding Observations on the Report submit-
      ted by New Zealand under Article 12 (1) of the Optional Protocol to the Convention on the
      Rights of the Child on the Sale of Children, Child Prostitution and Child Pornography,* UN
      Doc CRC/C/OPSC/NZL/CO/1 (2016) (hereinafter "CRC-OP-SC Concluding Observations").
39   See, Committee on the Rights of the Child, *Consideration of Reports submitted by States
      Parties under Article 12 (1) of the Optional Protocol to the Convention on the Rights of the
      Child on the Sale of Children, Child Prostitution and Child Pornography: New Zealand,* UN
      Doc CRC/C/OPSC/NZL/1 (2014).
40   See generally, CRC-OP-SC Concluding Observations.
41   Ibid.
42   See, CRC Fifth Periodic Report, above n 28, [2]–[3].
43   CRC-OP-SC Concluding Observations, above n 38, [4].

The Committee proceeds to offer a series of recommendations. Aside from general recommendations to aid in further implementation of the CRC-OP-SC,[44] it offers a series of specific recommendations in relation to prevention and prohibition of the sale of children, child prostitution and child pornography, as well as suggestions for the protection of the rights of child victims.

Regarding the prevention of the sale of children, child prostitution and child pornography, the Committee recommends a campaign to research the nature and root causes of the sexual exploitation of children in order to identify those at risk.[45] Furthermore, the Committee recommends preventative measures targeted against exploitation over the Internet, the implementation of social and economic development programmes and poverty reduction strategies[46] and the conduct of advocacy campaigns for the tourism industry to highlight the risk of child sex tourism.[47]

Concerning the prohibition of the sale of children, child prostitution and child pornography, the Committee recommends that New Zealand explicitly define and criminalize all offences in the context of the sale of children in accordance with CRC-OP-SC arts 2 and 3[48] as well the review of the *Prostitution Reform Act (2003)*[49] and the *Film, Videos and Publications Classifications Amendment Act (2005)* in order to ensure full compliance with these articles as regards attempted child pornography or complicity with child pornography.[50] Furthermore, it suggests that New Zealand revise its legislation to ensure that all legal persons, including corporations, can be held liable for offences under the CRC-OP-SC[51] and ensure that its legislation enables it to establish and exercise extraterritorial jurisdiction over all offences covered by the CRC-OP-SC.[52]

Finally, as regards the protection of the rights of child victims, the Committee makes a number of recommendations, directed towards the criminal justice system, regarding the legal protection and confidentiality of child victims and/ or witnesses in criminal proceedings. In particular, it recommends the enactment of the *Evidence Amendment Bill* to allow child victims and/or witnesses to provide evidence in alternative ways[53] as well as the ensuring that child

---

44   Ibid [8]–[21].
45   Ibid [23(a)].
46   Ibid [23(b), (c)].
47   Ibid [25].
48   Ibid [29].
49   Ibid [33].
50   Ibid [35].
51   Ibid [39].
52   Ibid [41].
53   Ibid [47(b)].

victims and/or witnesses are informed of their rights,[54] are able to voice their concerns[55] and that their identity and right to privacy is protected.[56]

2.4 Twenty-first and Twenty-second Periodic Report of New Zealand under the Convention of the Elimination of All Forms of Racial Discrimination

In March 2016, New Zealand submitted its Twenty-first and Twenty-second Periodic Report pursuant to its commitment under the *International Convention on the Elimination of All Forms of Racial Discrimination ("ICERD")*. It covers the period from December 2011 until December 2015 and responds to the Committee on the Elimination of Racial Discrimination's ("CERD") concluding observations following New Zealand's last report including detailed information on measures taken to implement the concluding observations as well as providing follow-up information on recommendations.[57]

It begins by noting the Government's commitment to the protection and promotion of international human rights as embodied by the *Universal Declaration on Human Rights* as well as other international human rights treaties. It notes that it is the continuing policy of New Zealand to eliminate discrimination, intolerance and violence based on colour, religion, race or ethnicity or national origin and that the law protects from discrimination on these grounds.[58] However, the report notes that racial discrimination is the most common form of discrimination experienced in New Zealand, with six per cent of respondents believing that racial discrimination was the reason for them being treated unfairly. People who identified as Asian reported the highest level of racial discrimination followed by Māori and Pacific peoples.[59] After an initial discussion of efforts to specifically promote and protect the rights of Indigenous peoples, the report turns to its core mission to respond to the concluding observations of the CERD as well as to provide it with follow-up information on its recommendations. The report organizes this response into specific articles of the *ICERD* including arts 2, 4, 5 and 7.

---

54   Ibid [47(e)].
55   Ibid [47(f)].
56   Ibid [47(g)].
57   Committee on the Elimination of Racial Discrimination, *Consideration of Reports submitted by States Parties under Article 9 of the Convention – Twenty-first and twenty-second Periodic Reports of States parties due in 2015: New Zealand*, UN Doc CERD/C/NZL/21-22 (2016) [1]–[3] ("CERD Twenty-First and Twenty-Second Periodic Report").
58   Ibid [5]–[7].
59   Ibid [9].

Regarding art 2, the report details the constitutional structure of New Zealand. It notes that New Zealand does not have a fully written constitution but rather it is found in formal legal documents, decisions of courts and in practices – some of which have crystalized into conventions that are almost always followed and that this framework increasingly reflects the fact that the *Treaty of Waitangi* is regarded as the founding document of the government of New Zealand.[60] It details some of these key constitutional features, including the *New Zealand Bill of Rights Act 1990*,[61] the New Zealand Human Rights Commission, the *Human Rights Act 1993*,[62] the Constitutional Advisory Panel – Te Ranga Kaupapa Ture[63] and the *Treaty of Waitangi* and the Tribunal.[64]

Regarding art 4, the report comments on the unlawfulness of racial disharmony and the offence of inciting racial disharmony. It notes that it is unlawful to excite hostility against, or to bring into contempt, any group of persons on grounds including colour, race or ethnic or national origins through published or distributed written matter or spoken words in public, and reports back to the CERD that, during the reporting period, 243 complaints were received on these grounds.[65] The government also notes that, during this reporting period, the *Harmful Digital Communications Act* was enacted by Parliament addressing harmful digital communications which include inciting racial hatred through digital communication[66] and was enacted in response to a finding by the New Zealand Law Commission that existing remedies for harmful communications do not effectively address new forms of harm made possible by digital communications.[67]

Article 5 addresses the ongoing inequalities faced by Māori and Pacific peoples in employment, education, health, social services and housing as well as the overrepresentation of Māori in the justice and prison system.[68] Overall, the government has set ambitious "Better Public" services targets to reduce crime by 20 per cent by June 2018.[69] Regarding overrepresentation of Māori in the justice and prison system, the report notes that significant progress has been made to improve the responsiveness of the criminal justice system to Māori

---

60   Ibid [24].
61   Ibid [25]–[30].
62   Ibid [31]–[38].
63   Ibid [39]–[42].
64   Ibid [47]–[59].
65   Ibid [126].
66   Ibid [129].
67   Ibid [130].
68   Ibid [142].
69   Ibid [144].

and Pacific peoples through rehabilitative programmes as well as interventions based on *tikanga* behavioural guidelines for daily life and interaction in Māori culture,[70] consultation with the Māori community[71] and the use of restorative justice.[72] Article 5 also addresses issues related to education, noting that in the CERD's Concluding Observations it suggested strengthening special measures to increase the level of education attainment of Māori and Pacific children. A central task for the Ministry of Education – Te Tahuhu o te Matauranga is to ensure that the education system meets the learning needs of all New Zealanders and while most learners are in English-language settings, the system also enables learning in Māori-medium, Pacific peoples' language or bilingual settings that recognize and build on language, culture and identity. Despite overall improvements in achievement of National Standards and National Certificate in Educational Achievement ("NCEA"), more needs to be done for students from low socio-economic, Māori and Pacific backgrounds.[73] For instance, the *Ka hikitia – Accelerating Success 2013–2017* programme is in its second phase of the government's strategy to realize Māori potential in secondary and tertiary education, and *The Māori Language – Te Reo Māori Bill* was introduced into Parliament in July 2014 to update the *Māori Language Act 1987* to give effect to various aspects of the Māori Language Strategy.[74] Further, the *Pasifika Education Plan* (*PEP*) *2013–17* sets out the education sector's vision to raise achievement in education for Pacific peoples by putting Pacific learners, their parents, families and communities at the centre of the education system in order to demand better outcomes.[75] Regarding health, the Committee recommended in its 2013 concluding observations that New Zealand intensify its effort to improve the health outcomes of Māori and Pasifika, and while equality has improved, there remain significant gaps in health outcomes across New Zealand.[76] Two schemes to address this inequality are the *He Korowai Oranga – Māori Health Strategy* and the *Ala Mo'ui: Pathways to Pacific Health and Well-being 2014–18*.[77] Article 5 also addresses issues in relation to employment. The government notes that all New Zealand residents are protected by the *Employment Relations Act 2000*.[78]

---

70   Ibid [145]–[149].
71   Ibid [153]–[157].
72   Ibid [161]–[162].
73   Ibid [181]–[182].
74   Ibid [188]–[199].
75   Ibid [207].
76   Ibid [234].
77   Ibid [237]–[243].
78   Ibid [254].

Highlights here include that the unemployment rate for all persons decreasing to 5.8 per cent of the labour force in the year to December 2014,[79] the recognition that cultural linkages are important to achieving improved labour market outcomes[80] and the launch of the *Pacific Economic Strategy 2015–2021* in August 2015.[81] In addition, art 5 addresses social services which, the report notes, were addressed by the implementation of welfare reform changes from July 2013.[82] As regards young persons and their families in particular, responsiveness is embedded in the *Ma Mātou Ma Tātou* strategy which is underpinned by *Puao te Atatu* and the *Children, Young Persons and their Families Act 1989*.[83] Finally, art 5 addresses housing. The report notes that Māori are disproportionally high users of social housing and that in response to the issue the Government has launched *He Whare Āhuru He Oranga Tāngata – the Māori Housing Strategy* in July 2014 which sets out six directions to improve Māori housing during the period of 2014–25.[84]

Finally, art 7 of the periodic report addresses issues in relation to culture. Highlights here include government efforts to fund a range of programmes and initiatives designed to assist iwi/Māori with their cultural objectives including *Te Matatini* (a Māori performing arts organization), Creative NZ (funder of Māori customary arts and contemporary arts practice) and Ngā Taonga Sound and Vision (an organization with audio-visual archives important to Māori, Pasifika and other ethnic communities).[85] Further, the New Zealand Film Commission has recognized the need to develop and expand the base of Māori filmmaking and in 2013–14 the Commission established a new initiative, *He Ara*, to empower groups of Māori and Pacific people film makers to develop films in a collaborative fashion.[86] Finally, the report notes that the Māori broadcasting sector has continued to grow and that the government has provided significant investment and developed various ownership interest in and regulatory mechanisms for Māori broadcasting.[87]

---

79   Ibid [255].
80   Ibid [256].
81   Ibid [257].
82   Ibid [264].
83   Ibid [268].
84   Ibid [277]–[279].
85   Ibid [290].
86   Ibid [293].
87   Ibid [295].

2.5   *Concluding Observation on the Sixth Periodic Report of New*
        Zealand, Addendum: Information Received from New Zealand
        in Follow-up to the Concluding Observations Concerning the
        Convention against Torture

Pursuant to its commitment under the UN *Convention against Torture and Other Cruel, Inhuman or Degrading Treatment or Punishment* ("CAT"), New Zealand submitted its Sixth Periodic Report to the Committee against Torture ("Committee") in December 2013, with general distribution to the UN in March 2014.[88] In response, in June 2015 the Committee released its *Concluding Observations on the Sixth Periodic Report of New Zealand.*[89] At the close of these observations, the Committee requested follow-up information from New Zealand on three of its recommendations within a year. These recommendations concern: the National Preventative Mechanism (para 9 of the concluding observations), the Independent Police Conduct Authority (para 10) and seclusion, solitary confinement and historic claims of abuse (para 15). The *Concluding Observation on the Sixth Periodic Report of New Zealand: Addendum Information received from New Zealand in follow-up to the Concluding Observations*[90] received in June 2016 provides further information about these topics.

2.5.1   National Preventative Mechanism

The Committee recommended New Zealand to:

· Support the National Preventative Mechanism ("NPM") in developing and maintaining a collective identity through, inter alia, joint visits and joint public reports, harmonized working methods, shared expertise and enhanced coordination.

New Zealand responded, detailing the coordination of the NPM which is led by the Human Rights Commission. In its role as the Central NPM, it identifies systemic issues, holds regular meetings and assists with NPM monitoring.[91]

---

88   See, Committee against Torture, *Consideration of Reports submitted by States Parties under Article 19 of the Convention pursuant to the Optional Reporting Procedure – Sixth Periodic Report of States parties due in 2013: New Zealand*, UN Doc CAT/C/NZL/6 (2014).

89   See, Committee against Torture, *Concluding Observations on the Sixth Periodic Report of New Zealand*, UN Doc CAT/C/NZL/CO/6 (2015).

90   Committee against Torture, *Concluding Observation on the Sixth Periodic Report of New Zealand: Addendum Information received from New Zealand in follow-up to the Concluding Observations*, UN Doc CAT/C/NZL/CO/6/Add.1 (2016).

91   Ibid [3].

· Increase NPM's funding and ensure that they are staffed appropriately.

New Zealand responded detailing the increased budgets of many of the main NPMs which include the Commission, the Independent Police Conduct Authority ("IPCA") and the Office of the Children's Commissioner ("OCC"). Independent Crown entities funded through the budget vote for different government agencies, these NPMs are encouraged to make the best use of current resources when funding is not available targeting high risk facilities.[92]

2.5.2   The Independent Police Conduct Authority
The Committee recommended New Zealand to:

· Ensure that the IPCA is fully independent and equipped with a broader mandate.

New Zealand responded stressing that the IPCA based its findings on the facts and the law, noting that it does not answer to the Police or the government regarding these findings. In turn, the independence of the IPCA is similar to that of a court and includes legislative and operational independence as well as a perception of independence through transparent procedures.[93]

2.5.3   Seclusion, Solitary Confinement and Historic Claims of Abuse
The Committee recommended New Zealand to:

· Limit the use of solitary confinement and seclusion.
· Prohibit its use for juveniles, persons with disabilities, pregnant women, women with infants and breastfeeding mothers.
· Compile and publish disaggregated data on the use of solitary confinement and seclusion.
· Conduct investigations into all allegations of ill-treatment, prosecute the perpetrators and provide effective remedies to the victims (in the context of Lake Alice hospital investigations).[94]

In addressing these recommendations, New Zealand focused on the use of seclusion in health-care facilities and the use of solitary confinement in prisons. Regarding the former, the response details New Zealand's mental health

---

92   Ibid [5]–[8].
93   Ibid [9]–[20].
94   Ibid [21].

legislation concerning seclusion. It stresses the Ministry of Health guidelines that monitor and limit its application, such as the standard that it is not used punitively or to modify unwanted behaviour and that potential physical and psychological effects must be carefully considered in advance of a decision to place a person in seclusion.[95] Regarding the use of solitary confinement in prisons, the response, again, emphasises the guidelines and mechanisms that limit its use such as the stipulation that separation can only be ordered if it is absolutely necessary to reduce risk posed to other prisoners and the possibility of judicial review.[96]

2.6   *Eighth Periodic Report of New Zealand under the Convention of the Elimination of All Forms of Discrimination against Women ("CEDAW")*

New Zealand's Eighth Periodic Report on the implementation of CEDAW covers the period between March 2012 to March 2016 and covers the key legislative, judicial, administrative and other measures adopted in the review period that give effect to the provisions of the Convention. The report, received in June 2016, identifies the priorities for women where more work is needed as to the following: supporting more women and girls in education and training; utilizing women's skills and growing the economy; encouraging and developing women leaders; and ensuring women and girls are free from violence.[97] Before concluding with the government's response to the recommendations made by the CEDAW Committee in its previous *Concluding Observations* on New Zealand's Seventh Periodic Report,[98] this present report addresses these issues in four principal parts.

Part One centres on discrimination and protections, human rights, prejudice and exploitation of women. It notes that New Zealand's legal framework provides for comprehensive protection against all forms of discrimination covered by CEDAW and its commitment to maintaining a legal and policy framework that provides universal protection against all forms of discrimination.[99] In particular, the Ministry for Women ("MfW") is the government's principal advisor on achieving better outcomes for women.[100] The main issues

---

95   Ibid [22]–[26].
96   Ibid [27]–[30].
97   Committee on the Elimination of All Forms of Discrimination against Women, *Consideration of Reports submitted by States parties under Article 18 of the Convention – Eighth Periodic Report of States parties due in 2016: New Zealand*, UN Doc CEDAW/C/NZL/8 (2016) [3] ("CEDAW Eighth Periodic Report").
98   See ibid [229].
99   Ibid [7]–[8].
100   Ibid [10].

it identifies includes advancing the rights of women with a disability through the *New Zealand Disability Strategy* which is currently being revised as well as through the *Disability Action Plan 2014–2018* which was developed between government agencies and representative organizations of disabled people and will benefit disabled women through priorities and actions including increased employment and economic opportunities, ensured personal safety, a transformed disability support system and the promotion of access in the community.[101] Further, this section focuses on advancing the rights of sexual and gender minorities,[102] marriage equality,[103] the advancement of the rights of migrant and refugee women[104] as well as maximizing opportunities for military women and New Zealand police women.[105]

Part Two concentrates on participation and equality in political and public life, representation and nationality. Its concern with participation and equality in political and public life spans both central and local government[106] as well as women in the law and their representation on statutory boards and private sector boards.[107] It notes that one of its areas of priority is the advancement of women's rights internationally through the diplomatic service, international conferences and organizations as well as the advancement of women issues in foreign policy and aid programmes.[108]

Part Three of the CEDAW Eighth Periodic Report concerns education, equal access, opportunities and conditions in relation to employment, health, social assistance and rural women. Regarding education, the report places priority on early childhood education[109] and Pacific education initiatives[110] as well as women's participation in tertiary education noting that the attainment rates between ethnic groups is decreasing and that women in general are more likely to participate in tertiary education[111] though fields of study still vary by gender with men still predominant in information technology, engineering and related technologies.[112] In relation to employment, the report notes that a priority remains boosting women's employment and skills in Canterbury which

---

101   Ibid [18]–[19].
102   Ibid [23]–[24].
103   Ibid [25]–[27].
104   Ibid [28]–[33].
105   Ibid [39]–[43].
106   Ibid [46]–[49].
107   Ibid [53]–[64].
108   Ibid [66]–[75].
109   Ibid [80]–[81].
110   Ibid [82].
111   Ibid [84]–[87].
112   Ibid [90].

suffered after the 2010 and 2011 earthquakes.[113] Furthermore, the government
is focused on flexible working arrangements, the extension of parental leave
and equal pay for work of equal value.[114] Regarding health, the government
notes that it wants to ensure that all New Zealanders have the same opportunities for good health and that women continue to have higher rates of utilization of primary health services than men, however, they also have reportedly
higher levels of unmet needs for such services.[115] Furthermore, though equity
has improved, significant gaps remain in health outcomes for New Zealanders,
with Māori, Pacific peoples, disabled people and socioeconomically disadvantaged groups generally experiencing worse health outcomes than other New
Zealanders.[116] Moreover, women continue to experience certain mental disorders at a higher rate than men such as eating disorders and mood disorders
and violence continues to have significant impacts on the physical and mental
health of women.[117] Noted improvements include better treatment of sexually
transmitted infections, declining rates of teen pregnancy and births as well as
a decrease in abortions.[118]

Part Four of the CEDAW Eighth Periodic Report concerns equality before the
law, and the elimination of discrimination against women in all matters relating to marriage and family relations. This section highlights that a review of the
legislation that sets out the response to family violence has been initiated by the
government to ensure that the legislation is fit for purpose. It is part of the Ministerial Group on Family Violence and Sexual Violence work programme.[119] The
review will focus on: enhancing victim safety, holding perpetrators accountable
for their actions and making them responsible for changing their behaviour and
improving links between family violence laws to support a better coordinated
system.[120] Furthermore, a new pilot programme has been launched to provide judges with better family violence information about defendants at bail
hearings.[121] Indeed, the government notes that violence against women in
New Zealand is a serious social problem and that it is widespread and takes
many different forms including physical, sexual and psychological.[122] In order
to combat the problem, the Government has developed projects specifically

---

113   Ibid [103]–[107].
114   Ibid [111]–[118].
115   Ibid [122].
116   Ibid [125].
117   Ibid [133]–[137].
118   Ibid [138]–[145].
119   Ibid [182].
120   Ibid.
121   Ibid [185]–[187].
122   Ibid [194]–[198].

focused on sexual violence, including: developing a long-term policy framework for responding to sexual violence, improving sector infrastructure, developing an approach for crisis service purchasing and planning, developing a national sexual violence primary prevention strategy and action plan and developing a national sexual violence strategy and action plan focused on youth.[123] Notable national campaigns geared at achieving these ends include: "It's not Ok", "are you that someone?" and "Mates & Dates".[124]

3   International Human Rights Law Jurisprudence: UN Cases Concerning New Zealand before the Human Rights Committee

After a host of cases before the HRC in 2015, no communications against New Zealand were examined in 2016. A number of new communications will be available in 2017.

4   Human Rights in the Domestic Context: The Activities of the New Zealand Humans Rights Commission

Deriving its statutory mandate from the *Human Rights Act 1993* (*"HRA"*) as set out in ss 5(1)–(2), the New Zealand Human Rights Commission ("Commission") is New Zealand's National Human Rights Institution ("NHRI"). It is accredited as an "A" status NHRI with the Global Alliance of National Human Rights institutions ("GANHRI") and so operates in accordance with the *Principles Relating to the Status of National Institutions* ("Paris Principles"). As such, the Commission is able to offer information to the UN Human Rights Council which is the principal Charter-based mechanism for the protection of human rights. The Commission continued its numerous activities this year for the promotion and protection of human rights in New Zealand, issuing a number of important reports.

4.1   *The New Zealand Human Rights Commission Annual Report 2016*
In November 2016, the Commission released the *New Zealand Human Rights Commission Annual Report* ("Annual Report").[125] The Annual Report details eight main areas highlighting notable developments from 2016.

---

123   Ibid [204].
124   Ibid [207]–[214].
125   New Zealand Human Rights Commission, *New Zealand Human Rights Commission Annual Report* (HRC, Wellington, 2016) ("Annual Report").

The first area of focus is in relation to developments in *Business and Human Rights*. The Annual Report notes that over the past year, the Commission has increased its focus on business and human rights reflecting recognition that the business and human rights landscape has changed. Notably in March 2016, the Commission published *The Business of Human Rights* which provides an overview for businesses on how to be good corporate citizens as well as the publication of the *A-Z Pre-Employment Guide to Human Rights for Employers and Employees* which offers a set of guidelines aimed at ensuring equality and fairness for all job applicants, regardless of gender, ethnicity, age, disability and religion.[126]

Regarding *Harmonious Relations,* the Annual Report notes key developments, which include the Commission's successful advocacy for an increase in the annual refugee resettlement quota from 750 to 1000 in 2016.[127] Specifically, in February 2016 the Commission published the *New Zealand Refugee Resettlement* report.[128] Aside from successfully advocating for an increased annual refugee quota, the Refugee Report advocated for a commitment to alternative forms of admission to people of refugee status to New Zealand, recommending that a generous, culturally sensitive and flexible definition of family should be applied in the case of refugees.[129] Further, regarding *Harmonious Relations*, the Annual Report notes that the Commission developed its first nationwide anti-racism campaign with aims of reducing the proportion of recent migrants who have experienced discrimination and will work towards creating a culture in which racist attitudes are considered unacceptable. To assist this campaign, an online platform to engage New Zealanders went live in the second half of 2016.[130]

Regarding *Discrimination and Inequality*, the Annual Report notes two main online developments. The first development is the updating of the Commission's "Tracking Equality at Work" web-based tool with the most recent data from 2015 which notes that the private sector lags significantly behind the public sector regarding female representation; respectively 17 per cent and 43.4 per cent. Second, the launch of a new online application entitled "1 in 3 Be Free" which is an education tool designed to help women screen for abuse in their

---

126   Ibid 6.

127   Ibid.

128   New Zealand Human Rights Commission, *New Zealand Refugee Resettlement* (HRC, Wellington, 2016) ("Refugee Report").

129   Annual Report, above n 125, 2.

130   Ibid 6–7.

relationship and thereby to empower more women to deal with or escape abusive or controlling relationships.[131]

Next, the Annual Report details the Commission's progress in relation to *Inclusive and Just Society*, noting that this past year the Commission led the publication of the CRPD Independent Monitoring Mechanism *Right to Education* interim report and worked with the Ministry of Education to support inclusive education and increased information-sharing and transparency among agencies. The Commission also held a multi-sector roundtable on the practice of normalizing intersex children in New Zealand.[132]

Regarding *Civil and Political Rights,* the Commission continued to make a significant impact participating in legal proceedings, appearing as an "intervener", in several major human rights-related cases over the past year. Of note, in February 2016 the Commission participated in *Spencer v Attorney-General* which was litigation concerning "parents as caregivers". After awarding Spencer more than $200,000 in damages, of particular significance, the court also accepted the Commission's submission that a training order should be made under the *HRA* and directed that the Ministry of Health should educate its officers on the importance of the human rights of disabled persons and their caregivers.[133] The Commission continued to influence law, policy and practice through making multiple submissions to various agencies and Parliamentary Select Committees and further made a successful application for funding from the UN Office of the High Commissioner for Human Rights to carry out a review of seclusion and restrain practices in detention settings.[134] In addition, significant work regarding housing, health and participation issues for vulnerable people impacted by the Canterbury earthquake was undertaken in 2016 by the Commission as a continuation of its monitoring of the recovery. It focused on a human rights impact analysis on the residential red zoning process and resulted in the October 2016 publication of the report *Staying the Red Zones: Monitoring Human Rights in the Canterbury Earthquake Recovery.*[135]

Concerning *Indigenous Rights,* the Annual Report notes that the Commission has actively developed the framework of Indigenous rights outlined in treaty instruments supporting the *UN Declaration on the Rights of Indigenous Peoples ("UNDRIP")*. Moreover, of note this year, the Commission, working with Te Puni Kokiri and the Ministry of Justice, developed a *Te mana i Waitangi*

---

131   Ibid 7.
132   Ibid 8.
133   Ibid.
134   Ibid 9.
135   Ibid.

training and development programme to increase the understanding of the human rights dimensions of the *Treaty of Waitangi* and it was delivered to identified state sector agencies.[136]

Regarding *The Human Rights Record*, the 2016 Annual Report notes that significant progress has been made in the reporting and monitoring frameworks New Zealand has adopted in relation to progress in human rights. Aside from review internationally through treaties and conventions,[137] New Zealand's human rights record is monitored and measured domestically through the National Plan of Action. In 2015, significant improvements in the way that human rights are monitored in New Zealand occurred through the online publication of the New Zealand Human Rights Commission's National Plan of Action 2015–2019 ("NPA").[138] The NPA details the government's actions in relation to New Zealand's second Universal Periodic Review ("UPR") at the UN under its Charter-based mechanisms for the protection of human rights and will be used as the basis of the mid-point UPR review.[139] Building on this initiative, in 2016 the Commission, the Ministry of Foreign Affairs and Trade, the New Zealand Treasury and the Ministry of Social Development initiated the first cross-agency effort to discuss the adoption of the Sustainable Development Goals ("SDG"). In particular, the future development of the NPA is linked to the implementation of the SDGs and so the Commission recognized the need for common indicators to measure and monitor achievement in both areas.[140]

Finally, regarding *Human Rights Remedy* the Annual Report notes that the Commission over the past year managed 1274 complaints of unlawful discrimination and successfully resolved or assisted in resolving 84 per cent of these complaints. Beyond this, 3754 other human rights complaints and enquiries were received last year through the Commission's Infoline service.[141]

4.2 The New Zealand Human Rights Commission Report: Staying in the Red Zones: Monitoring Human Rights in the Canterbury Earthquake Recovery

As aforementioned in the Commission's Annual Report 2016, significant work regarding housing, health and participation issues for vulnerable people

---

136 Ibid 9–10.
137 See, ibid. Section 2.
138 See, New Zealand Human Rights Commission, *National Action Plan 2015–2019* (6 June 2016) <http://npa.hrc.co.nz>.
139 Ibid.
140 Annual Report, above n 125, 11.
141 Ibid.

impacted by the Canterbury earthquake was undertaken in 2016 by the Commission as a continuation of its monitoring of the recovery. The culmination of much of this work is in the October 2016 report *Staying in the Red Zones: Monitoring Human Rights in the Canterbury Earthquake Recovery*.[142] Residential red zones ("RRZs") are properties that, after the earthquakes, were considered too uncertain, disruptive, lengthy and uneconomically viable in the short to medium term to repair or rebuild. The Crown offered to purchase RRZ properties from owners to help them avoid the complexities of the insurance process and allow them to move from areas with widespread damage.[143] Offers varied but 99 per cent of owners of RRZ properties accepted the Crown offer of purchase. However, as of March 2016, owners of 121 properties had not accepted the offer.[144] The Red Zone Report is based on results from surveys and interviews completed by people either living in or owning vacant land in Canterbury's RRZs. It approaches the issue from a human rights perspective and draws six main findings as follows:

- First, human rights need to be front and centre in disaster recovery, prevention and preparedness. The guiding principles of the *Sendai Framework*, adopted by the United Nations (including New Zealand) in 2015, place human rights at the centre of disaster risk reduction.
- Second, the right to property is fragile in New Zealand. Property rights need to be better enshrined in the *New Zealand Bill of Rights Act* by Parliament.
- Third, post-disaster it is particularly important for the Crown to exercise its powers carefully and in accordance with the relevant legislation.
- Fourth, the communication needs of people affected by disasters are not confined to the immediate post-disaster period. Affected people need information to make decisions, need to participate in decisions that affect them, and need co-ordinated service delivery. They also want to be treated with respect.
- Fifth, community engagement matters. The way in which government and non-government agencies pursue initiatives will determine how successful these are. The requirement to act swiftly must be weighed against the need to actively engage community in the design and implementation of solutions. A "nothing about us without us" approach requires time, resources,

---

142 New Zealand Human Rights Commission, *Staying in the Red Zones: Monitoring Human Rights in the Canterbury Earthquake Recovery* (HRC, Wellington, 2016) ("Red Zone Report").

143 Ibid 3.

144 Ibid 4.

and public and political will, but is essential to ensure that people are not passive recipients of disaster recovery response and risk reduction, but are actively involved in shaping it.

· Finally, there is no one-size-fits-all for disasters: flexibility to consider individual circumstances needs to be incorporated into the design of disaster planning, policies and services. Recognizing flexibility as an intrinsic goal in disaster preparedness results in better outcomes for people and organisations.[145]

4.3   The New Zealand Human Rights Commission Report: Investigation into End of Life Matters

In addition to the issues identified in the Annual Report 2016 and the Red Zone Report, the other major human rights issue that the Commission addressed in 2016 was the assisted dying debate; indeed, the Commission notes that it was the pre-eminent human rights issue of the year. The Commission made a submission to the Health Select Committee in its report *Investigation into End of Life Matters*.[146] The investigation resulted from a petition submitted by Hon. Maryan Street that the House of Representatives fully investigate public attitudes towards the introduction of legislation that would allow medically-assisted dying in the event of terminal illness or conditions that make life unbearable. This follows the landmark case of Lecretia Seales (*Seales v Attorney-General*) who sought a declaration from the High Court that her general practitioner would not be committing a crime if she were to assist her to end her life if the pain and indignity caused by her terminal brain cancer became too unbearable.[147] The ultimate decision confirmed that any action taken by a physician to assist a terminally ill person to take her/his own life continues to constitute a serious criminal offense under the *Crimes Act 1961* in the form of culpable homicide (s 160) and aiding and abetting suicide (s 179(b)).[148]

The *End of Life Report* focuses on two aspects of assisted dying: the current legal situation and international experiences.[149] The principal human rights issues identified in these contexts that form the basis of the report's

---

145   Ibid 10.

146   New Zealand Human Rights Commission, *Investigation into End of Life Matters* (HRC, Wellington, 2016) ("End of Life Report").

147   Ibid [1]–[2]; See, *Seales v Attorney-General* [2015] NZHC 1239.

148   Ibid [6]–[9].

149   Ibid [3].

structure include: the sanctity of life, respect for human dignity, respect for human autonomy and protection of the vulnerable.[150] The Commission's main conclusion is that a legal framework that would allow for assisted dying for a competent terminally ill adult to end her or his life (if she or he freely and autonomously chose to do so) could potentially be implemented if:

· It is developed in a manner consistent with core human rights principles;
· Is accompanied by adequate legal and procedural safeguards to protect vulnerable members of society; and
· Appropriate palliative care services are available and remain accessible for all.[151]

The Commission's non-exhaustive list of recommendations to achieve these ends can be categorized as follows:

· The need for high thresholds;
· Decisions must be free from any indication of coercion or influence and must be competently made;
· The need for supporting medical review/and perhaps psychiatric screening;
· A cooling-off period;
· The need for ongoing monitoring and independent review of the system;
· Judicial /expert oversight;
· Participation by medical professionals and others in the process must be voluntary – i.e. an "opt out" conscience clause;
· Awareness of cultural considerations;
· The need to ensure access to and standard of palliative care is not compromised and remains a viable and "first choice" option; and
· The importance of advanced care planning.[152]

---

150   Ibid [10].
151   Ibid [48].
152   Ibid [49].

Indigenous Peoples' Rights under International Law

Fleur Te Aho*†

1   Introduction

This note reviews New Zealand's state practice regarding Indigenous peoples' rights under international law in 2016 and traces key international developments concerning those rights. In 2016, New Zealand supported pioneering efforts to improve Indigenous participation in the United Nations ("UN") and revisions to the mandate of the UN Expert Mechanism on the Rights of Indigenous Peoples ("EMRIP") to promote implementation of the *UN Declaration on the Rights of Indigenous Peoples* ("UNDRIP").[1] New Zealand also showcased its domestic efforts to give effect to Māori rights before international fora. Indigenous peoples contributed to the operationalisation of the UN General Assembly's ("GA") Sustainable Development Goals ("SDGs") and the *UN Framework Convention on Climate Change's* ("UNFCCC")[2] *Paris Agreement*. Voluntary guidelines regarding Indigenous peoples drafted under the *Convention on Biological Diversity* ("CBD")[3] attracted controversy. Nationally, developments of international significance included Matike Mai Aotearoa releasing its report on constitutional transformation for Aotearoa and the Waitangi Tribunal's report on the *Trans-Pacific Partnership Agreement* ("TPPA"). The UN Human Rights Committee and the UN Committee on the Rights of the Child ("CRC") critically commented on the human rights situation of Māori. Various international bodies were also attentive to Indigenous peoples' rights in the course of their work.

---

*   *University of Auckland*
†   Ngāti Mutunga and English

1   *United Nations Declaration on the Rights of Indigenous Peoples*, GA Res 61/295, UN GAOR, 61st sess, 107th plen mtg, Supp No 49, UN Doc A/RES/61/295 (13 September 2007).
2   *United Nations Framework Convention on Climate Change*, opened for signature 4 June 1992, 1771 UNTS 107 (entered into force 21 March 1994).
3   *Convention on Biological Diversity*, opened for signature 5 June 1992, 1760 UNTS 79 (entered into force 29 December 1993).

© KONINKLIJKE BRILL NV, LEIDEN, 2018 | DOI 10.1163/9789004345911_010

2   Developments in Relation to International Resolutions,
     Recommendations and Other Forms of Non-binding or
     Soft Law Instruments

2.1   *Indigenous Peoples' Participation in the* UN

During 2016, groundbreaking consultations continued through the President of the UN GA on measures to enable the participation of Indigenous peoples' representatives and institutions in the meetings of UN bodies affecting them.[4] The consultations focused primarily on participation within the UN GA, a body that has historically been restricted to the participation of states and international organisations. The President of the GA's consultations are being guided by two Indigenous advisors who are prominent legal scholars – Claire Charters (from Aotearoa) and James Anaya (from the United States) – and two state advisors.[5] Consultations with representatives of Indigenous peoples, states and UN institutions were held between March and June 2016 with a compilation of the views expressed during the consultations released subsequently.[6] The consultations then moved to an inter-governmental phase, with the first of these consultations taking place in December. An *Elements for Discussion* document was prepared by the President of the GA's advisors to assist these consultations.[7] The document reflects the emerging agreement that Indigenous participation in the GA should generally include the opportunity for Indigenous organisations to speak and provide written contributions. It also promotes equitable participation by Indigenous peoples from different regions and outlines possible options for identifying eligible Indigenous organisations.[8]

---

4   *Rights of indigenous peoples,* GA Res 70/232, UNGA, 70th sess, 82nd plen mtg, UN Doc A/RES/70/232 (23 December 2015) [19].

5   Division for Social Policy and Development: Indigenous Peoples, *Participation at the* UN – *UNGA process,* United Nations <https://www.un.org/development/desa/indigenouspeoples /participation-of-indigenous-peoples-at-the-united-nations.html>.

6   *Compilation of views on possible measures necessary to enable the participation of indigenous peoples' representatives and institutions in relevant United Nations meetings on issues affecting them, and of good practices within the United Nations regarding indigenous peoples' participation,* UN GAOR, 70th sess, Agenda Item 69(a), UN Doc A/70/990 (25 July 2016).

7   Claire Charters and James Anaya, *Elements for discussion during the 71st Session of the General Assembly* (23 December 2016) United Nations <http://www.un.org/pga/71/wp-content/ uploads/sites/40/2015/08/Consultation-process-indigenous-issues.pdf>.

8   Ibid; Claire Charters, "Enhancing Indigenous Peoples' Participation in the UN" in Katrine Broch Hansen, Käthe Jepsen and Pamela Leiva Jacquelin (eds), *The Indigenous World 2017* (International Work Group for Indigenous Affairs, 2017) 554, 561–562.

New Zealand is an active participant in the consultations and a member of the Group of Friends on Indigenous issues who are supportive of efforts to improve Indigenous representation within the UN. In its statement before the UN GA's Third Assembly, New Zealand stated that it "continues to support the effective participation of indigenous peoples' representatives and institutions in relevant United Nations meetings on issues affecting them," and "stress[ed] the importance of continued participation of indigenous peoples" noting that "[i]t is only through continued participation and effective consultations with indigenous peoples that the final outcome of this process will have legitimacy and value."[9]

2.2   *2030 Agenda for Sustainable Development*

Indigenous peoples had some involvement in the High Level Political Forum's ("HLPF") July discussions on implementation of the SDGs through the Indigenous Peoples' Major Group ("IPMG") and the participation of members of the Permanent Forum on Indigenous Issues ("PFII"). During its statements, the IPMG emphasised the importance of giving effect to Indigenous peoples' rights, including to their lands and natural resources, in order to ensure Indigenous peoples are not left behind in the implementation of the SDGs.[10] Indigenous peoples were referenced, along with other especially vulnerable groups, as being in need of protection and empowerment in the Ministerial Declaration that was the outcome document of the HLPF.[11] New Zealand participated in the HLPF.[12] Additionally, in December the UN GA's resolution on the rights of Indigenous peoples emphasised the need for attention to

---

9   Phillip Taula, *Rights of Indigenous Peoples* (17 October 2016) Ministry of Foreign Affairs and Trade <https://www.mfat.govt.nz/en/media-and-resources/ministry-statements-and-speeches/unga71-third-committee-agenda-item-65a-and-b-rights-of-indigenous-peoples/>.

10   Lola García-Alix, "Indigenous Peoples and the 2030 Agenda for Sustainable Development" in Katrine Broch Hansen, Käthe Jepsen and Pamela Leiva Jacquelin (eds), *The Indigenous World 2017* (International Work Group for Indigenous Affairs, 2017) 598, 601–602.

11   Economic and Social Council, *Ministerial declaration of the high-level segment of the 2016 session of the Economic and Social Council on the annual theme "Implementing the post-2015 development agenda: moving from commitments to results"*, UN ESCOR, 43rd plen mtg, Agenda Item 5, UN Doc E/HLS/2016/1 (29 July 2016).

12   Hamish Cooper, *New Zealand National Statement: High Level Political Forum on Sustainable Development* (21 July 2016) Ministry of Foreign Affairs and Trade <https://www.mfat.govt.nz/en/media-and-resources/ministry-statements-and-speeches/new-zealand-national-statement-high-level-political-forum-on-sustainable-development/>.

Indigenous peoples' rights in the implementation of the 2030 Agenda for Sustainable Development.[13]

3   Developments in Relation to International Treaties

3.1   UN *Framework Convention on Climate Change*
At the *UNFCCC*'s 22nd Conference of the Parties ("COP"), Indigenous peoples participated in the first steps to agree the operationalisation and implementation of the Paris Agreement. Indigenous participants emphasised that states' National Determined Contributions ("NDCs"), which are states' intended reductions in greenhouse gas emissions, should be developed and implemented with the "full and effective participation of Indigenous Peoples and must be consistent with the recognition, respect, and promotion of Indigenous Peoples' rights," including the commitments in the Paris Agreement's preamble.[14] However, only 19 countries' NDCs refer to indigenous peoples;[15] New Zealand's NDC does not.[16] Positively, one COP22 decision invited the Paris Committee on Capacity Building to take human rights, gender equality and Indigenous peoples' knowledge into consideration in its work;[17] it was decided that a knowledge-sharing platform for Indigenous peoples and local communities would be established;[18] and the 15th Board meeting of the Green Climate Fund, which will help fund climate action globally, decided to develop an Indigenous peoples' policy.[19]

---

13   *Rights of indigenous peoples*, GA Res 71/178, UN GAOR, 71st sess, 65th plen mtg, Agenda Item, 65(a), UN Doc A/RES/71/178 (19 December 2016) [4].

14   Sherpa et al, "UN Framework Convention on Climate Change (UNFCCC)" in Katrine Broch Hansen, Käthe Jepsen and Pamela Leiva Jacquelin (eds), *The Indigenous World 2017* (International Work Group for Indigenous Affairs, 2017) 613, 615.

15   Ibid.

16   New Zealand, *Submission under the Paris Agreement – New Zealand's Nationally Determined Contribution* (2016) United Nations Framework Convention on Climate Change <http://www4.unfccc.int/ndcregistry/PublishedDocuments/New%20Zealand%20First /New%20Zealand%20first%20NDC.pdf>.

17   Conference of the Parties, United Nations Framework Convention on Climate Change, *Report of the Conference of the Parties on its twenty-second session, Held in Marrakech from 7 to 18 November 2016 – Addendum – Part 2: Action Taken by the Conference of the Parties at its Twenty Second Session*, UN Doc FCCC/CP/2016/10/Add.2 (31 January 2017) 8; Sherpa et al, above n 14, 615.

18   This was agreed during the COP22 plenary session in the early hours of 19 November 2016. See Sherpa et al, above n 14, 616.

19   Green Climate Fund, *Report of the fifteenth meeting of the Board, 13–15 December 2016*, GCF/B.15/25 (3 April 2017). See also Sherpa et al, above n 14, 617–618.

4   National Developments of International Significance

4.1   *Iwi Report on Constitutional Transformation*
In January, Matike Mai Aotearoa, an iwi-led working group on constitutional transformation for New Zealand, released its report. The report considers possible foundational values for a new constitution for the country and outlines six indicative models that emerged from its consultations. It recommends that discussion on constitutional transformation continue, identifying 2040 as an aspirational goal for some form of change.[20]

4.2   *Waitangi Tribunal Reports on the Trans-Pacific Partnership*
In March, the Waitangi Tribunal held an urgent hearing into claims that the Trans-Pacific Partnership Agreement breached Māori rights under the Treaty of Waitangi. The Tribunal found that the *TPPA*'s text did not breach the Treaty.[21] While the *TPPA* may now collapse following the United States' withdrawal from the agreement, the Tribunal's judgment is of broader import, emphasising that "Māori interests are entitled to a reasonable degree of protection when those interests are affected by international instruments entered into by the New Zealand Government."[22]

5   International Oversight of New Zealand's Compliance with
        Indigenous Peoples' Rights

5.1   *UN Human Rights Committee*
The UN Human Rights Committee recommended that New Zealand take action to address the human rights situation of Māori in its concluding observations on New Zealand's sixth periodic report under the *International Covenant on Civil and Political Rights*.[23] Its recommendations included that New Zealand "revise the Marine and Coastal Area (Takutai Moana) Act 2011 with a view to ensuring respect of the customary rights of Māori on their land and resources,

---

20   Matike Mai Aotearoa, *He Whakaaro Here Whakaumu Mō Aotearoa: The Report of Matike Mai Aotearoa – The Independent Working Group on Constitutional Transformation* (January 2016) Converge Peace Movement Aotearoa <http://www.converge.org.nz/pma/MatikeMaiAotearoaReport.pdf>.

21   Waitangi Tribunal, *Report on the Trans-Pacific Partnership Agreement* (Wai 2522, 2016).

22   Ibid 7.

23   Human Rights Committee ("HRCtee"), *Concluding observations on the sixth periodic report of New Zealand,* 116th sess, UN Doc CCPR/C/NZL/CO/6 (28 April 2016).

and their cultural development";[24] "[s]trengthen the role of the Treaty of Waitangi in the existing constitutional arrangements";[25] "[g]uarantee the informed participation of indigenous communities in all relevant national and international consultation processes";[26] "[i]mplement technical capacity programmes for indigenous communities aiming at their effective participation in all relevant consultation and decision-making processes";[27] "take all appropriate measures to enhance Māori ... representation in government positions at all levels, in particular at the local council level";[28] and evaluate the impact of law enforcement operational policies on Indigenous peoples and provide training to law enforcement officials to protect against racial profiling.[29] New Zealand made no formal response to the report.

5.2   *UN Committee on the Rights of the Child*

The UN Committee on the Rights of the Child also issued recommendations to address the human rights situation of Māori in its fifth periodic report on New Zealand under the *Convention on the Rights of the Child.*[30] Its recommendations included that New Zealand further efforts to preserve Māori identity, including intensifying "efforts to promote and foster Maori language, culture and history in education and increase enrolment in Maori language classes";[31] take "urgent measures to address disparities in access to education, health services and a minimum standard of living by Maori ... children and their families";[32] "address the root causes of youth suicide, with special attention to Maori children";[33] "introduce a systemic approach to addressing child poverty, in particular [regarding] Maori ... children";[34] and, "strengthen its efforts to address the overrepresentation of Maori ... children and young people in the juvenile justice system."[35] Again, New Zealand offered no formal response to the report.

---

24   Ibid [44].
25   Ibid [46(a)].
26   Ibid [46(b)].
27   Ibid [46(c)].
28   Ibid [48].
29   Ibid [24].
30   Committee on the Rights of the Child, *Concluding observations on the fifth periodic report of New Zealand*, 73rd sess, UN Doc CRC/C/NZL/CO/5 (30 September 2016).
31   Ibid [19(a)].
32   Ibid [15(a)].
33   Ibid [17].
34   Ibid [36(a)].
35   Ibid [45(e)].

6   Discussion of International Issues Related to Indigenous Peoples in
        International Fora

6.1   UN *General Assembly Third Committee*

In the UN GA's Third Committee, as well as commenting on Indigenous peoples' participation in UN meetings (discussed above) and the revised mandate of EMRIP (discussed below), New Zealand commented upon the UN Special Rapporteur on the rights of indigenous peoples' (Special Rapporteur) report on conservation measures and Indigenous peoples. New Zealand noted that "effective relationships and partnerships with tangata whenua ... is a critical element of achieving enhanced conservation of natural resources and historical and cultural heritage," identifying some of its own innovative approaches to the governance and management of natural resources negotiated as part of Treaty settlements.[36]

6.2   UN *Human Rights Council*

During the UN Human Rights Council's ("HRC") 33rd session in September, New Zealand responded to concerns expressed in the Special Rapporteur's annual report regarding the government's inadequate consultation with Indigenous peoples on the TPPA. New Zealand stated that it had been "active in engaging with stakeholders on New Zealand's negotiating objectives and the negotiating process." It acknowledged that Māori had expressed concerns regarding the consultation process and identified that "in recent months New Zealand has conducted nationwide engagement with New Zealand society, including Maori and iwi" on the TPPA. It noted that all of New Zealand's free trade agreements since 2001, including the TPPA, have included a Treaty of Waitangi exception clause, which "reflects the constitutional significance of the Treaty to New Zealand." It drew attention to the Waitangi Tribunal's finding that the TPPA did not breach the principles of the Treaty. New Zealand stated that it remains committed to strengthening the relationship between the government and Māori.[37]

6.3   UN *Expert Mechanism on the Rights of Indigenous Peoples*

A prime focus of the EMRIP's 9th session was the review of the mechanism's mandate. New Zealand stated that any changes to the mandate "should

---

36   Taula, above n 9.

37   Carl Allan Reaich, *Clustered Interactive Dialogue* (20 September 2016) Human Rights
       Council <http://webtv.un.org/meetings-events/human-rights-council/regular-sessions/
       33rd-session/watch/clustered-id-contd-indigenous-peoples-18th-meeting-33rd-regular
       -session-human-rights-council-/5131061166001#full-text>.

be aimed at creating a more effective, efficient, and fully representative mechanism that coordinates and interacts better with relevant agencies and mechanisms," that the "revised mechanism must reflect the precise legal status of the UN Declaration on the Rights of Indigenous Peoples," and that it did "not consider that radical modifications, for example, to make EMRIP similar in nature to a treaty body, are appropriate."[38] New Zealand's proposed revisions included that EMRIP be tasked "to assist in the follow-up on recommendations to Member States from indigenous-specific mandates and the broader UN human rights system, including identifying possible technical assistance" and "to facilitate dialogue between States and indigenous peoples at country level."[39]

EMRIP's mandate was ultimately revised by resolution of the HRC, without a vote, at its 33rd session.[40] EMRIP is now mandated to provide the HRC "with expertise and advice on the rights of indigenous peoples as set out in the United Nations Declaration on the Rights of Indigenous Peoples, and assist Member States upon request, to achieve the ends of the Declaration through the promotion, protection and fulfilment of the rights of indigenous peoples."[41] New features of the mandate include:

- upon request, assisting "Member States and/or indigenous peoples in identifying the need for and providing technical advice regarding the development of domestic legislation and policies relating to the rights of indigenous peoples";
- providing "Member States, upon their request, with assistance and advice for the implementation of recommendations made at the universal periodic review and by treaty bodies, special procedures or other relevant mechanisms";
- "[u]pon the request of Member States, indigenous peoples and/or the private sector" engaging and assisting "them by facilitating dialogue, when agreeable to all parties, in order to achieve the ends of the Declaration";

---

38   Jarrod Clyne, *9th session of the Expert Mechanism on the Rights of Indigenous Peoples Item 2: Follow-up to the World Conference on Indigenous Peoples including the review of the mandate of the Expert mechanism* (11 July 2016) Docip <http://cendoc.docip.org/collect/cendocdo/index/assoc/HASHe6d5/791b6ce9.dir/EM16Clyne018.pdf>.

39   Ibid.

40   *Expert Mechanism on the Rights of Indigenous Peoples,* HRC Res 33/25, 33rd sess, 41st mtg, Agenda Item 5, UN Doc A/HRC/RES/33/25 (30 September 2016).

41   Ibid [1].

- identifying, disseminating and promoting "good practices and lessons learned regarding the efforts to achieve the ends of the Declaration, including through reports to the Human Rights Council"; and
- the expansion of EMRIP's membership from five to seven experts, in order to reflect the seven Indigenous sociocultural regions.[42]

New Zealand welcomed the adoption of the resolution. It expressed the hope that "the new mandate will enable EMRIP to better guide states through drawing on best practice to work towards achieving the ends of the Declaration on the Rights of Indigenous Peoples."[43]

6.4   *Permanent Forum on Indigenous Issues*
During the PFII's 15th session, New Zealand reaffirmed its support for the UNDRIP and the *Outcome Document* from the World Conference on Indigenous Peoples, noting "the importance of continued understanding and commitment to the common objectives of the Declaration alongside the Treaty of Waitangi and New Zealand's existing legal and constitutional frameworks."[44] It asserted that it was "undertaking a range of actions consistent with the Outcome Document of the World Conference" although it acknowledged that "there is still more to do in New Zealand, particularly to increase social, cultural and health indicators for Maori."[45] It also highlighted its efforts to support the Māori language,[46] culture and heritage, and economic and social progress.[47]

6.5   *Convention on Biological Diversity Conference of the Parties*
The 13th COP to the CBD was held in December, along with the eighth meeting of the *Cartagena Protocol on Biosafety*, and the second meeting on the

---

42   Ibid [2], [4].

43   Taula, above n 9.

44   Jaclyn Williams, *New Zealand: Item 3(d): Follow-up to the World Conference* (2016) Docip <http://cendoc.docip.org/collect/cendocdo/index/assoc/HASH2a55/17e13f8e.dir/PF16 Jaclyn084a.pdf> 1.

45   Ibid.

46   Jaclyn Williams, *New Zealand Item 3(b): Follow-up to the recommendations of the Permanent Forum – Indigenous Languages: preservation and revitalisation* (2016) Docip <http://cendoc.docip.org/collect/cendocdo/index/assoc/HASH01aa/d517e13f.dir/PF16Jaclyn066a.pdf>.

47   Jaclyn Williams, *New Zealand Item 4: Implementation of the six mandated areas of the Permanent Forum with reference to the UNDRIP* (2016) Docip <http://cendoc.docip.org/collect/cendocdo/index/assoc/HASH8ca1/5125916b.dir/PF16Jaclyn021.pdf>.

Nagoya Protocol on Access to Genetic Resources and Benefit Sharing. New Zealand actively participated in the meetings. Of central importance to Indigenous peoples were the discussions on the *Mo'otz Kuxtal Voluntary Guidelines*, which are to guide the development of measures to ensure the consent of, and benefit-sharing with, Indigenous peoples and local communities where their traditional knowledge is accessed and used.[48] Controversy emerged over the language on consent to be used in the guidelines. A collection of states, supported the inclusion of the word "free" in the guideline's reference to "prior and informed consent." But the African Group, Timor Leste, India and Indonesia opposed its inclusion and Brazil suggested it could be included on the proviso that it accorded with national legislation. The International Indigenous Forum on Biodiversity ("IIFB") and members of the PFII emphasised the need for reference to free prior and informed consent, in accordance with the wording of the UNDRIP. Indigenous peoples eventually walked out of the negotiations in protest. The adopted guidelines now seemingly creating three different standards of protection as they refer to: "'prior and informed consent', 'free, prior and informed consent' or 'approval and involvement', depending on national circumstances, of indigenous peoples and local communities".[49] Another key development regarding Indigenous peoples was the decision to encourage parties to the *CBD* "[t]o recognize and integrate traditional knowledge, customary sustainable use as well as diverse approaches undertaken by indigenous peoples and local communities in efforts to maintain genetic diversity, reduce habitat and biodiversity loss, and to promote an equitable and participatory approach to the management and restoration of critical ecosystems."[50]

6.6   *World Intellectual Property Office*

WIPO's Intergovernmental Committee on Intellectual Property and Genetic Resources, Traditional Knowledge and Folklore ("IGC") resumed its work in 2016 after a year-long hiatus, with New Zealand participating in the negotiations. At the 30th session New Zealand "noted that it was not a small task to produce a text aimed at taking account of the many and varied views and proposals that

---

48   Polina Shulbaeva, "The Convention on Biological Diversity (CBD)" in Katrine Broch Hansen, Käthe Jepsen and Pamela Leiva Jacquelin (eds), *The Indigenous World 2017* (International Work Group for Indigenous Affairs, 2017) 607, 608.

49   Ibid 609.

50   Conference of the Parties, Convention on Biological Diversity, *Report of the Conference of the Parties to the Convention on Biological Diversity on its thirteenth meeting*, UN Doc CBD/COP/13/25 (17 December 2016) 20 [17(c)]. See Shulbaeva, above n 48, 609.

Member States and observers had put forward" and it provided some drafting suggestions regarding Article 3.1 of the draft instrument to protect genetic
resources.[51]

7   Developments Contributing to Customary International law or of Particular Relevance to New Zealand

7.1   *Committee on the Elimination of Racial Discrimination*
The Committee on the Elimination of Racial Discrimination's ("CERD") recommendations included that states protect Indigenous peoples' rights to own
their lands, territories and resources;[52] title Indigenous lands;[53] and provide
Indigenous peoples with compensation for land loss or damage.[54]

7.2   *Committee on Economic, Social and Cultural Rights*
The Committee on Economic, Social and Cultural Rights recommended, inter
alia, that Canada repeal the discriminatory provisions in the *Indian Act*.[55]

7.3   *Committee on the Elimination of Discrimination against Women*
The Committee on the Elimination of Discrimination against Women's recommendations included that Sweden ensure the representation of Indigenous
women in political life.[56]

---

51   World Intellectual Property Organization, *Intergovernmental Committee on Intellectual
      Property and Genetic Resources, Traditional Knowledge and Traditional Cultural Expres-
      sions Thirtieth Session Geneva, May 30 to June 3, 2016*, WIPO/GRTKF/IC/30/10 (23 Septem-
      ber 2016) [118].

52   Committee on the Elimination of Racial Discrimination, *Concluding observations on the
      combined twenty-first to twenty-third periodic reports of Argentina*, UN Doc CERD/C/ARG/
      CO/21-23 (11 January 2017) [21]; Committee on the Elimination of Racial Discrimination,
      Concluding observations on the combined fourth to sixth periodic reports of Paraguay, UN
      Doc CERD/C/PRY/CO/4-6 (4 October 2016) [20] ("CERD on Paraguay").

53   Committee on the Elimination of Racial Discrimination, *Concluding observations on the
      combined thirteenth to fifteenth periodic reports of Namibia*, UN Doc CERD/C/NAM/CO/13-
      15 (10 June 2016) [24].

54   CERD on Paraguay, above n 52, [20].

55   Committee on Economic, Social and Cultural Rights, *Concluding observations on the sixth
      periodic report of Canada*, UN Doc E/C.12/CAN/CO/6 (23 March 2016) [22].

56   Committee on the Elimination of Discrimination against Women, *Concluding observa-
      tions on the combined eighth and ninth periodic reports of Sweden*, UN Doc CEDAW/C/
      SWE/CO/8-9 (10 March 2016) [31].

7.4   Committee on the Rights of the Child

The Committee on the Rights of the Child's recommendations included that Gabon adopt a law for the protection of Indigenous peoples based on the UNDRIP.[57]

7.5   Human Rights Committee

The Human Rights Committee recommended, inter alia, that Namibia and Costa Rica secure the free, prior and informed consent of Indigenous peoples prior to the development of extractive industry projects.[58]

7.6   Human Rights Council Universal Periodic Review

During the HRC's Universal Periodic Review, states' recommendations regarding Indigenous peoples included that Tanzania legally protect Indigenous peoples' rights to land[59] and Papua New Guinea establish mechanisms for securing the prior informed consent of Indigenous peoples on issues affecting them.[60]

---

57   Committee on the Rights of the Child, *Concluding observations on the second periodic report of Gabon*, UN Doc CRC/C/GAB/CO/2 (8 July 2016) [61].

58   HRCtee, *Concluding observations on the sixth periodic report of Costa Rica*, UN Doc CCPR/C/CRI/CO/6 (21 April 2016) [42]; HRCtee, *Concluding observations on the second report of Namibia,* UN Doc CCPR/C/NAM/CO/2 (22 April 2016) [44].

59   Human Rights Council, *Report of the Working Group on the Universal Periodic Review: United Republic of Tanzania,* UN Doc A/HRC/33/12 (14 July 2016) [137.70].

60   Human Rights Council, *Report of the Working Group on the Universal Periodic Review: Papua New Guinea,* UN Doc A/HRC/33/10 (13 July 2016) [104.152].

International Economic Law

*Christian Riffel**

The year 2016 was marked by the successful conclusion of the *Trans-Pacific Partnership Agreement* ("*TPP*")[1] and the panel ruling in *Indonesia – Import Licensing Regimes*, a case brought by New Zealand (together with the United States) against several Indonesian import restrictions on horticultural and animal products.[2] Another highlight in the international economic law arena was the finalization of the legal text of the *Pacific Agreement on Closer Economic Relations* ("*PACER Plus*"), which aims at economic integration between Australia, New Zealand, and the Pacific Island countries.[3] At the same time, further trade integration has come under fire worldwide. Two events epitomize this: the outcome of the Brexit referendum to withdraw the United Kingdom from the European Union and the election of Donald Trump, an outspoken critic of the *TPP* and the *North American Free Trade Agreement*,[4] as the 45th president of the United States. It is expected that these developments will have significant implications for the trade landscape in 2017.

1 Preferential Trade

The government is negotiating free trade agreements ("FTAs") with a view to increasing export opportunities for New Zealand businesses as well as legal certainty, thus making the risks associated with cross-border trade more predictable.[5]

---

* University of Canterbury

1 Ministry of Foreign Affairs & Trade, *Trans-Pacific Partnership* <https://www.tpp.mfat.govt .nz/>.

2 Panel Report, *Indonesia – Importation of Horticultural Products, Animals and Animal Products*, WTO Doc WT/DS477/R, WT/DS478/R, modified by WT/DS477/R/Corr.1, WT/DS478/R/ Corr.1 (22 December 2016).

3 Radio New Zealand, *Pacific countries agree to trade agreement's legal text* (26 August 2016) <http://www.radionz.co.nz/international/pacific-news/311908/pacific-countries-agree -to-trade-agreement%27s-legal-text>.

4 *North American Free Trade Agreement*, signed 17 December 1992, (1993) 32 ILM 289 (entered into force 1 January 1994).

5 Ministry of Foreign Affairs & Trade, *Trade Agenda 2030*, 18–19 <https://www.mfat.Trade2030/ Trade-Agenda-2030-Strategy-document.govt.nz/assets/_securedfiles/pdf>.

© KONINKLIJKE BRILL NV, LEIDEN, 2018 | DOI 10.1163/9789004345911_011

1.1   Trans-Pacific Partnership

The *TPP* was signed in Auckland on 4 February 2016 and New Zealand has been designated as the depository for the *TPP*. It brings together the economies of New Zealand, Australia, Brunei Darussalam, Canada, Chile, Japan, Malaysia, Mexico, Peru, Singapore, the United States and Viet Nam into one mega trading bloc. The combined GDP of these 12 parties amounts to 36 per cent of world GDP.[6] The Agreement, once in force, will have a massive economic impact. For New Zealand, it would mean the first free trade agreement with Canada, Japan, Mexico, Peru, and the United States. 95.4 per cent of all customs duties on New Zealand exports to these countries will be eventually eliminated.[7] Furthermore, for the first time, an investor-state dispute settlement ("ISDS") mechanism would be in place, giving investors from those countries the right to take legal action against New Zealand government measures. In terms of regulatory impact, most changes concern New Zealand's intellectual property ("IP") laws, leading to a higher level of IP protection as compared to the *WTO Agreement on Trade-Related Aspects of Intellectual Property Rights* ("*TRIPS Agreement*").[8] Among other things, the protection of data in marketing approval procedures for new agricultural chemicals will be extended from five to 10 years; copyright protection will go up to life plus 70 years; and to compensate for unreasonable delays in the examination process, patent terms can be extended. Besides, New Zealand Customs Service is granted more powers to detain counterfeit goods and pirated copyright protected works at the border.[9] The *TPP Amendment Bill* was passed in November. Pursuant to s 2, the Bill will commence when the *TPP* enters into force. New Zealand is set to ratify the *TPP* in 2017.

There is one big caveat, however: the Agreement, as it stands, cannot enter into force without the United States. According to *TPP* art 30.5, at least 85 per cent of the combined GDP of the signatories in 2013 are required for the Agreement to enter into force. This requirement cannot be met without US participation.

1.2   Regional Comprehensive Economic Partnership

The negotiations for a *Regional Comprehensive Economic Partnership* ("*RCEP*") are ongoing. As of 2016, 16 negotiation rounds took place, the last one in Jakarta

---

6   Ministry of Foreign Affairs & Trade, *Trans-Pacific Partnership* <https://www.tpp.mfat.govt .nz/>.

7   Ministry of Foreign Affairs & Trade, *Trans-Pacific Partnership National Interest Analysis* (25 January 2016) 38.

8   *WTO Agreement on Trade-Related Aspects of Intellectual Property Rights*, signed 15 April 1994, 1869 UNTS 299 (entered into force 1 January 1995).

9   See the entire Trans-Pacific Partnership Agreement Amendment Bill at <http://www.legislation .govt.nz/bill/government/2016/0133/latest/whole.html#DLM6838023>.

in December. The leaders of the participating countries set out seemingly conflicting objectives in a joint statement, namely the "swift conclusion" of the negotiations while achieving a "high-quality" agreement at the same time.[10]

RCEP is of economic significance to New Zealand, as it would establish a free trade area with countries with which New Zealand currently has no bilateral agreement, i.e. India and Japan.[11] There are other designated signatories that have no bilateral free trade agreement in place at present, such as China/India, China/Japan, Japan/Korea, and Australia/India.

It should be stressed that the secrecy, criticised throughout the negotiations of the TPP, persist with respect to RCEP. Not even position papers, as is the modern practice of the European Commission when negotiating trade agreements, are provided by the government to the public.[12] In terms of transparency and accountability this is lamentable, since it is inconceivable that abstract statements, such as the formulation of negotiation goals and an outline of issues, would in any way jeopardize the government's room for manoeuvre. Also, more transparency would pre-empt the ever more prevalent leaking of documents. Generally speaking, to have a say in the outcome, people have to be able to influence the FTA negotiations. The ratification process, being a yes or no decision, is too late to alter the legal text.

1.3 New Zealand–India Free Trade Agreement

Aside from RCEP, New Zealand pursues trade liberalization with India through a second channel, namely bilaterally. The bilateral agreement is intended to form a safety net should the plurilateral negotiations come to nothing. It is clear, however, that should the liberalization level achieved plurilaterally exceed the bilateral deal, it will be of little practical import. In this connection, it should be noted that bilateral agreements usually include a most-favoured-nation ("MFN") obligation with respect to services and investment, not goods, so that further tariff reductions would not need to be plurilateralized.[13]

---

10   See *Joint Leaders' Statement on the Regional Comprehensive Economic Partnership* (8 September 2016, Vientiane, Laos) <http://asean.org/storage/2016/09/56-RCEP_Joint-Leaders-Statement_8-September-2016.pdf>.

11   Should the TPP enter into force, New Zealand would have an agreement with Japan, namely the TPP of which Japan would be just like New Zealand a constituent member.

12   The European Union even publishes draft texts. See, e.g., for the EU–Japan Economic Partnership Agreement, European Commission, *EU–Japan trade agreement: texts of the agreement in principle* (6 July 2017) <http://trade.ec.europa.eu/doclib/press/index.cfm?id=1684>.

13   See, e.g., *Free Trade Agreement Between The Government of New Zealand And The Government of the People's Republic of China* Ch. 3.

1.4 New Zealand–China Free Trade Agreement

New Zealand and China decided at the end of 2016 that it is time to upgrade their existing free trade agreement, as new business sectors have gained in importance.[14] Digital trade is a case in point. The agreement entered into force in 2008 and was the first free trade agreement to be concluded by China with a Western country. Since then the trade relationship with China has almost tripled over the past decade according to Statistics New Zealand.[15] It is likely that the upgrade will take account of the ongoing negotiations at the regional level, i.e. RCEP.

As to the protection of foreign investments, the national treatment obligation in the NZ–China FTA does not include the pre-establishment phase as of yet.[16] It bears noting, however, that, as a result of access granted to the residential property market in the *Free Trade Agreement Between New Zealand and the Republic of Korea*,[17] the government can no longer discriminate against Chinese house buyers because of the MFN clause in NZ–China FTA art 139(1), which encompasses "admission". The NZ–Korea FTA was after the entry into force of the NZ–China FTA[18] and the purchase of residential property is a covered investment (given the expected capital gains). The requirement of prior government approval, as set out in Annex II to the NZ–Korea FTA, does not relate to residential property, unless it is on protected areas, such as heritage sites or scenically valuable areas. According to Land Information New Zealand, Chinese were the biggest group of foreign house buyers in April–June 2016.[19] As a side note, under the TPP, New Zealand secured a reservation relating to the taxation of residential property in the Annex II Schedule.

---

14 Joint Statement Between New Zealand and the People's Republic of China on the Upgrade of the China-New Zealand Free Trade Agreement <https://www.mfat.govt.nz/assets/FTAs-agreements-in-force/China-FTA/China-NZ-JMS-FTA-upgrade.pdf>.

15 Statistics NZ, *Trade with China nearly tripled in past decade* (7 September 2016) <http://www.stats.govt.nz/browse_for_stats/industry_sectors/imports_and_exports/trade-china-tripled-decade.aspx>.

16 NZ–China FTA art 138.

17 The national treatment obligation in the investment chapter extends to the "establishment" and "acquisition" of investments, art 10.5.

18 This is relevant because of NZ–China FTA art 139(3).

19 Tom Pullar-Strecker, *3 per cent of NZ house buyers officially from overseas* (1 August 2016) Stuff <http://www.stuff.co.nz/business/industries/82682551/fresh-attempt-to-calculate-impact-of-overseas-home-buyers>.

1.5   *Pacific Agreement on Closer Economic Relations (PACER Plus)*

A Special Pacific Islands Trade Ministers Meeting took place in Christchurch on 26 August 2016. At that meeting, the ministers finalized the text of *PACER Plus*. The Agreement is not just a trade agreement, but is also conceived as an economic development agreement, as shown by the long timeframes to eliminate customs duties.[20] Its main focus is on increasing living standards.[21] The Agreement's investment chapter does not provide for ISDS, nor does the Agreement contain a chapter on intellectual property protection. This is reflective of the economic development of the Pacific Island countries. In the final analysis, the regime, as laid out in *PACER Plus,* is less integrative than the one under New Zealand's other free trade agreements.

Both Australia and New Zealand pledged to provide funds to help Pacific Island countries with the implementation of *PACER Plus.*[22] With a view to enhancing labour mobility within the region, the parties concluded a side agreement on labour mobility, which is not binding, however. This concerns unskilled and semi-skilled workers.

1.6   *New Zealand–European Union Free Trade Agreement*

Surprisingly, there are some pitfalls around the New Zealand-European Union FTA negotiations which should otherwise be a straightforward deal among two like-minded entities as far as trade matters are concerned. For good reason, New Zealand has been a latecomer in terms of countries with which the European Union launched trade negotiations, and remoteness is only part of the story. Mindful that New Zealand is an agricultural powerhouse, for the free trade agreement to be economically meaningful for New Zealand, it will have to make an impact on the notorious EU agricultural regime, the so-called Common Agricultural Policy, particularly its centrepieces: quotas, tariff quotas, and agricultural subsidies. Another area of contention, where New Zealand has a great economic interest, concerns the services sectors. New Zealand is a services provider, as shown by its increasing GDP from services.[23]

---

20   Ministry of Foreign Affairs & Trade, *Pacific Agreement on Closer Economic Relations (PACER) Plus National Interest Analysis* (6 June 2017) 8.

21   See recital 3 to the Preamble.

22   See *Implementing Arrangement for Development and Economic Cooperation under the Pacific Agreement on Closer Economic Relations Plus*, available at <https://www .mfat.govt.nz/en/trade/free-trade-agreements/agreements-under-negotiation/pacer/ pacer-plus-full-text/>.

23   Trading Economics, *New Zealand GDP From Services* (2017) <www.tradingeconomics .com/new-zealand/gdp-from-services>.

In October, the European Union and New Zealand signed the Partnership Agreement on Relations and Cooperation, according to European treaty practice, a precursor to a fully-fledged free trade agreement. An open question is the New Zealand-United Kingdom trade relationship after Brexit. Both countries started a trade policy dialogue with a view to sounding out the feasibility of a bilateral agreement.[24]

As to the future negotiation agenda, it will be interesting to see how the New Zealand government responds to the establishment of an investment court system promoted by Canada and the European Union through the Comprehensive Economic and Trade Agreement, which was signed on 30 October 2016. Slightly higher IP standards, notably with respect to geographical indications, can be expected following an FTA with the European Union. Those higher standards would need to be multilateralized, given that the *TRIPS Agreement* does not have an economic integration exception. As a corollary, the level of IP protection in New Zealand would be lifted in general.

2   World Trade

2.1   *Environmental Goods Agreement*
The negotiations for an Environmental Goods Agreement under the auspices of the World Trade Organization ("WTO") are ongoing. The objective is to reach an agreement on the full elimination of customs duties on goods that contribute to sustainable development and are used to combat pollution, for example, solar water heaters or recycling machinery.[25]

2.2   *Trade in Services Agreement ("TiSA")*
New Zealand is one of 23 parties to negotiate a Trade in Services Agreement, which has as its goal the liberalization of trade in services beyond the level laid down in the *General Agreement on Trade in Services*.[26] The negotiations, occurring outside the WTO, are testament to the growing importance of services to the global economy. In 2016 the parties conducted a stocktaking exercise.

---

24   Todd McClay, "NZ establishes trade policy dialogue with UK" (Press Release, 18 October 2016) <https://www.beehive.govt.nz/release/nz-establishes-trade-policy-dialogue-uk>.

25   Ministry of Foreign Affairs & Trade, *Environmental Goods Agreement* <https://www.mfat .govt.nz/en/trade/our-work-with-the-wto/environmental-goods-agreement-ega/>.

26   *General Agreement on Trade in Services*, signed 15 April 1994, 1869 UNTS 183 (entered into force 1 January 1995).

No conclusion has been reached yet. *TiSA* parties account for approximately 70 per cent of worldwide trade in services.[27]

2.3   *WTO Cases*
2.3.1   Indonesia – Import Licensing Regimes
The Indonesia-New Zealand trade dispute was decided in favour of New Zealand in December. New Zealand beef exports had fallen by 80 per cent as a result of Indonesian import restrictions.[28] The Panel found these restrictions inconsistent with WTO law.

The case is of systemic importance, as it clarified some moot points. As far as state responsibility for private actors is concerned, the Panel followed the ruling of the Appellate Body in the *US – COOL* case. WTO Members set the regulatory framework within which private actors operate. That framework can be challenged before the WTO, even though particular decisions within that given framework are taken by private actors. The prerequisite for state responsibility in this case is that the private actions have been incentivized by the set framework.[29]

On the procedural side, the Panel held that a change of the measure at issue after the establishment of the panel is immaterial to the panel's terms of reference.[30] In order to make a prima facie case, a complainant does not need to show that the measure at issue actually impinged on trade volumes. Even if trade volumes have gone up while a measure was in force, that measure may still constitute a quantitative restriction.[31] Conversely, data that demonstrates that trade has decreased since the entry into force of the measure can be used

---

27   Ministry of Foreign Affairs & Trade, *Trade in Services Agreement (TiSA)* <https://www.mfat.govt.nz/en/trade/free-trade-agreements/agreements-under-negotiation/tisa/>.

28   *Indonesia – Importation of Horticultural Products, Animals and Animal Products*, WTO Doc WT/DS466/1, G/L/1038, G/AG/GEN/113, G/LIC/D/46, G/PSI/D/2 (9 September 2013) (Request for Consultations by New Zealand) [2].

29   Panel Report, *Indonesia – Import Licensing Regimes*, WTO Doc WT/DS477/R, WT/DS478/R, modified by WT/DS477/R/Corr.1, WT/DS478/R/Corr.1, [7.6], [7.346], quoting Appellate Body Report, *United States – Certain Country of Origin Labelling (COOL) Requirements*, WTO Doc WT/DS384/AB/R, WT/DS386/AB/R (23 July 2012) [291].

30   Panel Report, *Indonesia – Import Licensing Regimes*, WTO Doc WT/DS477/R, WT/DS478/R, modified by WT/DS477/R/Corr.1, WT/DS478/R/Corr.1, [6.24].

31   See Panel Report, *Turkey – Restrictions on Imports of Textile and Clothing Products*, WTO Doc WT/DS34/R (19 November 1999) [9.204].

as evidence to buttress a claim of restriction.[32] As noted by Davies before, trade effects can be "a decisive evidential consideration."[33]

With respect to Article XI of the *General Agreement on Tariffs and Trade* ("*GATT*"),[34] the Panel ruled that automatic import licensing systems fall under its remit.[35] In order to ascertain whether a particular measure constitutes a quantitative restriction, the combined effect of its requirements has to be examined.[36] As regards trade in agricultural or fisheries products, the Panel held that *GATT* art XI:2(c)(ii) has been overridden by *Agreement on Agriculture* art 4.2.[37]

Indonesia invoked several exceptions of *GATT* art XX to defend its import licensing regimes. As to *GATT* art XX(d), the Panel observed that the ruling of the Appellate Body in *US – Carbon Steel* that 'a responding Member's law will be treated as WTO-consistent until proven otherwise'[38] does not relieve the respondent of the duty to provide the legal texts of the legal instruments it seeks compliance with. Merely enumerating national laws or regulations is not sufficient.[39] Indonesia's other attempts under *GATT* art XX failed as well because the measures did not refer to any of the policy objectives listed in art XX as their rationale. It is true that the burden of proof is incumbent upon "the party invoking an exception".[40] Who bears the burden of proof is one thing; another thing is the standard of proof. In this regard, Van den Bossche and Prévost noted that

---

32   Panel Report, *Indonesia – Import Licensing Regimes*, WTO Doc WT/DS477/R, WT/DS478/R, modified by WT/DS477/R/Corr.1, WT/DS478/R/Corr.1, [7.88], [7.323].

33   Arwel Davies, "Interpreting the Chapeau of GATT Article XX in Light of the 'New' Approach in *Brazil-Tyres*" (2017) 43(3) *Journal of World Trade* 507, 516.

34   *General Agreement on Tariffs and Trade 1994*, adopted 15 April 1994, 1867 UNTS 187 (entered into force 1 January 1995).

35   Panel Report, *Indonesia – Import Licensing Regimes*, WTO Doc WT/DS477/R, WT/DS478/R, modified by WT/DS477/R/Corr.1, WT/DS478/R/Corr.1, [7.56].

36   Ibid [7.109]–[7.111], [7.268], [7.317], [7.476].

37   Ibid [7.60]; *Marrakesh Agreement Establishing the World Trade Organization*, opened for signature 15 April 1994, 1867 UNTS 3 (entered into force 1 January 1995), annex 1A (*Agreement on Agriculture*) 1867 UNTS 190.

38   Appellate Body Report, *United States – Countervailing Duties on Certain Corrosion Resistant Carbon Steel Flat Products from Germany*, WTO Doc WT/DS213/AB/R and Corr.1 (19 December 2002) 157.

39   Panel Report, *Indonesia – Import Licensing Regimes*, WTO Doc WT/DS477/R, WT/DS478/R, modified by WT/DS477/R/Corr.1, WT/DS478/R/Corr.1, [7.581].

40   See, e.g., Panel Report, *United States – Standards for Reformulated and Conventional Gasoline*, WTO Doc WT/DS2/R (20 May 1996) [6.20], [6.35].

Although a Member's articulation of the objective(s) of the measure at issue should be taken into account, a panel is not bound by this and must take account of all evidence put before it in this regard including the texts of statutes, legislative history and other evidence regarding the structure and operation of the measure.[41]

In the present case, the Panel focussed on the text of the measures at issue and found that Indonesia did not meet the above threshold.[42] The reasoning was akin to the one adopted by the Panel in *China – Raw Materials*, where "China [the respondent] was unable to substantiate its claim that its [measures at issue] are part of a comprehensive programme maintained in order to reduce pollution".[43] To be justified, the measures must be *designed* to protect, for example, public morals (art XX(a)) or public health (art XX(b)). The true object and purpose of the import licensing regimes, however, was simplification and administration of the import process.[44] None of these is an accepted ground of justification under GATT art XX, whose list of justifiable policy objectives is exhaustive.[45]

Indonesia already announced that it will appeal the ruling.[46] In this context, it is worth noting that Indonesia is a designated signatory to RCEP.

2.3.2 Third Party Participation

The Dispute Settlement Understanding ("DSU")[47] enables non-disputing Members to make written submissions to WTO panels and the Appellate Body.[48] New Zealand's third party involvement relates to agricultural products, thus reflecting the country's export interests.

---

41   Peter Van den Bossche and Denise Prévost, *Essentials of WTO Law* (CUP, 2016) 89.

42   Panel Report, *Indonesia – Import Licensing Regimes*, WTO Doc WT/DS477/R, WT/DS478/R, modified by WT/DS477/R/Corr.1, WT/DS478/R/Corr.1, [7.631], [7.657], [7.678]–[7.679].

43   Panel Report, *China – Measures Related to the Exportation of Various Raw Materials*, WTO Doc WT/DS394/R, WT/DS395/R, WT/DS398/R (22 February 2012) [7.516].

44   Panel Report, *Indonesia – Import Licensing Regimes*, WTO Doc WT/DS477/R, WT/DS478/R, modified by WT/DS477/R/Corr.1, WT/DS478/R/Corr.1, [7.631], [7.657], [7.678], [7.739], [7.773f], [7.794].

45   Unlike *Agreement on Technical Barriers to Trade* art 2.2 ("inter alia").

46   World Trade Organization, *DS477: Indonesia – Importation of Horticultural Products, Animals and Animal Products* (2017) <www.wto.org/english/tratop_e/dispu_e/cases_e/ds477_e.htm>.

47   WTO Understanding on Rules and Procedures governing the Settlement of Disputes (adopted 15 April 1994, entered into force 1 January 1995) 1869 UNTS 401.

48   DSU arts 10.2, 17.4.

Korea – Radionuclides[49] is concerned with certain testing and certification requirements for radionuclides imposed by Korea on food products from Japan in the wake of the Fukushima nuclear accident.

Indonesia – Chicken[50] concerns measures similar to the ones challenged by New Zealand in *Indonesia – Import Licensing Regimes*, just in a different agricultural sector. New Zealand has an interest in transparent market access given the importance of Indonesia as an export market for New Zealand agricultural products.[51]

US – Tuna II[52] is about eco-labelling, in the present case regarding dolphin-safe harvesting. New Zealand has a stake in this foodstuff-related issue in terms of policy reforms. In 2016 the case has gone in its second round of compliance proceedings.

Another case of relevance to New Zealand is the *Tobacco Plain Packaging* case against Australia,[53] as New Zealand is poised to introduce similar legislation. However, as of 2016, the case has not been decided yet.

---

49   World Trade Organization, *DS495: Korea – Import Bans, and Testing and Certification Requirements for Radionuclides* <https://www.wto.org/english/tratop_e/dispu_e/cases_e/ds495_e.htm>.

50   World Trade Organization, *DS484: Indonesia – Measures Concerning the Importation of Chicken Meat and Chicken Products* <https://www.wto.org/english/tratop_e/dispu_e/cases_e/ds484_e.htm>.

51   Observatory of Economic Complexity, *What does Indonesia import from New Zealand?* (2016) <http://atlas.media.mit.edu/en/visualize/tree_map/hs92/import/idn/nzl/show/2016/>.

52   World Trade Organization, *DS381: United States – Measures Concerning the Importation, Marketing and Sale of Tuna and Tuna Products* <https://www.wto.org/english/tratop_e/dispu_e/cases_e/ds381_e.htm>.

53   *Australia – Certain Measures Concerning Trademarks, Geographical Indications and Other Plain Packaging Requirements Applicable to Tobacco Products and Packaging*, wto Doc WT/DS434, WT/DS435, WT/DS441, WT/DS458, WT/DS467.

International Environmental Law

*Josephine Toop**

1   Introduction

In 2016, Aotearoa/New Zealand signed and ratified the *Paris Agreement*[1] and submitted to the *United Nations Framework Convention on Climate Change* ("*UNFCCC*")[2] its Nationally Determined Contributions ("NDC") as well as its Initial Report and *Greenhouse Gas Inventory 1990–2014*. A New Zealander was also elected co-chair of the newly established Ad Hoc Working Group ("APA") on the *Paris Agreement*. New Zealand lodged its Aviation Emissions Reduction Action Plan with the International Civil Aviation Organization ("ICAO"). In the Pacific, New Zealand and the European Union worked together on renewable energy initiatives. New Zealand attended the 47th Pacific Islands Forum where climate change and other issues were considered. New Zealand signed the *Trans-Pacific Partnership Agreement* ("*TPP*") in 2016, which includes controversial investor-state dispute settlement provisions ("ISDS"), and has an environmental chapter containing a multilateral environmental agreement section, among other things.[3] New Zealand presented a Biodiversity Action Plan 2016–2020, and committed to making New Zealand predator free by 2050. A Memorandum with China was concluded to protect wetlands in both countries used by migratory birds. The Scientific Committee of the International Whaling Commission ("IWC SC") once again reiterated grave concerns about the survival of the critically endangered Māui dolphin and considered that protection measures taken thus far by New Zealand fell short. Nationally, New Zealand produced reports tracking net position and progress towards climate goals, as well as projections about how the climate of New Zealand may change under various low or high emissions scenarios. The New Zealand Emissions Trading Scheme ("NZETS") review continued, in the context of which the Parliamentary Commissioner for the Environment ("PCE") made submissions, and some decisions about the NZETS were taken, such as phasing out over three years the

---

* University of Canterbury
1 *Paris Agreement*, opened for signature 22 April 2016, Dec. 1/CP.21, Annex, UN Doc FCCC/CP/2015/10/Add.1 (entered into force 4 November 2016).
2 *United Nations Framework Convention on Climate Change*, opened for signature 9 May 1992, 1771 UNTS 107 (entered into force 21 March 1994).
3 *Trans-Pacific Partnership Agreement*, signed by all parties 4 February 2016 (not yet in force).

one for two transitional measure/subsidy which currently allows some businesses to pay only one emissions unit for every two tonnes of emissions. The hydrochlorofluorocarbons ("HCFC") wholesaler permit category was revoked, and changes to New Zealand legislation were made to enable ratification of the TPP. Predator Free 2050 Limited was established to help facilitate achieving New Zealand's pest control ambitions. The *Environmental Reporting Act 2015* came into effect in 2016 and the PCE provided some analysis of environmental reporting thus far undertaken. There were also national and international developments connected to fisheries, the marine environment and Antarctica in 2016. These are not addressed here because they are covered in the reviews of Joanna Mossop "Law of the Sea and Fisheries" and Alan Hemmings "The Antarctic Treaty System" (this issue).[4] Reference to those reviews is necessary for a full account of New Zealand's activities relating to international environmental law in 2016.

2   International Developments

2.1   *Biodiversity*

In March, the New Zealand Department of Conservation and the State Forestry Administration of China concluded a Memorandum to protect wetlands in both countries used by migratory birds. The Red Knot and the Bar-tailed Godwit make an annual 24,000km round trip between New Zealand and China. The Memorandum aims to enable the two countries to work together to

---

4   Omitted developments include the Kermadec Ocean Sanctuary Bill 2006 (120–2) (see Joanna Mossop, "Law of the Sea and Fisheries" (2016) 14 *New Zealand Yearbook of International Law* (this volume)); 2016 consultation on new legislation to replace the existing *Marine Reserves Act 1971* (see Mossop, cited above); statements on the *South China Sea* arbitration (see Mossop, cited above); a 2016 report identifying problems with the New Zealand fisheries management system, and a subsequent review of decisions not to prosecute for illegal dumping of fish (see Mossop, cited above); consultation on proposals to strengthen fisheries management (see Mossop, cited above); New Zealand's participation (including tabling papers) at the 39th Antarctic Treaty Consultative Meeting (ATCM) (see Alan Hemmings, "The Antarctic Treaty System" (2016) 14 *New Zealand Yearbook of International Law* (this volume)); participation (including tabling papers) at the 35th Meeting of the Commission for the Conservation of Antarctic Marine Living Resources (see Hemmings, cited above) and consensus on the designation of the Ross Sea Marine Protected Area which New Zealand has been a proponent of for a number of years (see Hemmings, cited above).

protect wetlands used by Red Knots, Godwits and other migratory shorebirds during their annual migrations.[5]

Māui dolphin (*Cephalorhynchus hectori Māui*) are an IUCN red list critically endangered subspecies of Hector's dolphin. They are the smallest and rarest marine dolphin in the world, and are found only on the west coast of the North Island of New Zealand. Fishing is the greatest threat, responsible for about three quarters of reported deaths with a known cause, with set nets that cause dolphins to drown being particularly damaging.[6] The June IWC SC's report notes that no new management actions have been enacted since 2013 and "concludes, as it has repeatedly in the past, that existing management measures in relation to bycatch mitigation fall short of what has been recommended previously."[7] The SC "reiterates its previous recommendation that highest priority should be assigned to immediate management actions to eliminate bycatch of Māui dolphins including closures of any fisheries within the range of Māui dolphins that are known to pose a risk of bycatch to dolphins (i.e. set net and trawl fisheries)" and "urges the New Zealand Government to commit to specific population increase targets and timelines for Māui dolphin conservation".[8] The SC "expresses continued grave concern over the status of this small, severely depleted subspecies. The human-caused death of even one individual will increase the extinction risk".[9]

In regard to the IUCN 2016 Honolulu Challenge on Invasive Alien Species which calls for urgent action to reduce the impact of invasive species on global biodiversity, New Zealand committed to making the country predator free by 2050.[10] "Predator Free 2050" has been heralded by the government as the "largest and most ambitious invasive species eradication project ever attempted".[11]

---

5   Nicky Wagner, "Supporting shorebirds' 24,000km flight" (Press Release, 18 March, 2016) <https://www.beehive.govt.nz/release/supporting-shorebirds%E2%80%99-24000km -flight>.

6   Ministry for Primary Industries, "Maui's and Hector's Dolphins" (26 January 2017) <https://www.mpi.govt.nz/protection-and-response/sustainable-fisheries/managing-our -impact-on-marine-life/protecting-hectors-and-maui-dolphins/>.

7   International Whaling Commission, *Report of the Scientific Committee of the IWC*, IWC/66/ Rep01(2016), (June 2016) 79.

8   Ibid.

9   Ibid.

10   IUCN, "Commitments towards achieving the Honolulu Challenge" <https://www.iucn.org/ theme/species/our-work/invasive-species/honolulu-challenge-invasive-alien-species/ commitments-towards-achieving-honolulu-challenge>.

11   Maggie Barry, "Predator Free 2050 leads global effort against invasive species" (Press Release, 30 November 2016) <https://www.beehive.govt.nz/release/predator-free-2050 -leads-global-effort-against-invasive-species>.

The goal is to preserve native species threatened with extinction through predation by completely eradicating invasive rats, stoats and possums from New Zealand by 2050. As an interim goal, the government has committed to eradicate all pests from all island nature reserves and develop a method for eradicating one of the key target pests from mainland New Zealand by 2025.[12]

In 2016, New Zealand participated in the *Convention on Biological Diversity*[13] COP-13, *Cartagena Protocol*[14] MOP-8, and *Nagoya Protocol*[15] MOP-2. Among other things, the conference led to the *Cancun Declaration on mainstreaming the conservation and sustainable use of biodiversity for well-being*.[16] At the meeting, New Zealand announced that it will take on a leadership role internationally and work with others to control and eradicate invasive alien species and protect native habitats to increase global efforts to achieve Aichi Target 9.[17] New Zealand presented its *Biodiversity Action Plan 2016–2020*; a targeted update of the *Biodiversity Strategy and Action Plan* published in 2000, to meet New Zealand's commitments under the Convention. The updated Action Plan sets out 20 national targets and includes examples of protecting biodiversity such as "Predator Free 2050", the "War on Weeds", and the "Battle for our Birds" (discussed in the national developments section below). New Zealand aims to increase landscape-scale predator control to more than 1 million hectares, remove 500,000 hectares of wilding conifer infestation and expand the "Healthy Nature, Healthy People" programme.[18]

---

12   Ibid; For more about "Predator Free 2050" see the national developments section.

13   *Convention on Biological Diversity,* opened for signature 5 June 1992, 1760 UNTS 79 (entered into force 29 December 1993).

14   *Cartagena Protocol on Biosafety to the Convention on Biological Diversity*, opened for signature 15 May 2000, 2226 UNTS 208 (entered into force 11 September 2003).

15   *Nagoya Protocol on Access to Genetic Resources and the Fair and Equitable Sharing of Benefits Arising from their Utilization to the Convention on Biological Diversity*, opened for signature 2 February 2011, UNEP/CBD/COP/DEC/X/1 (entered into force 12 October 2014).

16   *Cancun Declaration on mainstreaming the conservation and sustainable use of biodiversity for well-being* (3 December 2016) <https://www.cbd.int/cop/cop-13/hls/in-session/cancun-declaration-draft-dec-03-2016-pm-en.pdf>. For other conference outcomes see <https://www.cbd.int/conferences/2016>.

17   Maggie Barry, "NZ taking world leadership role against invasive species" (Press Release, 5 December 2016) <https://www.beehive.govt.nz/release/nz-taking-world-leadership-role-against-invasive-species>.

18   Maggie Barry, "Minister releases new Biodiversity Action Plan" (Press Release, 1 December 2016) <https://www.beehive.govt.nz/release/minister-releases-new-biodiversity-action-plan>.

2.2   Climate Change and Ozone

New Zealand signed the *Paris Agreement* in April and ratified it in October. The *Paris Agreement*, concluded in December 2015, agrees to limit global temperature rise to 2°C this century, with an aspirational goal of 1.5°C above pre-industrial levels. A global stocktake every five years from 2023 will review each country's progress. The *Paris Agreement* entered into force unexpectedly rapidly on 4 November. New Zealand submitted its NDC to the UNFCCC in 2016. New Zealand's NDC target is to reduce greenhouse gas ("GHG") emissions to 30 per cent below 2005 levels by 2030.[19] As reported last year, Climate Action Tracker (an independent scientific analysis produced by four research organisations) has rated New Zealand's target as "inadequate".[20] The CEO and Senior Scientist at Climate Analytics has stated that "[w]hile most other governments intend cutting emissions, New Zealand appears to be increasing emissions, and hiding this through creative accounting. It may not have to take any action at all to meet either its 2020 or 2030 targets."[21]

In May, former New Zealand Climate Change Ambassador Jo Tyndall was elected as co-chair of the newly established APA on the *Paris Agreement*. Although the *Paris Agreement* defines basic obligations and establishes new procedures and mechanisms, details must be further elaborated through adoption of an extensive set of decisions (the "Paris Rulebook") for these to be fully operational. The APA is to develop such rules and guidelines for the effective implementation of the *Paris Agreement* once it enters into force.[22]

In July, New Zealand submitted its Initial Report,[23] although it is not a mandatory reporting requirement for New Zealand (New Zealand did not make a

---

19   *Submission under the Paris Agreement: New Zealand's Nationally Determined Contribution* (2016) <http://www4.unfccc.int/ndcregistry/PublishedDocuments/New%20Zealand%20 First/New%20Zealand%20first%20NDC.pdf>.

20   Marcia Rocha and others, *New Zealand deploys creative accounting to allow emissions to rise: Climate Action Tracker Policy Brief* (July 2015) 2.

21   "New Zealand deploys creative accounting to allow emissions to rise" *Climate Action Tracker* (12 July 2015) <http://climateactiontracker.org/publications/briefing/214/New -Zealand-deploys-creative-accounting-to-allow-emissions-to-rise-.html> quoting Bill Hare, CEO and Senior Scientist at Climate Analytics.

22   Ministry of Foreign Affairs and Trade, *Annual Report 2015–16* (19 October 2016) 26 <https://www.mfat.govt.nz/assets/MFAT-Corporate-publications/MFAT-Annual-Report -2015-2016.pdf>.

23   Ministry for the Environment, *New Zealand's Report to facilitate the calculation of its emissions budget for the period 2013 to 2020* (2016).

commitment under the *Kyoto Protocol*[24] for the period 2013 to 2020, choosing instead to make its target under the UNFCCC). The Initial Report describes how New Zealand will account for its 2020 target and presents its calculations relating to its emission budget for the period 2013 to 2020. New Zealand also submitted its *Greenhouse Gas Inventory 1990–2014* ("GHG Inventory") which fulfils reporting requirements under the UNFCCC and *Kyoto Protocol*. The content of the GHG Inventory is discussed further below in the national developments section.

In November, New Zealand participated in COP-22 to the UNFCCC, MOP-12 to the *Kyoto Protocol*, and the first session of the COP serving as the MOP to the *Paris Agreement* ("CMA-1") in Marrakech, Morocco. One of the major outcomes of the climate conference was the Marrakech Action Proclamation which, inter alia, calls for the highest political commitment to combat climate change as a matter of urgent priority and calls for urgently raising ambitions and strengthening cooperation to close the gap between current emissions trajectories and the pathway needed to meet the long-term temperature goals of the *Paris Agreement*. It states that the extraordinary momentum on climate change worldwide is irreversible.[25] CMA-1 was extended beyond Marrakech because no decisions were yet ready for adoption. It was resolved that the "Paris Rulebook" decisions, needed to fully implement the *Paris Agreement,* are to be ready when CMA 1 resumes at COP 24 in 2018. More details and other outcomes and decisions of the conference can be found on the UNFCCC website.[26]

Also in 2016, New Zealand lodged its Aviation Emissions Reduction Action Plan with ICAO at its annual summit in September. Transport accounts for around 17 per cent of New Zealand's emissions. The plan outlines current and planned measures to address aviation emissions and covers four key parties – government, air traffic control, airports and airlines. The Minister for Transport has stated that, while international aviation is not included in the *Paris Agreement*, New Zealand intends to voluntarily join a global measure under

---

24 *Kyoto Protocol to the United Nations Framework Convention on Climate Change*, opened for signature 16 March 1998, 2303 UNTS 162 (entered into force 16 February 2005).

25 *Marrakech Action Proclamation For Our Climate And Sustainable Development* (2016) <http://unfccc.int/files/meetings/marrakech_nov_2016/application/pdf/marrakech_action_proclamation.pdf>.

26 A list of decisions from the meeting is available at <http://unfccc.int/meetings/marrakech_nov_2016/meeting/9567/php/view/decisions.php#c>.

development by the ICAO and participate from Phase I, which commences in 2021, provided other developed countries and the majority of major aviation states also agree to do so.[27]

New Zealand participated in the *Montreal Protocol*[28] MOP-28 held in October in Kigali, Rwanda, and welcomed the adoption of the *Kigali Amendment to the Montreal Protocol* to cut the production and consumption of hydrofluorocarbons ("HFCS"). HFCS have often been used as a substitute to CFCS (which were phased out earlier). Although better for the ozone than CFCS, HFCS are potent GHGs. The amendment adds HFCS to the list of substances controlled under the *Montreal Protocol* to be phased out. Countries will need to phase down HFCS within varying timeframes. New Zealand's Minister for the Environment has stated that "[f]or New Zealand, this will mean an 85 per cent phase down of HFCS by 2036, once the amendment is ratified. The first step of the phase down will happen in 2019, with a reduction of 10 per cent compared to 2011–2013 levels."[29] In New Zealand, HFCS are commonly used in refrigeration and air-conditioning and other smaller uses such as aerosols.[30] The *Kigali Amendment* will enter into force on 1 January 2019, provided that it is ratified by at least 20 parties to the *Montreal Protocol*.

2.3   *The Pacific*

New Zealand and the European Union work together to support renewable energy initiatives in the Pacific. In June, they led a joint mission to the Pacific.[31] New Zealand and the European Union also co-hosted the Pacific Energy Conference in Auckland in 2016, where donors committed over $1 billion for sustainable energy projects in the Pacific. New Zealand agreed to provide a

---

27   Simon Bridges, "Govt releases plan to tackle aviation emissions" (Press Release, 29 September 2016) <https://www.beehive.govt.nz/release/govt-releases-plan-tackle-aviation-emissions>.

28   *Montreal Protocol on Substances that Deplete the Ozone Layer,* opened for signature 16 September 1987, 1522 UNTS 3 (entered into force 1 January 1989).

29   Nick Smith, "Major agreement reached to phase down greenhouse gases" (Press Release, 16 October 2016) <https://www.beehive.govt.nz/release/major-agreement-reached-phase-down-greenhouse-gases>.

30   Ministry of Foreign Affairs, "Amendment to the Montreal Protocol on Substances that Deplete the Ozone Layer, Kigali 15 October 2016" *New Zealand Treaties Online* <http://www.treaties.mfat.govt.nz/search/details/p/213/780>.

31   Murray McCully, "Joint NZ EU development mission to the Pacific" (Press Release, 31 May 2016) <https://www.beehive.govt.nz/release/joint-nz-eu-development-mission-pacific>.

further $100 million to energy projects in nine Pacific countries, bringing its total contribution to $220 million.[32]

New Zealand attended the 47th Pacific Islands Forum in September 2016 in Pohnpei, the Federated States of Micronesia. In the *Forum Communiqué* leaders welcomed the *Paris Agreement* and reinforced that achieving the goal of limiting global temperature increase to 1.5°C above pre-industrialised levels is an existential matter for many Forum Members which must be addressed with urgency.[33] Leaders endorsed voluntary guidelines; the *Framework for Resilient Development in the Pacific: An Integrated Approach to Address Climate Change and Disaster Risk Management* ("FRDP")[34] and agreed for it to be fully elaborated and operationalised upon the entry into force of the *Paris Agreement* to support coordination and action on a number of key issues related to climate change and disaster risk management.[35] The Forum also produced, among other things, the *Pohnpei Statement: Strengthening Pacific Resilience to Climate Change and Disaster Risk*[36] to complement the FRDP and tasked the Forum Secretariat to convene a Working Group to elaborate on a Pacific Resilience Partnership process by December 2016 to implement the FRDP. Leaders also endorsed the *Pohnpei Oceans Statement: A Course to Sustainability*,[37] which, inter alia, calls for early action by all countries to ratify and implement the *Paris Agreement* and provide adequate and simplified access to finance for adaptation and mitigation by Pacific Small Islands Developing States to address the impacts of sea level rise and climate change. New Zealand announced at the Forum that it would be investing $5 million in renewable energy projects in Micronesia to enable the development of up to 400kW of solar generated power.[38]

---

32   Murray McCully, "$1 billion for Pacific energy projects" (Press Release, 7 June 2016) <https://www.beehive.govt.nz/release/1-billion-pacific-energy-projects>.

33   *Forum Communiqué*, PIFS(16) [14] <http://www.forumsec.org/resources/uploads/embeds/file/2016_Forum_Communique_11sept.pdf>.

34   *Framework for Resilient Development in the Pacific: An Integrated Approach to Address Climate Change and Disaster Risk Management (FRDP) 2017–2030* (11 September 2016) <http://www.forumsec.org/resources/uploads/embeds/file/Annex%201%20-%20Framework%20for%20Resilient%20Development%20in%20the%20Pacific.pdf>.

35   *Forum Communiqué*, above n 33, [15].

36   *Pohnpei Statement: Strengthening Pacific Resilience to Climate Change and Disaster Risk* (2016)   <http://www.fsmpio.fm/announcements/forum/Annex2_Strengthening_Pacific_Resilience_to_Climate_Change_and_Disaster_Risk.pdf>.

37   *Pohnpei Oceans Statement: A Course to Sustainability* (2016) <http://www.fsmpio.fm/announcements/forum/Annex3%20_A_Course_to_Sustainability.pdf>.

38   John Key, "NZ support for renewable energy in Micronesia" (Press Release, 10 September 2016) <https://www.beehive.govt.nz/release/nz-support-renewable-energy-micronesia>.

2.4   *Free Trade Agreements*

On 4 February 2016, the *TPP* between New Zealand, the United States, Australia, Canada, Brunei, Chile, Japan, Malaysia, Mexico, Peru, Singapore and Vietnam was signed in Auckland, New Zealand amidst street protests,[39] following the release of a legally verified text on 26 January 2016. The *TPP* is the largest regional trade agreement in history, covering one-third of all world trade. Some have argued it may actually be "the private interests of foreign investors that take centre stage".[40] Whilst proponents have argued that *TPP* will benefit New Zealand's environment,[41] others have suggested that "[t]he environment is a significant casualty" under the *TPP*.[42] See last year's report for more about the *TPP* and the environment.[43] In late 2016, the United States presidential election and the incoming administration with its stated anti-*TPP* position put the future of the agreement into some doubt, although New Zealand has indicated they remain interested in the *TPP* without the United States.[44]

3   National Developments

3.1   *Trade*

As noted above, the controversial *TPP* was signed in 2016. Nationally, the text of the agreement and its National Interest Analysis ("NIA")[45] were submitted for parliamentary treaty examination in early February, and were referred to the

---

39   Cherie Howie, "TPP protesters shut down central Auckland as ministers sign controversial deal" *New Zealand Herald* (4 February 2016) <http://www.nzherald.co.nz/business/news/article.cfm?c_id=3&objectid=11584458>.

40   Simon Terry, "Expert Paper #4: The Environment under TPPA Governance" (January 2016) 4 <https://tpplegal.files.wordpress.com/2015/12/tpp-environment.pdf>. This comprises part of a series of expert papers on the *TPP* available at <https://tpplegal.wordpress.com/>.

41   Nick Smith and Todd McClay, "TPP good for environment and trade" (Press Release, 6 April 2016) <https://www.beehive.govt.nz/release/tpp-good-environment-and-trade>.

42   Terry, above n 40, 5–6.

43   Josephine Toop, "International Environmental Law" (2015) 13 *New Zealand Yearbook of International Law* 250–266, 255–257.

44   Patrick O'Meara, "NZ still keen for TPP without US, Key tells APEC" (22 November 2016) <http://www.radionz.co.nz/news/business/318478/nz-still-keen-for-tpp-without-us,-key-tells-apec>.

45   Ministry of Foreign Affairs and Trade, *Trans-Pacific Partnership National Interest Analysis* (25 January 2016) <https://www.parliament.nz/resource/en-NZ/00DBSCH_ITR_68247_1/f2c7141dd41442fb6c1fa1c32107f39b0a889e7d>.

Foreign Affairs, Defence and Trade Committee. The Committee sought public submissions in March and reported back at the beginning of May. The government majority of the Committee recommended that New Zealand complete its domestic processes within two years of the TPP being signed, and provide notification of this; i.e., complete the legislative changes needed to ratify the agreement within this period.[46] The opposition parties' (New Zealand Labour Party, Green Party of Aotearoa, and the New Zealand First Party) minority views indicated that they could not support the ratification of the TPP due to a range of issues, including sovereignty concerns, concerns about ISDS, poor process (both for the multilateral negotiation and for domestic consultation and examination processes), inadequate modelling (flaws in the NIA), omissions in modelling, problems with the substantive content, uncertain gains, and harm to the environment and sustainability concerns.[47] On 9 May, the Trans-Pacific Partnership Agreement Amendment Bill (133–3) was introduced to Parliament. On 12 May it passed its first reading and was referred to the Foreign Affairs, Defence and Trade Committee who sought submissions by 22 July. The Committee reported back in October, and the bill passed its second reading on 3 November. A series of supplementary order papers were introduced and the Bill passed its third reading on 15 November. The resulting *Trans-Pacific Partnership Agreement Amendment Act 2016* made changes to New Zealand legislation consistent with the TPP.

3.2   *Biodiversity*
In September, the *New Zealand Biodiversity Action Plan* was published.[48] It shows progress towards the five goals of the Strategic Plan of the *Convention on Biological Diversity* by 2020.[49] It contains national targets and outlines the contribution that New Zealand will make toward stemming global loss of biodiversity over the next four years. The plan outlines some initiatives undertaken to try to halt the decline of New Zealand native species such as the "War on Weeds", which aims to rid New Zealand of wilding conifers and 12

---

46   *International treaty examination of the Trans-Pacific Partnership Agreement: Report of the Foreign Affairs, Defence and Trade Committee* (2016) 3 <https://www.parliament.nz/resource/en-NZ/51DBSCH_SCR68965_1/017c7d1eedfaa46cda74da3faa83982cee1ab4d3>.

47   Ibid 11–20.

48   *New Zealand Biodiversity Action Plan: 2016–2020* (2016) <http://www.doc.govt.nz/Documents/conservation/new-zealand-biodiversity-action-plan-2016-2020.pdf>.

49   Department of Conservation, "New Zealand Biodiversity Strategy and Action Plan" <http://www.doc.govt.nz/nature/biodiversity/nz-biodiversity-strategy-and-action-plan/>.

other problem weeds,[50] and the "Battle for our Birds",[51] a New Zealand predator control operation involving aerial 1080 drops and self-resetting traps in response to heavy beech tree mast years where heavy tree seeding led to extra food for pests and an associated boom in rat and stoat populations.[52] The plan outlines interim 2025 goals, including increasing the areas where predators are suppressed, removing all mammalian predators from offshore island nature reserves, and developing scientific solutions to lead to the removal of at least one small mammal predator species from mainland New Zealand.[53] New Zealand's commitment to make the country predator free by 2050 aims to preserve native species threatened with extinction through predation by completely eradicating invasive rats, stoats and possums from New Zealand by 2050. In November, Predator Free 2050 Limited ("PF2050 Ltd") was established and nine directors appointed. It is expected to be a key player in achieving New Zealand's Predator Free 2050 ambition. The company is to be funded by central government, local government, business and philanthropists. The board will work on each regional project with iwi and community conservation groups and will work to attract $2 of private sector and local government funding for every $1 of government funding.[54] It will direct investment into regionally significant predator eradication projects and the science needed to find solutions to achieve predator-free status.[55] In 2016, the PCE also released a report on saving New Zealand's birds, containing some discussion about developing a plan for "Predator Free 2050". The PCE recommended preparation of a portfolio of areas for sustained predator control, research about optimising the effectiveness of 1080 drops, habitat restoration, early engagement with the public over research into breakthrough genetic techniques, open discussion about genetic diversity in bird populations, the need to tackle feral cats, and

---

50   For more on the "war on weeds", see, Department of Conservation, "The Dirty Dozen" <http://www.doc.govt.nz/nature/pests-and-threats/war-on-weeds/the-dirty-dozen/>.

51   For more on "battle for our birds", see, Department of Conservation, "Battle for our Birds" <http://www.doc.govt.nz/battleforourbirds>, and Department of Conservation, "Battle for our Birds pest control operations in 2016 and 2017" <http://www.doc.govt.nz/our-work/battle-for-our-birds/pest-control-operations-in-2016/>.

52   Maggie Barry, "Budget 2016: Battle for our Birds 2016" (Press Release, 7 May 2016) <https://www.beehive.govt.nz/release/budget-2016-battle-our-birds-2016>.

53   *Biodiversity Action Plan*, above n 48, 7.

54   Steven Joyce, Nathan Guy, Maggie Barry, "Predator Free NZ 2050 to be a massive team effort" (Press Release, 25 July) <https://www.beehive.govt.nz/release/predator-free-nz-2050-be-massive-team-effort>.

55   Maggie Barry, "Predator Free 2050 Ltd board appointed" (Press Release, 30 November 2016) <https://www.beehive.govt.nz/release/predator-free-2050-ltd-board-appointed>.

the need to support and coordinate conservation community groups.[56] A new research facility was opened at Lincoln University to research new methods of pest control in 2016 as well.[57]

As discussed in the international developments section above, in June 2016 the New Zealand government was once again under scrutiny by the IWC SC regarding the critically endangered Māui dolphin. The IWC SC report notes that "no new management actions had been enacted since 2013" and "concludes, as it has repeatedly in the past, that existing management measures in relation to bycatch mitigation fall short of what has been recommended previously."[58] Although fishing is the greatest threat to Māui dolphin, other potential threats include marine tourism, construction, coastal pollution, vessels, mining, oil spills, plastic bags, sedimentation, marine farming and climate change. 2016 saw a new potential threat to the Māui dolphin emerge in Oil and Gas Block Offer 2016. Block Offer 2016 involves 525,515 km^2 made up of one onshore release area in Taranaki basin and four offshore release areas in the Reinga-Northland Basin, Taranaki Basin, Pegasus Basin and Great South-Canterbury Basin.[59] Māui habitat is thought to include large areas of the Taranaki coastline. The Green Party of Aotearoa has stated that this "largest ever oil and gas block offer ... including 2,600 km^2 in the Maui's dolphin sanctuary, is a disaster for our environment."[60] Potential issues with oil and gas projects in Māui territory include that "[e]xpert scientists say that seismic surveys, which are part of petroleum exploration, can harm dolphins' hearing and may push them into unprotected areas where they are more exposed to fishing nets', and "exploratory drilling is the riskiest phase of oil production" and an oil spill could wipe out the last remaining Māui dolphins.[61]

---

56 Jan Wright, PCE, *Taonga of an island nation: Saving New Zealand's birds* (May 2017) <http://www.pce.parliament.nz/media/1695/taonga-of-an-island-nation-web-final-small.pdf> 7–8.

57 Maggie Barry, "New research facility in war against pests" (Press Release, 9 June 2016) <https://www.beehive.govt.nz/release/new-research-facility-war-against-pests>.

58 International Whaling Commission, Report of the Scientific Committee of the IWC (IWC/66/Rep01(2016), June 2016) 79.

59 New Zealand Petroleum and Minerals, "Block Offer 2016 announced" (21 March 2016) <https://www.nzpam.govt.nz/about/news/block-offer-2016-announced/>.

60 Gareth Hughes, "Biggest ever Block Offer a disaster for the environment" (Press Release, 21 March 2016) <https://www.greens.org.nz/news/press-release/biggest-ever-block-offer-disaster-environment>.

61 Russel Norman, "Govt opening up Maui's dolphin habitat for petroleum exploration" (Press Release, 17 June 2014) <https://www.greens.org.nz/news/govt-opening-maui%E2%80%99s-dolphin-habitat-petroleum-exploration>.

3.3   *Climate Change & Ozone*

3.3.1   Climate-related Reports

New Zealand's Greenhouse Gas Inventory 1990–2014 was released in May 2016, along with a Snapshot report.[62] The GHG Inventory and Snapshot report show total (gross) emissions; emissions from the energy, industrial processes and product use ("IPPU"), agriculture and waste sectors, but not including net removals from land use, land-use change and forestry ("LULUCF"). They also show net emissions; gross emissions together with emissions and removals from the LULUCF sector. New Zealand's gross emissions were 65.8 million tonnes of carbon dioxide equivalent (Mt CO_2-e) in 1990. By 2014, gross emissions were 81.1 Mt CO_2-e. This represents an increase of 23.2 per cent. Agriculture contributed 49 per cent of New Zealand's gross emissions in 2014 (39.6 Mt CO_2-e), an increase of 15 per cent on 1990 levels. The energy sector contributed 30 per cent of gross emissions (32.2 Mt CO_2-e), up 36 per cent on 1990 levels. The IPPU sector contributed 6 per cent (5.2 Mt CO_2-e), an increase of 45 per cent on 1990 levels. The waste sector contributed 5 per cent (4.1 Mt CO_2-e) of gross emissions, down 0.5 per cent on 1990 levels, due to improved landfill management practices, particularly methane recovery. In 1990, New Zealand's net emissions were 36.9 Mt CO_2-e. In 2014, they were 56.7 Mt CO_2-e. This is an increase of 53.6 per cent.

New Zealand's 2020 target is to reduce emissions to five per cent below 1990 levels by 2020. New Zealand's gross emissions from 2013 to 2020 are projected to be 655.9 Mt CO_2-e. New Zealand is projected to hold 748.5 million units at the end of the period. This consists of a carbon budget of 516.7 million units, 108.1 million units due to removals from forestry and land-use activities included in the *Kyoto Protocol*, and a surplus of 123.7 million units from the first commitment period (2008–12). New Zealand's net position, as at July 2016, is that New Zealand is projected to meet its 2020 target with a surplus of 85.7 million units.[63]

In June, a report entitled *Climate Change Projections for New Zealand* was published. The report addresses expected changes in New Zealand's temperature and climate to 2120, drawing on climate model simulations from

---

62   Ministry for the Environment, *New Zealand's Greenhouse Gas Inventory 1990–2014* (May 2016) <http://www.mfe.govt.nz/publications/climate-change/new-zealand-greenhouse-gas -inventory-1990-2014>; Ministry for the Environment, *Snapshot: New Zealand's Greenhouse Gas Inventory 1990–2014* (May 2016, INFO 758) <http://www.mfe.govt.nz/sites/ default/files/media/Climate%20Change/greenhouse-gas-inventory-snapshot-2016.pdf>.

63   Ministry for the Environment, "Latest update on New Zealand's net 2020 position" (July 2016); Snapshot, above n 62, 5.

the Intergovernmental Panel on Climate Change ("IPCC") Fifth Assessment Report.[64] A snapshot summary of the report is also available.[65] Some of the report's key points include that New Zealand will likely experience higher temperatures with an increase of 0.7°C to 1°C by 2040 and an increase of 0.7°C to 3°C by 2090 (depending on low or high emissions scenarios); a change in rainfall patterns; increased frequency of dry days, droughts and of heavy rainfall events for various parts of the country; and increases in storm intensity.

3.3.2 New Zealand Emissions Trading Scheme ("NZETS")

The NZETS was originally introduced by the (centre-left) Labour Party-led government in 2008 and was significantly amended in 2009 and 2012 by the (centre-right) National Party-led government to slow its implementation and make it more business-friendly. One such measure was a transitional "two for one" surrender obligation which allows some businesses to pay only one emissions unit for every two tonnes of emissions. This transitional measure was extended by three years beyond what was initially envisaged. In November 2015, the government began a review of the NZETS focusing on what would come next for the transitional measures, how the NZETS needs to evolve to meet future targets and operational and technical improvements. The Government decided not to include agriculture in the review,[66] meaning that the agricultural sector, which comprises roughly half of New Zealand's GHG emissions, remains outside the NZETS.

In the context of the NZETS review, the PCE made two submissions in February and April. In the first of these, she recommends that the two-for-one surrender obligation be phased out as soon as possible, and that a ceiling price for carbon be retained, but be complemented by a floor price, and a commitment made for both the ceiling and floor price to rise over time.[67] In her April submission, the PCE notes various aspects of climate change policy where action is

---

64   Ministry for the Environment, *Climate Change Projections for New Zealand Atmospheric projections based on simulations undertaken for the IPCC 5th Assessment* (2016) <http://www.mfe.govt.nz/sites/default/files/media/Climate%20Change/nz-climate-change-projections-final.pdf>.

65   Ministry for the Environment, *Snapshot: Climate Projections for New Zealand* (June 2016, INFO 765) <http://www.mfe.govt.nz/sites/default/files/media/Climate%20Change/climate-projections-snapshot.pdf>.

66   Tim Groser, "Government begins review of ETS" (Press Release, 24 November 2015) <https://www.beehive.govt.nz/release/government-begins-review-ets>.

67   Jan Wright, PCE, Submission to the Minister for Climate Change Issues, *Emissions Trading Scheme Review 2015/16: Priority Issues* (18 February 2016) 5 <http://www.pce.parliament.nz/media/1669/pce-submission-on-ets-review.pdf>.

required. She recommends quantitative analysis to be sure that actions aimed at reducing emissions do reduce emissions; conducting a scan of all aspects of New Zealand laws, regulations, and policies to identify barriers to reducing GHG emissions; developing principles and guidelines for assessing economic and financial risks associated with climate change for different sectors of the economy; establishing a schedule for phasing out free allocation; and restoring the integrity of the NZETS. In regard to the latter, she notes that the purchase of "hot air" carbon units from Russia and Ukraine and the laundering of ERUS used to meet 2012 *Kyoto Protocol* target into AAUs to be used to meet the 2020 target has damaged integrity. She suggests that if the government resolved not to carry over any units beyond 2020 and restricted future purchases of offshore carbon credits to those that represent real and verifiable emission reductions, this may go some way to restoring NZETS integrity. The PCE notes that "New Zealand is the only country with an ETS that has put no limit on the purchase of offshore carbon credits. Other countries have set limits on the proportion of units that can be purchased offshore – typically around 10%."[68] She accordingly recommends that a limit on the proportion of carbon credits that can be purchased offshore be set for after 2020.[69] Finally, in regard to the agricultural sector, the PCE notes that it will be very difficult to meet Paris targets if the agricultural sector does not begin to take some responsibility for methane and nitrous oxide.[70] The PCE subsequently released a report in October entitled *Climate change and agriculture: Understanding the biological greenhouse gases*. This report examines the issue of agricultural GHGs – methane and nitrous oxide – which together form about half of New Zealand's GHG emissions. The report aims to develop a common understanding of the basic science.[71]

In October, the government reported that it was halfway through its NZETS review.[72] Some action has already been taken. The *Climate Change Response (Removal of Transitional Measure) Amendment Act 2016* phases out the one for two transitional measure/subsidy over three years. The government has

---

68   Jan Wright, PCE, Submission to the Minister for Climate Change Issues, *Emissions Trading Scheme Review 2015/16: Other Matters* (28 April 2016) 9 <http://www.pce.parliament.nz/media/1658/ets-review-submission-other-mattersfinal3.pdf>.

69   Ibid 10.

70   Ibid 7.

71   Jan Wright, PCE, *Climate change and agriculture: Understanding the biological greenhouse gases* (October 2016) <http://www.pce.parliament.nz/media/1678/climate-change-and-agriculture-web.pdf>.

72   Paula Bennett, "ETS one-for-two subsidy to be phased out" (Press Release, 26 May 2016) <https://www.beehive.govt.nz/release/ets-one-two-subsidy-be-phased-out>.

indicated that the price ceiling, which caps units at $25, will remain.[73] The review is ongoing and ministerial advice on in-principle decisions for the NZETS is expected in mid-2017, with legislative changes to follow in 2018.[74]

Various minor 2016 amendments to the NZETS included prescribing allocative baselines for eligible industrial activities;[75] amending allocation of New Zealand units for the eligible industrial activity of manufacturing iron and steel from iron sand; adding two more products of that manufacturing that must be used as the basis of allocation;[76] clarifications as to definitions and how to calculate age of a tree and carbon stocks in the forestry sector;[77] updating the emissions factor for natural gas from six fields in the stationary energy and industrial processes sector;[78] and specifying the price of carbon for the 2017 levy year and prescribing the rates of levy for leviable motor vehicles and goods for the 2017 levy year in the synthetic greenhouse gas sector.[79]

3.3.3   Ozone

In 2016, the *Ozone Layer Protection Amendment Regulations 2016* revoked the HCFC wholesaler permit category and clarified that exemptions do not apply to HCFC imports from member states that are not party to or compliant with the *Montreal Protocol on Substances that Deplete the Ozone Layer* (the "*Montreal Protocol*"); and clarified that the importation of bulk recycled substances is conditionally prohibited and subject to exemption requirements.[80]

3.3.4   Renewable Energy

New Zealand aims to have 90 per cent of its electricity generated by renewables by 2025.[81] In 2016, several *New Zealand Energy Quarterly* editions were released to help track progress towards this goal.[82] In the September quarter (published

---

73   Ibid.

74   Ministry for the Environment, "NZ ETS Review 2015/16: Stage two submissions" (1 June 2017) <http://www.mfe.govt.nz/climate-change/reducing-greenhouse-gas-emissions/new -zealand-emissions-trading-scheme/reviews-nz-e-2>.

75   *Climate Change (Eligible Industrial Activities) Amendment Regulations 2016*.

76   *Climate Change (Eligible Industrial Activities) Amendment Regulations (No 2) 2016*.

77   *Climate Change (Forestry Sector) Amendment Regulations 2016*.

78   *Climate Change (Stationary Energy and Industrial Processes) Amendment Regulations 2016*.

79   *Climate Change (Synthetic Greenhouse Gas Levies) Amendment Regulations 2016*.

80   *Ozone Layer Protection Amendment Regulations 2016*.

81   Simon Bridges, "Significant rise in renewable electricity" (Press Release, 26 March 2015) <https://www.beehive.govt.nz/release/significant-rise-renewable-electricity>.

82   Ministry for Business, Innovation and Employment, *New Zealand Energy Quarterly* (2016) <http://www.mbie.govt.nz/info-services/sectors-industries/energy/energy-data -modelling/publications/new-zealand-energy-quarterly/previous-energy-quarterly -editions>.

December 2016), renewable energy was reported to have contributed 86.1 per cent of New Zealand's electricity generation in the 2015 calendar year.[83]

3.4   Environmental Reporting

The *Environmental Reporting Act 2015* came into effect in 2016. As a result, every six months a report must be produced on one of five environmental domains: air, freshwater, land, marine and climate, and a synthesis report providing an analysis of cross-domain trends and interactions must be published once every three years. The *Environmental Reporting (Topics for Environmental Reports) Regulations 2016* prescribed the topics for the synthesis and domain reports.

In June 2016, the PCE released her commentary[84] on the pilot report *Environment Aotearoa 2015*.[85] As regards the state of the New Zealand environment itself, the PCE notes, inter alia, that little of the ocean that New Zealand is responsible for is protected by reserves; air quality is generally good in most places most of the time; water quality has declined markedly in many places; temperatures are increasing; surface waters of the ocean are acidifying and the level of the sea is rising; erosion and pests are a significant problem and more is needed to win the war against predators because our native plants and animals are in serious trouble.[86] The PCE highlights the importance of basing reports in a bedrock of scientific understanding. She identifies several areas for improvement in future state of the environment reports, including that emerging issues should be incorporated in environmental reports and that the choice of issues should not be dictated by the availability and quality of indicators. She makes recommendations about the purpose of the reports, structure and selection of environmental indicators, and recommends inclusion of outlook

83   Ministry of Business, Innovation and Employment, *New Zealand Energy Quarterly: September quarter 2016* (22 December 2016) <http://www.mbie.govt.nz/info-services/sectors -industries/energy/energy-data-modelling/publications/new-zealand-energy-quarterly/ previous-energy-quarterly-editions/2016/september-quarter-2016>; Judith Collins, "Significant increase in renewables and second lowest carbon emissions from electricity on record" (Press Release, 22 December 2016) <https://www.beehive.govt.nz/release/sig nificant-increase-renewables-and-second-lowest-carbon-emissions-electricity-record>.

84   Jan Wright, PCE, *The state of New Zealand's environment: Commentary by the Parliamentary Commissioner for the Environment on Environment Aotearoa 2015* (June 2016) <http:// www.pce.parliament.nz/media/1666/the-state-of-new-zealand-s-environment.pdf>.

85   Ministry for the Environment, *Environment Aotearoa 2015* (October 2015) <http://www .mfe.govt.nz/publications/environmental-reporting/environment-aotearoa-2015>.

86   Jan Wright, *The state of New Zealand's environment*, above n 84, 31, 36, 37, 38 and 41.

sections and conclusions on the relative significance of different environmental issues to give perspective on their seriousness.[87]

In October, an individual domain report was produced; the first national report on the marine environment.[88] The report notes that New Zealand's oceans, coasts, and marine wildlife are under growing pressure and identifies three top areas of concern. These are that GHG emissions are causing ocean acidification and warming which may cause widespread harm to New Zealand's marine ecosystems; that most of New Zealand's native marine birds and many mammals are threatened with, or at risk of, extinction; and that New Zealand's coastal marine habitats and ecosystems are degraded, indeed of all marine environments, our coastal ecosystems are under the most pressure from human activities due to introduced marine pests, sediment and nutrients washed off the land, and seabed trawling and dredging.[89] In the context of the release of the report, the Secretary for the Environment has noted, among other things, that

> [n]inety percent of our native seabirds and shorebirds are threatened with or at risk of extinction. More than a quarter of our native marine mammals are threatened with extinction. Fishing bycatch, introduced predators, and habitat change are among a raft of reasons for the poor state of much marine wildlife.[90]

The next national report which deals with freshwater is due to be released in April 2017.

---

87   Ibid 12, 13, 14, 16, 20, 22, 24, 41–47.

88   New Zealand Ministry for the Environment and Statistics New Zealand, *New Zealand's Environmental Reporting Series: Our Marine Environment 2016* (October 2016) <http://www.mfe.govt.nz/sites/default/files/media/Environmental%20reporting/our-marine-environment.pdf>.

89   Ibid 7.

90   New Zealand Ministry for the Environment, "Changes to our oceans pose serious concerns" (Media Release, 27 October 2016) <http://www.mfe.govt.nz/sites/default/files/media/Marine%20environment%20media%20release_0.pdf>.

Law of the Sea and Fisheries

*Joanna Mossop**

1 Marine Environmental Protection

1.1 *Kermadec Oceans Sanctuary*

In September 2015, the Government announced plans to establish a 620,000 km² marine sanctuary around the Kermadec Islands to the north of New Zealand.[1] Under the proposal, no fisheries quota would be issued in respect of the Sanctuary, effectively creating a no-take zone. According to the Regulatory Impact Statement prepared by the Ministry for the Environment in February 2016, there is limited commercial fishing taking place in the Kermadec region, with the existing quota held by Te Ohu Kaimoana (Māori Fisheries Trust).[2] The Sanctuary also overlaps with a minerals prospecting permit issued to Nautilus Minerals in 2007. The Regulatory Impact Statement noted that limited consultation was undertaken before the Government announced its plans for the Sanctuary.

A Bill was introduced to Parliament to give effect to the Sanctuary on 8 March 2016.[3] A parliamentary select committee recommended the Bill be passed with some amendments in July. However, the nature of the sanctuary was challenged by Te Ohu Kaimoana, which argued that the decision to prohibit fishing in the Sanctuary violated rights protected under the Treaty of Waitangi and the 1992 Fisheries Deed of Settlement. Te Ohu Kaimoana also argued that the Crown had failed to consult adequately on the substance of the Sanctuary. Subsequent negotiations failed to resolve the disagreement.

1.2 *Marine Protected Areas*

In 2016, the Ministry for the Environment undertook consultations on new legislation to replace the existing *Marine Reserves Act 1971*. Under the *Marine Reserves Act*, marine reserves are required to be no-take areas. As a result,

---

* Victoria University of Wellington

1 See Joanna Mossop, "Law of the Sea and Fisheries" (2015) 13 *New Zealand Journal of International Law* 267.

2 Environmental Systems Directorate, *Regulatory Impact Statement: Establishment of a Kermadec Ocean Sanctuary* (25 February 2016) Ministry for the Environment <http://www.mfe.govt.nz/sites/default/files/media/Legislation/RIS/RIS-for-kermadec-ocean-sanctuary-bill_0_0.pdf>.

3 Kermadec Ocean Sanctuary Bill 2006 (120–2).

marine protected areas that fall outside that model have to be established by special legislation. According to the consultation document, the new legislation would provide for four different types of marine protected areas: marine reserves; species-specific sanctuaries; seabed reserves; and recreational fishing parks.[4] A key feature of the proposal is that it only applies to New Zealand's territorial sea and not the exclusive economic zone. In answering questions about this geographical limitation in the House of Representatives, the Minister for the Environment replied that the Kermadec Oceans Sanctuary would mean that 15 per cent of New Zealand's exclusive economic zone would be included in protected areas. No legislation was introduced in 2016.

2   Law of the Sea

2.1   *South China Sea Arbitration*

The Minister of Foreign Affairs and Trade, the Honourable Murray McCully, issued a statement on the release of the decision on the merits in the *South China Sea* arbitration.[5] Mr McCully called on all parties to respect the Arbitral Tribunal ruling.[6] He stated that "[w]hile New Zealand does not take a position on the various territorial claims in the South China Sea we have consistently stated that the differing interests in the region should be managed peacefully and in accordance with international law." Mr McCully said it was in all parties' interests to respect the UN Convention on the Law of the Sea, and urged all parties to resolve their issues in the South China Sea.

2.2   *International Labour Organisation Maritime Labour Convention*

New Zealand ratified the ILO Maritime Labour Convention in March 2016. The Convention was incorporated into New Zealand law through *Maritime Rules Part 52*, which are regulations promulgated under the *Maritime Transport Act 1994*. The provisions of the Convention will come into force in March 2017.

---

4   Ministry for the Environment, *A New Marine Protected Areas Act: Consultation Document* (January 2016) <http://www.mfe.govt.nz/publications/marine/new-marine-protected-areas -act-consultation-document>.

5   *South China Sea Arbitration (Philippines v China) (Award)* (Permanent Court of Arbitration, 12 July 2016).

6   Murray McCully, "NZ Comment on South China Sea Tribunal Ruling" (Press Release, 12 July 2016) <https://www.beehive.govt.nz/release/nz-comment-south-china-sea-tribunal-ruling>.

2.3   United Nations General Assembly

New Zealand was active in relation to the following initiatives under the General Assembly's purview:

- Two Preparatory Committee meetings were held in relation to the decision to investigate an international legally binding instrument on the conservation and sustainable use of marine biological diversity in areas beyond national jurisdiction.
- The General Assembly agreed to hold a Conference in 2017 to focus on the implementation of Sustainable Development Goal 14.[7]
- The annual General Assembly Resolution on sustainable fisheries was adopted on 7 December 2016.[8]
- The annual General Assembly Resolution on oceans and the law of the sea was adopted on 23 December 2016.[9]

3   Fisheries

Fisheries management and prosecutions of fisheries offences by the Ministry for Primary Industries ("MPI") received considerable attention in 2016. In May, an academic paper identified problems with the fisheries management system, arguing that fish were routinely dumped in New Zealand waters without being reported.[10] As a result, the authors argued, the actual catch was approximately 2.7 times the catch reported to the Food and Agriculture Organisation

---

7   *Modalities for the United Nations Conference to Support the Implementation of Sustainable Development Goal 14: Conserve and sustainably use the oceans, seas and marine resources for sustainable development*, GA Res 70/303, UN GAOR, 70th sess, 116th plen mtg, Agenda Items 20 and 79(a), UN Doc A/RES/70/303 (23 September 2016, adopted 9 September 2016).

8   *Sustainable fisheries, including through the 1995 Agreement for the Implementation of the Provisions of the United Nations Convention on the Law of the Sea of 10 December 1982 relating to the Conservation and Management of Straddling Fish Stocks and Highly Migratory Fish Stocks, and related instruments*, GA Res 71/123, UN GAOR, 71st sess, 55th plen mtg, Agenda Item 73(b), UN Doc A/RES/71/123 (13 February 2017, adopted 7 December 2016).

9   *Oceans and the Law of the Sea*, GA Res 71/257, UN GAOR, 71st sess, 68th plen mtg, Agenda Item 73(a), UN Doc A/RES/71/257 (20 February 2017, adopted 23 December 2016).

10   Glenn Simmons et al, "Reconstruction of Marine Fisheries Catches for New Zealand (1950–2010)" (Working Paper 2015-87, Institute for Oceans and Fisheries, 2016) <http://www.seaaroundus.org/doc/PageContent/OtherWPContent/Simmons+et+al+2016+-+NZ+Catch+Reconstruction+-+May+11.pdf>.

("FAO").[11] Also in May, two MPI internal reviews were made public that revealed that fishermen had been filmed dumping fish during a trial using cameras to monitor fishing activities.[12] At least one review was critical of previous decisions not to prosecute for the illegal discarding of fish.

As a result of the latter's publicity, the Government commissioned a review of the decisions not to prosecute in relation to three operations undertaken by MPI. This was conducted by Michael Heron QC and the report was released on 15 September 2016.[13] Heron remarked that, in general, the MPI prosecution process was robust and professional.[14] In relation to two of the operations, Heron concluded that the decisions made by MPI were understandable and appropriate. However, the third operation, Achilles, received some criticism.

Operation Achilles concerned the operation of fishing vessels upon which cameras had been placed in order to monitor the interactions between the vessels and protected species, including Hector's dolphins. The project was run by the Fisheries Management directorate of MPI and the cameras were installed with the consent of the fishing companies. Heron found that there was no written agreement in relation to the use of the footage and that there was a misunderstanding as to undertakings made in this context. The fishers had understood MPI would not prosecute on the basis of the video footage. An investigation found evidence of illegal discarding by five of the six boats carrying cameras. Although the investigation report recommended prosecution of the offences, no prosecutions occurred.

Mr Heron found that the decision not to prosecute was influenced by factors that were irrelevant, including potential reputational damage to MPI. However, he concluded that the decision could have been reached had relevant factors been considered. Heron also noted that the problem of illegal discards has been an issue for the quota management system since its inception. The report was accepted by MPI.

---

11   MPI has challenged the methodology and conclusions in the report. See, Ministry for Primary Industries, *The Health of New Zealand's Fisheries* (22 June 2017) <www.mpi.govt.nz/law-and-policy/legal-overviews/fisheries/the-health-of-new-zealands-fisheries/>.

12   Michael Morrah, "MPI Reports Reveal Widespread Illegal Dumping of Fish" *Newshub* (online) 18 May 2016 <http://www.newshub.co.nz/home/new-zealand/2016/05/exclusive-internal-mpi-reports-reveal-widespread-illegal-dumping-of-fish.html>.

13   Ministry for Primary Industries, *Independent review of prosecution decisions* (1 May 2017) <www.mpi.govt.nz/protection-and-response/environment-and-natural-resources/sustainable-fisheries/independent-review-of-prosecution-decisions/>.

14   Michael Heron, *Independent Review of MPI/Mfish Prosecution Decisions Operation Achilles, Hippocamp and Overdue* (15 September 2016) [4.1.12].

In a further development, the government undertook a consultation process called "The Future of Our Fisheries" on proposals to strengthen fisheries management in November and December 2016.[15] The proposals centred around a review of the fisheries management system, a proposed integrated electronic monitoring and reporting system, and a proposed law change to allow for new trawl technologies. Consultations on the proposals closed in December 2016.

3.1   *Fisheries Surveillance*

A Defence White Paper was released in June and a Capability Plan in November. New Zealand currently conducts naval and air patrols in the Southern Ocean and in the South Pacific for the detection of illegal fishing. The White Paper states that the Government's highest priority is for the defence force "to be able to undertake tasks in New Zealand and its Exclusive Economic Zone, Antarctica and the Southern Ocean."[16] The plan is to obtain a third ice-strengthened offshore patrol vessel that will be able to undertake patrols in the Southern Ocean and in the Pacific. Four inshore patrol vessels will be retired over time.

---

15   Ministry for Primary Industries, *Future of our Fisheries* <http://mpi.govt.nz/news-and
        -resources/consultations/future-of-our-fisheries>.
16   New Zealand Government, *Defence White Paper 2016* (2016) New Zealand Defence Force,
        [4.33]   <http://www.nzdf.mil.nz/downloads/pdf/public-docs/2016/defence-white-paper
        -2016.pdf>.

The Antarctic Treaty System

Alan D. Hemmings[*]

1 Introduction

The key Antarctic Treaty System ("ATS")[1] events of 2016 were, again, its two annual diplomatic meetings: the Antarctic Treaty Consultative Meeting ("ATCM")
and the Meeting of the Commission for the Conservation of Antarctic Marine Living Resources ("Commission"). These diplomatic meetings include
the main sessions of the advisory bodies, the Committee for Environmental
Protection ("CEP") and the Scientific Committee for the Conservation of Antarctic Marine Living Resources ("SC-CAMLR"), established under the relevant
international instruments.[2] The ATCM received reports (generally as Working
Papers – "WPS") from a number of intersessional contact groups operating
through electronic means between the 38th and 39th ATCMs. No Meeting of
Experts was held between these ATCMs. In relation to the Commission, and
following normal practice, three intersessional meetings of Working Groups of
SC-CAMLR (Ecosystem Monitoring and Management; Statistics, Assessments
and Modelling; and Fish Stock Assessment), and a meeting of the Subgroup on
Acoustic Survey and Analysis Methods were held during 2016. New Zealand
was an active and significant participant across all the major issues before the
ATS institutions. In 2016, the most significant legal (and political) event across
the ATS (and for New Zealand as joint proponent with the United States) was
the achievement of consensus, finally, on the designation of the Ross Sea
Marine Protected Area, which has been a major New Zealand Antarctic policy objective since 2011, when both New Zealand and the United States first
tabled papers on MPAs to SC-CAMLR.[3] Whilst not adopted as a legally binding

---

[*] Gateway Antarctica, University of Canterbury

[1] "'Antarctic Treaty system' means the Antarctic Treaty, the measures in effect under that Treaty, its associated separate international instruments in force and the measures in effect under
those instruments": *Protocol on Environmental Protection to the Antarctic Treaty,* opened for
signature 4 October 1991, 30 ILM 1455 (entered into force 14 January 1998) ("*Madrid Protocol*")
art 1.

[2] *Madrid Protocol*, arts 11 and 12; *Convention for the Conservation of Antarctic Marine Living
Resources,* opened for signature 5 May 1980, 1329 UNTS 48 (entered into force 7 April 1982)
("*CCAMLR*") arts XIV and XV, respectively.

[3] See generally, Alan D. Hemmings, "Year in Review: The Antarctic Treaty System" (2011) 9 *New
Zealand Yearbook of International Law* 339.

Measure,[4] the ATCM's reiteration of Parties' commitment, 25 years on from its adoption, to the *Madrid Protocol's* art 7 prohibition of mineral resource activities was politically significant.

2   1959 Antarctic Treaty[5]

The 39th ATCM[6] was convened in Santiago, Chile, from 23 May – 1 June 2016.[7] This was the second ATCM to be held in Chile. It hosted the 4th ATCM in 1966, and two Special Antarctic Treaty Meetings ("SATCM") in Viña del Mar in 1990 – a short 10th SATCM to consider applications for Consultative Party status and the three-week 11th SATCM that began the negotiations and set the substantive shape for what become the *Madrid Protocol.* ATCMs are rotated around the Consultative Parties, in a rough alphabetical sequence (in English).

For the seventh successive year, all nine of the legally-binding Measures adopted related to Protected Areas or Historic Sites and Monuments.[8] Three of the Measures related to areas of particular research interest to New Zealand (and to areas in the Ross Sea region that New Zealand claims as the Ross Dependency). Two of these (*Measure 1 (2016): Antarctic Specially Protected Area No 116 (New College Valley, Caughley Beach, Cape Bird, Ross Island): Revised Management Plan*; and *Measure 6 (2016): Antarctic Specially Protected Area No 131 (Canada Glacier, Lake Fryxell, Taylor Valley, Victoria Land): Revised Management Plan*) arise directly from Working Papers, with attached Draft Revised Management Plans, tabled by New Zealand.[9] The third (*Measure 3*

---

4   On Measures, Decisions and Resolutions generally, see Decision 1 (1995) <http://www.ats.aq/documents/keydocs/vol_2/vol2_3_Rules_of_Procedure_and_Admin_Decision1_e.pdf>.

5   *Antarctic Treaty,* opened for signature 1 December 1959, 402 UNTS 71 (entered into force 23 June 1961).

6   ATCMs address the full range of obligations under both the Antarctic Treaty and the Madrid Protocol, and the presently more limited reporting obligations under the *Convention on the Conservation of Antarctic Seals* (opened for signature 1 June 1972, entered into force 11 March 1978).

7   Antarctic Treaty Secretariat, *Final Report of the Thirty-ninth Antarctic Treaty Consultative Meeting* (Santiago, 2016).

8   Fewer than in recent years. For a comparison (1998–2015) see, Table 1, Alan D. Hemmings, "Year in Review: The Antarctic Treaty System" (2015) 13 *New Zealand Yearbook of International Law* 274.

9   New Zealand, "Revision of the Management Plan for Antarctic Specially Protected Area (ASPA) No 116: New College Valley, Caughley Beach, Cape Bird, Ross Island" (Working Paper

(*2016*): *Antarctic Specially Protected Area No 122* (*Arrival Heights, Hut Point Peninsula, Ross Island*): *Revised Management Plan*) arises directly from a WP, with attached Draft Revised Management Plan, tabled by the United States.[10]

Six administrative Decisions (D) were adopted: (D1) *Observers to the Committee for Environmental Protection*; (D2) *Revised Rules of Procedure for the Antarctic Treaty Consultative Meeting*; (D3) *Secretariat Report, Programme and Budget*; (D4) *Procedure for Selection and Appointment of the Executive Secretary of the Secretariat of the Antarctic Treaty*; (D5) *Exchange of Information*; and (D6) *Multi-Year Strategic Work Plan for the Antarctic Treaty Consultative Meeting*.

Six hortatory Resolutions (R) were adopted: (R1) *Revised Guidelines for Environmental Impact Assessment in Antarctica*; (R2) *Site Guidelines for Visitors*; (R3) *Code of Conduct for Activity within Terrestrial Geothermal Environments in Antarctica* (to which was annexed a *Code of Conduct* produced by the Scientific Committee for Antarctic Research ("SCAR")); (R4) *Non-native Species Manual*; (R5) *Revised Guide to the Presentation of Working Papers Containing Proposals for Antarctic Specially Protected Areas, Antarctic Specially Managed Areas or Historic Sites and Monuments*; and (R6) *Guide to the Presentation of Working Papers Containing Proposals for Antarctic Specially Protected Areas, Antarctic Specially Managed Areas or Historic Sites and Monuments*.

The ATCM again conducted its work through four forums: the Committee for Environmental Protection and three Working Groups. However, the Working Groups differed from those of recent years: Working Group 1 on Policy, Legal and Institutional Issues (previously "Legal and Institutional Affairs"); Working Group 2 on Operations, Science and Tourism (combining the previously separate "Tourism and Non-governmental Activities" and "Operational Matters" Working Groups);[11] and a special Group 3 on the 25th Anniversary of the *Protocol on Environmental Protection*, which saw a number of presentations by delegations (including Jillian Demptser, Head of the New Zealand Delegation) and former Prime Ministers of Australia (Bob Hawke) and France

---

No 26, 2016); New Zealand, "Revision of the Management Plan for Antarctic Specially Protected Area (ASPA) No 131: Canada Glacier, Lake Fryxell, Taylor Valley, Victoria Land" (Working Paper No 27, 2016).

10   United States, "Revised Management Plan for Antarctic Specially Protected Area No. 122 – Arrival Heights, Hut Point Peninsula, Ross Island" (Working Paper No 3, 2016).

11   Chaired by the head of the Argentine delegation and the Director of the British Antarctic Survey from the UK delegation – novel in both its joint chairing and combination of Argentine and UK officials.

(Michel Rocard).[12] Jillian Dempster's presentation identified "three key areas to attend to:

1. Wise management of the natural Antarctic environment and human activities;
2. Further developing an enduring and resilient Antarctic Treaty System; and,
3. The full realisation of the Treaty System's global responsibilities."[13]

A major outstanding item of the *Madrid Protocol*, still to be brought into force, now 25 years after the *Protocol* itself was adopted, is its *Annex VI, Liability Arising from Environmental Emergencies*, adopted as Measure 1 in 2005.[14] The United States, as Depository Government, advised that it had received notification of only 12 of the necessary 28 Consultative Parties approvals necessary for the *Annex* to enter into force.[15]

New Zealand tabled far fewer papers at the ATCM in 2016 than in recent years,[16] with just eight, comprising seven Working Papers (WP) and one Information Paper (IP). The sole IP was tabled by New Zealand alone.[17]

The two WPs concerned with revision of Antarctic Specially Protected Area Management Plans, already referred to,[18] were tabled by New Zealand alone. One WP was tabled by New Zealand and India;[19] one by Australia, New Zealand, Norway and the United States;[20] one by Norway, France, Netherlands,

---

12   "Presentations at the Special Working Group on the 25th Anniversary of the Protocol on Environmental Protection" in Antarctic Treaty Secretariat, *Final Report of the Thirty-ninth Antarctic Treaty Consultative Meeting* (Santiago, 2016) 219–255.

13   Ibid 252.

14   See, Alan D. Hemmings, "Year in Review: The Antarctic Treaty System" (2015) 13 *New Zealand Yearbook of International Law* 276–278.

15   Antarctic Treaty Secretariat, *Final Report of the Thirty-ninth Antarctic Treaty Consultative Meeting* (Santiago, 2016) [128].

16   See, Hemmings, "Year in Review: The Antarctic Treaty System" (2015), above n 14, 275.

17   New Zealand, "A tool to support regional scale environmental management" (Information Paper No 53, 2016).

18   Note 9.

19   New Zealand and India, "Report of the Intersessional Contact Group 'Developing a Strategic Approach to Environmentally Managed Tourism and non-Governmental Activities'" (Working Paper No 28, 2016).

20   Australia, New Zealand, Norway and United States, "A methodology to assess the sensitivity of sites used by visitors: prioritising future management attention" (Working Paper No 16, 2016).

New Zealand and the United Kingdom;[21] one by Australia, Japan, New Zealand, Norway, SCAR, Spain and the United States;[22] and one involving 21 Consultative Parties (the largest number of Parties ever to have been involved in tabling a paper at an ATCM) – United States, Argentina, Australia, Belgium, Chile, Czech Republic, Finland, France, Germany, Italy, Japan, Republic of Korea, Netherlands, New Zealand, Norway, Poland, South Africa, Spain, Sweden, United Kingdom and Uruguay.[23] This last WP (WP 38) argued for a recommitment, at the 25th anniversary of the adoption of the *Madrid Protocol*, to its critical art 7 – Prohibition of Mineral Resource Activities – which reads in full: "Any activity relating to mineral resources, other than scientific research, shall be prohibited".

Working Paper 38 led to the ATCM's adoption by consensus of Resolution 6 (2016) "Confirming ongoing commitment to the prohibition on Antarctic mineral resource activities, other than for scientific research; support for the Antarctic Mining Ban" (below). Whilst as a Resolution it is not legally binding (as a Measure would be), it must be taken as – precisely because it could not have been adopted other than through the consensus of all current Antarctic Treaty Consultative Parties – a substantive statement of intent. Of course the very fact that the majority of Consultative Parties clearly felt that such a reiteration was necessary, or at least useful, may itself say something about the sorts of concerns that have swirled around in recent years about the supposed interests and intentions of some states in relation to future Antarctic mining.[24]

At adoption of the *Madrid Protocol* there were 26 Consultative Parties; there are now 29. Of the three additions, two (Bulgaria and Ukraine) were not, and one (Czech Republic) was amongst the tablers of WP 38. Surprisingly, six Consultative Parties involved in negotiation of the *Protocol* (Brazil, China, Ecuador, India, Peru and the Russian Federation) were *not* amongst the WP 38 tablers.

---

21   Norway, France, Netherlands, New Zealand and United Kingdom, "Communication mechanisms: National Competent Authorities" (Working Paper No 35, 2016).

22   Australia, Japan, New Zealand, Norway, SCAR, Spain and United States, "Antarctic Environments Portal" (Working Paper No 10, 2016).

23   United States, Argentina, Australia, Belgium, Chile, Czech Republic, Finland, France, Germany, Italy, Japan, Republic of Korea, Netherlands, New Zealand, Norway, Poland, South Africa, Spain, Sweden, United Kingdom and Uruguay, "Confirming Ongoing Commitment to the Prohibition of Mining Activity in Antarctica other than for Scientific Research. Antarctic Mining Ban" (Working Paper No 38, 2016).

24   In Western media, China and the Russian Federation, in particular, have periodically been identified as insincere in relation to the present minerals prohibition.

Does this speak to mere administrative failure or difficulties in engaging these states (since plainly their subsequent concurrence in the consensus necessary to adopt Resolution 6 indicates that they were in the final instance not opposed to the sentiment of the Resolution), or were some (or all) of them identified as potentially unreliable on the prohibition of minerals activity, and thus in a sense the object of the WP and the Resolution?

Resolution 6 (2016)

Confirming ongoing commitment to the prohibition on Antarctic mineral resource activities, other than for scientific research; support for the Antarctic Mining Ban

The Representatives,

Recognising that the Protocol on Environmental Protection to the Antarctic Treaty ("the Protocol"), which was signed twenty-five years ago, is an essential element of current efforts to protect the Antarctic environment;

Noting that Article 7 of the Protocol provides that in the Antarctic Treaty area any activity relating to mineral resources, other than scientific research, shall be prohibited;

Taking into account that outside the Antarctic Treaty system there are many in the public and media who incorrectly believe that the Protocol expires in 2048;

Recalling that in accordance with its Article 25, the Protocol does not expire in 2048;

Recalling that in paragraph 5 of the Washington Ministerial Declaration on the Fiftieth Anniversary of the Antarctic Treaty the Consultative Parties reaffirmed their commitment to Article 7 of the Protocol;

Recommend that their Governments:

1. acknowledge the benefits to the Antarctic environment and dependent and associated ecosystems that have resulted from the prohibition on activities relating to mineral resources, other than scientific research, under Article 7 of the Protocol;

2. reaffirm their commitment to Article 7 of the Protocol; and

3. declare their firm commitment to retain and continue to implement this provision as a matter of highest priority to achieve the comprehensive protection of the Antarctic environment and dependent and associated ecosystems.

3   1980 Convention on the Conservation of Antarctic Marine Living
         Resources ("CCAMLR")

The regular 2016 (35th) Meeting of the Commission for the Conservation of
Antarctic Marine Living Resources ("Commission") was held at the CCAMLR
Secretariat in Hobart, Tasmania, Australia from 17–28 October 2016.[25]

   The Ministry of Foreign Affairs and Trade describes New Zealand as having
"a particular interest in the exploratory toothfish fisheries in the Ross Sea",[26]
and this is also the primary area of fisheries activity by New Zealand operators. The Ross Sea is divided between CCAMLR Statistical Subareas 88.1 and
88.2.[27] For the 2016/17 season, New Zealand vessel activity was, again, confined
to these two subareas. In Subarea 88.1 the precautionary catch limit ("PCL")
for the 2016/17 season was set at 2,870 tonnes (identical to the previous season albeit spread across 18 vessels compared to the 16 of the previous season)
across a maximum of three New Zealand, one Australian, one Japanese, four
South Korean, three Russian, one Spanish, three Ukrainian and one United
Kingdom flagged vessels.[28] For Subarea 88.2, an identical PCL was set to that
for the previous two seasons (619 tonnes, spread across 16 vessels compared to
15 for the previous season) across a maximum of three New Zealand, one Australian, three South Korean, one Norwegian, three Russian, three Ukrainian,
one United Kingdom and one Uruguayan flagged vessels.[29] As usual, decisions
in relation to both subarea catch limits across the CCAMLR area and various
generic obligations were codified as *Conservation Measures*.[30]

   New Zealand tabled four papers in the Commission and, unusually, none in
the Scientific Committee. These papers comprised the final (and as it proved,
successful) New Zealand and United States joint proposal for the Ross Sea
Marine Protected Area;[31] two papers on CCAMLR Inspections – one jointly

---

25   CCAMLR Secretariat, *Report of the Thirty-fifth Meeting of the Commission*, CCAMLR-XXXV
      (Hobart, 2016).
26   Ministry of Foreign Affairs and Trade, *The Antarctic Treaty System* <https://www.mfat
      .govt.nz/en/environment/antarctica/the-antarctic-treaty-system>.
27   CCAMLR Secretariat, *Convention Area* <https://www.ccamlr.org/en/organisation/
      convention-area>.
28   *CCAMLR Conservation Measure 41-09 (2016): Limits on the exploratory fishery for Dissosti-
      chus mawsoni in Statistical Subarea 88.1 in the 2016/17 season.*
29   *CCAMLR Conservation Measure 41-10 (2016): Limits on the exploratory fishery for Dissosti-
      chus mawsoni in Statistical Subarea 88.2 in the 2016/17 season.*
30   CCAMLR Secretariat, *Schedule of Conservation Measures in Force 2016/17* (Hobart, 2016).
31   New Zealand and United States, "A proposal for the establishment of a Ross Sea Region
      marine protected area", CCAMLR-XXXV/25 Rev 1.

with the United Kingdom and Australia undertaken from the Royal Navy's HMS *Protector*,[32] and the other a solely New Zealand inspection undertaken from the Royal New Zealand Navy's HMNZ *Otago*.[33] The fourth paper concerned seabird mortality mitigation measures.[34]

The most substantive, and certainly the highest profile, outcome of the 35th Meeting of the Commission was that, after further discussion in Hobart, consensus was reached on the designation of the Ross Sea region Marine Protected Area.[35] The MPA was adopted by the Commission through a 17-page Conservation Measure ("CM") including three annexes detailing: (a) Boundaries and zones within the MPA; (b) Management Plan; and (c) Priorities for scientific research and monitoring.[36] The MPA, which will commence on 1 December 2017, is designated for 35 years. The area is divided into three zones: a "General Protection Zone", a "Special Research Zone", and a "Krill Research Zone". Fishing activities are prohibited within the MPA, except as authorised under three paragraphs of the CM, which allow continued toothfish (*Dissostichus* spp.) fishing within the Special Research Zone and krill (*Euphausia superba*) fishing within the Krill Research Zone and Special Research Zone. As can be seen from the map of the MPA, found in Annex 1 of the CM (reproduced below), these two research zones comprise substantial parts of the total MPA area. In order to reach consensus on its designation, concessions had to be made by the proponents in relation to the duration of the designation, the area covered, and marine harvesting (fishing) activities.

Many observers (including the present author, who suggested "little prospect" of any MPA being designated in the "near future")[37] had not believed that it would be possible to reach consensus on this MPA at the 35th meeting of the Commission. Only on the eve of the meeting did more positive

---

32 United Kingdom, Australia and New Zealand, "Policy issues arising from CCAMLR inspections undertaken from HMS *Protector* during 2015/16", CCAMLR-XXXV/02.

33 New Zealand, "CCAMLR inspections undertaken by New Zealand from HMNZS Otago during 2015/16" CCAMLR-XXXV/BG/36.

34 New Zealand, "CCAMLR seabird mortality mitigation measures with a particular reference to offal and discard discharging in high latitude fisheries", CCAMLR-XXXV/BG/19.

35 CCAMLR Secretariat, *Report of the Thirty-fifth Meeting of the Commission*, CCAMLR-XXXV (Hobart, 2016) [8.37]–[8.73]. The "specific objectives" of the MPA are itemised at [8.48].

36 *CCAMLR Conservation Measure 91-05 (2016): Ross Sea region marine protected area.*

37 See, particularly, Hemmings, "Year in Review: The Antarctic Treaty System" (2015), above n 14, 280.

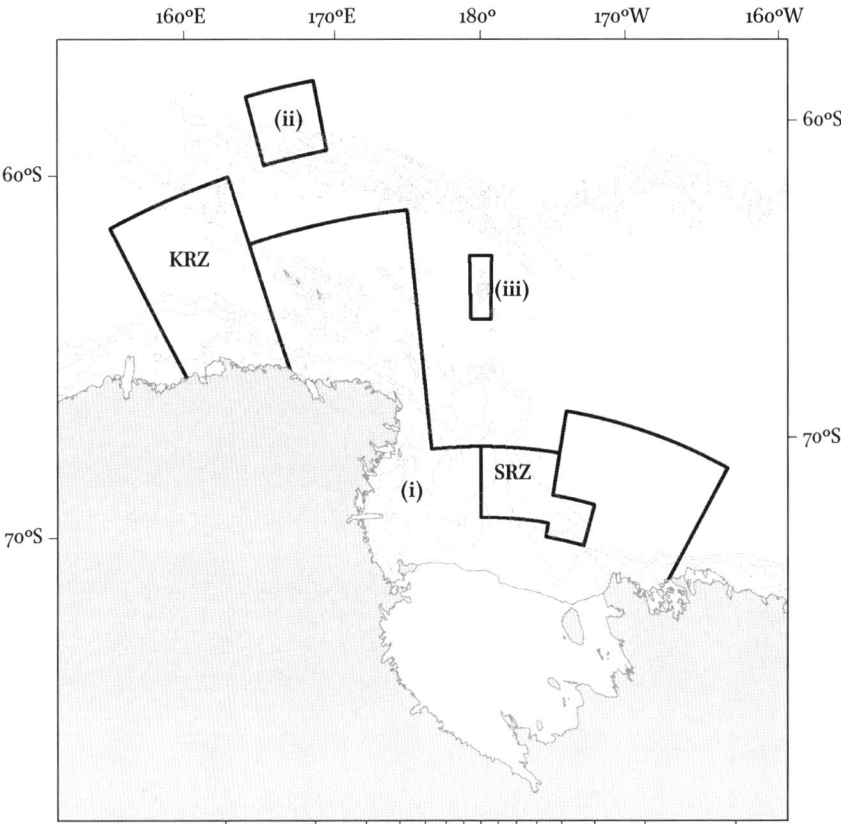

FIGURE 1   *The Ross Sea region marine protected area, including the boundaries of the*
          General Protection Zone, composed of areas (i), (ii), and (iii), the Special
          Research Zone (SRZ), and the Krill Research Zone (KRZ). Depth contours
          are at 500, 1 500 and 2 500 m.

assessments appear.[38] The fact that it was achieved was widely welcomed, with media releases from CCAMLR,[39] the New Zealand Minister of Foreign Affairs

---

38   See, e.g., Michael Slezak, *Antarctic marine reserves deal within reach as Russia thaws environmental stance* (17 October 2016) The Guardian <https://www.theguardian .com/world/2016/oct/17/antarctic-marine-reserves-deal-within-reach-as-russia-thaws -environmental-stance>.

39   Commission for the Conservation of Antarctic Marine Living Resources, *CCAMLR to create world's largest marine protected area* (28 October 2016) <https://www.ccamlr.org/ node/92518>.

and Trade,[40] the US Secretary of State,[41] and in hundreds of media reports worldwide,[42] including in New Zealand.[43]

The achievement of the second MPA in Antarctic waters, and what is now the largest MPA on the planet, is a major development. However, the MPA is not yet operational, and it will in any case be several years before it is possible to assess its effectiveness. For beyond the undoubted relief at its designation and pride in New Zealand and United States diplomatic, scientific and non-governmental communities (and elsewhere) in its achievement, and hopes for its success, it is finally effectiveness on-the-water that counts. Similarly, in relation to understanding the diplomatic negotiations that made agreement possible in Hobart in October 2016. But, in relation to the latter, perhaps significant factors included: high-level political engagement with the issue in the United States, New Zealand and Russia; rigorous official level engagement in capitals and on the margins of the UN in New York; the fact that the Russian Federation (and a very experienced Russian diplomat, Mr Vasily Titushkin) was the Chair of the CCAMLR Commission in 2016; and the broad support for an MPA designation after a number of years of impasse amongst other states on the Commission.

4 New Zealand Legislative Activity

No substantive legislative activity relating to Antarctica occurred during 2016. The *Antarctica (Environmental Protection: Liability Annex) Amendment Act 2012*[44] has not yet entered into force. Under s 2 (Commencement) of the Act, "[t]his Act comes into force on a date appointed by the Governor-General by

---

40   Murray McCully, *Agreement to protect Ross Sea reached* (28 October 2016) <https://www .beehive.govt.nz/release/agreement-protect-ross-sea-reached>.

41   John Kerry, *On the new marine protected area in Antarctica's Ross Sea* (27 October 2016) <https://2009-2017.state.gov/secretary/remarks/2016/10/263763.htm>.

42   See, e.g., Chelsea Harvey, *In historic agreement, nations create world's largest marine reserve in* Antarctica (27 October 2016) The Washington Post <https://www.washingtonpost .com/news/energy-environment/wp/2016/10/27/in-historic-agreement-nations-forge -the-worlds-largest-marine-reserve-in-antarctica/?utm_term=.eeb71b3fded4>.

43   Isaac Davison, *Major diplomatic coup for New Zealand as world's largest marine reserve finally gets the tick* (28 October 2016) New Zealand Herald <http://www.nzherald.co.nz/ world/news/article.cfm?c_id=2&objectid=11737669>.

44   See Alan D. Hemmings, "Year in Review: The Antarctic Treaty System" (2012) 10 *New Zealand Yearbook of International Law* 243.

Order in Council." The trigger for this will be the attainment of the threshold 28 approvals by states which were Consultative Parties at the time the *Annex* was adopted in 2005, which is necessary for the *Annex* to enter into force. The US ATCM report (above), which notes that only 12 of the requisite 28 approvals of the *Annex* have been notified, indicates entry into force is not close.

International Criminal Law and International Humanitarian Law

Treasa Dunworth[*]

1 Introduction

The most significant development in 2016, discussed in Part 2 below, was the coming to fruition of the humanitarian consequences of the nuclear weapons initiative – a project that New Zealand has been strongly committed to over the past several years.[1]

In contrast, there was a decided lack of progress in international criminal law. Seven years on from the Kampala Review Conference for the International-al Criminal Court, neither of the two amendments to the Statute agreed at that Conference have been ratified by New Zealand.[2] The first amendment, which extends the three war crimes relating to weapons (the use of poison or poisoned weapons (art 8(2)(b)(xvii)); the use of asphyxiating, poisonous or other gases (art 8(2)(b)(xviii)); and the use of expanding bullets (art 8(2)(b)(xix))) to non-international armed conflict, is entirely uncontentious for New Zealand, and is currently in force for 34 states. Despite that, there are no indi-cations that New Zealand is even close to ratification. The second amendment, defining the crime of aggression and putting in place modalities for the Court to operationalise its jurisdiction over the crime, raises more complex issues than its weapons counterpart. It, too, remains unratified by New Zealand and is discussed more fully in Part 3 below.

2 Nuclear Weapons and the Humanitarian Initiative

As 2015 came to an end, New Zealand joined the vote at the United Nations General Assembly to convene an open-ended working group ("OEWG") to "substantively address concrete effective legal measures, legal provisions and

---

[*] University of Auckland

[1] See Treasa Dunworth, "International Criminal Law and International Humanitarian Law" (2015) 13 *New Zealand Yearbook of International Law* 282, 282–284.

[2] See Treasa Dunworth, "International Criminal Law and International Humanitarian Law" (2014) 12 *New Zealand Yearbook of International Law* 240, 240–241.

norms that will need to be concluded to attain and maintain a world without nuclear weapons".[3]

The OEWG was to meet in Geneva in 2016 for up to 15 working days.[4] The resolution had been the culmination of efforts over several years to gain traction on nuclear disarmament using the lens of the humanitarian consequences of nuclear weapons (whether accidentally released or deliberately used) to bring pressure to bear on states to agree to seriously discuss nuclear disarmament.

The precise language of the authorisation from the Assembly was important: New Zealand, for example, had expressed concern that the 2016 meeting would not simply be a repeat of the work back in 2013, that there would be some tangible outcomes and that it would not be simply further discussion. As Ambassador Higgie expressed it in her statement to the General Assembly's First Committee:

> It is indeed the catastrophic consequences, and increasing risk, of a nuclear weapon detonation which remain the primary motivation for urgent progress on nuclear disarmament. It is New Zealand's hope that any body – such as an Open-Ended Working Group – to be established by this Committee will have a mandate which reflects the urgency of progress on nuclear disarmament and offers us the real prospect of this.[5]

The OEWG duly convened for sessions in February, May and August. New Zealand participated fully, including as a member of the New Agenda Coalition and on its own account. As with many other states, attention continued to be drawn to the humanitarian consequences of nuclear weapons. For example, in New Zealand's second statement, it focused on the long-term harmful effects of nuclear testing in the Pacific and concluded by reflecting that 'adoption of legally-effective measures to prohibit nuclear weapons would enshrine international humanitarian law and humanitarian values which we hold dear'.[6]

---

3   *Taking Forward Multilateral Nuclear Disarmament Negotiations*, GA Res 70/33, UN GAOR, 70th sess, 67th plen mtg, Agenda Item 97bb, UN Doc A/Res/70/33 (11 December 2015, adopted 7 December 2015) [2].

4   Ibid [5].

5   H.E. Dell Higgie, Ambassador for Disarmament, *UNGA70: New Zealand Statement to the First Committee* (13 October 2015) Ministry of Foreign Affairs and Trade <https://www.mfat .govt.nz/en/media-and-resources/ministry-statements-and-speeches/unga70-first -committee/> [5].

6   H.E. Dell Higgie, Ambassador for Disarmament, (*untitled*) *statement to the Open Ended Working Group* (*Panel II*) (23 February 2016) Reaching Critical Will.

As had been widely hoped, the OEWG completed its work by recommending in its Report that a United Nations conference be convened in 2017 to negotiate a legally binding instrument to prohibit nuclear weapons, leading to their total elimination.[7] The Report was adopted by a vote, rather than by consensus as had been expected, a matter that caused New Zealand some difficulty. As Ambassador Higgie explained:

> New Zealand has been participating in the negotiations on this final report on the basis of our shared understanding that we were all working together to reach agreement on the text – and that this text would be adopted by consensus in line with the stated intention of the Chair and of OEWG delegations. We wish, then, to express our surprise and regret that a vote has been called on the text and, in particular, without any prior notice and so late in our proceedings this afternoon. The New Zealand Delegation has urgently sought instructions from our Minister. However, we have been unable to secure instructions given the last minute nature of these developments and the lack of a finalised written text. As a result we have not been able to participate in either of the votes which have taken place just now.[8]

The reason for the sudden shift from consensus to the call for a vote lay with Australia. Unable to accept the text as it was evolving (even though it had been weakened in some respects in an attempt to accommodate its views), Australia called for a vote on the text. As a result, a vote took place (on a re-strengthened text) and in this way the Report was adopted, with its recommendation intact for 2017 negotiations. Although the vote was unrecorded, it seems that the 22 states voting against it were all states under extended nuclear deterrence. The inability of New Zealand to cast a positive vote in favour of the Report was disappointing, but as explained by Ambassador Higgie, without instructions, New Zealand could not participate in the vote.

In any event, the OEWG's Report and recommendation to convene negotiations was duly considered by the First Committee in October, and New Zealand joined as a co-sponsor of that resolution.[9] And so, on 23 December 2016,

---

7   *Report of the Open-Ended Working Group taking forward multilateral nuclear disarmament negotiations,* 71st sess, Agenda Item 99(kk), UN Doc A/71/371 (1 September 2016) [67].

8   H.E. Dell Higgie, Ambassador for Disarmament, *Explanation of Vote* (19 August 2016) Converge <http://www.converge.org.nz/pma/nz-oewg190816.pdf>.

9   H.E. Dell Higgie, Ambassador for Disarmament, *UNGA71 New Zealand Statement to the First Committee* (17 October 2016) Converge <http://www.converge.org.nz/pma/nz-17oct16.pdf>.

the General Assembly adopted that recommendation and agreed to convene nuclear disarmament negotiations in 2017.[10]

3   Crime of Aggression

2016 brought no progress on New Zealand's ratification of the Kampala Amendment to the Rome Statute for the International Criminal Court on the Crime of Aggression. Reflecting the particular sensitivities around including this crime in the Rome Statute, the overall pace of ratifications has been slow. However, during 2016, both Palestine and Iceland deposited their instruments of ratification, bringing the total number of ratifying states to 30. This is a significant first step towards bringing the Amendment into force, as it paves the way now for the Conference of the States Parties to vote again on activating the Court's jurisdiction.[11] However, because that vote requires a 7/8th majority, with only 30 states having ratified it, it would seem that any such decision to actually activate the Court's jurisdiction is still quite a way off.

In New Zealand, nothing has happened towards ratification despite a recommendation back in 2013 from the Foreign Affairs Defence and Trade Select Committee ('FADTC') that New Zealand ought to make ratification a priority in light of New Zealand's traditional support for international law and of maintaining international peace and security.[12] At the time of FADTC's report, the government indicated that it would take a formal decision on ratification in the first quarter of 2014.[13] That has not eventuated, nor has any explanation for the failure. The New Zealand statement at the General Debate at the Fifteenth Session of the Assembly of the States Parties held in November made no mention of the Crime of Aggression, although New Zealand welcomed the 30th ratification when speaking in the Security Council having received the report

---

10   *Taking forward multilateral nuclear disarmament negotiations*, GA Res 71/258, UN GAOR 71st sess, 68th plen mtg, Agenda Item 98, UN Doc A/Res/71/258 (11 January 2017).

11   *Resolution RC/Res.6 of the Review Conference of the Rome Statute: The crime of aggression*, RC/Res.6, 13th plen mtg, UN Doc RC/11 (11 June 2010) Annex I, Article 15bis(3).

12   Foreign Affairs Defence and Trade Committee, *Briefing on the International Criminal Court and the Kampala Amendment on the Crime of Aggression* (19 December 2013) New Zealand Parliament <https://www.parliament.nz/resource/en-NZ/50DBSCH_SCR5986_1 /9503a0b44b42634193b9dad23750b78f4e8c5538> 3–4.

13   Government Response to Report of the Foreign Affairs, *Defence and Trade Committee on Briefing on the International Criminal Court and the Kampala Amendment on the Crime of Aggression* (19 December 2013).

of the International Criminal Court.[14] On 11 July 2016, at a seminar in Wellington, Attorney-General Christopher Finlayson spoke on the issue (responding to a speech by visiting Professor Roger Clark who was critical of New Zealand's tardiness), and stressed that despite the failure to move forward on ratification, New Zealand was 'serious about the task' and was not simply ignoring it.[15] He went on to set out what he saw as the arguments in favour and arguments against in some detail, which would indicate that at least he has been briefed and engaged with the issues – but as yet, there is no sign that this will translate into anything more, nor was anything more concrete indicated in his comments.

---

14   Statement by Van Boehemen, Security Council.
15   Hon Christopher Finlayson, *Making aggression a leadership crime in 2017* (11 July 2016) New Zealand Centre for Global Studies <http://nzcgs.org.nz/wp-content/uploads/2013/11/11-July-2016-Making-aggression-a-leadership-crime.pdf>.

International Law and Security

*Anna Hood**

1 Introduction

In 2016, the primary international security law issues in New Zealand arose from New Zealand's role as an elected member of the United Nations Security Council ("Security Council" or "Council"). In that forum, New Zealand raised a range of substantive security law issues with varying degrees of success. It also took small but significant steps to address some of the many procedural issues that frequently stymie the Council's work. This report begins with an overview of New Zealand's work on the Security Council in 2016. It then turns to examine two other international law and security matters from the year: the visit of the USS Sampson to New Zealand waters, which raised issues under both New Zealand's nuclear free legislation and the Security Treaty between Australia, New Zealand and the United States of America ("ANZUS"); and changes that took place with New Zealand's troop commitment to Iraq.

2 New Zealand's Second Year on the United Nations Security Council

2016 was the second year of New Zealand's two-year term on the Security Council. The *New Zealand Foreign Affairs and Trade Annual Report 2015–2016* noted that during its time on the Council, New Zealand was "active across the Council's agenda and demonstrated that we are willing to take on major issues and challenge the Council to do better."[1] Two of the key issues that New Zealand focused on during its time on the Council in 2016 were the Syrian crisis and Middle East Peace Process. Outside of these efforts, it also put considerable time and energy into trying to improve the Council's processes.

New Zealand had a particular opportunity to encourage a focus on the Syrian crisis when it assumed the Presidency of the Council in the month of September. Despite the reluctance of a number of member states on the Council to look at the issue of Syria in the Council chamber, New Zealand succeeded in making it one of the key themes of the Council's work programme for the month. New Zealand sought to make progress on "information sharing of certain locations to avoid airstrikes", proposals for ceasefire talks and a statement

---

* University of Auckland
1 Ministry of Foreign Affairs and Trade, *Annual Report 2015–16* (2016) 10.

© KONINKLIJKE BRILL NV, LEIDEN, 2018 | DOI 10.1163/9789004345911_016

about the use of chemical weapons in Syria.[2] The Council held sessions on Syria on 17 September and 29 September. Those sessions did not, however, result in any concrete plan for action in Syria and New Zealand's representative on the Council, Gerard van Bohemen, expressed "deep disappointment" at the lack of progress that was made.[3]

New Zealand worked throughout its time on the Council to try to revive and energise the Middle East Peace Process. In 2015, it put forward a draft resolution on the issue but the resolution did not make it to the Council chamber for debate. Towards the end of 2016, Egypt developed a draft resolution that highlighted the illegality of Israeli settlements in occupied Palestinian territory[4] and demanded that "Israel immediately and completely cease all settlement activities in the occupied Palestinian territory."[5] New Zealand joined forces with Malaysia, Senegal and Venezuela to sponsor the resolution. The text became Resolution 2334 and was passed on 23 December 2016 with 14 votes in favour of it and the United States abstaining.

Resolution 2334 has been controversial, both legally and politically. Legally, questions have been raised about the extent to which it is legally binding[6] and whether it simply confirms existing international practice or extends the legal understanding of the Israeli/Palestinian conflict in certain respects.[7] Politically, Israel was very upset by the passage of the Resolution and withdrew its

---

2   Stacey Kirk, "NZ back in charge at the world's most powerful table as security council president", *Stuff* (online) 2 September 2016 <http://www.stuff.co.nz/national/politics/83811340/ NZ-back-in-charge-at-the-worlds-most-powerful-table-as-Security-Council-President>.

3   UN SCOR, 71st sess, 7780th mtg, UN Doc S/PV.7780 (29 September 2016) 7. Mr van Bohemen did note, however, that the Council had made progress on "Colombia, aviation security, the Comprehensive Nuclear-Test-Ban Treaty and Afghanistan" during the month of September.

4   This point was included in Operative Paragraph 1 of the final Resolution: SC Res 2334, UN SCOR 71st sess, 7853rd mtg, UN Doc S/RES/2334 (23 December 2016) ("Resolution 2334").

5   This language was included in Operative Paragraph 2 of Resolution 2334.

6   Daniel Joyner, *Legal Bindingness of Security Council Resolutions Generally, and Resolution 2334 on the Israeli Settlements in Particular* (9 January 2017) EJIL Talk! <https://www.ejiltalk .org/legal-bindingness-of-security-council-resolutions-generally-and-resolution-2334-on -the-israeli-settlements-in-particular/>. The Resolution was not passed under Chapter VII but questions have been raised as to whether the language in Operative Paragraph 2 is sufficiently strong to mean that paragraph is binding under Article 25 of the UN Charter.

7   Andreas Zimmermann, *Security Council Resolution 2334 (2016) and its Legal Repercussions Revisited* (20 January 2017) EJIL Talk! <https://www.ejiltalk.org/security-council-resolution -2334-2016-and-its-legal-repercussions-revisited/>. For example, the Resolution refers to Palestinian "territory" rather than "territories" which could be read as an indication that the Security Council acknowledges a Palestinian entity with a defined territory.

Ambassador from New Zealand in protest.[8] Further questions have been raised about whether New Zealand's Foreign Minister, Murray McCully, should have sought Cabinet approval for the Resolution before consenting to New Zealand sponsoring it.[9]

With respect to process matters in the Council, New Zealand pursued a number of initiatives in 2016. It spearheaded efforts to get the process for determining who chairs Council committees changed so that elected members can have a say in such decisions.[10] At least one of the P5 States was reluctant to accept the change. In order to get agreement to the change, New Zealand threatened to put a resolution to the Council on the matter. It is likely that such a resolution would have passed, as procedural resolutions do not require the consent of P5 members and the elected members were in favour of it. In the end, however, it was not necessary for New Zealand to take this step and the issue was resolved in accordance with New Zealand's wishes.[11] New Zealand also organised a Council meeting to review the use of the veto, took steps to improve peacekeeping operations, and set up a monthly meeting for permanent representatives to review the most significant problems on the Council's agenda.[12]

The impact that New Zealand had on the Council during its 24-month tenure is an issue that will no doubt be debated in years to come. In the second half of 2016, Gerard von Bohemen questioned the extent to which New Zealand had affected international peace and security issues while on the Council, stating "[w]e're focusing on the facts on the ground, and there we haven't had the impact I would have liked to have had, because the situations have been so intractable."[13] I would add that the difficulties New Zealand faced on the Council may not just be due to the fact that many international peace and security situations are intractable; it may also be the case that the Council is not always

---

8   Audrey Young, "Israeli ambassador recalled from NZ after UN resolution", *NZ Herald* (online), 24 December 2016 <http://www.nzherald.co.nz/nz/news/article.cfm?c_id=1& objectid=11772739>.

9   Richard Harman, "That UN vote on Israel – the inside story. Why NZ did what it did", *Politik* (online) 16 March 2017 <http://politik.co.nz/en/content/foreignaffairs/1052/That -UN-vote-on-Israel---the-inside-story-Why-NZ-did-what-it-did-UN-Security-Council -Murray-McCully-Gerard-Van-Bohemen.htm>.

10   *Annual Report 2015–16*, above n 1, 11.

11   Stacey Kirk, "NZ has made waves on the UN Security Council, but has it made a difference?" *Stuff* (online), 20 August 2016 <http://www.stuff.co.nz/national/politics/83377293/ NZ-has-made-waves-on-the-UN-Security-Council-but-has-it-made-a-difference>.

12   *Annual Report 2015–16*, above n 1, 11.

13   Kirk, above n 11.

the most appropriate body to look to to resolve the many and varied issues unfolding around the world. In the future, we may need to take different approaches to addressing some of the security concerns facing the international community.

3   ANZUS Matters

In 2015, New Zealand issued an invitation to the United States to send a ship to New Zealand in 2016 for the Royal New Zealand Navy's 75th anniversary celebration. At the time it was issued, the invitation was controversial as it was the first time since the passage of the *New Zealand Nuclear Free Zone, Disarmament Arms Control Act 1987* ("the Act")[14] that New Zealand had invited a United States' ship to enter its waters and doubt existed about whether the United States could send a ship without breaching the Act.[15]

The Act requires the Prime Minister to ascertain that any ships entering New Zealand waters are nuclear free.[16] As the United States has a policy of neither confirming nor denying whether its ships are nuclear powered or carry nuclear weapons, there were questions as to whether the Prime Minister would be able to issue the requisite assurance under the Act. The United States decided to send the USS Sampson to the celebrations and the Prime Minister, John Key, determined that the ship was nuclear free. He stated, "As you would expect I went through a thorough formal process that included receiving advice from Foreign Affairs, from the Department of Prime Minister and Cabinet, the Attorney-General and from the Minister of Foreign Affairs ... On the back of that advice I feel quite comfortable signing the declaration, which gives approval for the ship to come."[17]

A further issue connected to the USS Sampson's visit was whether the presence of a United States ship in New Zealand waters would rekindle the ANZUS treaty relationship between New Zealand and the United States.[18] However, Key quashed any such idea saying in July 2016 that "[i]f the question is will

---

14   *New Zealand Nuclear Free Zone, Disarmament, and Arms Control Act 1987* (NZ).

15   "Will the US navy be able to visit NZ?" *Radio NZ* (online), 31 October 2015, <http://www .radionz.co.nz/news/political/289192/us-naval-ships-invited-to-visit-nz>.

16   *New Zealand Nuclear Free Zone, Disarmament, and Arms Control Act 1987* (NZ) s 9.

17   Vernon Small and Tracy Watkins, "US warship to break final ANZUS barrier as veteran protestor claims victory", *Stuff* (online), 18 October 2016 <http://www.stuff.co.nz/national/ politics/85464508/us-warship-to-break-final-anzus-barrier>.

18   When New Zealand first passed the Act, the United States deemed this a breach of the ANZUS treaty and suspended its obligations to New Zealand.

there be step back into Anzus then the answer is no. We run an independent foreign policy. We are happy with the defence tie-up we have with the United States and others, which is we make those decisions on a case by case basis of what we want to do."[19]

4   Troops in Iraq

In February 2015, the New Zealand government announced that it was deploying 143 troops to Iraq for a two-year period to undertake non-combat training exercises.[20] The decision was controversial as it was not put to a parliamentary vote.[21]

On 20 June 2016, Cabinet announced that it was extending the period that New Zealand troops would be in Iraq by 18 months to November 2018.[22] Additionally, Cabinet decided to alter New Zealand's mission in Iraq in two ways. First, it determined that New Zealand troops would train Iraqi soldiers in Besmaya, as well as in Taji, where their activities had been originally based. Second, it determined that New Zealand troops would be authorised to provide training to stabilisation forces such as the Iraqi Federal Police.[23] The decision to extend New Zealand's mission in Iraq raised concerns in the Labour Party, Green Party and New Zealand First. In particular, the Labour Party said it was worried that mission creep was occurring.[24]

A further controversial incident regarding New Zealand troops in Iraq arose in October 2016 when reports appeared in the *Guardian* that New Zealand SAS troops were active in Iraq.[25] When troops were first deployed to Iraq in 2015, the government had said that the SAS would not be involved in the mission.

---

19   Audrey Young, "United States ship to visit NZ for the first time in 33 years", *New Zealand Herald* (online), 21 July 2016 <http://www.nzherald.co.nz/nz/news/article.cfm?c_id=1& objectid=11678267>.

20   New Zealand, *Parliamentary Debates,* 24 February 2015, vol 703, 1813 (John Key).

21   New Zealand, *Parliamentary Debates,* 24 February 2015, vol 703, 1828 (Annette King).

22   Gerry Brownlee, "Government extends Iraq deployment" (Press Release, 20 June 2016) <https://www.beehive.govt.nz/release/government-extends-iraq-deployment>.

23   Ibid.

24   Jo Moir, "Kiwi troop deployment to Iraq has been extended by 18 months', *Stuff* (online), 20 June 2016 <http://www.stuff.co.nz/national/politics/81265744/kiwi-troop-deployment -to-iraq-has-been-extended-by-18-months>.

25   Martin Chulov, 'Kurdish forces vow no retreat until Nineveh plains are retaken from Isis", *The Guardian* (online), 21 October 2016 <https://www.theguardian.com/world/2016/ oct/20/kurdish-forces-vow-no-retreat-until-nineveh-plains-are-retaken-from-isis>.

In 2016, the government denied the claims in the *Guardian* with Defence Minister Gerry Brownlee stating that "the government has ruled out sending SAS, or any troops into combat roles in Iraq ... We have also been clear that special forces could be deployed for short periods – for example, to provide advice on issues like force protection or to help with high profile visits."[26]

---

26   Vernon Small and Laura Walters, "Government denies report NZ SAS in combat in Iraq", *Stuff* (online), 22 October 2016 <http://www.stuff.co.nz/timaru-herald/news/national/85603946/NZ-SAS-in-northern-Iraq-reports>.

New Zealand State Conduct

∴

Treaty Action and Implementation

*Mark Gobbi**

1 Overview

This article documents governmental activity undertaken to implement New Zealand's international obligations during the current interval.[1] It concludes that the level of activity in the current interval, relative to the previous interval,[2] decreased for the judicial branch but has increased for the parliamentary and executive branches. This overview summarises that activity and compares it with the activity undertaken during the previous interval.

1.1 *Parliamentary Activity*
1.1.1 Acts of Parliament

During the current interval, Parliament enacted 45 bills with implications for New Zealand's international obligations. Thirty-nine simply amended Acts that had implemented treaties, four improved compliance with treaties that had already been implemented, and two implemented new treaties. Thirty-two of these bills involved multilateral agreements, nine involved bilateral agreements, three concerned recommendations, and one involved a code.

In terms of Acts, this level of activity is more than the previous interval. During the previous interval, Parliament enacted 42 bills with implications for New Zealand's international obligations. Thirty-nine simply amended Acts that had implemented treaties, two improved compliance with treaties that had already been implemented, and one implemented amendments to a treaty. Forty-one of these bills involved multilateral agreements and one involved a code.[3]

---

* The author is currently serving as Parliamentary Counsel in New Zealand's Parliamentary Counsel Office. However, the views expressed herein are the author's own and may not be attributed to the Parliamentary Counsel Office or the Attorney-General. The excellent research work of Jasper Fawcett-Griffiths and Ruby King, who gathered the material found in Parts 3 and 4 (apart from Section C), is gratefully acknowledged.

1 The current interval began on 1 July 2015 and ended on 30 June 2016.

2 The previous interval began on 1 July 2014 and ended on 30 June 2015.

3 Mark Gobbi, "Treaty Action and Implementation" (2015) 13 *New Zealand Yearbook of International Law* 295, 295, 303–312.

1.1.2 Treaty Examination Reports

During the current interval, the House of Representatives considered 12 select committee reports on treaties (12 agreements in all). Eleven reports brought matters to the attention of the House. Public submissions featured in six of these reports, and none warranted a Government response.[4]

In terms of reports, this level of activity is more than during the previous interval (one more report). In terms of agreements examined, this level of activity is also more than during the previous interval (one more agreement). During the previous interval, the House of Representatives considered 11 select committee reports on treaties (11 agreements in all). Seven reports brought substantive matters to the attention of the House. Public submissions featured in one of these reports, and none warranted a Government response.[5]

1.2 *Executive Activity*

1.2.1 Regulations

During the current interval, the Executive made 33 regulations relevant to New Zealand's international obligations. Three of these regulations implemented a bilateral agreement, two implemented recommendations, one implemented standards, and 27 implemented multilateral agreements. Fourteen concerned environmental agreements, six dealt with civil aviation, four adopted resolutions of the United Nations Security Council, three concerned trade, two dealt with money laundering, two dealt with labour, one dealt with taxes, and one dealt with drugs.

This level of activity is more than the level of activity that took place during the previous interval. During the previous interval, the Executive made 27 regulations relevant to New Zealand's international obligations. One of these regulations implemented a bilateral agreement, two implemented standards, one implemented aspects of code, and twenty-three implemented multilateral agreements. Fifteen concerned environmental agreements, five dealt with money laundering, one dealt with various maritime rules, one concerned lighting fitted to vehicles, one dealt with drugs, one dealt with driving requirements, one implemented a bilateral tax agreement, one dealt with banks, and one adopted a resolution of the United Nations Security Council.[6]

1.2.2 Treaty Actions

During the current interval, the Executive was involved in 38 treaty actions with respect to five multilateral agreements and 22 bilateral agreements. Of the

---

4   See Standing Order 252 (2014).

5   Gobbi (2015), above n 3, 295, 301–303.

6   Ibid 296, 312–321.

five multilateral agreements (7 actions), the Executive signed three, ratified one, accepted one, and acceded to one. One came into force. Of the 22 bilateral agreements (31 actions), the Executive signed 22. Nine came into force.

This level of activity is more than the level of activity that took place during the previous interval. During the previous interval, the Executive was involved in 22 treaty actions with respect to six multilateral agreements and 16 bilateral agreements. Of the six multilateral agreements, the Executive ratified three. Six came into force. Of the 16 bilateral agreements, the Executive notified one, ratified one, and signed 9. Eight came into force.[7]

1.2.3 Periodic Reports

New Zealand is required to provide periodic reports to the United Nations regarding its compliance with the following human rights treaties: the International Covenant on Civil and Political Rights (1966), the International Covenant on Economic, Social and Cultural Rights (1966), the International Convention on the Elimination of All Forms of Racial Discrimination (1966), the Convention on the Elimination of All Forms of Discrimination against Women (1979), the Convention against Torture and Other Cruel, Inhuman or Degrading Treatment or Punishment (1984), the Convention on the Rights of the Child (1989), and the Convention on the Rights of Persons with Disabilities (2006).[8]

During the current interval, the Executive submitted New Zealand's twenty-first and twenty-second period reports in respect of the International Convention on the Elimination of All Forms of Racial Discrimination (1966)[9] and New Zealand's fifth periodic report in respect of the Convention on the Rights of the Child (1989).[10] It also submitted further information[11] following a review of

---

7   Ibid 296, 300–301.

8   For an online record of New Zealand's periodic reporting under these agreements, see, OHCHR <http://tbinternet.ohchr.org/_layouts/TreatyBodyExternal/Countries.aspx? CountryCode=NZL&Lang=EN>; see also, <https://www.justice.govt.nz/justice-sector -policy/constitutional-issues-and-human-rights/human-rights/international-human -rights/>.

9   Committee on the Elimination of Racial Discrimination, International Convention on the Elimination of All Forms of Racial Discrimination, *Consideration of reports submitted by States parties under article 9 of the Convention: Twenty-first and twenty-second periodic reports of States parties due in 2015: New Zealand*, UN Doc CERD/C/NZL/21-22 (20 April 2016).

10   Committee on the Rights of the Child, Convention on the Rights of the Child, *Consideration of reports submitted by States parties under article 44 of the Convention: Fifth periodic reports of States parties due in 2015: New Zealand*, UN Doc CRC/C/NZL/5 (11 January 2016).

11   Committee against Torture, Convention against Torture and Other Cruel, Inhuman or Degrading Treatment or Punishment, *Request for further information from New Zealand*

New Zealand's sixth periodic report under the Convention against Torture and Other Cruel, Inhuman or Degrading Treatment or Punishment (1984).[12]

In terms of periodic reports, this level of activity is more than the level of activity that took place during the previous interval. During the previous interval, the Executive submitted New Zealand's sixth period report in respect of the International Covenant on Civil and Political Rights (1966).[13]

1.3   *Judicial Activity*

During the current interval, the judiciary delivered 63 judgments that referenced New Zealand's international obligations. Seven of these judgments were reported in the New Zealand Law Report series; the Supreme Court delivered two, the Court of Appeal delivered three, and the High Court delivered two. Fifty-six were reported in other series; the Supreme Court delivered three, the Court of Appeal delivered 12, the High Court delivered 30, the District Court delivered one, the Family Court delivered eight, the Youth Court delivered one, and the Human Rights Review Tribunal delivered one. None were unreported.

Of these 63 judgments, 17 dealt with family law, nine with immigration, seven with judicial review, five with criminal law, four with civil procedure, two with evidence law, two with extradition, two with human rights law, two with social security, one with arbitration, one with criminal procedure, one with legal aid, one with constitutional law, one with criminal justice, one with contract law, one with sentencing, one with privacy, one with social welfare, one with employment law, one with youth justice, one with environmental law, and one with cross-border insolvency.

These 63 judgments referred to 27 different international instruments (one of which does not have New Zealand as a party), of which 24 are multilateral agreements, one is a bilateral agreement, one is a declaration, and one is a set of principles and guidelines. In total, these judgments have 101 references. In these cases, the most frequently cited international agreements are the United Nations Convention on the Rights of the Child (1989) (26 references), the International Covenant on Civil and Political Rights (1966) (18 references),

---

following the review of New Zealand's 6th periodic report under the Convention against Torture, UN Doc CAT/C/NZL/CO/6.Add.1 (3 June 2016).

12   For a copy of this report, see, Committee against Torture, Convention against Torture and Other Cruel, Inhuman or Degrading Treatment or Punishment, *Consideration of reports submitted by States parties under article 19 of the Convention pursuant to the optional reporting procedure: Sixth periodic reports of States parties due in 2013: New Zealand*, UN Doc CAT/C/NZL/6 (4 March 2014).

13   Gobbi (2015), above n 3, 297.

United Nations Convention Relating to the Status of Refugees (1951) (10 references), the European Convention for the Protection of Human Rights and Fundamental Freedoms (1950) (nine references), the Hague Convention on the Civil Aspects of International Child Abduction (1980) (six references), the Protocol Relating to the Status of Refugees (1967) (four references), the United Nations Convention on the Rights of Persons with Disabilities (2006) (three references), and the Convention against Torture and Other Cruel, Inhuman or Degrading Treatment or Punishment (1984) (three references). Three other instruments are referenced twice and 16 others are referenced once.

In terms of the number of judgments delivered, the level of activity is less than the activity that took place during the previous interval. During the previous interval, the judiciary delivered 108 judgments that referenced New Zealand's international obligations. Nineteen of these judgments were reported in the New Zealand Law Report series; the Supreme Court delivered five, the Court of Appeal delivered six, and the High Court delivered eight. Eighty-nine were reported in other series; the Supreme Court delivered three, the Court of Appeal delivered 14, the High Court delivered 39, the Family Court delivered 25, the Employment Court delivered four, the Youth Court delivered one, the Māori Land Court delivered one, and the Human Rights Review Tribunal delivered two. None were unreported.

Of these 108 judgments, 31 dealt with family law, 14 with judicial review, nine with immigration, six with employment law, five with criminal procedure, five with criminal law, four with civil procedure, four with land law, four with evidence, three with costs, three with accident compensation, two with arbitration, two with civil matters, two with copyright, two with maritime law, one with bankruptcy, one with equity, one with habeas corpus, one with privacy, one with company law, one with local government, one with contract law, one with environmental law, one with resource management law, one with the Bill of Rights, one with media law, and one with constitutional law.

These 108 judgments referred to 36 different international instruments (two of which do not have New Zealand as a party), of which 35 are multilateral agreements and one is a guide to an aspect of a multilateral agreement. In total, these judgments have 135 references. In these cases, the most frequently cited international agreements are the International Covenant on Civil and Political Rights (1966) (22 references), the United Nations Convention on the Rights of the Child (1989) (20 references), the Hague Convention on the Civil Aspects of International Child Abduction (1980) (17 references), the European Convention for the Protection of Human Rights and Fundamental Freedoms (1950) (11 references), the Universal Declaration of Human Rights (1948) (eight references), United Nations Convention Relating to the

Status of Refugees (1951) (six references), the United Nations Convention on the Rights of Persons with Disabilities (2006) (five references), the United Nations Declaration on the Rights of Indigenous Peoples (2007) (four references), the Hague Convention on Protection of Children and Co-operation in respect of Intercountry Adoption (1993) (four references), the International Covenant on Economic, Social and Cultural Rights (1966) (three references), and the UNCITRAL Model Law on International Commercial Arbitration (1985) (three references). Six other instruments are referenced twice and 19 others are referenced once.[14]

1.4   Conclusion

During the current interval, each of the three branches of government contributed to the implementation of New Zealand's international obligations. The level of activity for the current interval decreased relative to the previous interval for the Judiciary, but increased for Parliament and the Executive. International agreements are an important source of law in New Zealand.

2   Treaty Action

This Part sets out the treaty actions taken by the Executive during the current interval. It lists the agreements that New Zealand has signed, ratified, accepted, approved, or acceded to, or that entered into force for New Zealand. It also sets out the reports on treaties that the Executive tabled in the House during the current interval.

2.1   Executive Treaty Action[15]

2.1.1   Multilateral Treaties

Agreement on Government Procurement done at Marrakesh on 15 April 1994 as amended by the Protocol Amending the Agreement on Government Procurement done at Geneva on 30 March 2012 (acceded to on 10 July 2015)

World Trade Organization: Trade Facilitation Agreement (accepted 29 September 2015)

Asian Infrastructure Investment Bank Articles of Agreement (signed 29 June 2015 and entered into force 25 December 2015)

---

14   Ibid 297–298, 321–332.

15   See, New Zealand Ministry of Foreign Affairs and Trade, *Annual Report 2015–16*, A.1 AR (2016) 89–90; see, also New Zealand Treaties Online, MFAT <www.treaties.mfat.govt.nz/>.

Maritime Labour Convention 2006 (signed 9 March 2016 and ratified 9 March 2016)

Paris Agreement on climate change (signed 22 April 2016)

2.1.2   Bilateral Treaties

Agreement between the Government of Samoa and the Government of New Zealand for the Elimination of Double Taxation with Respect to Taxes on Income and the Prevention of Tax Evasion and Avoidance (signed 8 July 2015 and entered into force 23 December 2015)

Protocol Amending the Air Services Agreement between the Swiss Federal Council and the Government of New Zealand (signed 19 November 2014 and entered into force 27 July 2015)

Air Services Agreement between the Government of the Kingdom of Cambodia and the Government of New Zealand (signed 19 August 2015)

Exchange of Letters constituting an Agreement to Amend the Agreement between the Government of New Zealand and the Government of the United Arab Emirates on Air Services (signed and entered into force 7 September 2015)

Agreement between the Government of the State of Qatar and the Government of New Zealand for Air Services (signed 9 September 2015)

Amendment of the Agreement related to Air Transport dated 9 November 1967 between France and New Zealand (signed and entered into force 22 September 2015)

Air Services Agreement between the Government of New Zealand and the Government of the Republic of Seychelles (signed and entered into force 29 September 2015)

Air Services Agreement between the Government of New Zealand and the Government of the Oriental Republic of Uruguay (signed 30 September 2015)

Agreement on a Working Holiday Scheme Between the Government of the Republic of Lithuania and the Government of New Zealand (signed 1 October 2015)

Agreement between the Government of New Zealand and the Government of the Republic of Poland Concerning the Co-Production of Films (signed 21 October 2015 and entered into force 29 February 2016)

Air Services Agreement between the Government of the State of Kuwait and the Government of New Zealand (signed 23 October 2015)

Free Trade Agreement between New Zealand and the Republic of Korea (signed 23 March 2015 and entered into force 20 December 2015)

Third Protocol to the Agreement between the Government of New Zealand and the Government of Malaysia for the Avoidance of Double Taxation and Prevention of Fiscal Evasion with Respect to Taxes on Income (signed 6 November 2012 and entered into force 12 January 2016)

Trans-Pacific Partnership Agreement (signed 4 February 2016)

Air Services Agreement between the Government of New Zealand and the Government of the Kingdom of Saudi Arabia (signed 4 February 2016)

Agreement on Film Co-Production Between the Government of New Zealand and the

Government of the State of Israel (signed 1 March 2016)

Protocol to Amend the Agreement between the Government of the Socialist Republic of Viet Nam and the Government of New Zealand on Air Services (signed 19 March 2015 and entered into force 11 March 2016)

Agreement between the Government of New Zealand and the Government of the Republic of San Marino on the Exchange of Information with Respect to Taxes (signed 1 April 2016)

Air Services Agreement between the Government of New Zealand and the Government of the Republic of India (signed 1 May 2016)

Exchange of Letters Amending the Air Transport Agreement between the Government of New Zealand and Government of the French Republic (signed and entered into force 2 May 2016)

Air Services Agreement between the Government of New Zealand and the Government of the Hellenic Republic (signed 28 May 2015 and entered into force 11 May 2016)

Agreement between the Government of New Zealand and the Government of the United States of America on Technology Safeguards Associated with United States Participation in Space Launches from New Zealand (signed 16 June 2016)

2.2   *Reports on Treaties Tabled in the House of Representatives*
2.2.1   Reports Where No Substantive Matters Were Drawn to the
             Attention of the House

International treaty examination of the Agreement between the Government of New Zealand and the Government of Samoa for the Elimination of Double Taxation with Respect to Taxes on Income and the Prevention of Tax Evasion and Avoidance; Finance and Expenditure Committee (19 August 2015)

2.2.2   Reports Where Substantive Matters Were Drawn to the Attention
             of the House

International treaty examination of the Cape Town Agreement of 2012 on the implementation of the provisions of the Torremolinos Protocol of 1993 relating to the Torremolinos International Convention for the Safety of Fishing Vessels, 1977; Transport and Industrial Relations Committee (6 May 2016)

> While in support of the Agreement, the Committee noted that the potential effect on New Zealand's ship-building industry is relatively minor because New Zealand does not build many fishing vessels.

International treaty examination of the Convention on Limitation of Liability for Maritime Claims, 1976; Transport and Industrial Relations Committee (6 May 2016)

> The Committee noted that New Zealand is a party to the 1976 Convention and to the 1996 Protocol that effectively supersedes it. It reached the view that New Zealand need not be a party to both, and recommended that New Zealand denounce the 1976 Convention.

International treaty examination of the International Convention on Standards of Training, Certification and Watchkeeping for Fishing Vessel Personnel, 1995; Transport and Industrial Relations Committee (6 May 2016)

> The Committee supported becoming a party to the Convention. In doing so, it noted several advantages, including its application to all vessels in New Zealand waters, whether they come from states that are party to it or not.

International treaty examination of the Trans-Pacific Partnership Agreement; Foreign Affairs, Defence and Trade Committee [6,351 submissions (3,150 on forms), heard 255] (4 May 2016)

> The Committee split along party lines. The majority, which reflected the position of the government of the day, supported the Agreement on economic grounds. It pointed out that the Agreement would require New Zealand to alter some of its laws and to become a party to the following international agreements: the Budapest Treaty on the International Recognition of the Deposit of Microorganisms for the Purposes of Patent Procedure (1977), the WIPO Copyright Treaty (1996), the Berne Convention for the protection of Literary and Artistic Works (1971), and the WIPO Performance and Phonograms Treaty (1996) [each of which was the subject of a separate treaty examination report]. The minority, which

reflected the positions of several non-government parties, opposed the Agreement. It raised issues regarding sovereignty, consultation and transparency and process, and progress being made on the World Trade Organization front.

International treaty examination of the Berne Convention for the Protection of Literary and Artistic Works; Foreign Affairs, Defence and Trade Committee [eight submissions, six heard] (4 May 2016)

The Committee noted that New Zealand would need to accede to the Convention if it wishes to ratify the Trans-Pacific Partnership Agreement. The Committee also noted that acceding to the Convention would impose no new legal obligations on New Zealand because New Zealand already meets its standards of protection of literary and artistic works.

International treaty examination of the Budapest Treaty on the International Recognition of the Deposit of Micro-organisms for the Purposes of Patent Procedure; Foreign Affairs, Defence and Trade Committee [six submissions, five heard] (4 May 2016)

The Committee noted that New Zealand would need to accede to the Treaty if it wishes to ratify the Trans-Pacific Partnership Agreement. The Committee also noted that acceding to the Treaty would impose no additional costs on patent applicants, businesses, the Government, or the public. The main obligation imposed on parties to the Treaty is that they recognise, for the purposes of patent procedure, the deposits of micro-organisms in 42 international depository authorities recognised under the Treaty.

International treaty examination of the WIPO Copyright Treaty; Foreign Affairs, Defence and Trade Committee [eight submissions, six heard] (4 May 2016)

The Committee noted that New Zealand would need to accede to the Treaty if it wishes to ratify the Trans-Pacific Partnership Agreement. The Committee also noted that, although New Zealand copyright law already substantially complies with the obligations of the Treaty, acceding to it would require New Zealand to ensure that works distributed over the Internet are protected, to ensure that rights enjoyed under the Agreement on Trade-Related Aspects of Intellectual Property Rights are not removed, and to accept limits on its ability to modify New Zealand's copyright settings.

International treaty examination of the wipo Performances and Phonograms Treaty; Foreign Affairs, Defence and Trade Committee [eight submissions, seven heard] (4 May 2016)

> The Committee noted that New Zealand would need to accede to the Treaty if it wishes to ratify the Trans-Pacific Partnership Agreement. The Committee also noted that, although New Zealand copyright law already complies with most of the Treaty, acceding to it would require New Zealand to give performers new rights for the reproduction and distribution of their live performances and sound recordings of their performances.

International treaty examination of the Doha Amendment to the Kyoto Protocol; Foreign Affairs, Defence and Trade Committee (one submission) (12 November 2015)

> The majority of the Committee supported the Agreement. It noted that the implications for New Zealand were minimal because the obligations relating to emission reduction commitments would not apply to New Zealand because it chose a target of reducing emissions to five per cent below 1990 levels for the period 2013 to 2020 rather than commit to limit or reduce emissions under the Kyoto Protocol for the second commitment period. The minority dissociated itself from the report for process reasons (the Agreement was tabled three years after New Zealand adopted it yet the public was given only two weeks to make submissions), and because it disagreed with New Zealand's commitment choice.

International treaty examination of the World Trade Organization Agreement on Trade Facilitation; Foreign Affairs, Defence and Trade Committee (11 September 2015)

> The Committee supported the Agreement, noting that its provisions are generally consistent with existing best practice for customs policies and procedures and that no legislative or regulatory changes are needed because its provisions reflect New Zealand's existing border practices. It also expressed the hope that the Agreement would pave the way for a broader outcome on the Doha Round.

International treaty examination of the Asian Infrastructure Investment Bank, Articles of Agreement, Final Text, adopted at 5th Chief Negotiators' Meeting, 22 May 2015; Foreign Affairs, Defence and Trade Committee (21 August 2015)

> The Committee supported the Agreement. As indicated in the National Interest Analysis appended to the report, becoming a party to the Agreement would require amending the International Finance Agreements Act 1961 to provide the legal basis for a permanent legislative authority for New Zealand's capital injections.

3   Legislation Related to New Zealand's International Obligations

This Part sets out the legislation dealt with during the current interval that concerns New Zealand's international obligations. It is divided into two sections, the first listing the Acts that were enacted and the second listing the regulations that were made.

3.1   *Acts of Parliament*

Acts of Parliament relating to New Zealand's international obligations are identified as: (1) Acts simply amending legislation that has implemented treaties; (2) Acts improving compliance with treaties that have already been implemented; or (3) Acts implementing new treaty obligations.

3.1.1   Acts Simply Amending Legislation that Implemented Treaties
Crimes Amendment Act 2015

This Act amends the Crimes Act 1961 which implements the Convention relating to the Status of Refugees (1951) [art 31], the International Covenant on Civil and Political Rights (1966), the Convention on the Elimination of All Forms of Discrimination against Women (1979) [arts 3, 4, 6 and 15], the Convention on the Physical protection of Nuclear Material and Nuclear Facilities (1980), the Convention Against Torture and Other Cruel, Inhuman or Degrading Treatment or Punishment (1984), the Recommendations of the Financial Action Task Force (Task Force established 1989), the Convention on the Rights of the Child (1989), the Convention on the Marking of Plastic Explosives for the Purpose of Detection (1991), the ILO Convention 182 (1999): Concerning the Worst Forms of Child Labour, the Convention on Combating Bribery of Foreign Public Officials in International Business Transactions (1997), the Optional Protocol to the Convention on the Rights of the Child on the Sale of Children, Child Prostitution and Child Pornography (2000), the Convention against Transnational Organised Crime (2000), the Protocol against the Smuggling of Migrants by Land, Sea and Air, supplementing the Convention against Transnational Organised Crime (2000), and the Protocol to Prevent, Suppress and Punish Trafficking of Persons, especially Women and Children, supplementing the Convention against Transnational Organised Crime.

Crimes (Indecency) Amendment Act 2015
This Act amends the Crimes Act 1961, which implements the Convention relating to the Status of Refugees (1951) [art 31], the International Covenant on Civil and Political Rights (1966), the Convention on the Elimination of All Forms of Discrimination against Women (1979) [arts 3, 4, 6, and 15], the Convention on the Physical Protection of Nuclear Material and Nuclear Facilities (1980), the Convention against Torture and Other Cruel, Inhuman or Degrading Treatment or Punishment (1984), the Recommendations of Financial Action Task Force (Task Force established 1989), the Convention on the Rights of the Child (1989), the Convention on the Marking of Plastic Explosives for the Purpose of Detection (1991), the ILO Convention 182 (1999): Concerning the Worst Forms of Child Labour, the Convention on Combating Bribery of Foreign Public Officials in International Business Transactions (1997), the Optional Protocol to the Convention on the Rights of the Child on the Sale of Children, Child Prostitution and Child Pornography (2000), the Convention against Transnational Organised Crime (2000), the Protocol against the Smuggling of Migrants by Land, Sea and Air, supplementing the Convention against Transnational Organised Crime (2000), and the Protocol to Prevent, Suppress and Punish Trafficking of Persons, especially Women and Children, supplementing the Convention against Transnational Organised Crime (2000).

Criminal Proceeds (Recovery) Amendment Act 2015
This Act amends the Criminal Proceeds (Recovery) Act 2009, which implements the Recommendations of Financial Action Task Force (Task Force established 1989).

Customs and Excise Amendment Act (No 2) 2015
This Act amends the Customs and Excise Act 1996 which implements the Customs Convention on the Temporary Importation of Private Road vehicles (1954), the Customs Convention on Containers (1972), the Recommendations of Financial Action Task Force (Task Force established 1989), the Protocol of Amendment to the International Convention on the Simplification and Harmonization of Customs Procedures (1999), the Free Trade Agreement

between the Government of New Zealand and the Government of the People's Republic of China (2008), and the ASEAN-Australia-New Zealand Free Trade Area (2009). The Customs and Excise Act also implements a standard for motor fuel testing established by the American Society for Testing and Materials International (ASTM D2699:79).

Customs and Excise (Objectionable Publications) Amendment Act 2015

This Act amends the Customs and Excise Act 1996, which implements the Customs Convention on the Temporary Importation of Private Road Vehicles (1954), the Customs Convention on Containers (1972), the Recommendations of Financial Action Task Force (Task Force established 1989), the Protocol of Amendment to the International Convention on the Simplification and Harmonization of Customs Procedures (1999), the Free Trade Agreement between the Government of New Zealand and the Government of the People's Republic of China (2008), and the ASEAN-Australia-New Zealand Free Trade Area (2009). The Customs and Excise Act 1996 also implements a standard for motor fuel testing established by the American Society for Testing and Materials International (ASTM D2699:79).

Customs and Excise (Tobacco Products – Budget Measures) Amendment Act 2016

This Act amends the Customs and Excise Act 1996, which implements the Customs Convention on the Temporary Importation of Private Road Vehicles (1954), the Customs Convention on Containers (1972), the Recommendations of Financial Action Task Force (Task Force established 1989), the Protocol of Amendment to the International Convention on the Simplification and Harmonization of Customs Procedures (1999), the Free Trade Agreement between the Government of New Zealand and the Government of the People's Republic of China (2008), and the ASEAN-Australia-New Zealand Free Trade Area (2009). The Customs and Excise Act 1996 also implements a standard for motor fuel testing established by the American Society for Testing and Materials International (ASTM D2699:79).

Education Amendment Act (No 2) 2015

This Act amends the Education Act 1989, which implements the ILO Convention 10 (1921): Minimum Age (Agriculture), the ILO Convention 58 (1936): Minimum Age (Sea), the ILO Convention 59 (1937): Minimum Age (Industry), the Convention against Discrimination in Education (1960), and the ILO Convention 122 (1964): Employment Policy.

Employment Relations Amendment Act 2016

This Act amends the Employment Relations Act 2000, which implements the ILO Convention 11 (1921): Right of Association (Agriculture), the ILO Convention 14 (1921): Weekly Rest (Industry), the ILO Convention 22 (1926): Seamen's Articles of Agreement, the ILO Convention 32 (1932): Protection against Accidents (Dockers), the ILO Convention 122 (1964): Employment Policy, and the Act also incorporates the principles underlying ILO Convention 87 (1948): Freedom of Association and ILO Convention 98 (1949): Right to Organise and Bargain Collectively.

Exclusive Economic Zone and Continental Shelf (Environmental Effects) (Transitional Provisions) Amendment Act 2015

This Act amends the Exclusive Economic Zone and Continental Shelf (Environmental Effects) Act 2012, which implements the Convention on the Prevention of Marine Pollution by Dumping Wastes and Other Matter (1972), the International Convention for the Prevention of Pollution from Ships (1973), the United Nations Convention on the Law of the Sea (1982), and the Convention on Biological Diversity (1993).

Extradition Amendment Act 2015

This Act amends the Extradition Act 1999, which governs the execution of bilateral extradition agreements.

Films, Videos, and Publications Classification (Objectionable Publications) Amendment Act 2015

This Act amends the Films, Videos, and Publications Classification Act 1993, which implements the Convention for the Suppression of the Circulation of, and Traffic in, Obscene Publications (1923), the Protocol to amend the Convention for the Suppression of the Circulation of, and Traffic in, Obscene Publications (1947), the International Covenant on Civil and Political Rights (1966) [arts 3, 15, and 19], the Convention on the Elimination of All Forms of Discrimination against Women (1979) [art 5], the ILO Convention 182 (1999): Worst Forms of Child Labour, and the Optional Protocol to the Convention on the Rights of the Child on the Sale of Children, Child Prostitution and Child Pornography (2000).

Financial Service Providers (Registration and Dispute Resolution) Amendment Act 2015

This Act amends the Financial Service Providers (Registration and Dispute Resolution) Act 2008, which implements the 40 Recommendations that the Financial Action Task Force ("FATF") adopted at its plenary meeting on 20

June 2003, the Special Recommendations on Terrorist Financing that the FATF adopted at its plenary meeting on 31 October, and the Special Recommendation IX on Terrorist Financing that the FATF adopted as its plenary meeting between 20 and 22 October.

Financial Transactions Reporting Amendment Act 2015

This Act amends the Financial Transactions Reporting Act 1996, which implements the Recommendations of Financial Action Task Force (Task Force established 1989).

Hazardous Substances and New Organisms Amendment Act 2015

This Act amends the Hazardous Substances and New Organisms Act 1996, which implements the Convention on Persistent Organic Pollutants (2001).

Holidays Amendment Act 2016

This Act amends the Holidays Act 2003, which implements the ILO Convention 52 (1936): Holidays with Pay and the ILO Convention 101 (1952): Holidays with Pay Agriculture.

Income Tax Amendment Act 2015

This Act amends the Income Tax Act 2007, which implements aspects of the United Nations Framework Convention on Climate Change (1992), and the Kyoto Protocol to the United Nations Framework Convention on Climate Change (1997). The Act enumerates a grey list of jurisdictions where tax exemption or relief laws might apply (schedule 24). A number of double taxation agreements with other jurisdictions are given effect via regulations made under the Act.

Marine Mammals Protection Amendment Act 2015

This Act amends the Marine Mammals Protection Act 1978, which implements the Convention on the Prevention of Marine Pollution by Dumping of Wastes and other Matter (1972).

Minimum Wage Amendment Act 2016

This Act amends the Minimum Wage Act 1983 which implements the ILO Convention 14 (1921): Weekly Rest (Industry) and the ILO Convention 26 (1928): Minimum Wage-Fixing Machinery.

Misuse of Drugs Amendment Act 2015

This Act amends the Misuse of Drugs Act 1975, which implements the Single Convention on Narcotic Drugs (1961), the Convention on Psychotropic

Substances (1971), the Protocol to the Single Convention on Narcotic Drugs (1972), the Convention on the Physical Protection of Nuclear Material and Nuclear Facilities (1980), the Convention against Illicit Traffic in Narcotic Drugs and Psychotropic Substances (1988), the Recommendations of Financial Action Task Force (Task Force established 1989), and the Convention on the Marking of Plastic Explosives for the Purpose of Detection (1991).

Misuse of Drugs Amendment Act 1978 Amendment Act 2015

This Act amends the Misuse of Drugs Amendment Act 1978, which is read as part of the Misuse of Drugs Act 1975. The Misuse of Drugs Act 1975 implements the Single Convention on Narcotic Drugs (1961), the Convention on Psychotropic Substances (1971), the Protocol to the Single Convention on Narcotic Drugs (1972), the Convention on the Physical Protection of Nuclear Material and Nuclear Facilities (1980), the Convention against Illicit Traffic in Narcotic Drugs and Psychotropic Substances (1988), the Recommendations of Financial Action Task Force (Task Force established 1989), and the Convention on the Marking of Plastic Explosives for the Purpose of Detection (1991).

Mutual Assistance in Criminal Matters Amendment Act 2015

This Act amends the Mutual Assistance in Criminal Matters Act 1992, which implements the Single Convention on Narcotic Drugs (1961), the Convention for the Suppression of Unlawful Seizure of Aircraft (1970), the Convention on Psychotropic Substances (1971), the Protocol to the Single Convention on Narcotic Drugs (1972), the Convention for the Suppression of Unlawful Acts against the Safety of Civil Aviation (1973), the Convention on the Prevention and Punishment of Crimes against Internationally Protected Persons, Including Diplomatic Agents (1973), the Convention against the Taking of Hostages (1979), the Convention against Torture and Other Cruel, Inhuman, or Degrading Treatment or Punishment (1984), the Convention against Illicit Traffic in Narcotic Drugs and Psychotropic Substances (1988), the Protocol for the Suppression of Unlawful Acts of Violence at Airports Serving International Civil Aviation (1988), the Convention for the Suppression of Unlawful Acts against the Safety of Maritime Navigation (1988), the Protocol for the Suppression of Unlawful Acts against the Safety of Fixed Platforms Located on the Continental Shelf (1988), the Recommendations of Financial Action Task Force (Task Force established 1989), the Convention on the Safety of United Nations and Associated Personnel (1994), the Convention against Transnational Organised Crime (2000), the Protocol against the Smuggling of Migrants by Land, Sea and Air, supplementing the Convention against Transnational Organised Crime (2000), and the Protocol to Prevent, Suppress and Punish Trafficking of Persons, especially Women and Children, supplementing the Convention against Transnational Organised Crime (2000).

National Animal Identification and Tracing Amendment Act 2015

This Act amends the National Animal Identification and Tracing Act 2012, which implements Chapter 4.2 of the World Organisation for Animal Health's Terrestrial Animal Health Code.

Official Information Amendment Act 2015

This Act amends the Official Information Act 1982, which implements the Universal Declaration of Human Rights (1948), the Convention relating to the Status of Refugees (1951) [art 12], and the International Covenant on Civil and Political Rights (1966) [arts 14, 17, and 19].

Parental Leave and Employment Protection Amendment Act 2016

This Act amends the Parental Leave and Employment Protection Act 1987, which implements the ILO Convention 11 (1958): Discrimination (Employment and Occupation). The Act also amends the Employment Relations Act 2000, which implements the ILO Convention 11 (1921): Right of Association (Agriculture), the ILO Convention 14 (1921): Weekly Rest (Industry), the ILO Convention 22 (1926): Seamen's Articles of Agreement, the ILO Convention 32 (1932): Protection against Accidents (Dockers), and the ILO Convention 122 (1964): Employment Policy, and incorporates the principles underlying the ILO Convention 87 (1948): Freedom of association and ILO Convention 98 (1949): Right to Organise and Bargain Collectively. The Act also amends the Income Tax Act 2007, which implements the United Nations Framework Convention on Climate Change (1992), the Kyoto Protocol to the United Nations Framework Convention on Climate Change (1997) and enumerates a grey list of jurisdictions where tax exemption or relief laws might apply (schedule 24). A number of double taxation agreements with other jurisdictions are given effect via regulations made under the Act.

Passports Amendment Act 2015

This Act amends the Passports Act 1992, which implements the Convention relating to the Status of Refugees (1951), the Protocol relating to the Status of Refugees (1967), the Convention against Transnational Organised Crime (2000), the Protocol against the Smuggling of Migrants by Land, Sea and Air, supplementing the Convention against Transnational Organised Crime (2000), and the Protocol to Prevent, Suppress and Punish Trafficking of Persons, especially Women and Children, supplementing the Convention against Transnational Organised Crime (2000).

Sale and Supply of Alcohol Amendment Act 2015

This Act amends the Sale and Supply of Alcohol Act 2012, which implements the International Covenant on Civil and Political Rights (1966) [article 14], and the ILO Convention 59 (1937): Minimum Age (Industry).

Sale and Supply of Alcohol (Anzac Day Trading Hours for Licensed RNZRSA Clubs) Amendment Act 2016

This Act amends the Sale and Supply of Alcohol Act 2012 which implements the international Covenant on Civil and Political Rights (1966) [art 14] and the ILO Convention 59 (1937): Minimum Age (Industry).

Sale and Supply of Alcohol (Rugby World Cup 2015 Extended Trading Hours) Amendment Act 2015

This Act amends the Sale and Supply of Alcohol Act 2012, which implements the International Covenant on Civil and Political Rights (1966) [art 14], and the ILO Convention 59 (1937): Minimum Age (Industry).

Sentencing Amendment Act 2015

This Act amends the Sentencing Act 2002, which implements the Convention on the Physical Protection of Nuclear Material and Nuclear Facilities (1980), and the Convention on the Marking of Plastic Explosives for the Purpose of Detection (1991).

Social Assistance (Portability to Cook Islands, Niue, and Tokelau) Act 2015

This Act Amends the Social Security Act 1964, which implements the ILO Convention 44 (1934): Unemployment Provision, ILO Convention 122 (1964): Employment Policy, and the Convention on Social Security between the Government of the United Kingdom of Great Britain and Northern Ireland and the Government of New Zealand (1969).

Social Security Amendment Act 2015

This Act amends the Social Security Act 1964, which implements the ILO Convention 44 (1934): Unemployment Provision, the ILO Convention 122 (1964): Employment Policy, and the Convention on Social Security between the Government of the United Kingdom of Great Britain and Northern Ireland and the Government of New Zealand (1969).

Social Security Amendment Act (No 2) 2015

This Act amends the Social Security Act 1964, which implements the ILO Convention 44 (1934): Unemployment Provision, the ILO Convention 122 (1964):

Employment Policy, and the Convention on Social Security between the Government of the United Kingdom of Great Britain and Northern Ireland and the Government of New Zealand (1969).

Social Security (Commencement of Benefits) Amendment Act 2015

This Act amends the Social Security Act 1964, which implements the ILO Convention 44 (1934): Unemployment Provision, the ILO Convention 122 (1964): Employment Policy, and the Convention on Social Security between the Government of the United Kingdom of Great Britain and Northern Ireland and the Government of New Zealand (1969).

Summary Proceedings Amendment Act 2015

This Act amends the Summary Proceedings Act 1957, which implements the International Covenant on Civil and Political Rights (1966) [arts 10, 12, and 14], the Convention on the Elimination of All Forms of Discrimination against Women (1979) [arts 6 and 11], the Convention on the Physical Protection of Nuclear Material and Nuclear Facilities (1980), the Convention against Torture and Other Cruel, Inhuman or Degrading Treatment or Punishment (1984) [art 3], and the Convention on the Marking of Plastic Explosives for the Purpose of Detection (1991).

Tariff Amendment Act 2015

This Act amends the Tariff Act 1988, which implements the General Agreement on Tariffs and Trade (1947 and 1994), the Agreement between New Zealand and Singapore on Closer Economic Partnership (2001), the New Zealand-Thailand Closer Economic Partnership Agreement (2005), the Trans-Pacific Strategic Partnership Agreement among Brunei Darussalam, Chile, New Zealand, and Singapore (2005), the Free Trade Agreement between the Government of New Zealand and the Government of the People's Republic of China (2008), the Malaysia-New Zealand Free Trade Agreement (2009), the Agreement Establishing the ASEAN-Australia-New Zealand Free Trade Area (2009) and the New Zealand-Hong Kong, China Closer Economic Partnership Agreement (2010).

Taxation (New Zealand Superannuation and Retirement Income) Act 2015

This Act amends the Income Tax Act 2007, which implements aspects of the United Nations Framework Convention on Climate Change (1992) and the Kyoto Protocol to the United Nations Framework Convention on Climate Change (1997). The Act enumerates a grey list of jurisdictions where tax exemption or relief laws might apply (schedule 24). A number of double taxation agreements with other jurisdictions are given effect via regulations made under the Act.

Tokelau (Territorial Sea and Exclusive Economic Zone) Amendment
Act 2015

This Act amends the Tokelau (Territorial Sea and Exclusive Economic Zone) Act 1977, which implements the Convention on the Territorial Sea and Contiguous Zone (1958).

Trade in Endangered Species Amendment Act 2015

This Act amends the Trade in Endangered Species Act 1989, which implements the Convention on International Trade in Endangered Species of Wild Fauna and Flora (1973).

Wages Protection Amendment Act 2016

This Act amends the Wages Protection Act 1983 which implements the ILO Convention 95 (1949): Protection of Wages.

3.1.2   Acts Improving Compliance with Treaties Already Implemented
Human Rights Amendment Act 2016

This Act amends the Human Rights Act 1993, which implements the Universal Declaration of Human Rights (1948), the ILO Convention 97 (1949): Migration for Employment, the ILO Convention 100 (1951): Equal Remuneration, the Convention relating to the Status of Refugees (1951) [arts 2 and 4], the ILO Convention 111 (1958): Discrimination (Employment and Occupation), the Convention on the Elimination of All Forms of Racial Discrimination (1963), the ILO Convention 122 (1964): Employment Policy, the International Covenant on Civil and Political Rights (1966), the International Covenant on Economic, Social and Cultural Rights (1966), the Optional Protocol to the International Covenant on Civil and Political Rights (1966), the Convention on the Elimination of All Forms of Discrimination against Women (1979), and the United Nations Convention on the Rights of Persons with Disabilities (2006). The Act amends the functions of the Human Rights Commission, to include promotion and compliance with all international instruments on human rights ratified by New Zealand, and the promotion of the development of new international instruments on human rights.

Patents (Trans-Tasman Patent Attorneys and Other Matters)
Amendment Act 2016

This Act amends the Patents Act 2013, which implements the Budapest Treaty on the International Recognition of the Deposit of Microorganisms for the Purposes of Patent Procedure (1977), and the Patent Cooperation Treaty (1970). The amendments are designed to give better effect to the joint registration regime in accordance with the Arrangement between the Government of Australia and the Government of New Zealand Relating to Trans-Tasman Regulation of Patent Attorneys (2013).

Policing Amendment Act 2015

This Act amends the Policing Act 2008, which implements art 43 of the Charter of the United Nations (1945). The amendments allow the Commissioner of Police to disclose information to corresponding overseas agencies in accordance with international disclosure instruments (which include international agreements providing for the disclosure of information by the Police to overseas agencies).

Radiation Safety Act 2016

This Act replaces the Radiation Protection Act 1965, which implements the International Atomic Energy Agency Regulations for the Safe Transport of Radioactive Material (early 2000s). The Radiation Safety Act 2016 enables New Zealand to better meet its international obligations relating to radiation protection, radiation safety and security, and nuclear non-proliferation, including (but not limited to) its obligations under the Convention on the Physical Protection of Nuclear Material and Nuclear Facilities (1980), the Convention for the Suppression of Acts of Nuclear Terrorism (2005) and the Agreement between New Zealand and the International Atomic Energy Agency for the Application of Safeguards in Connection with the Treaty on the Non-Proliferation of Nuclear Weapons (1972). The Act also amends the Terrorism Suppression Act 2002, which implements the Convention on the Physical Protection of Nuclear Material and Nuclear Facilities (1980), the Recommendations of Financial Action Task Force (Task Force established 1989), the Convention on the Marking of Plastic Explosives for the Purpose of Detection (1991), the International Convention for the Suppression of Terrorist Bombing (1997), the International Convention for the Suppression of the Financing of Terrorism (1999), the United Nations Security Council Resolution 1267 (1999), the United Nations Security Council Resolution 1333 (2000), the Anti-Terrorism Resolution 1373 passed by the Security Council of the United Nations Organisation (2001), the United Nations Security Council Resolution 1390 (2002), and the Convention for the Suppression of Acts of Nuclear Terrorism.

3.1.3 Acts Implementing New Treaties

International Finance Agreements Amendment Act 2015

This Act amends the International Finance Agreements Act 1961, which implements the Articles of Agreement of the International Monetary Fund (1945), the Articles of Agreement of the International Finance Corporation (1945), the Articles of Agreement of the International Finance Corporation (1955), the Resolution of Board of Governors Setting Forth the Terms and Conditions Governing Admission to Membership in the International Monetary Fund (1961), the Resolution of Board of Governors Setting Forth the Terms and Conditions Governing Admission to Membership in the International Bank for Reconstruction and Development (1961), the Resolution of Board of Governors Setting Forth the Terms and Conditions Governing Admission to Membership in the International Finance Corporation (1961), and the Convention Establishing the Multilateral Investment Guarantee Agency (1985). The amendments implement the Asian Infrastructure Investment Bank Articles Agreement (2015), which enables the Government of New Zealand to be a member of the Asian Infrastructure Investment Bank.

> *Tariff (Free Trade Agreement between New Zealand and the Republic of Korea) Amendment Act 2015*

This Act amends the Tariff Act 1988, which implements the General Agreement on Tariffs and Trade (1947 and 1994), the Agreement between New Zealand and Singapore on Closer Economic Partnership (2001), the New Zealand-Thailand Closer Economic Partnership Agreement (2005), the Trans-Pacific Strategic Partnership Agreement among Brunei Darussalam, Chile, New Zealand, and Singapore (2005), the Free Trade Agreement between the Government of New Zealand and the Government of the People's Republic of China (2008), the Malaysia-New Zealand Free Trade Agreement (2009), the Agreement Establishing the ASEAN-Australia-New Zealand Free Trade Area (2009) and the New Zealand-Hong Kong, China Closer Economic Partnership Agreement (2010). The Act also implements New Zealand's obligations under the Free Trade Agreement between New Zealand and the Republic of Korea (2015).

3.2 *Regulations*[16]

This section sets out the regulations made during the current interval that relate to New Zealand's international obligations.[17]

---

16 The regulations listed under this heading supplement the list of regulations known to have implications for New Zealand's international obligations set out in Part V of Mark Gobbi, "In Search of International Standards and Obligations relevant to New Zealand Regulations" (2007–2008) 5 *New Zealand Yearbook of International Law* 327, 343–372.

17 This list of regulations does not include commencement orders for Acts that implement international obligations. See, e.g., International Finance Agreements Amendment Act 2013 Commencement Order 2016, International Finance Agreements Amendment Act 2015 Commencement Order 2015, and Tariff (Free Trade Agreement between New Zealand and the Republic of Korea) Amendment Act 2015 Commencement Order 2015.

3.2.1 Anti-Money Laundering and Countering Financing of Terrorism (Class Exemptions) Amendment Notice 2015

This notice is made under s 157(1) of the Anti-Money Laundering and Countering Financing of Terrorism Act 2009. The Act implements the Recommendations of the Financial Action Task Force (established 1989). This notice amends the Anti-Money Laundering and Countering Financing of Terrorism (Class Exemptions) Notice 2014, which sets out class exemptions to some of the rules contained within the principal Act. The exemptions are consistent with New Zealand's international obligations as a member of the Financial Action Task Force and the Asia Pacific Group on Money Laundering. The amendment adds a class to the class exemptions set out in the Schedule.

3.2.2 Anti-Money Laundering and Countering Financing of Terrorism (Class Exemptions) Amendment Notice (No 2) 2015

This notice is made under s 157(1) of the Anti-Money Laundering and Countering Financing of Terrorism Act 2009. The Act implements the Recommendations of the Financial Action Task Force (established 1989). This notice amends the Anti-Money Laundering and Countering Financing of Terrorism (Class Exemptions) Notice 2014, which sets out class exemptions to some of the rules contained within the principal Act. The exemptions are consistent with New Zealand's international obligations as a member of the Financial Action Task Force and the Asia Pacific Group on Money Laundering. The amendment adds two classes to the class exemptions set out in the Schedule.

3.2.3 Climate Change (Eligible Industrial Activities) Amendment Regulations 2016

These regulations are made under s 161A of the Climate Change Response Act 2002. The Act implements the United Nations Framework Convention on Climate Change (1992), and the Kyoto Protocol to the United Nations Framework Convention on Climate Change (1997). These regulations amend the Climate Change (Eligible Industrial Activities) Regulations 2010 to change the allocative baseline figures for the product produced by aluminium smelting.

3.2.4 Climate Change (Forestry Sector) Amendment Regulations 2015

These regulations are made under s 163 of the Climate Change Response Act 2002. The Act implements the United Nations Framework Convention on Climate Change (1992) and the Kyoto Protocol to the United Nations Framework Convention on Climate Change (1997). These regulations amend the Climate Change (Forestry Sector) Regulations 2008 by extending the pre-calculated values of carbon stock per hectare for exotic hardwoods to include forests older than 25 years. This allows an accurate estimate of carbon stocks in those forests.

3.2.5   Climate Change (Liquid Fossil Fuels) Amendment
Regulations 2015

These regulations are made under s 163 of the Climate Change Response Act 2002. The Act implements the United Nations Framework Convention on Climate Change (1992) and the Kyoto Protocol to the United Nations Framework Convention on Climate Change (1997). These regulations amend the Climate Change (Liquid Fossil Fuels) Regulations 2008 to allow opt-in participants to deduct from their emissions calculations emissions related to liquid fossil fuels that are exported from New Zealand. As these deductions can currently be made by obligation participants, the effect of the amendments is to address the inconsistency of treatment between opt-in participants and obligation participants.

3.2.6   Climate Change (Stationary Energy and Industrial Processes)
Amendment Regulations 2015

These regulations are made under s 163 of the Climate Change Response Act 2002. The Act implements the United Nations Framework Convention on Climate Change (1992) and the Kyoto Protocol to the United Nations Framework Convention on Climate Change (1997). These regulations amend the Climate Change (Stationary Energy and Industrial Processes) Regulations 2009 to adjust the requirements for collecting and recording information in relation to mined coal, to provide for the deduction of such coal from an annual emissions return, to clarify that an opt-in natural gas participant may calculate its emissions obligations using a unique emissions factor that the Environmental Protection Authority has approved the participant to use, and to update emissions factors to ensure that stationary energy and industrial process emissions reporting remains as accurate as possible.

3.2.7   Climate Change (Synthetic Greenhouse Gas Levies) Amendment
Regulations 2015

These regulations are made under ss 233(4)(a), 235(4), and 245(1) of the Climate Change Response Act 2002. The Act implements the United Nations Framework Convention on Climate Change (1992) and the Kyoto Protocol to the United Nations Framework Convention on Climate Change (1997). These regulations amend the Climate Change (Synthetic Greenhouse Gas Levies) Regulations 2013 to specify the price of carbon for the 2016 levy year and prescribe the rates of levy for leviable motor vehicles and goods for the 2016 levy year.

3.2.8 Climate Change (Unique Emissions Factors) Amendment Regulations 2015

These regulations are made under ss 163 and 164 of the Climate Change Response Act 2002. The Act implements the United Nations Framework Convention on Climate Change (1992) and the Kyoto Protocol to the United Nations Framework Convention on Climate Change (1997). These regulations amend the Climate Change (Unique Emissions Factors) Regulations 2009 to align with the default emissions factor in the Climate Change (Waste) Regulations 2010, and to allow historical annual landfill input tonnage data to be used when calculating landfill methane gas emissions, rather than the average filling rate, if the Environmental Protection Authority is satisfied it is reliable.

3.2.9 Climate Change (Waste) Amendment Regulations 2015

These regulations are made under s 163 of the Climate Change Response Act 2002. The Act implements the United Nations Framework Convention on Climate Change (1992) and the Kyoto Protocol to the United Nations Framework Convention on Climate Change (1997). These regulations amend the Climate Change (Waste) Regulations 2010 to update the default emissions factor used in calculating emissions from operating disposal facilities, so that it aligns with updated average waste composition data.

3.2.10 Customs and Excise (Rules of Origin for Republic of Korea FTA Goods) Amendment Regulations 2015

These regulations are made under ss 65 and 287A of the Customs and Excise Act 1996. The Act implements the Australia and New Zealand Closer Economic Relations Trade Agreement (1983), the International Convention on the Harmonised Commodity Description and Coding System (1983), the New Zealand-Thailand Closer Economic Partnership Agreement (2005), the Trans-Pacific Strategic Economic Partnership Agreement among Brunei Darussalam, Chile, New Zealand and Singapore (2005), the International Convention on the Harmonised Commodity Description and Coding System (1950), the ASEAN-Australia-New Zealand Free Trade Area Agreement (2008), the New Zealand-Hong Kong, China Closer Economic Partnership Agreement (2010), and the Agreement between New Zealand and the Separate Customs Territory of Taiwan, Penghu, Kinmen, and Matsu on Economic Cooperation (ANZTEC) (2013). These regulations amend the Customs and Excise Act 1996 to prescribe the rules of origin and product specific rules for goods imported from the Republic of Korea. These regulations also implement the Free Trade Agreement between New Zealand and the Republic of Korea (2015).

3.2.11   Double Tax Agreements (Samoa) Order 2015

This order is made under s BH 1 of the Income Tax Act 2007. The Act implements the ILO Convention 9 (1949): Migration for Employment, the Convention relating to the Status of Refugees (1951), the Covenant on Civil and Political Rights (1966), the Protocol Relating to the Status of Refugees (1967), the Convention Against Torture and Other Cruel, Inhuman and Degrading Treatment or Punishment (1984), the Convention against Transnational Organised Crime (2000), the Protocol against the Smuggling of Migrants by Land, Sea and Air, supplementing the Convention against Transnational Organised Crime (2000), and the Protocol to Prevent, Suppress and Punish Trafficking of Persons, especially Women and Children, supplementing the Convention against Transnational Organised Crime (2000). This order replaces the Double Tax Agreements (Samoa) Order 2010, which implemented two agreements between New Zealand and Samoa, once the Agreement between the Government of New Zealand and the Government of Samoa for the elimination of double taxation with respect to taxes on income and the prevention of tax evasion and avoidance (2015) comes into force.

3.2.12   Fisheries (Commercial Fishing) Amendment Regulations 2015

These regulations are made under s 297 of the Fisheries Act 1996. The Act implements the Agreement for the Implementation of the Provisions of the United Nations Convention on the Law of the Sea of 10 December 1982 relating to the Conservation and Management of Straddling Fish Stocks and Highly Migratory Fish Stocks (1982), and the United Nations Fish Stocks Agreement (1995). These regulations amend the Fisheries (Commercial Fishing) Regulations 2001 to change the restriction for eel fishing from a net mesh-based limit to a weight-based limit. These regulations also implement the Western and Central Pacific Fisheries Commission Conservation and Management Measure 2014–05, by inserting a new regulation 80A to prohibit the use of wire traces or shark lines by commercial tuna and billfish fishers.

3.2.13   Fisheries (High Seas Fishing Notifications: Western and Central
          Pacific Fisheries Commission) Amendment Notice 2016

This notice is made under s 113C of the Fisheries Act 1996. The Act implements the Agreement for the Implementation of the Provisions of the United Nations Convention on the Law of the Sea of 10 December 1982 relating to the Conservation and Management of Straddling Fish Stocks and Highly Migratory Fish Stocks (1982) and the United Nations Fish Stocks Agreement (1995). This notice amends the Fisheries (High Seas Fishing Notifications: Western and Central Pacific Fisheries Commission) Notice 2009, which gives notice that the Western and Central Pacific Fisheries Commission is an organisation or arrangement within the definition of a global, regional, or sub-regional fisheries organisation or arrangement in Part 6A of the Fisheries Act 1996. Notice is also given of a host of international conservation and management measures that the Commission has adopted. These measures apply to ships that are on the high seas in an area that the Commission covers and that are registered under the Ship Registration Act 1992 or fly the New Zealand flag. The 2016 amendment notice updates the list of international conservation and management measures that have been adopted by the Western and Central Pacific Fisheries Commission.

3.2.14   Fisheries (High Seas Fishing Notifications – Commission for the Conservation of Antarctic Marine Living Resources) Amendment Notice 2015

This notice is made under s 113C of the Fisheries Act 1996. The Act implements the Agreement for the Implementation of the Provisions of the United Nations Convention on the Law of the Sea of 10 December 1982 relating to the Conservation and Management of Straddling Fish Stocks and Highly Migratory Fish Stocks (1982) and the United Nations Fish Stocks Agreement (1995). This notice amends the Fisheries (High Seas Fishing Notifications – Commission for the Conservation of Antarctic Marine Living Resources) Notice 2009, which gives notice of a list of international conservation and management measures that the Commission for the Conservation of Antarctic Marine Living Resources has adopted. These measures apply to ships that are on the high seas in an area that the Commission covers and that are registered under the Ship Registration Act 1992 or fly the New Zealand flag. The 2015 amendment updates the list of international conservation and management measures that have been adopted by the Commission for the Conservation of Antarctic Marine Living Resources.

3.2.15   Fisheries (High Seas Fishing Notifications – Commission for the Conservation of Southern Bluefin Tuna) Amendment Notice 2015

This notice is made under s 113C of the Fisheries Act 1996. The Act implements the Agreement for the Implementation of the Provisions of the United Nations Convention on the Law of the Sea of 10 December 1982 relating to the Conservation and Management of Straddling Fish Stocks and Highly Migratory Fish Stocks (1982) and the United Nations Fish Stocks Agreement (1995). This notice amends the Fisheries (High Seas Fishing Notifications – Commission for the Conservation of Southern Bluefin Tuna) Notice 2009, which gives notice of a number of international conservation and management measures that the Commission for the Conservation of Southern Bluefin Tuna has adopted. These measures apply to shops that are on the high seas in an area that the Commission covers and that are registered under the Ship Registration Act 1992 or fly the New Zealand flag. The 2015 amendment notice updates the list of international conservation and management measures that have been adopted by the Commission for the Conservation of Southern Bluefin Tuna.

3.2.16   Food Regulations 2015

These regulations are made under ss 2(1), 8(3), 43, 76, 381, 383, 384, 386 to 392, and 418 of the Food Act 2014. The Act implements the Agreement between the Government of Australia and the Government of New Zealand concerning a Joint Food Standards System (1995). These regulations implement the new food safety regime established by the Act regarding how persons trade in food.

3.2.17   Marine Protection (Offences) Amendment Regulations 2015

These regulations are made under s 394 of the Maritime Transport Act 1994. The Act implements the International Convention for the Unification of Certain Rules of Law relating to Bills of Lading (1924), the Protocol to International Convention for the Unification of Certain Rules of Law relating to Bills of Lading (1968), the Convention on Civil Liability for Oil Pollution Damage (1969), International Convention on Tonnage Measurement of Ships (1969), the International Convention on the Establishment of an International Fund for Compensation for Oil Pollution Damage (1971), the Convention on the Prevention of Marine Pollution by Dumping of Wastes and other Matter (1972), the Protocol relating to Intervention on the High Seas in Cases of Pollution by Substances other than Oil (1973), the International Convention for the Prevention of Pollution from Ships (1973), the Convention on Limitation of Liability for Maritime Claims (1976), the Protocol to the International Convention for the Prevention of Pollution from Ships (1978), the International Convention on Standards of Training, Certification and Watchkeeping for Seafarers (1978), the Protocol to International Convention for the Unification of Certain Rules of Law relating to Bills of Lading (1979), the United Nations Convention on the Law of the Sea (1982), the International Convention on Salvage (1989), the Protocol to the Convention on Limitation of Liability for Maritime Claims (1996), the Protocol to the Convention on the Prevention of Marine Pollution by Dumping of Wastes and other Matter (1996), and the Protocol of 1996 to Amend the Convention on the Limitation of Liability for Maritime Claims (1976). These regulations amend the Marine Protection (Offences) Regulations 1998. The amendments make consequential changes to ensure consistency with the revocation of the Marine Protection Rules Part 124: the amendments to the Marine Protection Rules Part 170, which implement the International

Convention for the Prevention of Pollution from Ships (1973); the amendments to the Marine Protection Rules Part 150, which implement the International Convention for the Prevention of Pollution from Ships (1973) and the IMO International Maritime Dangerous Goods Code; and the new Marine Protection Rules Part 131 (which, among other things, will revoke the Marine Protection Rules Part 200). These regulations also give effect to New Zealand's international obligations following amendments to Annex V of the International Convention for the Prevention of Pollution from Ships (1973) as modified by the Protocol of 1978 (MARPOL) (2013).

3.2.18   Medicines Amendment Regulations (No 2) 2015

These regulations are made under s 105(1)(j) of the Medicines Act 1981. The Act implements the Single Convention on Narcotic Drugs (1961), the International Covenant on Civil and Political Rights (1966) [art 14], Convention on Psychotropic Substances (1971), the Protocol to the Single Convention on Narcotic Drugs (1972), and the Convention against Illicit Traffic in Narcotic Drugs and Psychotropic Substances (1988). These regulations amend the Medicines Regulations 1984, which implement the United Nations Convention on Psychotropic Substances (1971). These regulations set out an updated list of specified medicines and their classifications.

3.2.19   Minimum Wage Order 2016

This order is made under ss 4, 4A and 4B of the Minimum Wage Act 1983. The Act implements ILO Convention 14 (1921): Weekly Rest (Industry) and ILO Convention 26 (1928): Minimum Wage-Fixing Machinery. This order increases the minimum rates of pay for adult workers, starting-out workers, and trainees.

3.2.20   Product Safety Standards (Children's Nightwear and Limited Daywear Having Reduced Fire Hazard) Regulations 2016

These regulations are made under s 29 of the Fair Trading Act 1986. The Act implements the UN Guidelines for Consumer Protection (1985) and Annex 14 of the Free Trade Agreement between the Government of New Zealand and the Government of the People's Republic of China (2008), which sets out the Agreement between the Government of New Zealand and the Government of the People's Republic of China on Cooperation in the Field of Conformity Assessment in Relation to Electrical and Electronic Equipment and Components (2008). These regulations replace the Product Safety Standards (Children's Nightwear and Limited Daywear Having Reduced Fire Hazard) Regulations 2008 (the "2008 regulations"). The 2008 regulations declared the Australian/New Zealand Standard AS/NZS 1249:2003 (Children's nightwear and limited daywear having reduced fire hazard), with some variations, to be a product safety standard. That standard has now been updated and replaced with AS/NZS 1249:2014, and these regulations declare that new standard to be a product safety standard.

3.2.21 United Nations (Iran – Joint Comprehensive Plan of Action) Regulations 2016

These regulations are made under s 2 of the United Nations Act 1946. The Act implements art 41 of the Charter of the United Nations (1945). These regulations replace the current United Nations Sanctions (Iran) Regulations 2010 by imposing a new suite of restrictions in relation to Iran to give effect to Resolution 2231 of the Security Council of the United Nations, adopted under the United Nations Charter on 20 July 2015.

3.2.22 United Nations (South Sudan) Sanctions Regulations 2015

These regulations are made under s 2 of the United Nations Act 1946. The Act implements art 41 of the Charter of the United Nations (1945). These regulations give effect to Resolution 2206 (2015) of the Security Council of the United Nations, adopted pursuant to the United Nations Charter on 3 March 2015, which prevents certain persons from entering or transiting through New Zealand, and freezes the property of certain individuals or entities.

3.2.23 United Nations Sanctions (Yemen) Amendment Regulations 2015

These regulations are made under s 2 of the United Nations Act 1946. The Act implements art 41 of the Charter of the United Nations (1945). These regulations amend the United Nations Sanctions (Yemen) Regulations 2014 in order to give effect to Resolution 2216 (2015) of the Security Council of the United Nations, adopted pursuant to the United Nations Charter on 14 April 2015, which prohibits the exportation, transfer, or sale of arms that are intended for certain persons. New Zealand craft are also prohibited from carrying such arms, and persons in New Zealand (and New Zealand citizens in places outside New Zealand) are prohibited from providing training or assistance to certain persons in relation to military activities or the use and maintenance of arms.

3.2.24 United Nations (Syrian Cultural Property) Regulations 2015

These regulations are made under s 2 of the United Nations Act 1946. The Act implements art 41 of the Charter of the United Nations (1945). These regulations give effect to Resolution 2199 (2015) of the Security Council of the United Nations, adopted pursuant to the United Nations Charter on 12 February 2015, which prohibits the trade, transfer, import, and export of cultural property that was illegally removed from any place in Syria after 15 March 2011. The prohibition extends to property in respect of which there are reasonable grounds to suspect that it was illegally removed.

3.2.25   Various Civil Aviation Rules

Civil Aviation Act 1990 s 30 empowers the Minister to make rules for the designation, classification and certification of aircraft, pilots, crew members and other services, for the setting of standards, specifications, restrictions and licensing requirements, the conditions of operation of foreign aircraft and international flights to, from, or within NZ, and for a number of other purposes. Many of these rules incorporate international standards or implement international obligations. The following rules were made during the current interval:

> *Part 1: Definitions and Abbreviations Amendment 2015*
> *(Amendment 49)*

This rule amends Part 1 of the Civil Aviation Rules, which sets out the definitions and abbreviations contained in the rules. This rule inserts new definitions and abbreviations into the Civil Aviation Rules to align the rules with current international standards, definitions, abbreviations and measurements according to the International Civil Aviation Organization ("ICAO").

> *Part 47: Aircraft Registration and Making Amendment 2015*
> *(Amendment 5)*

This rule amends Part 47 of the Civil Aviation rules, which provide the framework and administrative machinery necessary for keeping the New Zealand Register of Aircraft. This rule addresses the current gap in the regulation of unmanned aircraft systems by establishing a new rule part to regulate the activity of these aircraft. Such amendments are in line with amendments to the Convention on International Civil Aviation (1944) that include implications for the regulations of international operations of unmanned aircraft systems.

> *Part 100: Safety Management 2016*

This rule was enacted under s 28 of the Civil Aviation Act 1990 to prescribe certification requirements for Safety Management Systems, which aim to improve New Zealand's aviation safety performance. The requirements prescribed in Part 100 include a safety policy, a process for risk management, safety assurance measures and training for personnel. This rule also ensures New Zealand meets its international obligations as a signatory to the Convention on International Civil Aviation (1944). There is an obligation on New Zealand to implement the ICAO's standards and recommended practices where practicable. Of relevance, these include a state safety programme in the form of a safety management system. Certificated organizations will have a Safety Management System in accordance with Part 100, and therefore this rule also includes amendments to the following parts: 115, 119, 121, 125, 135, 139, 141, 145, 146, 148, 149, 171, 173, 174, and 175.

Part 102: Unmanned Aircraft Operator 2015

This rule, which was made under ss 28, 29, and 30 of the Civil Aviation Act 1990, was enacted to address the immediate safety risks associated with the use of Unmanned Aircraft Systems, and take steps to achieve compliance with international standards and recommended practices with regard to unmanned aircraft as established by the International Civil Aviation Organization and the Convention on International Civil Aviation (1944). This rule also makes consequential amendments to the following parts: 1, 12, 19, 47, 91, and 101.

Part 139: Aerodromes – Certification, Operation and Use Amendment 2015 (Amendment 10)

This rule amends Part 139 of the Civil Aviation Rules, which provides the regulatory requirements relating to the certification and operation of aerodromes, the security measures applicable to aerodromes and the use of aerodromes by aircraft operators. This rule amends Part 139 in order to achieve greater compliance with Annex 14 of the Convention on International Civil Aviation (1944). The rule does this by providing a regulatory structure for the provision of air traffic services and developing appropriate transitional arrangements as necessary, to facilitate means of greater regulatory authority. This rule also makes consequential amendments to the following Parts: 1, 121, 125, 135, and 129.

Part 172: Air Traffic Service Organisations – Certification Amendment 2015 (Amendment 10)

This rule amends Part 172 of the Civil Aviation Rules, which prescribes the certification requirements, for the issue of an aviation document, for organizations currently providing, or intending to provide, any air traffic service. This rule updates the reference to surveillance in the rules in order to be consistent with international convention.

3.2.26   Various Land Transport Rules
Part 11 of the Land Transport Act 1998 provides for the making of rules with respect to various aspects of land transport. Many of these rules incorporate international standards or implement international obligations. None of the amendments made during the current interval affected New Zealand's international obligations.

3.2.27   Various Marine Protection Rules

Maritime Transport Act 1994 s 386(1) provides for the making of rules for the purposes of implementing New Zealand's obligations under any marine protection convention, to enable New Zealand to become a party to a convention, protocol or agreement relating to the protection of the marine environment and to implement international practices and standards relating to the protection of the marine environment that the International Maritime Organisation recommends. The following rules were made during the current interval:

Part 131: Offshore Installations – Oil Spill Contingency Plans and Oil Pollution Prevention Certification 2015

Part 131, which was made under ss 386, 387, 388, 390, and 451 of the Maritime Transport Act 1994, entered into force on 31 October 2015. The objective of Part 131 is to ensure that offshore installations operating in New Zealand continental waters and in the internal waters of New Zealand have oil spill contingency plans that will support an efficient and effective response to an oil spill at sea. It also ensures certain pollution prevention equipment and arrangements and on-board installations meet international performance standards and inservice maintenance requirements. Part 131 gives effect to the provisions of the International Convention for the Prevention of Pollution from Ships 1973/78 (MARPOL) concerning certification of certain equipment and arrangements for the prevention of oil pollution on board offshore installations, and the International Convention on Oil Pollution Preparedness, Response and Cooperation 1990 (OPRC) in respect of offshore installations.

Part 132: New Zealand Oil Spill Control Agents 2016

Part 132 entered into force on 11 January 2016. The objective of Part 132 is to ensure that New Zealand is prepared and able to respond to potential oil pollution incidents. Part 132 helps contribute to New Zealand meeting its international obligations in respect of protecting the marine environment. Part 132 gives effect to the provisions of the International Convention for the Prevention of Pollution from Ships 1973/78 (MARPOL) concerning the control of substances used to combat pollution incidents at sea, and the International Convention on Oil Pollution Preparedness, Response and Cooperation 1990 (OPRC) in respect of such incidents.

3.2.28   Various Maritime Rules

Maritime Transport Act 1994 s 36(1) provides for the making of rules for the purposes of the implementation of technical standards, codes of practice, performance standards and other requirements of certain conventions. Section 36(1)(u) of the Act provides for the making of rules for prescribing or providing for such matters as may be necessary to enable New Zealand to become a party to any international convention, protocol, or agreement relating to maritime transport as may be recommended by the International Maritime Organization. The following rule was made during the current interval:

Part 52: Maritime Labour Convention 2016

Part 52, which was made under s 36 of the Maritime Transport Act 1994, came into force on 1 October 2015. The objective of Part 52 is to give effect to the provisions of the Maritime Labour Convention 2006 (adopted by the International Labour Organisation) not covered elsewhere in New Zealand law, including other Maritime Rules. Part 52 does this by requiring registration of certain ships, imposing minimum requirements for seafarers to work on certain ships, requiring maritime labour certificates, and imposing rules regarding conditions of employment, accommodation and catering, and health and welfare.

4 Judicial Decisions Related to New Zealand's International Obligations

This Part sets out the reported and unreported judicial decisions rendered during the current interval that concern New Zealand's international obligations. It divides the reported cases into those cases reported in the New Zealand Law Reports ("NZLR") and those cases reported in other series. It also identifies the international agreements that were referenced and sets out the distribution of these references among the various courts.

4.1 *Reported Cases*

4.1.1 NZLR Cases

Air New Zealand Ltd v Disputes Tribunal [2016] NZHC 393, [2016] 2 NZLR 713 (High Court, Christchurch, Nation J), judicial review case that cites the Convention for the Unification of Certain Rules for International Carriage by Air (1999) [Montreal Convention].

B v Waitemata District Health Board [2016] NZCA 184, [2016] 3 NZLR 569 (Court of Appeal, Stevens, Cooper and Kós JJ), judicial review case that cites the United Nations Convention on the Rights of Persons with Disabilities (2006).

Chief Executive of the Ministry of Social Development v Black [2016] NZHC 1274, [2016] 3 NZLR 341 (High Court, Dunedin, Nation J), social security case that cites the United Nations Convention on the Rights of the Child (1989).

DP v R [2015] NZCA 476, [2016] 2 NZLR 306 (Court of Appeal, Harrison, Wild and Miller JJ), criminal procedure case that cites the United Nations

Convention on the Rights of the Child (1989) and the International Covenant on Civil and Political Rights (1966).

Marteley v Legal Services Commissioner [2015] NZSC 127, [2016] 1 NZLR 633 (Supreme Court, Elias CJ, William Young, Glazebrook, Arnold and O'Regan JJ), legal aid case that cites the International Covenant on Civil and Political Rights (1966) and the European Convention for the Protection of Human Rights and Fundamental Freedoms (1950).

R v Wichman [2015] NZSC 198, [2016] 1 NZLR 753 (Supreme Court, Elias CJ, Young, Glazebrook, Arnold, and O'Regan JJ), evidence law case that cites the United Nations Basic Principles and Guideline on the Right to a Remedy and Reparation of Victims of Gross Violations of International Human Rights Law and Serious Violations of International Humanitarian Law (2005), the United Nations Convention on the Rights of the Child (1989), and the United Nations Declaration of Basic Principles of Justice for Victims of Crime and Abuse of Power (1985).

Thompson v Attorney-General [2016] NZCA 215, [2016] 3 NZLR 206 (Court of Appeal, Wild, French and Cooper JJ), constitutional law case that cites the International Covenant on Civil and Political Rights (1966).

4.1.2   Cases Reported in Other Series that Reference International
          Obligations

Adoption Action Inc v Attorney-General [2016] NZHRRT 9, [2016] NZFLR 113, (2016) 10 HRNZ 622 (Human Rights Review Tribunal, Haines (Chairperson), Keefe, and Scott (Members)), family law case that cites the United Nations Convention on the Rights of the Child (1989) and the United Nations Convention on the Rights of Persons with Disabilities (2006).

AQ v Immigration and Protection Tribunal [2016] NZHC 367 (High Court, Auckland, Woodhouse J), judicial review case regarding immigration that cites the United Nations Convention Relating to the Status of Refugees (1951) and the Protocol Relating to the Status of Refugees (1967).

ASM v DPM [2016] NZHC 137, [2016] NZHC BCL 120, [2016] NZFLR 747 (High Court, Auckland, Venning J), family law case that cites the Convention Relating to the Status of Refugees (1951) and the Hague Convention on the Civil Aspects of International Child Abduction (1980).

Barrera v Cruz [2015] NZSC 135, [2015] BCL 348 (Supreme Court, Elias CJ, William Young, O'Regan JJ), family law case that cites the Hague Convention on the Civil Aspects of International Child Abduction (1980) and the Vienna Convention on Diplomatic Relations (1961).

Brown v R [2015] NZCA 325 (Court of Appeal, Wild, Keane and Kós JJ), criminal law case that cites the United Nations Convention on the Rights of the Child (1989).

BK v CJ [2015] NZHC 2990, [2016] BCL 87 (High Court, Whangarei, Duffy J), family law case that cites the Hague Convention on the Civil Aspects of International Child Abduction (1980).

BSC Construction Ltd v Withers [2015] NZHC 1988 (High Court, New Plymouth, Heath J), contract law case that cites the UNCITRAL Model Law on International Commercial Arbitration (1985).

BZ (Sri Lanka) v Immigration and Protection Tribunal of Auckland [2015] NZHC 2883 (High Court, Auckland, Whata J), immigration case that cites the United Nations Convention Relating to the Status of Refugees (1951).

Cardona v Valdez [2016] NZFC 2268 (Family Court, Porirua, O'Dwyer J), family law case that cites the United Nations Convention on the Rights of the Child (1989).

CF v Attorney-General [2016] NZHC 918, [2016] NZAR 848 (High Court, Auckland, Katz J), judicial review case regarding immigration that cites the Convention Relating to the Status of Refugees (1951).

Chief Executive of the Ministry of Business, Innovation and Employment v Nair [2016] NZCA 248, [2016] NZAR 836 (Court of Appeal, Ellen France P, Randerson and Miller JJ), judicial review case that cites the International Covenant on Civil and Political Rights (1966), the Convention on the Rights of the Child (1989), and the Convention Relating to the Status of Refugees (1951).

Chief Executive of the Ministry of Social Development v TM [2016] NZFC 1627 (Family Court, Hutt Valley, Judge AP Walsh), family law case that cites the United Nations Convention on the Rights of the Child (1989).

Chief Executive of the Ministry of Social Development (MSD) v LA [2016] NZFC 1640 (Family Court, Auckland, Judge E Smith), family law case that cites the United Nations Convention on the Rights of the Child (1989).

CP v Chief Executive, Ministry of Business, Innovation and Employment [2015] NZHC 3332 (High Court, Auckland, Duffy J), immigration case that cites the Convention against Torture and Other Cruel, Inhuman or Degrading Treatment or Punishment (1984), the International Covenant on Civil and Political Rights (1966), the Protocol Relating to the Status of Refugees (1967), the United Nations Convention Relating to the Status of Refugees (1951), and the Vienna Convention on the Law of Treaties (1969).

D v Immigration and Protection Tribunal [2015] NZHC 2458, [2015] NZAR 1940 (High Court, Auckland, Gilbert J), immigration case that cites the United Nations Convention Relating to the Status of Refugees (1951).

Delany v Mulloy [2016] NZFC 243 (Family Court, Christchurch, Judge E Smith), family law case that cites the United Nations Convention on the Recovery Abroad of Maintenance (1956).

Do v Police [2015] NZHC 2235 (High Court, Wellington, Clifford J), sentencing case that cites the International Covenant on Civil and Political Rights (1966).

Domb v Real Estate Agents Authority [2016] NZHC 3157, [2016] NZAR 47 (High Court, Wellington, Collins J), privacy law case that cites the European Convention for the Protection of Human Rights and Fundamental Freedoms (1950).

Fang v Ministry of Business, Innovation and Employment [2015] NZHC 2059 (High Court, Auckland, Fogarty J), immigration case that cites the United Nations Convention on the Rights of the Child (1989), the International Convention on Civil and Political Rights (1966), and the International Convention on Economic, Social and Cultural Rights (1966).

Gebrien v Todd [2015] NZFC 4949 (Family Court, Wellington, Judge JF Moss), family law case that cites the United Nations Convention on the Rights of the Child (1989).

Harlen v Chief Executive of the Ministry of Social Development [2015] NZHC 2663 (High Court, Auckland, Faire J), social security case that cites the International Covenant on Economic, Social and Cultural Rights (1966) and the United Nations Convention on the Rights of the Child (1989).

JS v Immigration and Protection Tribunal [2015] NZHC 2832, [2016] NZAR 111 (High Court, Auckland, Muir J), judicial review and immigration case that cites the Convention against Torture and Other Cruel, Inhuman or Degrading Treatment or Punishment (1984), the International Covenant on Civil and Political Rights (1966), and the Convention Relating to the Status of Refugees (1951).

JVF v PGF [2015] NZHC 2967 (High Court, Auckland, Moore J), evidence law case that cites the Hague Convention on the Civil Aspects of International Child Abduction (1980).

Kyburn Investments Ltd v Beca Corporation Holdings Ltd [2015] NZCA 290, [2015] BCL 289 (Court of Appeal, White, Fogarty, and Dobson JJ), arbitration case that cites the UNCITRAL Model Law on International Commercial Arbitration (1985).

Lawson v Chief Executive of the Ministry of Social Development [2016] NZHC 910 (High Court, New Plymouth, Dobson J), social welfare case that cites the United Nations Convention on the Rights of Persons with Disabilities (2006).

MAGB v GQC [2015] NZHC 1595, [2015] BCL 347 (High Court, Wellington, MacKenzie J), family law case that cites the United Nations Convention on the Rights of the Child (1989) and the Vienna Convention on Diplomatic Relations (1961).

Mailley v District Court at North Shore [2016] NZCA 83, [2016] BCL 81 (Court of Appeal, Randerson, Wild and Kós JJ), immigration case that cites the European

Convention for the Protection of Human Rights and Fundamental Freedoms (1950).

MGT v ACT [2015] NZHC 1857 (High Court, Auckland, Faire J), family law case that cites the Hague Convention on the Civil Aspects of International Child Abduction (1980).

Nathan v C3 Ltd [2015] NZCA 350, (2015) 13 NZELR 72, [2015] BCL 336 (Court of Appeal, Randerson, White and Winkelmann JJ), employment law case that cites the Right to Organise and Collective Bargaining Convention (1949) [ILO Convention 98] and the Freedom of Association and Protection of the Right to Organise Convention (1948) [ILO Convention 87].

Neville v Attorney-General [2015] NZHC 1946, [2015] NZAR 1537 (High Court, Auckland, Venning J), human rights case that cites the International Covenant on Civil and Political Rights (1966) and the European Convention for the Protection of Human Rights and Fundamental Freedoms (1950).

New Zealand Carbon Farming Ltd v Mighty River Power Ltd [2015] NZCA 605 (Court of Appeal, Wild, French, and Cooper JJ), environmental law case that cites the United Nations Framework Convention on Climate Change (1992) and the Protocol to the United Nations Framework Convention on Climate Change (1997).

New Zealand Police v VT [2016] NZYC 819, [2016] DCR 67 (Youth Court, Manukau, Judge AJ Fitzgerald), youth justice case that cites the United Nations Convention on the Rights of the Child (1989).

Nguyen v Mayer [2016] NZFC 1371 (Family Court, Tokoroa, Judge AC Willis), family law case that cites the Hague Convention on the Civil Aspects of International Child Abduction (1980).

Open Home Foundation v DP [2016] NZFC 2853 (Family Court, Masterton (held in Wellington), Walsh J), family law case that cites the United Nations Convention of the Rights of the Child (1989).

Peterson v Lucas [2015] NZCA 627 (Court of Appeal, Winkelmann, Courtney and Clifford JJ), civil procedure case that cites the Berne Convention for the Protection of Literary and Artistic Works (1886 as amended 1971).

Philip Grant Wallis v New Zealand Police [2015] NZHC 2904 (High Court, Auckland, Venning J), criminal law case that cites the United Nations Convention on the Rights of a Child (1989).

R v DP [2015] NZHC 1765 (High Court, Auckland, Lang J), criminal law case that cites the United Nations Convention on the Rights of the Child (1989).

Radhi v District Court at Manukau [2016] NZHC 3347 (High Court, Auckland, Woolford J), extradition case that cites the United Nations Convention on the Rights of the Child (1989).

Rangitonga v Parker [2016] NZCA 166, [2016] NZAR 768 (Court of Appeal, Randerson, Lang and Clifford JJ), criminal law case that cites the International Covenant on Civil and Political Rights (1966) and the European Convention for the Protection of Human Rights and Fundamental Freedoms (1950).

Re (1921) Livingstone v Livingstone [2015] NZHC 2575, [2015] NZAR 1827 (High Court, Wellington, Ellis J), civil procedure case that cites the International Covenant on Civil and Political Rights (1966) and the European Convention for the Protection of Human Rights and Fundamental Freedoms (1950).

RM v Immigration and Protection Tribunal [2016] NZHC 735 (High Court, Auckland, Palmer J), immigration law case that cites the United Nations Convention on the Rights of the Child (1989), the Convention against Torture and Other Cruel, Inhuman or Degrading Punishment (1984), the International Convention on Civil and Political Rights (1966), the Protocol Relating to the Status of Refugees (1967), and the United Nations Convention Relating to the Status of Refugees (1951).

Seward v Goosen [2016] NZFC 1884 (Family Court, New Plymouth, Barkle J), family law case that cites the United Nations Convention on the Rights of the Child (1989).

Siemer v Attorney-General [2016] NZSC 75, [2016] NZAR 765 (Supreme Court, Elias CJ, Glazebrook, and O'Regan JJ), civil procedure case that cites the International Covenant on Civil and Political Rights (1966).

Singh (Kulbir) v Chief Executive, Ministry of Business, Innovation and Employment [2015] NZCA 592, [2016] NZAR 93 (Court of Appeal, Harrison, Stevens and Wild JJ), judicial review case that cites the International Covenant on Civil and Political Rights (1966), the United Nations Convention on the Rights of the Child (1989), the European Convention for the Protection of Human Rights and Fundamental Freedoms (1950), and the Convention Relating to the Status of Refugees (1951).

S W v Chief Executive Office of the Ministry of Social Development [2016] NZHC 461 (High Court, Auckland, Palmer J), family law case that cites the United Nations Convention on the Rights of the Child (1989).

Taylor v Attorney-General [2015] NZHC 1706, [2015] BCL 350, [2015] 3 NZLR 791 (High Court, Auckland, Heath J), human rights case that cites the International Covenant on Civil and Political Rights (1966).

Taylor v Chief Executive of Department of Corrections [2015] NZCA 477, [2015] NZAR 1648 (Court of Appeal, Randerson, Harrison and Cooper JJ), judicial review case that cites the International Covenant on Civil and Political Rights (1966), the United Nations Standard Minimum Rules for the Treatment of Prisoners (1955), and the European Convention for the Protection of Human Rights and Fundamental Freedoms (1950).

Teitiota v Chief Executive of the Ministry of Business, Innovation and Employment [2015] NZSC 107 (Supreme Court, Elias CJ, William Young, Glazebrook, Arnold and O'Regan JJ), civil procedure case that cites the International Covenant on Civil and Political Rights (1966), the Convention on the Rights of the Child (1989), and the Convention Relating to the Status of Refugees (1951).

Thorpe v Barrett [2015] NZHC 3344 (High Court, Auckland, Courtney J), family law case that cites the United Nations Convention on the Rights of the Child (1989).

Toia v Prison Manager, Auckland Prison [2015] NZCA 624 (Court of Appeal, Ellen France P, French and Winkelmann JJ), criminal justice case that cites the European Convention for the Protection of Human Rights and Fundamental Freedoms (1950).

Tuitupou v New Zealand Immigration and Protection Tribunal [2015] NZHC 3158 (High Court, Auckland, Edwards J), immigration case that cites the United Nations Convention on the Rights of the Child (1989), and the International Covenant on Civil and Political Rights (1966).

United States of America v Dotcom CRI-2012-092-001647 Dec 23, 2015 (District Court, North Shore, Judge NR Dawson), extradition case that cites the Convention against Transnational Organised Crime (2000), the Extradition (United States of America) Order (1970), and the Vienna Convention on the Law of Treaties (1969).

Waitere v Chief Executive Office of Ministry of Social Development [2016] NZHC 461 (High Court, Auckland, Palmer J), family law case that cites the United Nations Convention on the Rights of the Child (1989).

Whittman v UCI Holdings Ltd [2016] NZHC 1228, [2016] NZAR 1008 (High Court, Auckland, Palmer J), cross-border insolvency case that cites the United Nations Model Law on Cross-Border Insolvency (1997).

Wu v Minister of Immigration [2016] NZHC 1309 (High Court, Auckland, Palmer J), immigration case that cites the United Nations Convention on the Rights of the Child (1989).

Yu v New Zealand Customs Service [2016] NZCA 140, [2016] NZAR 626 (Court of Appeal, Miller, Fogarty, and Toogood JJ), criminal law case that cites the United Nations Convention against Transnational Organised Crime and the Protocols Thereto (2000).

4.2   *Unreported Cases*

Owing to the advent of various electronic case law services and the timing of this publication, unreported judicial decisions rendered during the current interval that concern New Zealand's international obligations has become a rarity. This interval has none.

4.3   *Distribution of References to International Agreements among Various Courts, NZLR Cases, Other Reported Cases, and Unreported Case*[18]

International obligations	NZLR	Other	Unrep	All	Total
Convention on the Rights of the Child (1989)	SC: 1 CA: 1 HC: 1	SC: 1 CA: 3 HC: 12 FC: 5 YC: 1 HT: 1		SC: 2 CA: 4 HC: 13 FC: 5 YC: 1 HT: 1	26
Covenant on Civil and Political Rights (1966)	SC: 1 CA: 2	SC: 2 CA: 4 HC: 9		SC: 3 CA: 6 HC: 9	18
Convention Relating to the Status of Refugees (1951)		SC: 1 CA: 2 HC: 7		SC: 1 CA: 2 HC: 7	10
European Convention for the Protection of Human Rights and Fundamental Freedoms (1950)*	SC: 1	CA: 5 HC: 3		SC: 1 CA: 5 HC: 3	9
Convention on the Civil Aspects of International Child Abduction (1980)		SC: 1 HC: 4 FC: 1		SC: 1 HC: 4 FC: 1	6
Protocol Relating to the Status of Refugees (1967)		HC: 4		HC: 4	4
Convention on the Rights of Persons with Disabilities (2006)	CA: 1	HC: 1 HT: 1		CA: 1 HC: 1 HT: 1	3
Convention against Torture and Other Cruel, Inhuman or Degrading Treatment or Punishment (1984)		HC: 3		HC: 3	3
UNCITRAL Model Law on International Commercial Arbitration (1985)		CA: 1 HC: 1		CA: 1 HC: 1	2

---

18   **Key:** SC = Supreme Court, CA = Court of Appeal, HC = High Court, FC = Family Court, YC = Youth Court; DC = District Court, HT = Human Rights Review Tribunal, * = New Zealand is not a party to this Convention.

International obligations	NZLR	Other	Unrep	All	Total
Convention on the Law of Treaties (1969)		HC: 1 DC: 1		HC: 1 DC: 1	2
Convention on Economic, Social and Cultural Rights (1966)		HC: 2		HC: 2	2
Convention on Diplomatic Relations (1961)		SC: 1		SC: 1	1
United Nations Model Law on Cross-Border Insolvency (1997)		HC: 1		HC: 1	1
United Nations Convention against Transnational Organised Crime and the Protocols Thereto (2000)		CA: 1		CA: 1	1
Treaty on extradition between New Zealand and the United States of America (1970)		DC: 1		DC: 1	1
Convention against Transnational Organised Crime (2000)		DC: 1		DC: 1	1
United Nations Standard Minimum Rules for the Treatment of Prisoners (1955)		CA: 1		CA: 1	1
Convention for the Protection of Literary and Artistic Works (1886 as amended 1971)		CA: 1		CA: 1	1
United Nations Framework Convention on Climate Change (1992)		CA: 1		CA: 1	1
Protocol to the United Nations Framework Convention on Climate Change (1997)		CA: 1		CA: 1	1
Right to Organise and Collective Bargaining Convention (1949) [ILO Convention 98]		CA: 1		CA: 1	1

4.3   *Distribution of References to International Agreements* (cont.)

International obligations	NZLR	Other	Unrep	All	Total
Freedom of Association and Protection of the Right to Organise Convention (1948) [ILO Convention 87]		CA: 1		CA: 1	1
Convention on Diplomatic Relations (1961)		HC: 1		HC: 1	1
Convention as to the Recovery Abroad of Mainte-nance (1956)		FC: 1		FC: 1	1
Convention for the Unification of Certain Rules for International Carriage by Air (1999)	HC: 1			HC: 1	1
United Nations Basic Principles and Guideline on the Right to a Remedy and Reparation of Victims of Gross Violations of International Human Rights Law and Serious Violations of Humanitarian Law (2005)	SC: 1			SC: 1	1
United Nations Declaration of Basic Principles of Justice for Victims of Crime and Abuse of Power (1985)	SC: 1			SC: 1	1
Totals	11	90	0	101	101

5 Update of Master List of Implementing Acts

This Part updates the master list of implementing Acts set out in Part 5 of "In Search of International Standards and Obligations Relevant to New Zealand Acts" (2007) 4 *New Zealand Yearbook of International Law* 366–93 (as amended).[19] The master list entries should be amended as follows:

International Finance Agreements Act 1976
Add the following item:
Asian Infrastructure Investment Bank Articles Agreement (2015)

Tariff Act 1988
Add the following item:
Free Trade Agreement between New Zealand and the Republic of Korea (2015)

6 Update of Master List of Implementing Regulations

This Part updates the master list of implementing regulations set out in Part 5 of "In Search of International Standards and Obligations relevant to New Zealand Regulations" (2007–2008) 5 *New Zealand Yearbook of International Law* 327–72 (as amended).[20] The master list should be amended as follows:

---

19   For previous amendments to the master list, see Gobbi (2015), above n 3, 335–336; Mark Gobbi, "Treaty Action and Implementation" (2014) 12 *New Zealand Yearbook of International Law* 247, 286; Mark Gobbi, "Treaty Action and Implementation" (2013) 11 *New Zealand Yearbook of International Law* 285, 326–328; Mark Gobbi, "Treaty Action and Implementation" (2012) 10 *New Zealand Yearbook of International Law* 261, 302–303; Mark Gobbi, "Treaty Action and Implementation" (2011) 9 *New Zealand Yearbook of International Law* 351, 386; Mark Gobbi, "Treaty Action and Implementation" (2010) 8 *New Zealand Yearbook of International Law* 283, 328–329; Mark Gobbi, "Treaty Action and Implementation" (2009) 7 *New Zealand Yearbook of International Law* 381, 424–431; Mark Gobbi, "Treaty Action and Implementation" (2008) 6 *New Zealand Yearbook of International Law* 379, 418–420; Mark Gobbi, "Treaty Action and Implementation" (2007–2008) 5 *New Zealand Yearbook of International Law* 279, 326.

20   For previous amendments to the master list, see Gobbi (2015), above n 3, 336–339; Mark Gobbi, "Treaty Action and Implementation" (2014) 12 *New Zealand Yearbook of International Law* 247, 287–290; Mark Gobbi, "Treaty Action and Implementation" (2013) 11 *New Zealand Yearbook of International Law* 285, 328–332; Mark Gobbi, "Treaty Action and Implementation" (2012) 10 *New Zealand Yearbook of International Law* 261, 303–306; Mark Gobbi, "Treaty Action and Implementation" (2011) 9 *New Zealand Yearbook of International Law* 351, 386–389; Mark Gobbi, "Treaty Action and Implementation" (2010) 8

6.1   *New Entries*

Add the following entries in their appropriate alphabetical order:

Civil Aviation Rules: Part 100 – Safety Management 2016
Civil Aviation Act 1990, s 28
Convention on International Civil Aviation (1944)

Civil Aviation Rules: Part 102 – Unmanned Aircraft Operator 2015
Civil Aviation Act 1990, ss 28, 29, and 30
Convention on International Civil Aviation (1944)

Civil Aviation Rules: Part 139 – Aerodromes – Certification, Operation and Use 1992
Civil Aviation Act 1990, s 30
Convention on International Civil Aviation (1944)

Fisheries (Commercial Fishing) Regulations 2001
Fisheries Act 1996, s 297
Western and Central Pacific Fisheries Commission Conservation and Management Measure 2014–05

Food Regulations 2015
Food Act 2014, ss 2(1), 8(3), 43, 76, 381, 383, 384, 386 to 392, and 418
Agreement between the Government of Australia and the Government of New Zealand concerning a Joint Food Standards System (1995)

Marine Protection (Offences) Regulations 1998
Maritime Transport Act 1994, ss 394 and 201
Annex 5 of the International Convention for the Prevention of Pollution from Ships (1973), as modified by the Protocol of 1978 (MARPOL), which came into effect on 1 January 2013

Marine Protection Rules: Part 131 – Offshore Installations – Oil Spill Contingency Plans and Oil Pollution Prevention Certification 2015
Maritime Transport Act 1994, ss 386, 387, 388, 390, and 451

New Zealand Yearbook of International Law 283, 330–335; Mark Gobbi, "Treaty Action and Implementation" (2009) 7 *New Zealand Yearbook of International Law* 381, 425–431; Mark Gobbi, "Treaty Action and Implementation" (2008) 6 *New Zealand Yearbook of International Law* 379, 421–423.

International Convention for the Prevention of Pollution from Ships (1973)
International Convention on Oil Pollution Preparedness, Response and Cooperation (1990)

Maritime Rules: Part 52 – Maritime Labour Convention 2016
Maritime Transport Act 1994, s 36
Maritime Labour Convention (2006)

Minimum Wage Order 2016
Minimum Wage Act 1983, ss 4, 4A and 4B
ILO Convention 14 (1921): Weekly Rest (Industry)
ILO Convention 26 (1928): Minimum Wage-Fixing Machinery

United Nations (Iran – Joint Comprehensive Plan of Action) Regulations 2016
United Nations Act 1946, s 2
Resolution 2231 of the Security Council of the United Nations (2015)

United Nations (South Sudan) Sanctions Regulations 2015
United Nations Act 1946, s 2
Resolution 2206 of the Security Council of the United Nations (2015)

United Nations (Syrian Cultural Property) Regulations 2015
United Nations Act 1946, s 2
Resolution 2199 of the Security Council of the United Nations (2015)

6.2   *Changes to Entries*
Customs and Excise Regulations 1996
Add "Free Trade Agreement between New Zealand and the Republic of Ko-
rea (2015)" after "Agreement between New Zealand and the Separate Customs
Territory of Taiwan, Penghu, Kinmen, and Matsu on Economic Cooperation
(ANZTEC) (2013)".

Double Tax Agreements (Samoa) Order 2010
Replace with the following item:[21]

Double Tax Agreements (Samoa) Order 2015
Income Tax Act 2007, s BH 1

---

21   This change is anticipatory. The new 2015 order will, in effect, displace the 2010 order
     when the 2015 Agreement comes into force.

Agreement between the Government of New Zealand and the Government of Samoa for the elimination of double taxation with respect to taxes on income and the prevention of tax evasion and avoidance (2015)

Marine Protection Rules: Part 131 – Offshore Installations – Oil Spill Contingency Plans and Oil Pollution Prevention Certification 2015
Add the following item:

International Convention on Oil Pollution Preparedness, Response and Co-operation (1990)

Product Safety Standards (Children's Nightwear and Limited Daywear Having Reduced Fire Hazard) Regulations 2008
Replace with the following item:

Product Safety Standards (Children's Nightwear and Limited Daywear Having Reduced Fire Hazard) Regulations 2016
Fair Trading Act 1986, s 29
Australian Standard AS 1182 1997 size coding scheme for infants' and children's clothing underwear and outerwear
Australian/New Zealand Standard AS/NZS 1249:2014 children's nightwear and limited daywear having reduced fire hazard

United Nations Sanctions (Yemen) Amendment Regulations 2015
Add the following item:

Resolution 2216 of the Security Council of the United Nations (2015)

Book Reviews

∵

Research Handbook on International Law and Natural Resources

By Elisa Morgera and Kati Kulovesi (eds)
[Cheltenham: Edward Elgar Publishing Limited, 2016, 551 pp. ISBN 978-1-78347-832-3]

Elizabeth Macpherson*

As we enter the *Anthropocene*, we humans find ourselves in the unenviable position of having demands for natural resources that may soon exceed the available, clean, supply.[1] The existing attention to natural resources in scholarly debate, at least at the international level, has typically been organised by resource, inhibiting the analysis of cross-cutting themes.[2] By contrast, the *Research Handbook on International Law and Natural Resources* sets out to synthesise the complicated web of international laws, frameworks and institutions bearing on the regulation of all natural resources. The authors seek to elevate the position of apparently disparate rules affecting natural resources as a discrete field of international law, concerned with materials that exist in nature and are of benefit to humans (preface, x). Doing so with success, the book might have been called the research handbook on the "international law *of* natural resources".

Impressive in its breadth, the book provides a systematic doctrinal (and sometimes theoretical) survey of environmental, human rights and economic law and the law of the sea, at an international, regional and transnational level, on a wide range of natural resources. The content is organised principally by resource, including the usual suspects of natural resource studies: land, water, minerals, fisheries, forests and energy. Yet it extends to natural resources of new and emerging extraction technologies, including biofuels, genetic resources, and resources of the polar extremes, the deep and high seas, and even

* University of Canterbury

1 The "Anthropocene" is known as the new geological epoch in which people have a devastating and overwhelming impact on the earth and its system. See Louis J Kotzé, "Rethinking Global Environmental Law and Governance in the Anthropocene" (2014) 32(2) *Journal of Energy & Natural Resources Law* 121.

2 An exception to this is Aileen McHarg, Barry Barton, Adrian Bradbrook and Lee Godden (eds), *Property and the Law in Energy and Natural Resources* (Oxford University Press, 2010), which is an excellent comparative case study analysis of property law theory across a range of natural resources, drawing primarily on domestic law, with some international content.

outer space. Although legal analysis is front and centre and the book's repertoire of international instruments is extensive, the contributors give due attention to the increasing influence of non-state actors, international cooperation
and "soft law" in the creation and enforcement of international norms, giving
the book a distinctive institutional focus. Thus, the reader gains a crucial understanding of the interplay between rules of international law and the processes that monitor and adjudicate them.

The book begins, in Part 1, by setting up key concepts in the international
regulation of natural resources, which are touched upon in the resource-
specific analyses in Parts 2 and 3. In Chapter 1, Virginie Barral provides a useful sketch of the historical framing of natural resources in international law:
the idea that natural resources are the demise of sovereign states (p. 5). Yet
shared international concerns about natural resource management, including transboundary ownership and global environmental degradation, have led
international norms to encroach upon the national sphere in the pursuit of
"sustainable development" (p. 8), beginning with the *Stockholm Declaration* in
1972.[3] Chapters 2 and 3 address the relationships between international trade
and investment law and natural resources, a relationship through which many
resource conflicts have played out (Viñuales, p. 26 and Kulovesi, p. 46 respectively). These chapters use high-profile and interesting cases to illustrate arguments, such as the *Chevron and Texaco Petroleum* contamination controversy
in Ecuador (p. 38). Chapter 4 examines the way international human rights
law has been used by communities to protect natural resources from development, including the co-option of the right to "property" by indigenous peoples
to protect collective, territorial rights in international and regional fora (Francioni, p. 72).[4] In Chapter 5, Emanuela Orlando discusses the "resource curse"
theme recurring in many of the chapters: the idea that countries blessed with
the most ample supplies of natural resources are often the poorest (p. 87).
Orlando argues this is due, in large part, to corruption and often precipitates
localised conflict. To round off the theoretical framework, Morgera addresses
corporate accountability in Chapter 6 (p. 109). This is of increasing concern
to international theorists of natural resources because of the use of corporate
structures to minimise environmental compliance and the growing influence
of "soft-law" pressures towards environmental accountability in commercial

---

3 *United Nations Conference on the Human Environment,* GA Res 2994, UN GAOR, 27th sess,
   2112th plen mtg, UN Doc A/Res/2994 (12 December 1972).

4 *American Convention on Human Rights,* opened for signature 2 November 1969, 1144 UNTS 123
   (entered into force 18 July 1978) art 21.

arrangements, like the OECD *Guidelines for Multinational Enterprises*[5] and the UN's *"Global Compact"* (pp. 113–116).

The core of the book is the analysis of the international law treatment of a wide array of natural resources, logically divided between resources within national jurisdiction (Part 2) and resources beyond national jurisdiction (Part 3). The research-specific studies include biological resources, energy and minerals, and resources of the oceans, Arctic and Antarctic. All contributions to this part are useful, although some are particularly interesting. Trouwborst's chapter (p. 198) provides an interdisciplinary analysis of the less prominent field of wildlife and landscapes in natural resources law, referring principally to the 1992 *Convention on Biological Diversity*.[6] The chapter also makes the theoretical distinction between the (often conflated) international law of natural resources and international environmental law, the former of which has been mostly concerned with national sovereignty over the benefits of resource extraction and use, and the latter with the need for environmental protection (and sustainability) as a common, perhaps global, concern (p. 205). The chapters on minerals (Kidd, p. 327) and high seas fisheries (Barnes and Massarella, p. 369) are particularly well structured, covering the historical evolution of international law dealing with these common resources and providing a clear roadmap for future research.

The resource-specific studies in Parts 2 and 3 refer extensively to international law doctrine in a range of international documents of varying force. Yet from a conceptual perspective, the chapters exhibit common themes of international law, despite the diversity of the natural resources addressed. The commonalities lend weight to the editors' claim that a distinct branch of international law has emerged with respect to national resources. Common themes across the resource-specific studies include: the "resource curse"; "permanent sovereignty" over natural resources; what is meant by "sustainability" and required by "biodiversity"; the difficulty of enforcing international rules and standards; and the growing importance of transnational cooperation and "soft-law". The position of indigenous peoples with respect to natural resources, and the relevance of the *United Nations Declaration on the Rights of Indigenous Peoples*[7] and International Labour Organisation *Convention 169*[8] is also touched

---

5   OECD, *Guidelines on Multinational Enterprises* (OECD Publishing, 2011).

6   *Convention on Biological Diversity*, opened for signature 5 June 1992, 1760 UNTS 382 (entered into force 29 December 1993).

7   *United Nations Declaration on the Rights of Indigenous Peoples*, GA Res 61/295, UN GAOR, 61st sess, 107th plen mtg, Supp No 49, UN Doc A/RES/61/295 (13 September 2007).

8   *Convention Concerning Indigenous and Tribal Peoples in Independent Countries* (*ILO No. 169*), opened for signature 27 June 1989, 28 ILM 1382 (entered into force 5 September 1991).

upon in many chapters (Koivurova on Arctic resources, pp. 360–361 and Cotula on land, pp. 140–145). These discussions highlight the developing influence of non-state actors (including indigenous and local communities) in driving international legal developments.

In Part 4 the book delves further into the role of actors and institutions in international law-making, although institutions certainly feature in many of the resource-specific studies (for example, Koivurova's discussion of the Arctic Council, p. 349). Included in this part is a particularly good chapter on global governance by Kim and van Asselt, which highlights "problem shifting" in international natural resources law: the way in which addressing a concern about the regulation of one natural resource often displaces the problem towards a different resource (p. 475). This, the contributors argue, is a consequence of the disjointed historical regulation of natural resources, requiring a more holistic and earth-centred approach to the treatment of natural resources in international law.

The main task of the book, as research handbook, is to set an agenda for future legal research. This is done to varying degrees in the conclusions of individual chapters and in the final chapter written by the editors (p. 517). The gaps identified include: the conceptual underpinnings of sustainable development; indigenous perspectives on natural resources; the impact of, and potential for, soft law in international natural resource regulation; the growing influence of international trade law on natural resources (including the question of when resources leave a natural state and become goods); the use of market-based frameworks to allocate resource rights; how to integrate natural resource institutions across jurisdictions and sectors; and international frameworks needed for new and emerging uses of natural resources. Yet, as a researcher in the field of natural resources, I found myself hungering for more: more scrutiny of research gaps and more discussion of unanswered questions. After all, that is the benefit of combining so much expertise into one book.

Which leads me to a new subject in the global regulation of natural resources, prefaced by the editors as worthy of further attention (preface, xi), although it enjoys only passing consideration in this book. That is, the tendency towards a more *ecocentric* view of natural resources, in which natural resources are governed in a way that benefits the earth itself, not merely the humans that inhabit it. I would have expected some acknowledgement of calls within global debates (officially recognised or otherwise) for "rights for nature", including legal personality for natural resources,[9] and the ensuing need for further

---

9   See Michelle Maloney, "Building an Alternative Jurisprudence for the Earth: The International Rights of Nature Tribunal" (2016) 1 *Vermont Law Review* 129. In line with this ecocentric

research in this area. The editors of the *Research Handbook* are well-known in the field of international law and natural resources, and the contributors have also been well-selected for their expertise, although conspicuously for an international law text, they are predominantly from European institutions. Perhaps if the book had included more contributions from the southern hemisphere, demands for an ecocentric shift, including legal personality for natural resources, would have featured more strongly.

That aside, as a research handbook, the book has wide appeal to students, scholars and practitioners alike. Its primary appeal is to those approaching new areas of research, as it identifies key areas requiring further research attention. The contentions made by the contributors rest upon a solid primary and secondary research base and are well-referenced, well-edited and accessible to a variable audience. The book is undoubtedly a valuable source of knowledge (to which I will certainly refer in my own teaching and research), representing the most comprehensive analysis of the international regulation of natural resources to date.

---

tendency, domestic courts and legislation have recognised the "rights" of natural resources in Ecuador, Bolivia, India, Colombia and, notably, New Zealand with the *Te Awa Tupua* (*Whanganui River Claims Settlement*) *Act 2017* (NZ).

The International Criminal Court in an Effective Global Justice System

By Linda E Carter, Mark S Ellis and Charles Chernor Jalloh
[Cheltenham, Edward Edgar Publishing, 2016, 353 pp. ISBN:
978-1-78471-981-4. GB£ 95]

Cassandra Mudgway*

This book is particularly timely, with the future of the International Criminal Court (ICC) on somewhat uncertain footing. The African Union (AU), for example, has accused the Court of unfairly targeting the African continent and has supported member states that have signalled withdrawal from the ICC.[1] With African States being overrepresented in situations within the jurisdiction of the Court, such tensions may have serious implications for the enforcement of international criminal law. Written in the background of non-compliance and a general lack of cooperation from state and non-state parties, *The International Criminal Court in an Effective Global Justice System* nevertheless presents an overall optimistic assessment of the Court's (potential and actual) relationships with a diverse range of international actors. As the ICC is founded on the principle of complementarity, the book's six chapters argue that positive partnerships between the Court and national jurisdictions can help develop a more effective system of international criminal justice. Each chapter examines different types of relationships and so offers recommendations and analysis that are multifaceted and thus relevant for this multifaceted problem.

Chapter 1 addresses the different relationships that exist in international criminal justice generally. In doing so, the chapter outlines the goals of the book, which includes analysing the practice of international criminal courts, comprising: the International Criminal Tribunals for the former Yugoslavia (ICTY) and Rwanda (ICTR); The Special Courts of Sierra Leone (SCSL); The Extraordinary Chambers in the Court of Cambodia (ECCC); the Special Tribunal for Lebanon (STL); and the ICC itself. The book aims to identify best practice and lessons learned with regard to the courts' interactions with multiple international actors, such as: national criminal courts; the Security Council; regional organisations; and non-governmental organisations (NGOs). Four themes are used as tools for evaluation:

---

* Auckland University of Technology

1 Aljazeera "South Africa to Quit International Criminal Court" *Aljazeera English*, 22 October 2016 <http://video.aljazeera.com/channels/eng/videos/south-africa-set-to-quit-international -criminal-court/5181115917001>.

(1)   Accountability;
(2)   Tension between international justice and politics;
(3)   National capacity; and
(4)   Legitimacy.

These themes are weaved throughout the book, although not always specifically drawn upon when making recommendations or in conclusions.

Chapters 2 and 3 focus on the principal relationships between international criminal courts and national jurisdictions. As national criminal courts have the primary task of prosecuting atrocity crimes, Chapter 2 explores the international criminal courts' role in assisting and building state capacity to investigate and prosecute such international crimes. This chapter balances the themes of accountability and the need to protect state sovereignty. Various challenges to prosecution at the national level are discussed, including the difficulties in implementing the necessary legislation to allow prosecutions to take place, the existence of amnesties or immunities for key individuals, and the lack of expertise and security in post-conflict contexts. Chapter 2 argues that international criminal courts are best placed to offer assistance and capacity building, while equally acknowledging that the ICC is not currently resourced to allow for such capacity building. This chapter explores the past practice of the ICTY and ICTR in supporting local prosecution. Analysis reveals it was a rocky road for both Tribunals in transferring cases to national judicial systems and the follow-up of training local personnel. The chapter progresses with an exploration of ICC practice, highlighting the particular role of the Legal Tools Project and the Office of the Prosecutor (OTP). Consistent with the overall tone of the book itself, despite the acknowledged mixed success of past practice, the chapter is optimistic about the potential for collaborative enterprise. The book makes recommendations for the ICC to initiate a "conceptual shift" to emphasise national prosecutions and strengthen efforts in national capacity building (68).

Leading on from the previous chapter's emphasis on national jurisdictions, Chapter 3 examines the methods employed by international criminal courts to secure cooperation from states. Such cooperation includes executing arrest warrants, extradition and other necessary legal assistance. Chapter 3 illustrates that a lack of political will and inadequate funding has hindered state cooperation with the ICTY, ICTR, ECCC and STL. However, the SCSL is singled out as an overall success story because of its positive interactions with the Sierra Leone government. The role of the Security Council is highlighted as having unique relationships with each court. The chapter then assesses immunities as a bar to cooperation with particular reference to the ICC arrest warrant for Omar Hassan Al-Bashir, sitting President of Sudan, which has failed to be executed by African state parties. Continuing on from this, the chapter considers the issue of non-compliance, which has plagued all international criminal courts to varying extents. This discussion is contrasted with successful examples of cooperation secured by the exertion of international pressure from a diverse range of actors such as the North Atlantic Treaty Organisation, the European Union, and other states. Returning once more to the role of the Security Council, the chapter concludes with an argument for more robust enforcement measures. The Security Council's potential role in compelling compliance from states and regional organisations, such as the AU, appears contradictory to the chapter's emphasised importance of political will. For example, there is no discussion around how compelling the AU to comply with the ICC will improve political will of African States to positively engage with the Court.

As the ICC is moving towards promoting a mixed retributive-restorative approach to international criminal justice and the importance of transitional justice in post-conflict states, Chapter 4 is an essential addition to the book. This chapter assesses the extent to which non-judicial measures, such as truth commissions, amnesties and traditional mediation practices, could be considered under arts 17 and 53 in the Rome Statute. After introducing the concept and purpose of non-judicial proceedings, this chapter presents a detailed analysis of admissibility (art 17) and the Prosecutor's discretion not to prosecute in the "interests of justice" (art 53) using the tools of treaty interpretation. Overall, the analysis leads into a conclusion where blanket and self-imposed amnesties, most truth commissions and traditional mediation, would be precluded from consideration under both articles. The chapter ends with recommendations for an expert panel to review the same question and, if required, propose amendments to the Rome Statute.

Illustrating another alternative to national prosecution, Chapter 5 investigates the intersection between international law and international politics, focusing on the relationship between the ICC and African States in light of the AU developing a regional court with jurisdiction over atrocity crimes. Instead of focussing solely on the rising tensions between African States and the ICC, this chapter presents a variety of historic factors that fuelled the desire for regional prosecution of international crimes, including the creation of the AU itself. Chapter 5 is perhaps the most optimistic; instead of arguing that African States should be compelled to cooperate directly with the ICC (as argued in Chapter 3), this chapter contends that regionalisation of enforcement is a potential step forward for eliminating impunity. However, the authors note that the challenges of inadequate resources and political will remains. Using the development of regional human rights courts as an example, the authors argue that regional criminal courts could offer another layer of enforcement.

Being localised, these courts would operate within the historic, cultural and legal context of affected countries (and thus have perceived legitimacy). As the ICC has the same goal of ending impunity, Chapter 5 recommends that the Court should "keep an open mind" and engage more closely with regional organisations (262).

Chapter 6 considers the role that NGOs (and other international actors) can have in the development of international criminal justice. This chapter provides a detailed analysis of submissions made by NGOs through amicus curiae briefs in the international criminal courts. The chapter summarises the submissions that were either accepted or rejected by the ICC, ICTY, ICTR, ECCC, SCSL and STL. Chapter 6 analyses the potential influence of these briefs on judgments. Assessment of such influence reveals a general lack of transparency and inconsistent practice. Judgments of the ICC and ICTY make limited reference to amicus curiae briefs and thus, it is difficult to assess their influence. However, where amicus curiae briefs were referenced, they were revealed to be powerful tools for both legal and factual considerations. The *Jean-Paul Akayseu* case in the ICTR is a prime example, where NGO amicus briefs influenced the OTP to amend charges to include sexual violence.[2] The ultimate decision of *Jean-Paul Akayseu* was the first to link rape and genocide. Additionally, both the SCSL and STL are found to have relied on amicus curiae briefs. The chapter concludes that the ICC should utilise the unique perspective of NGOs, particularly when assessing admissibility under art 17 of the Rome Statute.

Overall, this book is a welcome addition to the continued development of international criminal justice and a positive perspective on the future of the International Criminal Court. In an era where increasing global compliance with international obligations means punishing non-compliant states, this book, for the most part, suggests ways in which the ICC may foster beneficial partnerships with national jurisdictions and so encourage cooperation. Both academics and practitioners will find *The International Criminal Court in an Effective Global Justice System* a worthwhile read and a necessary injection of optimism.

---

2   *The Prosecutor v. Jean-Paul Akayesu* (*Judgment*) (International Criminal Tribunal for Rwanda, Trial Chamber I, Case No ICTR-96-4-T, 2 September 1998).

Call for Papers

The *New Zealand Yearbook of International Law* is an annual, international refereed publication.

The Editors call for both short notes and commentaries, and longer in-depth articles, for publication in the 2017 edition of the *Yearbook*. Notes and commentaries should be between 3,000 to 7,000 words. Articles may be from 8,000 to 15,000 words.

The Editors seek contributions on all current topics in international law. The Editors particularly also encourage submissions that are relevant to the Pacific, the Southern Ocean and Antarctica, and New Zealand.

Submissions Will be Considered on a Rolling Basis. However, the Closing Date for Submissions is 1 May 2018.

Submissions should be provided in English, using *MS Word*-compatible word processing software, and delivered by email to the General Editor at roisin.burke@canterbury.ac.nz. Contributions must be original unpublished works and submission of contributions will be held to imply this. Manuscripts must be word-processed and in compliance with the *Australian Guide to Legal Citation*. The Guide is available online at: <http://law.unimelb.edu.au/mulr/aglc/about>.

LLM International Law & Politics

Located in Christchurch, the major city on the magnificent South Island of New Zealand, the School has a long and proud tradition of academic endeavour and boasts a number of dedicated teachers and researchers in the field of international law who have made it possible for the School of Law, together with the School of Language, Social and Political Sciences, to offer a specialist programme in international law and politics.

The Degree

The LLM is a partly taught and partly research-based degree aimed at students with a law background whose main interest is in developing their knowledge of international law, but who also have an interest in examining the political nature of the international order. The degree requires students to successfully complete a dissertation on a topic of their own choice as well as four courses from the list set out below. Two of the four courses must be Advanced

© KONINKLIJKE BRILL NV, LEIDEN, 2018 | DOI 10.1163/9789004345911_020

Principles of Public International Law and Principles and Practice of International Relations and Diplomacy.

The full list of international law and politics courses is set out below:

· Advanced Principles of Public International Law (*compulsory*)
· Principles and Practice of International Relations and Diplomacy (*compulsory*)
· International Criminal Law
· World Trade Law
· International Investment Law
· International Human Rights Law
· Antarctic Legal Studies
· International Environmental Law
· Law of the Sea
· European Union Law
· European Public Law

Not every course will be offered in any one year.

Enrolment Requirements and Start Dates

A candidate for the LLM (International Law and Politics) must, before enrolling for the degree, *either* qualify for the Degree of Bachelor of Laws, *or* on the basis of an equivalent qualification be admitted *ad eundem statum* as entitled to enrol for the degree LLM (International Law and Politics). The degree may be studied full-time for a year or part-time for two years or more.

For Further Information Contact

Ms Margaret Ricketts
Academic Manager
School of Law
University of Canterbury
Private Bag 4800
Christchurch 8020
New Zealand
Email: margaret.ricketts@canterbury.ac.nz
Web: www.laws.canterbury.ac.nz
Phone: +64 3 369 3662